Prague

THE ROUGH GUIDE

Rough Guide Credits

Text Editor:	Sophie Martin
Series Editor:	Mark Ellingham
Editorial:	Martin Dunford, Jonathan Buckley, Jo Mead, Kate Berens, Amanda Tomlin, Ann-Marie Shaw, Paul Gray, Helena Smith, Judith Bamber, Olivia Eccleshall, Orla Duane, Ruth Blackmore, Geoff Howard, Claire Saunders, Gavin Thomas, Alexander Mark Rogers, Polly Thomas, Joe Staines, Lisa Nellis, Andrew Tomičíc, Richard Lim, Claire Fogg, Duncan Clark, Peter Buckley (UK); Andrew Rosenberg, Mary Beth Maioli (US)
Online Editors:	Kelly Cross, Loretta Chilcoat (US)
Production:	Susanne Hillen, Andy Hilliard, Link Hall, Helen Ostick, Julia Bovis, Michelle Draycott, Katie Pringle, Robert Evers, Neil Cooper, Niamh Hatton
Picture Research:	Louise Boulton, Sharon Martins
Cartography:	Melissa Baker, Maxine Repath, Nichola Goodliffe, Ed Wright
Finance:	John Fisher, Gary Singh, Edward Downey, Mark Hall, Tim Bill
Marketing & Publicity:	Richard Trillo, Niki Smith, David Wearn, Jemima Broadbridge (UK); Jean-Marie Kelly, Myra Campolo, Simon Carloss (US)
Administration:	Tania Hummel, Charlotte Marriott, Demelza Dallow

Acknowledgements

Special thanks for this edition go to Sophie for her patience and warmth, to Simon Oatley and Andy Doyle for making my Prague ramblings enjoyable; and thanks, too, as usual, to Kate, Stan and Josh, and the support team back at home, particularly Gordon, Val, Gren, Ju and Nat. Thanks, too, from the editor to Maxine Burke for cartography, Neil Cooper for typesetting and Laurence Larroche for proofreading.

This fourth edition published March 2000 by Rough Guides Ltd, 62–70 Shorts Gardens, London WC2H 9AH. Reprinted April 2001. Previous editions published 1992, 1995, 1998.

Distributed by the Penguin Group:
Penguin Books Ltd, 27 Wrights Lane, London W8 5TZ.
Penguin Putnam Inc, 375 Hudson Street, New York 10014, USA.
Penguin Books Australia Ltd, 487 Maroondah Highway, PO Box 257, Ringwood, Victoria 3134, Australia.
Penguin Books Canada Ltd, 10 Alcorn Avenue, Toronto, Ontario, Canada M4V 1E4.
Penguin Books (NZ) Ltd, 182–190 Wairau Road, Auckland 10, New Zealand.

Printed in England by Clays Ltd, St Ives PLC
Typography and **original design** by Jonathan Dear and The Crowd Roars.
Illustrations throughout by Edward Briant.

320pp. Includes index.

A catalogue record for this book is available from the British Library.

ISBN 1-85828-525-9

Prague

THE ROUGH GUIDE

Written and researched by
Rob Humphreys

With additional research by
Tim Nollen

THE ROUGH GUIDES

Help us update

A lot of effort has gone in to ensure that this edition of *The Rough Guide to Prague* is up to date and accurate. However, things are still changing at an extraordinary speed in Prague and if you find we've missed something good or covered something which has now gone, then please write; suggestions, comments or corrections are much appreciated. We'll credit all contributions, and send a copy of the next edition (or any other Rough Guide if you prefer) for the best letters.

Please mark all letters "Rough Guide to Prague Update" and send to:
Rough Guides, 62–70 Shorts Gardens, London WC2H 9AH or
Rough Guides, 375 Hudson St, 4th Floor, New York, NY 10014.

Email should be sent to: *mail@roughguides.co.uk*

Online updates about *Rough Guide* titles can be found on our Web site at *www.roughguides.com*

The Author

Rob Humphreys joined Rough Guides in 1989, having worked as a failed actor, taxi driver and male model. He has travelled extensively in central and eastern Europe, writing guides to Prague, the Czech and Slovak Republics, and St Petersburg, as well as London. He has lived in London since 1988.

Readers' letters

A big thank you to the readers who took the trouble to write in with their comments and suggestions (apologies for any misspellings or omissions): Kathy Barlow, Slavomar Beliš, Bobbie and Andy Bolam, Richard Bowring, Janet Brown, Bob Cann, P. J. Carr, Vanda and David Cash, Valerie Coombs, David Creighton, Emma Donaldson, Mark Foreman, Matthew Heath, Alex Hetwer, Basil Howitt, Judie and Kevin, David and Beverley Jost, Paul Lewington, Philippe Lintern, Katrina Manson, Helen Massy-Beresford, John Perkins, Geoff Piper, Aparna and Radhika Piramal, Miroslav Pošta, Fiona Renton, J.W. van Sandick, Sheila Spencer, Caitlin Porter, Esther Semple and Barbara Taylor.

Rough Guides

Travel Guides • Phrasebooks • Music and Reference Guides

We set out to do something different when the first Rough Guide was published in 1982. Mark Ellingham, just out of University, was travelling in Greece. He brought along the popular guides of the day, but found they were all lacking in some way. They were either strong on ruins and museums but went on for pages without mentioning a beach or taverna. Or they were so conscious of the need to save money that they lost sight of Greece's cultural and historical significance. Also, none of the books told him anything about Greece's contemporary life – its politics, its culture, its people, and how they lived.

So with no job in prospect, Mark decided to write his own guidebook, one which aimed to provide practical information that was second to none, detailing the best beaches and the hottest clubs and restaurants, while also giving hard-hitting accounts of every sight, both famous and obscure, and providing up-to-the-minute information on contemporary culture. It was a guide that encouraged independent travellers to find the best of Greece, and was a great success, getting shortlisted for the Thomas Cook travel guide award, and encouraging Mark, along with three friends, to expand the series.

The Rough Guide list grew rapidly and the letters flooded in, indicating a much broader readership than had been anticipated, but one which uniformly appreciated the Rough Guides' mix of practical detail and humour, irreverence and enthusiasm. Things haven't changed. The same four friends who began the series are still the caretakers of the Rough Guide mission today: to provide the most reliable, up-to-date and entertaining information to independent-minded travellers of all ages, on all budgets.

We now publish 150 titles and have offices in London and New York. The travel guides are written and researched by a dedicated team of more than 100 authors, based in Britain, Europe, the USA and Australia. We have also created a unique series of phrasebooks to accompany the travel series, along with the acclaimed series of music guides, and a best-selling pocket guide to the Internet and World Wide Web. We also publish comprehensive travel information on our Web site: *www.roughguides.com*

Contents

Part Four: Contexts 251

Index 287

List of maps

MAP SYMBOLS

- Railway
- Road
- Passageway
- Steps
- Pedestrianized roads
- Path
- Ferry route
- Waterway
- Chapter division boundary
- Mountain peak
- Hotel
- Tourist office
- Post office
- Metro station
- Building
- Synagogue
- Church
- Christian cemetery
- Jewish cemetery
- Park

Introduction

Prague (Praha to the Czechs) is one of the least "Eastern" European cities you could imagine. Architecturally, and in terms of city sights, it is a revelation: few other cities, anywhere in Europe, look so good – and no other European capital can present six hundred years of architecture so completely untouched by natural disaster or war. Culturally, it has always looked towards Paris rather than Moscow, and after four decades of Soviet-imposed isolation the city is now keen to re-establish its position as the political and cultural centre of *Mitteleuropa*.

One of Prague's most appealing characteristics is that its artistic wealth is not hidden away inside grand museums and galleries, but displayed in the streets and squares. Its town planning took place in medieval times, its palaces and churches were decorated with a rich mantle of Baroque, and the whole lot has escaped the vanities and excesses of postwar redevelopment. Prague's unique compactness allows you to walk from the grandeur of the city's castle district, via a series of intimate Baroque lanes, across a medieval stone bridge, through one of the most alluring central squares on the continent, and end up sipping coffee on Wenceslas Square, the modern hub of the city, in under half an hour.

As well as having a rich history, Czechs have been at the forefront of European **culture** for much of the modern era. Before World War I, Prague boasted a Cubist movement second only to Paris, and, between the wars, a modernist architectural flowering to rival Bauhaus. Today, its writers, artists and film directors continue to exert a profound influence on European culture, out of all proportion to their numbers.

The city's recent history has attracted the attention of the west like no other capital in the former eastern bloc. The 1968 **Prague Spring** captured the imagination of a generation, with an explosion of cultural energy which, for a moment, made the "third way" between communism and capitalism seem a real possibility. Then, in the messy, sometimes bloody, upheavals of 1989, Czechoslovakia, and in particular Prague, outshone the rest with its

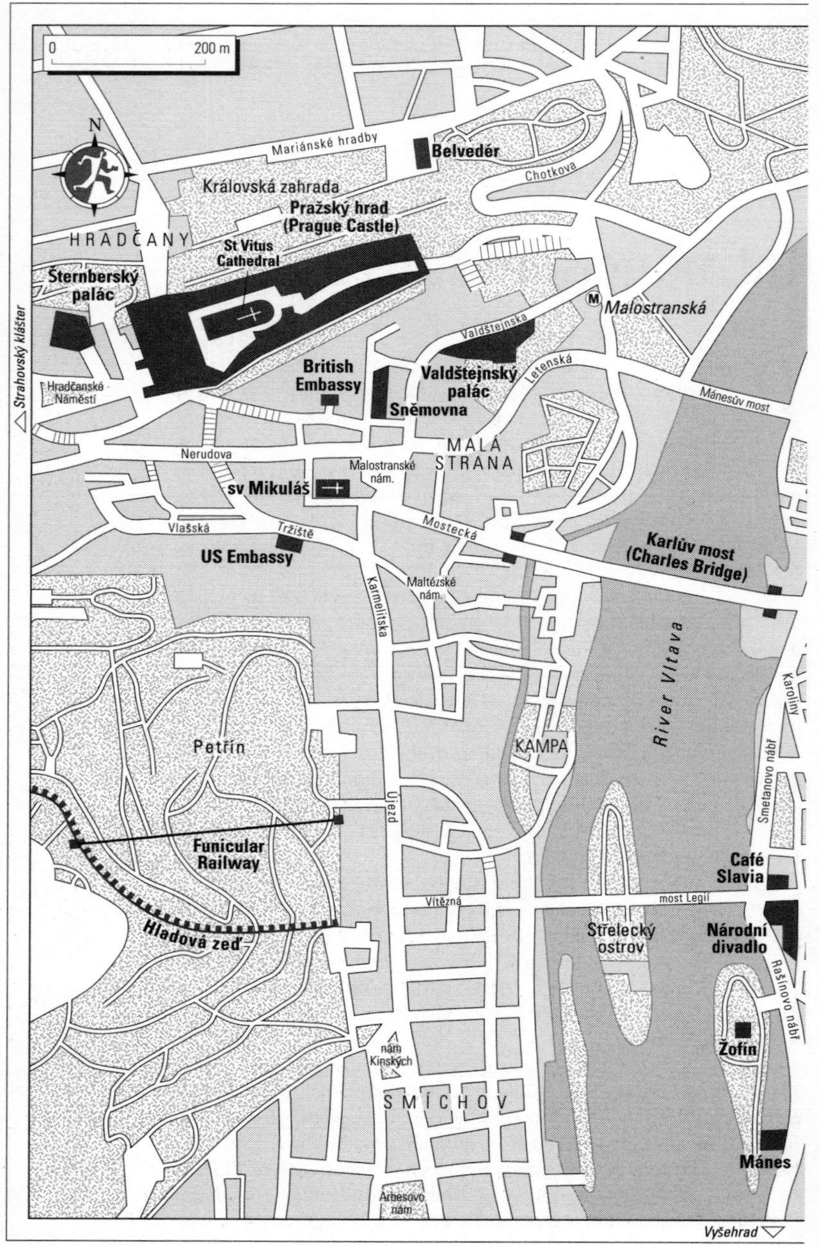
0
200 m
N
Mariánské hradby
Belvedér
Chotkova
Královská zahrada
Pražský hrad
(Prague Castle)
HRADČANY
St Vitus
Cathedral
Šternberský
palác
Strahovský klášter
Malostranská
Valdštejnská
Letenská
British
Embassy
Valdštejnský
palác
Hradčanské
Náměstí
Sněmovna
Mánesův most
MALÁ
STRANA
Nerudova
Malostranské
nám.
sv Mikuláš
Vlašská
Tržiště
Mostecká
US Embassy
Karlův most
(Charles Bridge)
Karmelitská
Maltézské
nám.
River Vltava
Karoliny
Petřín
KAMPA
Újezd
Smetanovo nábř
Funicular
Railway
Café
Slavia
Vítězná
most Legií
Hladová zeď
Střelecký
ostrov
Národní
divadlo
Rašínovo nábř
Žofín
nám
Kinských
SMÍCHOV
Mánes
Arbesovo
nám
Vyšehrad

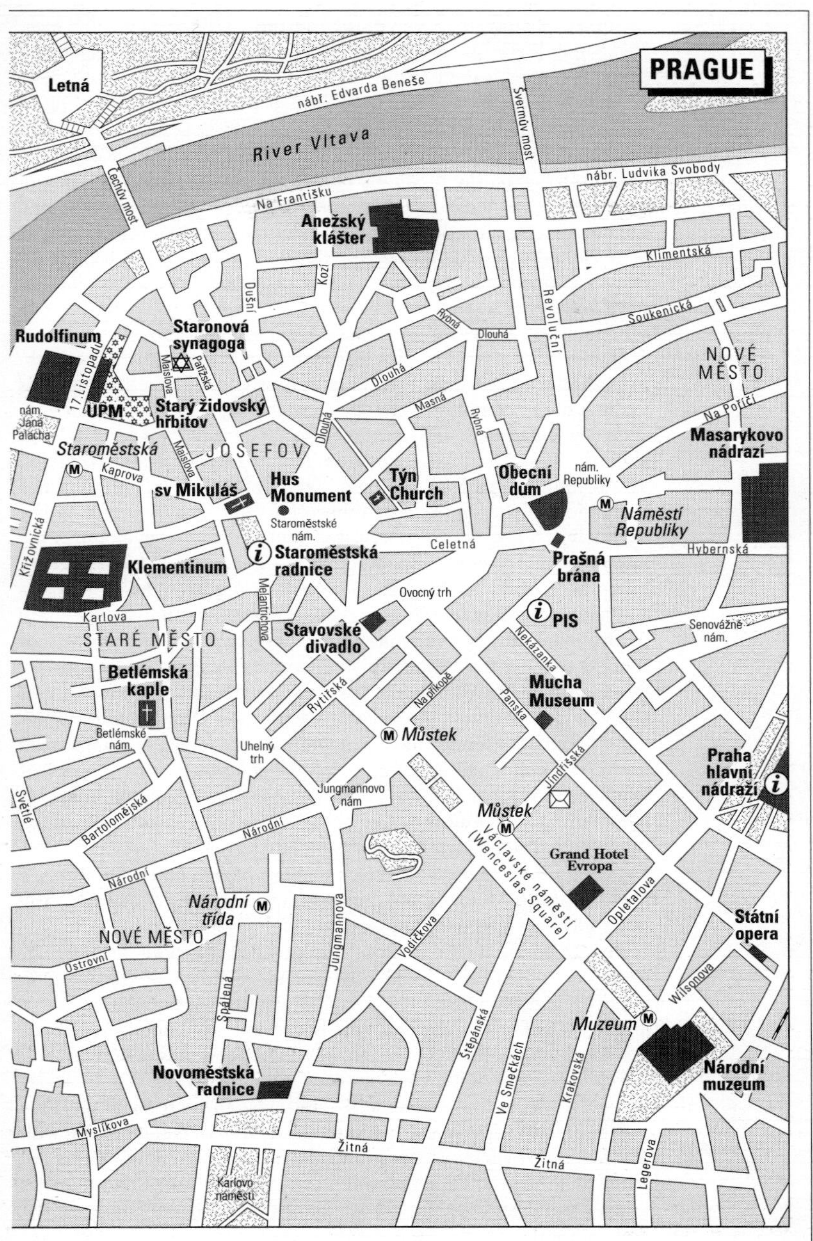
PRAGUE
Letná
nábř. Edvarda Beneše
River Vltava
Švermův most
nábř. Ludvika Svobody
Čechův most
Na Františku
Anežský klášter
Klimentská
Dušní
Kozí
Revoluční
Soukenická
Staronová synagoga
Rybná
Dlouhá
Rudolfinum
17. Listopadu
Maislova
Pařížská
NOVÉ MĚSTO
UPM
Starý židovský hřbitov
Masná
Na Poříčí
nám. Jana Palacha
Staroměstská
JOSEFOV
Masarykovo nádraží
Kaprova
sv Mikuláš
Hus Monument
Týn Church
Obecní dům
nám. Republiky
Náměstí Republiky
Staroměstské nám.
Křižovnická
Klementinum
Staroměstská radnice
Celetná
Prašná brána
Hybernská
Melantrichova
Ovocný trh
Karlova
PIS
STARÉ MĚSTO
Stavovské divadlo
Senovážné nám.
Nekázanka
Betlémská kaple
Mucha Museum
Rytířská
Na příkopě
Panská
Můstek
Betlémské nám.
Uhelný trh
Jindřišská
Praha hlavní nádraží
Jungmannovo nám.
Světlé
Bartolomějská
Národní
Václavské náměstí (Wenceslas Square)
Grand Hotel Evropa
Národní třída
Jungmannova
Vodičkova
Opletalova
Státní opera
NOVÉ MĚSTO
Ostrovní
Spálená
Wilsonova
Muzeum
Štěpánská
Ve Smečkách
Krakovská
Novoměstská radnice
Národní muzeum
Myslíkova
Žitná
Legerova
Karlovo náměstí

unequivocally positive "**Velvet Revolution**". True to its pacifist past, the country shrugged off forty years of communism without so much as a shot being fired.

The exhilarating popular unity of that period, and the feeling of participating in history itself have now gone. Few Czechs continue to talk about the events of 1989 as a "revolution". Disorientation at the speed of change, the break with Slovakia, and the first real taste of western vices in the capital have taken their toll. **Economically**, too, the country is going through some difficult times. Ninety percent of state-owned property has been "restituted", that is given back to its pre-1948 owners in various states of disrepair. Foreign companies have bought up huge slices of Czech industry for a song, and the traditional heavy industrial base has shrunk considerably.

Walking the streets of the city centre, you'd be forgiven for thinking otherwise. But then Prague is in a privileged position vis-à-vis the rest of the country – as the place where the majority of the country's new businesses and corporations have made their head offices, and, of course, thanks to its potential for attracting western tourists. The feeling in much of the rest of the country is that Prague has prospered at the expense of other cities and regions. This is not surprising, however, given that it is something like seven times the size of any other city in Bohemia, all the government ministries are based here, and it's where all the big decisions are made.

That's not to say that Prague doesn't have more than its fair share of problems. Its recent mini-boom may have brought crowds of tourists and hordes of, mostly American, expats, but it has done little to improve life for much of the city's population. The westernized shops and restaurants in the centre, with their glitzy window-dressing, are out of reach for most Praguers. Racial tensions, suppressed under the police state, have surfaced once more, with a spate of skinhead attacks on the city's considerable Romany and Vietnamese communities, which the police seem either powerless or unwilling to prevent. The lifestyle gulf between Party and non-Party members has been replaced by the western malaise of rich and poor. There's nothing new in this, but it does serve as a sobering footnote to the city's glowing image in the west.

Prague is also trying to come to terms with its more distant past. Both the forced, and frequently violent, removal of the German minority and the virtual extinction of the Jewish population had a marked effect on the city, but were never discussed openly under the previous regime. Much of the current retrospection is positive, a cultural rediscovery of the cosmopolitan interwar period, when the city was ethnically far more diverse. There is also the extremely sensitive matter of the events of the last war: the degree of collaboration with the Nazis and of acquiescence towards the fate of the Jews. These are issues that need to be addressed if the city is to break free from its monocultural straitjacket, which makes it stand out amongst the multicultural capitals of the west.

When to go

Lying at the heart of central Europe, Prague has a continental climate: winters can be bitterly cold, summers correspondingly scorching. The best times to visit, in terms of weather, are late spring and early autumn. Summer in the city can be pretty stifling, but the real reason for avoiding the peak season is that it can get uncomfortably crowded in the centre – finding a place to eat in the evening, let alone securing a room, can become fraught with difficulties. If you're looking for good weather, April is the earliest you can expect at least some sunny days, and October is the last warm month. If you don't mind the cold, the city looks beautiful in the snowy winter months.

Average temperatures (°F) and Rainfall

	Jan	Feb	Mar	April	May	June	July	Aug	Sept	Oct	Nov	Dec
Min °C	-5	-4	-1	3	8	11	13	13	9	5	1	-3
Max °C	0	1	7	12	18	21	23	22	18	12	5	1
mm	18	18	18	27	48	54	68	55	31	33	20	21

Part 1

Basics

Getting there from Britain and Ireland

By far the most convenient way to get to Prague is **by plane**. The flight from London takes just under two hours (compared with around nineteen hours by train), and there are now plenty of daily direct flights from London throughout the year.

By plane

Both British Airways (BA) and Czech Airlines (ČSA) run two daily **scheduled flights** from London Heathrow to Prague. British Airways fly from Terminal 1, while ČSA fly out of Terminal 2, and less frequently from Stansted. BA's low-cost airline, Go, also fly daily from Stansted, while British Midland fly daily out of Heathrow (Terminal 1). Currently, ČSA run the only direct service from Manchester.

Go tend to offer the cheapest fares, although you'll have to book well in advance to get their very lowest fare of £100 return (including tax). You've more chance of catching one of their £130 return fares, and for a fully flexible ticket you're looking at £260 return. Go are deliberately no frills: they don't give out free meals and drinks, though you can buy sandwiches and coffee on board.

The other airlines can't really compete with Go on price, but they do have more flights to choose from. As with Go, their budget tickets usually require you to stay at least one Saturday night, and don't allow for change or cancellation. However, to get the cheapest fares, you usually have to fly out mid-week as well. Booking tickets direct through the airlines themselves is rarely the cheapest option, though prices are usually fairly competitive: from as little as £160 return from London (£200 from Manchester). Fares vary according to season – they tend to be highest from April to October and in the two weeks around Christmas – though some kind of economy fare is usually available all year round. Be sure to enquire whether the fare you are being quoted includes tax (currently around £20–25 per person).

Discounted flights to Prague now feature in most of the "bucket shop" adverts of the various London freebie magazines, *Time Out*, *The Evening Standard* and the travel sections of the quality Sunday papers, where return fares can be bought for as little as £130. You might also try specialist agents, such as Campus Travel or STA (see box on p.4 for details), or one of the following Web sites: *www.cheapflights.co.uk*, *www.lastminute.co.uk*, or Bob Geldof's *www.deckchair.com*. Note, however, that in peak season, discount flights are often booked up weeks in advance. If this is the case, it might be worth considering flying to a neighbouring European city like Berlin, Leipzig or Vienna, for which return fares can be as little as £100 –

Airlines

British Airways ☎ 0345/222111; *www.british-airways.com*

British Midland ☎ 0870/607 0555; *www.britishmidland.com*

Czech Airlines (ČSA) *www.csa.cz*
London ☎ 0207/255 1898
Manchester ☎ 0161/489 0241

Go ☎ 0845/605 4321; *www.go-fly.com*

Agents and operators in Britain

Bohemian Promotions 61 Mere Rd, Erdington, Birmingham B23 7LL ☎0121/373 9107. Offers a full range of accommodation in Prague.

Bridgewater Travel P.O Box 2333, Kidderminster DY14 0YT ☎01299/271717; *www.bridgewater-travel.co.uk.* Accommodation and package deals.

ČEDOK 4th Floor, 53–54 Haymarket, London SW1 ☎0171/836 4414. Unreconstructed former state-owned tourist board offering flights, accommodation and package deals.

Czech & Slovak Tourist Centre 16 Frognal Parade, Finchley Rd, London NW3 ☎0207/794 3263; *www.czech-slovak-tourist.co.uk.* Accommodation, bus tickets, flights and lots more.

Czech Travel Ltd Trinity House, 1 Trinity Square, South Woodham Ferrers, Essex CM3 5JX ☎01245/328647; *www.czechtravel.freeuk.com.* Rooms and flats for rent in Prague.

Czechbook Agency Jopes Mill, Trebrownbridge, Near Liskeard, Cornwall PL14 3PX ☎01503/240629. Cheap private and self-catering accommodation in Prague.

Czechdays 89 Valence Road, Lewes BN7 1SJ ☎01273/474738. Cheap rooms in Prague suburbs.

Czechscene 1 Thon Lea, Evesham, Worcestershire WR11 6TN ☎01386/442782. B&B and self-catering flats available in Prague.

Hotel Connect Berkeley House, 18–24 High Street, Edgware HA8 7RP ☎0208/731 5005; *www.hotelconnect.co.uk.* Accommodation in Prague.

Martin Randall Travel 10 Barley Mow Passage, London W4 4PH ☎0208/742 3355. Pricey, specialist cultural guided tours of Prague.

North South Travel Moulsham Mill Centre, Parkway, Chelmsford, Essex CM2 7PX ☎01245/492882. Friendly, competitive travel agency offering discounted fares worldwide – profits are used to support projects in the developing world.

STA Travel *www.statravel.co.uk* 86 Old Brompton Rd, London SW7 3LH; 117 Euston Rd, London NW1 2SX; 38 Store St, London WC1E 7BZ ☎0207/361 6161; 25 Queen's Rd, Bristol BS8 1QE ☎0117/929 3399; 38 Sidney St, Cambridge CB2 3HX ☎01223/366966; 27 Forest Rd, Edinburgh ☎0131/226 7747; 88 Vicar Lane, Leeds LS1 7JH ☎0113/244 9212; 75 Deansgate, Manchester M3 2BW ☎0161/834 0668; 36 George St, Oxford OX1 2OJ; ☎01865/792800. Independent travel and discount flight specialists; offices also in Aberdeen, Glasgow, Liverpool, Newcastle, and on university campuses in Birmingham, Bristol, Canterbury, Cardiff, Coventry, Durham, Glasgow, Leeds, London, Loughborough, Nottingham, Sheffield and Warwick.

Travellers' Czech Ltd 203 Main Road, Biggin Hill, Kent TN16 3JU ☎01959/540700; *www.travellerscities.co.uk.* Private accommodation in, and packages to, Prague.

Travelscene 11–15 St Ann's Rd, Harrow, Middlesex HA1 ☎0208/427 4445; *www.travelscene.co.uk.* Two-night breaks and upwards in Prague.

USIT Campus Travel *www.campustravel.co.uk* 52 Grosvenor Gardens, London SW1W 0AG ☎0207/730 3402; 541 Bristol Rd, Selly Oak, Birmingham B29 6AU ☎0121/414 1848; 61 Ditchling Rd, Brighton BN1 4SD ☎01273/570226; 39 Queen's Rd, Clifton, Bristol BS8 1QE ☎0117/929 2494; 5 Emmanuel St, Cambridge CB1 1NE ☎01223/324283; 53 Forest Rd, Edinburgh EH1 2QP ☎0131/668 3303; 166 Deansgate, Manchester M3 3FE ☎0161/833 2046; 105–106 St Aldates, Oxford OX1 1DD ☎01865/242067. Student/youth travel specialists; branches also in YHA shops and universities around Britain.

again, you'll find the cheapest fares in the sources quoted above.

Package deals and city breaks

Numerous tour operators offer simple flight and accommodation **package deals** to Prague, which for a short trip can often be much better value than travelling independently. Most of the companies listed above will put together some kind of package for you. Travelscene, for example, offer a two-night city break including flights and accommodation for around £300. With these packages, there's no compulsion to go on any organized tours once you're there. If you're flying with Go, you can claim a discount if you book your accommodation through Hotel Connect. A list of the main agents can be found in the box opposite.

Flights from Ireland

There are no direct flights from anywhere in Ireland to Prague. The cheapest way of making the journey is to fly to London and pick up a connecting flight or package (see p.3). Discount travel agents, such as USIT, should be able to organize both flights. As usual, the cheapest tickets are only available if you make sure you stay away over a Saturday night, and fly mid-week.

Most airlines can offer budget return tickets **from Dublin** to London from IR£60 and under. Ryanair fly to Gatwick, Stansted and Luton from Dublin (as well as Cork, Derry, Kerry and Knock) and tend to be the cheapest – their best deals are on flights into Stansted – although Aer Lingus, who fly out of Dublin, Shannon and Cork into Heathrow and from Dublin into Stansted, offer similar budget fares, as do British Airways, who fly into Gatwick from Dublin, and CityJet, who fly from Dublin to London City Airport.

Flying **from Belfast**, however, your best bet is British Midland, who fly into Heathrow from Belfast International for around £70 return; BA cover the same route, but are usually a little more expensive. It's also worth checking with Jersey European, who fly from Belfast City airport to Gatwick and Stansted, and can usually match – and often undercut – the prices of their competitors.

All the above prices are for economy tickets, which are usually non-changeable, non-refundable, and assume you're prepared to travel mid-week and stay over a Saturday night. Note that **airport tax** out of Dublin is IR£5, and can be as much as a further IR£20 into London.

By train

Thanks to the Eurostar service through the Channel Tunnel, you can travel from London to Prague in around nineteen hours by **train**.

Airlines in Ireland

Aer Lingus
Dublin ☎01/705 3333 *www.aerlingus.ie*

British Airways
Belfast ☎0345/222111
Dublin ☎01800/626747
www.british-airways.com

British Midland
Belfast ☎0870/607 0555
www.iflybritishmidland.com

CityJet
Dublin ☎01/844 5566
www.cityjet.com

Jersey European
Belfast ☎0990/676676
www.jersey-european.co.uk

Ryanair
Dublin ☎01/677 4422
www.ryanair.com

Agents and operators in Ireland

Aran Travel Granary House, 58 Dominick St, Galway ☎091/562595; *arantvl@iol.com*

Joe Walsh Tours 34 Grafton St, Dublin 2 ☎01/671 8751; 69 Upper O'Connell St, Dublin 2 ☎01/676 3053; 8–11 Baggot St, Dublin 2 ☎01/676 8915; 117 St Patrick St, Cork ☎021/277959. General budget fares agent.

Student & Group Travel 1st Floor, 71 Dame St, Dublin 2 ☎01/677 7834. Student and group specialists.

Thomas Cook *www.tch.thomascook.com*
11 Donegal Place, Belfast ☎01232/242341; 118 Grafton St, Dublin ☎01/677 1721. Package holiday and flight agent with occasional discount offers.

Trailfinders 4–5 Dawson St, Dublin 2 ☎01/677 7888; *www.trailfinders.com.* General discount agent.

USIT *www.usitcampus.com*
Fountain Centre, College St, Belfast BT1 ☎01849/324073; 10–11 Market Parade, Patrick Street, Cork ☎021/270900; 33 Ferryquay St, Derry ☎01504/371888; Aston Quay, Dublin 2 ☎01/602 1600; Victoria Place, Eyre Square, Galway ☎091/565177; Central Buildings, O'Connell St, Waterford ☎051/872601. Student/youth specialists for flights and trains.

USEFUL INTERNET SITES FOR TRAVELLERS

British Foreign and Commonwealth Office
www.fco.gov.uk
Constantly updated advice for travellers on circumstances affecting your safety in over 130 countries.

UK Meteorological Office
www.met-office.gov.uk
Weather forecasts and links to other sites.

Online Tourist Information
www.travel.yahoo.com
Incorporates a lot of Rough Guide material in its coverage of destination countries and cities across the world, with information about places to eat and sleep etc.

The routes

The quickest way to get from London to Prague by train is on the **Eurostar via Brussels**. By catching the train at around noon from London Waterloo International, you arrive at Brussels Midi with around forty minutes to change onto the Brussels–Köln service. From Köln, there's an overnight service to Prague, which gets into the Czech capital just after 8am the following morning.

Travelling **Eurostar via Paris** is more expensive and more hassle. For a start, you have to cross Paris, and, as there is no direct overnight service to Prague, either stay the night in Paris and catch the daytime train, or change at Frankfurt in order to join up with the overnight service.

Travelling **via ferry to Ostend** is more difficult to organize than it used to be, as it can only be booked separately through Hoverspeed. Trains leave London Charing Cross, and use the Dover to Ostend crossing, the journey taking roughly eight hours. The return fare from London to Brussels is £49 for a five-day return, or £65 for a ticket valid for one year.

Although you can simply crash out on the seats on the overnight service from Köln to Prague, it makes sense to book a **couchette** which costs around £10 one-way in a six-berth compartment, rising to £13.50 in a four-berth compartment. Couchettes are mixed-sex and allow little privacy; for a bit more comfort, you can book a bed in a single-sex two-berth **sleeper** for around £35 one-way. You should be able to book your couchette or sleeper when you buy your ticket, but if you have any problems, contact German Railways (Deutsche Bahn). However you

TRAIN INFORMATION

European Rail ☎ 0207/387 0444
Eurostar ☎ 0990/186186; *www.eurostar.com*
USIT Campus ☎ 0207/730 3402; *www.campustravel.co.uk*
German Railways ☎ 0207/317 0919; *www.bahn.de*
Rail Europe ☎ 0990/848848; *www.sncf.fr*
Wasteels ☎ 0207/834 7066; *www.wasteels.dk*

BUS INFORMATION

Capital Express ☎ 0207/243 0488; *www.capitalexpress.demon.co.uk*
Eurolines ☎ 0990/808080; *www.eurolines.co.uk*
Kingscourt Express ☎ 0208/673 7500; *www.kce.cz*

CROSS-CHANNEL INFORMATION

Eurotunnel ☎ 0990/353535; *www.eurotunnel.com* Folkstone–Calais through the tunnel.
Hoverspeed ☎ 0990/240241; *www.hoverspeed.co.uk* Dover–Calais, Folkstone–Boulogne and Dover–Ostend.
P&O Stena Line ☎ 0870/600 0600; *www.posl.com* Dover–Calais.

decide to sleep, you'll be woken up in the early hours of the morning when the train crosses the Czech border.

Tickets and passes

Fares for continental rail travel are much more flexible than they used to be, so it's worth shopping around for the best deal, rather than taking the first offer you get. The cheapest deals for a return ticket from London – Prague tend to hover around £200. To qualify for the most heavily discounted fares, however, there are usually various restrictions: you may have to stay over a Saturday night, and your ticket may well be non-exchangeable and non-refundable. If you're travelling with one or more companions, you may well be eligible for a further discount, which can bring the fare down as low as £160 return. You should also be able to get through-ticketing, including the tube journey to Waterloo International, from mainline train stations in Britain, when you buy your ticket.

Those under 26 can purchase a discounted **BIJ** ticket, available from Rail Europe, USIT Campus or Wasteels, thus saving around £30 on the return fare. USIT Campus also offer a range of **Eurotrain Explorer** passes, which allow unlimited travel within the Czech Republic (£16 for seven consecutive days, or for five days in a month). Travellers over 60 can get a thirty percent discount on rail travel between, but not within, European countries by purchasing a **RES Card** (Rail Europe Senior Card) at a cost of £5. However, before you can buy this card, you must already possess a British Senior Card (£18); both are valid for a year.

If you're planning to visit Prague as part of a more extensive trip around Europe, it may be worth purchasing an **InterRail pass**, which gives you unlimited rail travel within certain countries; you must, however, have been resident in Europe for at least six months. InterRail tickets are currently zonal: to travel to Prague and back, you'll need at least a three-zone pass, costing £229 for one month for those under 26, and £309 a month for those aged 26 and over. Passes are not valid in the UK, though you're entitled to discounts in Britain and on Eurostar and cross-Channel ferries. Either way, though, you're only really going to get your money back if you do a lot of travelling.

By bus

The cheapest way to get to Prague is by **bus**. There are direct services from London's Victoria Station more or less daily throughout the year, all of which take around 24 hours to reach Prague's main bus terminal, Florenc. Prices between companies vary very slightly so it's worth ringing round to find the best deal; a return ticket currently costs around £80 for those under 26, or around £90 for those over 26. Addresses and telephone numbers for all current operators are in the box opposite.

The journey is long but just about bearable – make sure you bring along enough to eat, drink and read, and a small amount of Belgian and German currency for coffee and any spending en route. There are stops for around half an hour every four hours or so, and the routine is broken by the Channel crossing (included in the cost of the ticket).

For those keen on bus travel, and intent on visiting other parts of Europe, there's a **Eurolines Pass**, allowing free travel between 48 cities (including London and Prague) in 21 countries. Between June and September, the month-long pass costs £199 for under 26s, and £229 for those aged 26 and over; the rest of the year, the passes cost £159 and £199 respectively. A two-month long pass is also available.

By car

Driving to Prague is not the most relaxing option – even if you're into driving virtually non-stop, it'll take the best part of two days – but with two or more passengers it can work out relatively inexpensive. The quickest way of taking your car over to the continent is to drive to the **Channel Tunnel** near Folkestone, where Eurotunnel operates a 24-hour service carrying cars, motorcycles, buses and their passengers to Calais. At peak times, services run every fifteen minutes, making advance bookings for the 35-minute journey unnecessary. However, if you simply turn up unannounced, you'll have to pay from £169 return per carload, whereas if you give fixed dates for your travel, you can bring the price down to between £80 and £110 return.

The alternative cross-Channel options for most travellers are the conventional **ferry**, **catamaran** or **hovercraft** links between Dover and Calais or Ostend, Folkestone and Calais or Boulogne. Fares vary enormously with the time of year, month and even day that you travel, and the size of your car. If you book in advance, the cheapest standard fare on the Dover–Calais run, for example, can be as little as £100 return per carload.

Once you've made it onto the continent, you've got some 1000km of driving ahead of you. Theoretically, you could make it in twelve hours' solid, but realistically it will take you longer. The most direct route from Calais or Ostend is via Brussels, Liège (Luik), Cologne (Köln), Frankfurt, Würzburg and Nuremberg (Nürnberg), entering the country at the **Waidhaus–Rozvadov** border crossing. Motorways in Belgium and Germany are free, but to travel on any motorways within the Czech Republic, you need authorization in the form of a sticker or *dálniční známka*, which can be purchased from all border crossings and most garages and post offices. A ten-day sticker costs 100Kč, a month-long one costs 200Kč, and one valid for a year costs 800Kč.

If you're travelling by car, you'll need proof of ownership, or a letter from the owner giving you permission to drive the car. A British or other EU driving licence is fine; all other drivers are advised to purchase an International Driving Licence. You also need a red warning triangle in case you break down, a first-aid kit (both these are compulsory in the Czech Republic), and a "Green Card" for third party insurance cover at the very least. An even better idea is to sign up with one of the national motoring organizations, who offer continental breakdown assistance and, in extreme circumstances, will get you and your vehicle brought back home if necessary. Look into the RAC's European Cover (☎0800/550055; *www.rac.co.uk*) or the AA's Five-Star Europe cover (☎0800/444500; *www.theaa.co.uk*).

Travel insurance

Though not compulsory for a trip to Prague, **travel insurance** including medical cover is a good idea. Check before shelling out, however, that you are not already covered: many credit cards (particularly American Express) often have certain levels of medical or other insurance included, especially if you use them to pay for your trip; in addition, if you have a good "all risks" home insurance policy it may well cover your possessions against loss or theft even when overseas, and many private medical schemes also cover you while abroad.

Most travel agents and tour operators will offer you travel insurance – those policies offered by Campus Travel or STA in the UK, and USIT in Ireland, are usually reasonable value. If you feel the cover is inadequate, or you want to compare prices, any insurance broker, bank or specialist travel insurance company should be able to help: try Columbus Travel Insurance (☎0207/375 0011; *www.columbusdirect.co.uk*). Two weeks' cover for a trip to Prague should cost around £20 in both Britain and Ireland.

If you do have to pay for any medical treatment or drugs when in Prague, keep the receipts for claiming on your insurance once you're home. If you have anything stolen (including money) register the loss immediately with the local police – without their report you won't be able to claim. For the address of the main police stations in Prague, see p.28.

Getting there from the US and Canada

The quickest and easiest way to reach Prague from the US or Canada is **to fly**. Czech Airlines (ČSA) offer one of the most convenient options, with direct flights from New York, Chicago, Toronto and Montréal. In addition, the major carriers offer dozens of one- and two-stop flights from any number of North American gateways via major European cities. However, peak season flights from North America to Prague are still comparatively expensive, so it may be worth your while flying to Munich, Berlin or Leipzig and making your way overland from there. If you plan on travelling overland, it is worth noting that Eurail passes are not valid in the Czech Republic. While the Europe East Railpass includes the Czech Republic, along with Austria, Hungary and Slovakia, at $205 for five days' travel its cost-effectiveness is debatable. The New York–Prague **flying time** is about eight and a half hours. Toronto–Prague is around ten hours.

Shopping for tickets

Outside of frequent special offers, the cheapest of the airlines' published fares is usually an **Apex** ticket, although this will carry certain restrictions: you have to book – and pay – at least 21 days before departure (and in some cases 90 days), spend at least seven days abroad (maximum stay three months), and you tend to get penalized if you change your schedule. On transatlantic routes, there are also winter **Super Apex** tickets, sometimes known as "Eurosavers" – slightly cheaper than an ordinary Apex, but limiting your stay to between 7 and 21 days. Some airlines also issue **Special Apex** tickets to people younger than 24, often extending the maximum stay to a year. Many airlines offer youth or student fares to **under 26s**; a passport or driving licence is sufficient proof of age, though these tickets are subject to availability and can have eccentric booking conditions.

You can normally cut costs further by going through a **specialist flight agent** – either a **consolidator**, who buys up blocks of tickets from the airlines and sells them at a discount, or a **discount agent**, who in addition to dealing with discounted flights may also offer special student and youth fares and a range of other travel-related services such as travel insurance, rail passes, car rentals, tours and the like. Bear in mind, though, that penalties for changing your plans can be stiff. Some agents specialize in **charter flights**, which may be cheaper than anything available on a scheduled flight, but again departure dates are fixed and withdrawal penalties are high (check the refund policy). If you travel a lot, **discount travel clubs** are another option – the annual membership fee may be worth it for benefits such as cut-price air tickets and car rental.

Don't automatically assume that tickets purchased through a travel specialist will be cheapest – once you get a quote, check with the airlines and you may turn up an even better deal. Be advised also that the pool of travel companies is swimming with sharks – exercise caution and never deal with a company that demands cash upfront or refuses to accept payment by credit card.

Regardless of where you buy your ticket, **fares** will depend on the season, and are highest from around mid-June to the end of August, plus a

Airlines

Air Canada US ☎ 1-800/776-3000, Canada ☎ 1-800/555-1212 for local toll-free number; *www.aircanada.ca*

Air France US ☎ 1-800/237-2747, Canada ☎ 1-800/667-2747; *www.airfrance.dk*

American US ☎ 1-800/433-7300; *www.aa.com*

Austrian Airlines US ☎ 1-800/843-0002; *www.austrianair.com*

British Airways US ☎ 1-800/247-9297, Canada ☎ 1-800/668-1059; *www.british-airways.com*

CSA Czech Airlines US ☎ 1-212-765-6022 or 1-800/223-2365, Canada ☎ 1-800/555-1212; *www.csa.cz*

Delta US ☎ 1-800/241-4141, Canada ☎ 1-800/555-1212; *www.delta-air.com*

Finnair US ☎ 1-800/950-5000; *www.finnair.com*

KLM US ☎ 1-800/777-5553, Canada ☎ 1-800/361-5073; *www.klm.com* or *www.nwa.com*

Lufthansa US ☎ 1-800/645-3880, Canada ☎ 1-800/563-5954; *www.lufthansa.com*

SAS US & Canada ☎ 1-800/221-2350; *www.sas.se*

Swissair US ☎ 1-800/221-4750, Canada ☎ 1-800/267-9477; *www.swissair.com*

United US ☎ 1-800/538-2929; *www.ual.com*

Discount agents, consolidators and travel clubs

Airhitch 2641 Broadway, 3rd Fl #100, New York, NY 10025 ☎ 800/326-2009; *www.airhitch.org.* Stand-by tickets at reduced prices; offices in the U.S. and Europe.

Council Travel 205 E 42nd St, New York, NY 10017 ☎ 212/822-2700 or 1-800/226-8624; *www.counciltravel.com* Nationwide US organization, with branches in many US cities. Specializes in student travel.

Encore Travel Club 4501 Forbes Blvd, Lanham, MD 20706 ☎ 1-800/444-9800. Discount travel club.

Interworld 800 Douglass Rd, Miami, FL 33134 ☎ 305/443-4929 or 1-800/468-3796. Consolidator.

Moment's Notice 7301 New Utrecht Ave, Brooklyn, NY 11204 ☎ 718/234-6295 or 212/486-0500; *www.moments-notice.com.* Discount travel club.

New Frontiers/Nouvelles Frontières 12 E 33rd St, New York, NY 10016 ☎ 212/779-0600 or 1-800/366-6387; *www.newfrontiers.com*; 1001 Sherbrook East, Suite 720, Montréal, PQ H2L 1L3 ☎ 514/526-8444. Discount travel firm, with other branches in LA, San Francisco and Québec City.

STA Travel 10 Downing St, New York, NY 10014 ☎ 212/627-3111 or 1-800/777-0112; *www.sta-travel.com.* Worldwide specialists in independent travel, with branches in many US cities.

Travac 989 6th Ave, New York, NY 10018 ☎ 1-800/872-8800. Consolidator and charter broker; has another office in Orlando.

Travel Avenue 10 S Riverside, Suite 1404, Chicago, IL 60606 ☎ 1-800/333-3335; *www.travel-avenue.com.* Discount travel agent.

Travel Cuts 187 College St, Toronto, ON M5T 1P7 ☎ 416/979-2406 or 1-800/667-2887; ☎ 1-888/238-2887 from US; *www.travelcuts.com.* Canadian student travel organization, with branches across the country.

Travelers Advantage 3033 S Parker Rd, Suite 900, Aurora, CO 80014 ☎ 1-800/548-1116. Discount travel club.

Unitravel 11737 Administration Blvd, Ste 120, St Louis, MO 63146 ☎ 1-800/325-2222; *www.unitravel.com.* Consolidator.

Worldwide Discount Travel Club 1674 Meridian Ave, Miami Beach, FL 33139 ☎ 305/534-2082. Discount travel club.

two-week spell up to Christmas, and lowest from November through mid-December, and late December to the end of March; the rest of the year, shoulder fares operate. Note also that the ticket prices quoted opposite are for midweek travel. Weekend flights cost around $50 extra. All prices are round-trip, exclusive of taxes and subject to availability and change.

Flights from the US

ČSA is the only airline flying **non-stop** from the US **to Prague**, departing daily from New York and Chicago in the summer and on certain days the rest of the year (check with the airline as their flight days are variable). Various airlines offer **flights to Prague** from US hub cities, with stops in European hubs: Air France (via Paris), Delta (via Frankfurt or Vienna), Finnair (via Helsinki), Lufthansa (via Frankfurt), SAS (via Copenhagen) and KLM (via Amsterdam). Barring sales, which can drop fares by as much as thirty percent, **Apex fares** are pretty much identical whichever airline you choose, with rates from New York starting at around $600 (low season), $1000 (high); from Chicago add on about $100 and from LA $250. However, as airlines often run special limited offers, it's definitely worth shopping around. Also, since direct flights to Prague are usually more expensive than flights to other European cities, it may pay to fly to another country and continue overland from there. Another possible option would be an "open-jaw" fare. These provide more flexibility, enabling you to fly into one city and out of another. Again, Lufthansa is currently offering a limited special fare from New York into Berlin, then out of Prague two weeks later, for around $430 (low season).

Independent travel agencies such as Council Travel, STA and Nouvelles Frontières can often undercut the Apex fares on major carriers like British Airways or Air France, and they are especially useful if you are a full-time student or under 26. Student fares often allow you to stop over en route for little or no extra charge, something you can't do on an Apex ticket. For real bargain basement tickets, try the discount agents, discount travel clubs or seat consolidators, where you may be able to track down non-student, low season, round-trip fares to Prague for as little as $370 (from New York), $460 (from Chicago) or $600 from LA. Note, however, that these tickets are basically impossible to change once you've paid for them, so be sure about your dates and ask about the routing of the flight – many involve lengthy stopovers and multiple changes of plane. Finally, hype aside, the **Internet** has become a valuable shopping tool, allowing travellers to compare rates and bid on tickets, the risk being that it is often unclear who exactly you're dealing with; travellers should bear in mind that Internet commerce remains a somewhat risky, unregulated frontier.

If you're visiting Prague as part of a more extensive tour of Europe, it may be worth considering buying a **Eurail Pass**, though travellers should bear in mind that they are not valid in the Czech Republic. The all-country pass, which you must purchase before you leave for Europe, allows unlimited free travel on the railways of seventeen European countries. The **Eurail Youthpass** (for under-26s) costs US$365 for fifteen days, $587 for one month or $832 for two months; if you're 26 or over you'll have to buy a first-class pass, available in fifteen-day ($522), 21-day ($678), one-month ($838), two-month ($1188) and three-month ($1468) increments.

You stand a better chance of getting your money's worth out of a **Eurail Flexipass**, which is good for a certain number of travel days in a two-month period. This, too, comes in under-26/first-class versions: ten days, $431/$616; fifteen days, $568/$812. If you're travelling in a group of two or more, you might also want to consider the **Eurail Saverpass**. This costs $444 for fifteen consecutive days, $576 for 21; $712 for a month; $1010 for two months or $1248 for three. There's also a **Flexi Saverpass** at $524 for ten days or $690 for fifteen.

Another possibility is the **European East pass**, valid for travel in Hungary, Austria, Poland, Slovakia and the Czech Republic. Any five days in one month costs $195; and you can add on a maximum of five extra days for $21 per day. Finally, there's a **Czech Flexipass** which is valid for travel within the Czech Republic for five days out of fifteen and costs around $69.

Flights from Canada

ČSA is the only airline flying non-stop from **Canada to Prague**, departing daily from Montréal and Toronto in the summer and two (variable) days the rest of the year. The lowest scheduled Apex fares from either city are around CDN$1050 (low season) or CDN$1500 (high). Outside Montréal, your best bet is Lufthansa, which flies more or less daily from several major Canadian airports (sometimes in conjunction with Air Canada) to Prague via Frankfurt. Fares from Vancouver start at around CDN$1350 (low season) or CDN$1800 (high).

For discounted flights, check out Travel Cuts or Nouvelles Frontières where you may be able to find non-student, low season, round-trip fares to Prague for as little as CDN$729 (from Toronto) or CDN$988 (from Vancouver).

SPECIALIST AGENTS

American-International Homestays, Inc PO Box 1754, Nederland, CO 80466 ☎303/642-3088 or 1-800/876-2048. Accommodation with English-speaking families.

Backroads 801 Cedar St, Berkeley, CA 94710 ☎1-800/462-2848; *www.backroads.com* Hiking/canoeing/rafting tours starting and finishing in Prague.

Central Europe Holidays 10 E 40th St, suite 3601, New York, NY 10016 ☎1-800/800-8879, *ceheurope@aol.com* Tour packages to Prague.

Czech & Slovak Travel Service 7033 Sunset Blvd, Suite 210, Los Angeles, CA 90028 ☎213/389-2157. Travel agent specializing in Central/Eastern Europe.

Delta Vacations 53 Summer St, Keene, NH 03431 ☎1-800/872-7786; *www.deltavacations.com* City breaks to Prague.

Eastern Europe Tours 600 Stewart St, Suite 524, Seattle, WA 98101 ☎1-800/641-3456. Customized tours to the Czech Republic, with a "Chateaux, Museums and Spas" set package.

Europe Train Tours 198 E Boston Post Rd, Mararoneck, NY 10543 ☎1-800/551-2085. Customized tours by rail, with special rates on Swiss Air.

Fugazy International 770 US-1, North Brunswick, NJ 08902 ☎1-800/828-4488; *www.fugazy.com*. Customized tours and agents for package deals.

La Boheme 875 N Michigan Ave, Suite 3530, Chicago, IL 60611 ☎312/440-0866 or 1-888/LA BOHEME; email: *info@la-boheme.com* Customized tours in the Czech Republic and Central Europe.

Summit International Travel 789 Springfield Ave, Summit, NJ 07901 ☎1-800/527-8664. Highly-regarded specialists in the area. Walking, bicycling and car packages plus customized tours.

Tradesco 6033 Century Blvd, Suite 670, Los Angeles, CA 90045 ☎1-800/833-3402. Wide variety of packages.

Package tours

Since the situation regarding tourism is still very changeable, along with everything else in the former eastern bloc, **travel agencies specializing in eastern Europe**, such as the Czech & Slovak Travel Service, are good sources of up-to-date information, as well as being the best way to find out about any other cheap flight deals. Unfortunately, ČEDOK, the old state tourist monopoly, which once offered the broadest range of all-inclusive tours, no longer has an office in North America, although with US–Czech/Slovak tourism on the rise, they are rumoured to be considering returning. (Currently, an entirely different, American, company operates, from the same address, under the name ČEDOK.) A list of specialist travel agents is given in the box above.

Travel insurance

Before buying an **insurance policy**, check that you're not already covered. Some homeowners' or renters' policies are valid on vacation, and credit cards such as American Express often include some medical insurance, while most Canadians' provincial health plans typically provide limited overseas medical coverage. If you're not covered or you want to take additional precautions you might want to contact a specialist travel insurance company; see the box below or ask your travel agent for a recommendation.

TRAVEL INSURANCE SUPPLIERS

Access America ☎1-800/284-8300; *www.accessamerica.com*

Carefree Travel Insurance ☎1-800/323-3149

Council Travel ☎1-800/226-8624; *www.counciltravel.com*

Desjardins Travel Insurance (Canada only) ☎1-800/463-7830

STA Travel ☎1-800/781-4040; *www.sta-travel.com*

Travel Guard ☎1-800/826-1300; *www.travel-guard.com*

Travel Insurance Services ☎1-800/937-1387; *www.travelinsure.com*

Worldwide Assistance ☎1-800/821-2828; *www.worldwideassistance.com*

The cheapest coverage is currently with STA Travel, whose comprehensive policy for fifteen days in the Czech Republic starts at $55. Rates for a month start at $115.

Note that most North American travel policies apply only to items lost, stolen or damaged while in the custody of an identifiable, responsible third party – hotel porter, airline, luggage consignment, etc. Even in these cases, you will have to contact the local police within a certain time limit to have a complete report made out so that your insurer can process the claim.

Getting there from Australia and New Zealand

Although there are no direct **flights** to Prague from Australia or New Zealand, several mid-priced airlines, such as Czech Airlines (ČSA), Alitalia, Olympic Airways, Lufthansa and KLM (often in conjunction with Qantas/Air New Zealand), can get you there via Asia or Europe for around A$1760/NZ$2199. And as travelling time between Australasia and the Czech Republic can be 20 hours plus, the chance of a stopover and a good night's sleep can be a positive bonus.

Another alternative is to get a cheap flight to another European city and complete your journey by road or rail. Major carriers such as Qantas and British Airways include free return trips to Prague and stopovers en route on their London service, with fares from A$1900–2500/NZ$2475–2775. Cheaper operators include Garuda, Gulf, Japan, Korean and Malaysia airlines, with extra stopovers in Bali/Jakarta, Abu Dhabi, Tokyo, Seoul or Kuala Lumpur respectively, from around A$1350/NZ$2275. Cheapest of the lot are the Airtours/Britannia charter flights to London during their limited charter season from November to March, when you can pick up a fare for A$1100–1760/NZ$1620–2110.

Round the World (RTW) fares, valid for up to a year, are another good option, especially from New Zealand, where airlines offer fewer incentives to fly with them. Qantas, British Airways, Global Explorer and One World fares, starting at A$2400/NZ$3000, are probably the most versatile, taking in four continents, including Europe (with stops in Prague or Bratislava). The Star Alliance fare (from A$2699/NZ$3299) incorporating Air New Zealand, Ansett, Air Canada, Varig, Thai, United and SAS also includes stops in Europe on a mileage basis.

Fares vary according to the season, loosely defined as high (mid-May to end Aug & Dec to mid-Jan), shoulder (March to mid-May & Sept) and low (rest of year), with a A$/NZ$500–600 difference between high- and low-season prices.

Tickets purchased direct from the airlines tend to be expensive; you'll get much better deals, as well as the latest information on limited specials and packages from your local travel agent. Some of the best fares are through discount agents like Flight Centres and STA (for students and under 26s), who can also advise on visa regulations. Seat availability on most interna-

AIRLINES IN AUSTRALIA AND NEW ZEALAND

Aeroflot Australia ☎02/9262 2233. No NZ office.

Air New Zealand Australia ☎13 2476, New Zealand ☎09/366 2424 or 0800/737 000.

Airtours/Britannia Australia ☎02/9247 4833. No NZ office.

Alitalia Australia ☎1300/653 747, New Zealand ☎09/379 4455.

Ansett Australia Australia ☎13 1414, New Zealand ☎09/9652 9665.

British Airways Australia ☎02/8904 8800, New Zealand ☎09/356 8690.

Czech Airlines Australia ☎02/9247 6196. No NZ office.

Garuda Australia ☎1300/365 330, New Zealand ☎09/366 1855.

Gulf Air Australia ☎02/9244 2199, New Zealand ☎09/9244 2199.

Japan Airlines Australia ☎02/9272 1111, New Zealand ☎09/379 9906.

KLM Australia ☎02/9231 6333 or 1800/505 747. No NZ office.

Korean Airlines Australia ☎02/9262 6000, New Zealand ☎09/307 3687.

Lufthansa Australia ☎02/9367 3888, New Zealand ☎09/303 1529.

Malaysia Airlines Australia ☎13 2627, New Zealand ☎09/373 2741.

Olympic Airlines Australia ☎02/9251 2044. No NZ office.

Qantas Australia ☎13 1313, New Zealand ☎09/357 8900 or 0800/808 767.

Swissair Australia ☎02/9232 1744, New Zealand ☎09/358 3925.

Thai Airways Australia ☎1300/651 960, New Zealand ☎09/377 3886.

tional flights out of Australia and New Zealand is often limited, so it's best to book at least three weeks ahead.

Flights from Australia

Flights from eastern cities are common-rated (they all cost the same), so if you're travelling from Perth or Darwin deduct A$200–400.

The nearest to a direct flight to Prague is with Czech Airlines in conjunction with Qantas via Bangkok/Singapore for around A$1760 low season, to A$2100 high season. For a little more (A$1900–2200), Ansett/SAS get there via Copenhagen and Singapore. Additional flights to Prague only are with Olympic Airways via Athens and Lufthansa via Frankfurt starting around A$1700, while KLM's fares via Amsterdam start at A$1650.

Flights from New Zealand

There are even fewer options from New Zealand, and all involve a combination of airlines that take you via Asia or the US to a European hub city, and thence to Prague. The best deal is with Qantas to Los Angeles, Singapore or Bangkok, where you connect with Alitalia via Rome; and with Air New Zealand/United Airlines via LA and New York, both for around NZ$2199 in low season and NZ$2899 in high.

Most flights leave from Auckland, so you'll need to add on around NZ$100–300 for Christchurch and Wellington connections.

Travel insurance

Travel insurance is put together by the airlines and specialist groups such as those listed above and opposite, in conjunction with insurance companies. Policies are broadly comparable in premium and coverage, though Ready Plan usually give the best value for money. A typical policy for the Czech Republic costs A$110/NZ$140 for two weeks, and A$190/NZ$240 for one month.

INSURANCE COMPANIES IN AUSTRALIA AND NEW ZEALAND

AFTA ☎02/9956 4800

Cover More ☎02/9202 8000 in Sydney; elsewhere ☎1800/251881; New Zealand ☎09/377 5958 or ☎0800/657 744

Ready Plan Australia ☎03/9791 5077 in Melbourne; elsewhere ☎1300/555 017; New Zealand ☎09/300 5333

UTAG ☎02/9744 7833 in Sydney; elsewhere ☎1800/809 462

Agents and operators in Australia and New Zealand

Anywhere Travel, 345 Anzac Parade, Kingsford, Sydney ☎02/9663 0411; *anywhere@ozemail.com.au*

Budget Travel, 16 Fort St, Auckland, plus branches around the city ☎09/366 0061 or 0-800/808 040

Destinations Unlimited, 3 Milford Rd, Auckland ☎09/373 4033

Flight Centres 82 Elizabeth St, Sydney, plus branches nationwide ☎13 1600; 205 Queen St, Auckland ☎09/309 6171, plus branches nationwide; *www.flightcentre.com.au*.

Status Travel, 22 Cavenagh St, Darwin ☎08/8941 1843

STA Travel, 702 Harris St, Ultimo, Sydney, plus branches nationwide. Nearest branch ☎13 1776, fastfare telesales ☎1-300/360 960; 10 High St, Auckland ☎09/309 0458, fastfare telesales ☎09/366 6673, and other offices countrywide; *www.statravel.com.au*; email: *traveller@statravelaus.com.au*

Student Uni Travel, 92 Pitt St, Sydney ☎02/9232 8444, plus branches in Brisbane, Cairns, Darwin, Melbourne and Perth.

Thomas Cook, 175 Pitt St, Sydney, plus branches in other state capitals (local branch ☎13 1771, Thomas Cook Direct telesales ☎1-800/063 913); New Zealand: 159 Queen St, Auckland ☎09/359 5200; *www.thomascook.com.au*

Trailfinders, 8 Spring St, Sydney ☎02/9247 7666; 80 Clarence St, Sydney ☎02/9290 1500; *www.travel.com.au*; email: *consultant@travel.com.au*

Usit Beyond, corner of Shortland St and Jean Batten Place, Auckland ☎09/379 4224, plus branches in Christchurch, Hamilton, Palmerston North and Wellington; *www.usitbeyond.co.nz*.

Specialist operators

Australians Studying Abroad 1/970 High St, Armadale, Melbourne ☎03/9509 1955 or 1800/645 755. Art and cultural tours drawing on the significance of the Habsburg cities of Budapest, Prague and Vienna.

Contal Travel 40 Roma St, Brisbane ☎07/3236 2929. Prague accommodation, car rental and day tours.

Eastern Europe Travel Bureau 75 King St, Sydney ☎02/9262 1144, and branches in Melbourne, Adelaide, Perth and Brisbane. Packages to Prague.

Eastern Eurotours Level 9, Seabank, 12-14 Marine Parade, Southport, QLD 4215 ☎07/5591 0326 or 1-800 242 353. City and spa town coach tours.

Eurolynx 3/20 Fort St, Auckland ☎09/379 9716. Sightseeing tours to Prague.

Gateway Travel 48 The Boulevarde, Strathfield, Sydney ☎02/9745 3333. Accommodation and tours.

Red tape and visas

■ CZECH EMBASSIES AND CONSULATES

US, Canadian, New Zealand and all EU nationals need only a **full passport** to enter the Czech Republic, though the passport itself must be valid for at least two months beyond your return date. US citizens can stay for up to 30 days; UK and Canadian citizens can stay up to 180 days; all other EU citizens and New Zealanders can stay up to 90 days. If you're staying for over a month, you must register with the police within thirty days of your arrival (if you're staying in a hotel, this will be done for you). To extend your stay beyond the limits quoted above, you need a visa extension or a residence permit (see below). Note that entry requirements do change, sometimes at very short notice, so if in doubt, check with your nearest embassy or consulate before you leave.

At the time of writing Australians still needed a **visa** (valid for up to thirty days), available from a Czech embassy or consulate; it costs around £20 and should take no more than three days to obtain. Along with your application form you'll need a valid passport and two passport photographs (four for a multiple entry visa) and a SAE if applying by post. Visas are available at Prague airport, and at the chief road border crossings of Rozvadov, Dolní Dvořiště and Hatě, but cost nearly twice as much. Those entering on a visa must register with the police within three days of arrival (again, if you're at a hotel, they will do this for you).

To extend your visa, you either need a really good excuse, or a **residence permit** (*občanský průkaz*), which is difficult to obtain unless you're studying here or have a job (and, therefore, a work permit). Many people avoid this bureaucratic nightmare – which can take up to six months – by simply leaving the country for a few days when their time runs out, making sure they get their passport stamped upon re-entry, but the

Czech embassies and consulates

Australia 169 Military Rd, Dover Heights, Sydney, NSW 2030 ☎02/9371 0860

Austria Penzingerstrasse 11–13, 1140 Vienna ☎0222/894 1200

Belgium 555 rue Engeland, 1180 Bruxelles-Uccle ☎02/374 1203

Canada 541 Sussex Drive, Ottawa, Ontario K1N 6Z6 ☎613/562 3875; 1305 Avenue des Pins Ouest, Montréal, Quebec H3G 1B2 ☎514/849-4495

France 15 avenue Charles Floquet, 75343 Paris ☎40 65 13 00

Germany Wilhelmstrasse 44, 10117 Berlin ☎030/226380

Ireland 57 Northumberland Rd, Ballsbridge, Dublin 4 ☎01/668 1135

New Zealand 48 Hair St, Wainuiomata, Wellington ☎44/564 6001

UK 28 Kensington Palace Gdns, London W8 4QY ☎0207/243 1115
Visa hotline ☎0891/171267

USA 3900 Spring of Freedom St, NW, Washington DC 20008 ☎202/274 9100; 1109 Madison Ave, New York, NY 10028 ☎212/535-8814; 10990 Wilshire Blvd, Suite 1100, Los Angeles, CA ☎310/473-0889

Foreign consulates and embassies in Prague are listed on p.247.

legality of this is somewhat doubtful, and the Prague police frequently clamp down on foreigners working or staying here illegally.

If you already have a work permit and need a residence permit, you'll have to fill in the application form known as *povolení k pobytu*, which you can only get by going in person to the second floor of the Úřad práce (Department of Employment), Zborovská 11, Smíchov. Then go to the Cizinecká policie (Foreigners' Police), Olšanská 2, Žižkov. You should bring with you your passport, your work permit, a 1000Kč stamp (*kolková známka*) and a letter from the owner of the property you're staying in. You also need to bring with you a certificate saying that you have a clean criminal record, known as a *výpis z trestního rejstříku*, obtainable in person from the Rejstřík trestu, náměstí Hrdinů, Nusle, as long as you go armed with a 50Kč *kolková známka*.

Customs allowances into the Czech Republic are 250 cigarettes or 50 cigars, 1 litre of spirits and 2 litres of wine. Allowances when taking goods from the Czech Republic into EU countries are the same. These allowances may change in the future, though, so if in doubt, check with customs before you leave for Prague.

Health matters

No inoculations are required for the Czech Republic, and on a short visit you're unlikely to fall victim to anything worse than an upset stomach. However, if you suffer from a respiratory problem, avoid coming to Prague during the winter months, when sulphur dioxide levels in the city centre regularly breach World Health Organisation safety levels (see box on p.18).

Pharmacies, doctors and hospitals

Reciprocal arrangements between the Czech Republic and the EU mean that EU citizens are entitled to free emergency medical care, with a charge only for imported drugs and certain specialized treatments. Citizens from all other countries should have their own health insurance, and even EU residents would be well-advised to take out their own health policies, as the reciprocal agreement only covers emergency treatment and not a visit to a doctor.

If you should become ill, the easiest course of action is to go to a **pharmacy** (*lékárna*). Pharmacists are willing to give advice (though language may be a problem), and are able to dispense many drugs available only on prescription in other countries. They usually keep normal

Pharmacies

Central pharmacy

Václavské náměstí 64, Nové Město; metro Muzeum; Mon–Fri 8am–noon & 2–4pm.

24-hr pharmacies

Belgická 37, Vinohrady; metro náměstí Míru; ☎24 23 72 07

Štefánikova 6, Břevnov; metro Anděl; ☎53 70 39

Emergency dentist

Vladislavova 22, Nové Město ☎24 22 76 63; Mon–Thurs 7pm–7am; Fri–Sun 24hr.

Pollution in Prague

Don't be fooled by the outward beauty of Prague's buildings. The city is sick, suffering some of the highest levels of sulphur dioxide of any European capital. And the worst place to be is the old town itself: every winter the **pollution** in the Staré Město exceeds the WHO safety limits. On at least ten days during each winter, pollution levels rise to double the WHO safety levels, forcing the municipal authorities to introduce a total ban on non-essential traffic, domestic and foreign, within the city.

Between October and March, Prague is plagued by a lethal cocktail of winter weather, the city's basin-like topography, and the brown coal which provides energy for industry and most of the city's heating. The heavy, cold air sits in the basin, trapped in by the warmer air above, and thus preventing the sulphur dioxide and carbon monoxide from dispersing. Car ownership looks set to rise dramatically over the next decade, and a year-round ban on cars in the city centre is a serious possibility.

shop hours, but several outlying ones are open round the clock (there's a couple listed on p.17).

If language proves an insurmountable barrier, and you wish to see an **English-speaking doctor**, you should go to the Nemocnice na Homolce, Roentgenova 2, Motol; ☎52 92 11 11; bus #167 from metro Anděl. This is a privately run **hospital** specifically geared towards foreigners – take your passport and at least 1000Kč to put down as a deposit. They run a 24-hour emergency call-out service (☎52 92 20 43), but if it's a real **emergency**, then dial ☎155 for an ambulance and you'll be taken to the nearest hospital.

Information and maps

The Czech tourist board – known as the Czech Centre – is finally coming of age. The offices themselves have a handful of good maps and pamphlets to give away, and the staff are generally helpful and should be able to answer any queries you have about the country. There are also one or two fairly useful Web sites (see opposite).

Maps

For wandering round the centre of Prague, the **maps** produced in this book should be sufficient, but if you crave greater detail, or are staying out in the suburbs, you may need to buy something more comprehensive. The best maps of Prague are produced by Kartografie Praha, whose 1:20,000 booklet (*plán města*) covers the whole city and includes the tram and bus routes, too.

To get hold of one of the above maps of Prague in the UK, try Stanfords, 12–14 Long Acre, London WC2 (☎0171/836 1321; *sales@stanfords.co.uk*). In the US, Rand McNally should be able to help (call ☎1-800/333-0136 ext 2111 for the location of their nearest store and for direct-mail details). In

Surfing Prague

Central Europe On-Line News and information on the countries of the former Eastern Bloc, including Czech Republic, with lots of links to other Czech sites. *www.centraleurope.cz*

Do města/Downtown Prague's useful fortnightly listings leaflet on-line in English and Czech.*www.downtown.cz*

Prague Post A very useful site, not just for getting the latest news, but also for finding out what's on in Prague over the coming week. *www.praguepost.cz*

Radio Prague An informative site well worth visiting, with updated news and weather as audio or text. *www.radio.cz*

Ticketpro Prague's largest ticket agency is on-line so you can book concert tickets ahead. *www.ticketpro.cz*

Welcome to the Czech Republic Basic information on the country in English, and on the worldwide network of Czech Centres, run by the Czech Foreign Ministry. *www.czech.cz*

Australasia, Mapland, 372 Little Bourke St, Melbourne (☎03/9670 4383), the Travel Bookshop, Shop 3, 175 Liverpool St, Sydney (☎02/9261 8200) and Worldwide Maps and Guides, 187 George St, Brisbane (☎07/3221 4330), are worth contacting, as are Speciality Maps, 58 Albert St, Auckland (☎09/307 2217).

Otherwise, you can wait until you get to Prague, where you'll get more choice and it'll cost you a lot less. Try any PIS office (Prague Information Service), bookstore (*knihkupectví*) or even your hotel.

Czech centres abroad

Austria Herrengasse 17, 1010 Vienna ☎535 2361; *ccwien@czech.cz*

Belgium Boulevard Leopold II Laan 262, 1080 Brussels ☎02/644 9527; *ccbrussels@czech.cz*

Germany Karl Liebknecht Str. 3, 10178 Berlin ☎030/204 47 70; *ccberlin@czech.cz*

Slovakia nám. SNP 12, 812 34 Bratislava ☎07/381 4188; *ccbratislava@czech.cz*

UK 95 Great Portland St, London W1 5RA ☎0207/291 9925; *cclondon@czech.cz*

USA 1109 Madison Ave, New York, NY 10028 ☎212/288 0830; *nycenter@pop.net*

Costs, money and banks

In general terms, Prague is still incredibly cheap for westerners. The one exception is accommodation, which is comparable with many EU countries. At the time of writing, inflation was pretty much under control, though before you get to thinking everything is rosy in the Czech Republic, it's worth bearing in mind that the average monthly wage for Czechs is currently around 6500Kč (£125/$200).

You'll find more precise costs for accommodation, food and drink in the relevant sections of the book: see "Accommodation" (p.199) and "Eating and Drinking" (p.207). At the bottom end of the scale, if you stay in a hostel and stick to pubs and takeaways, you could get by on as little as £10/$16 a day. If you stay in private accommodation or cheapish hotels, and eat in slightly fancier restaurants, then you could easily spend £25/$40 a day. The good thing about Prague, however, is that once you've accounted for your room, most restaurants, pubs, museums and galleries, beer and even taxis and nightclubs are far from expensive.

Tipping is normal practice in cafés, bars, restaurants and taxis, though this is usually done by simply rounding up the total. For example, if the waiter tots up the bill and asks you for 74Kč, you should hand him a 100Kč note and say "take 80Kč".

Czech currency

The currency in the Czech Republic is the Czech crown or *koruna česká* (abbreviated to Kč), which is divided into one hundred relatively worthless hellers or *halíře* (abbreviated to h). At the time of going to press there were around 60Kč to the pound sterling and around 35Kč to the US dollar. The crown's value is likely to fall further in the future as the political and economic stability of the country is looking uncertain.

Notes come in 20Kč, 50Kč, 100Kč, 200Kč, 500Kč, 1000Kč (less frequently 2000Kč and 5000Kč) denominations; coins as 1Kč, 2Kč, 5Kč, 10Kč, 20Kč and 50Kč, plus 10h, 20h and 50h.

Travellers' cheques and credit cards

Travellers' cheques are the safest and easiest way to carry money. American Express and Thomas Cook are the most widely used – available for a small commission (usually one percent of the amount ordered) from any bank and some building societies, whether or not you have an account, and from branches of American Express and Thomas Cook. The cheques can be exchanged commission-free at the companies' respective Prague branches (for addresses, see box opposite).

Even if you have travellers' cheques, it's a good idea to take a **credit card** with a PIN as well. You can pay with plastic (Visa, Master Card/Access and Amex are the most acceptable) in most upmarket hotels, restaurants and shops, though it's not as widely used as in the UK or the US. You can also withdraw cash from the automatic teller machines (ATMs) or cashpoints, which are now a feature of downtown Prague. It's also a good idea to keep at least some hard currency in **cash** for emergencies, as it will be accepted almost anywhere. If you lose your Visa card, phone ☎24 23 24 23; if you lose your Mastercard, phone ☎24 24 81 10.

Changing money

The 24-hour exchange desk at the **airport** run by the Československá obchodní banka is, somewhat surprisingly, an excellent place to change money, regularly charging a mere one or two percent commission. Most Czech **banks** will be pre-

Central moneychanging outlets

American Express, Václavské náměstí 56, Nové Město; ☎24 21 99 92

Československá obchodní banka, Na příkopě 14, Nové Město; ☎24 11 11 11

Komerční banka, Na příkopě 33, Nové Město; ☎22 43 21 11

Thomas Cook, Staroměstské náměstí 5, Staré Město; ☎24 81 71 73

Živnostenká banka, Na příkopě 20, Nové Město; ☎24 12 11 11

pared to change travellers' cheques, accept Eurocheques, and give cash advances on credit cards – look for the window marked *směnárna*. Commissions at banks are fairly reasonable (generally under three percent), but the queues and the bureaucracy can mean a long wait. Quicker, but more of a rip-off in terms of either commission or exchange rate, are the exchange outlets which can be found on just about every street corner in the centre of Prague.

Banking hours are usually Monday to Friday 8am to 5pm, often with a break at lunchtime. Outside of these times, you may find the odd bank open, but otherwise you'll have to rely on the exchange outlets and the international hotels.

Cash emergencies

When you buy your travellers' cheques, make a note of the emergency phone number given. On your trip keep a record of all cheques and note which ones you spend – and report any loss or theft immediately. All being well, you should get the missing cheques reissued within a couple of days. Things can get trickier if you lose your credit card: your bank should be able to give you details of the number to call if this happens, but you won't be provided with a replacement card until you get home.

Assuming you know someone who is prepared to send you the money, the quickest and easiest way to have funds sent out to you in an emergency is to do it through **Western Union**, who will wire the money to you in a couple of hours (some banks will also do this via Western Union); get your sponsor to phone ☎0800/833833 in the UK or ☎1-800/325-6000 in North America. The Prague office of Western Union is at Sport Turist Special, Národní třída 33 (Mon–Fri 9am–12.30pm & 1.30–6pm, Sat & Sun 10am–12.30pm & 1.30–4.30pm; ☎24 22 85 18).

If you have a few days' leeway, you can simply get your bank to wire your money to a Czech bank, a process that shouldn't take more than a couple of working days. If you can last out the week, then an **international money order**, exchangeable at any post office, is by far the cheapest way of sending money.

If you're in really dire straits, get in touch with your **consulate** in Prague, who will usually let you make one phone call home free of charge, and will – in worst cases only – repatriate you, but will never, under any circumstances, lend you money.

Disabled travellers

Under the Communists very little attention was paid to the needs of the disabled. Attitudes are slowly changing – a law was passed in 1994 stipulating that all new buildings must have disabled access – but there is still a long way to go, and the country's chronic shortage of funds makes matters worse.

Transport is a major problem, since buses and all except the newest trams are virtually impossible for wheelchairs, though some metro stations now have facilities for the disabled, and the two railway stations (Hlavní nádraží and Nádraží Holešovice) actually have self-operating lifts.

At the time of writing, none of the **car rental** companies could offer vehicles with hand controls in Prague. If you're driving to Prague, most cross-Channel ferries now have adequate facilities, as does British Airways for those who are flying.

For a list of wheelchair-friendly **hotels**, restaurants, metro stations and so forth, order the guidebook *Accessible Prague/Přístupná Praha*) from the Prague Wheelchair Association, listed below.

CONTACTS FOR DISABLED TRAVELLERS

Australia

ACROD (Australian Council for Rehabilitation of the Disabled), PO Box 60, Curtin, ACT 2605; ☎02/6282 4333; 24 Cabarita Rd, Cabarita ☎02/9743 2699.

Britain

Holiday Care Service, 2nd Floor, Imperial Building, Victoria Rd, Horley, Surrey RH6 7PZ; ☎01293/774535. Information on all aspects of travel.

RADAR (The Royal Association for Disability and Rehabilitation), 12 City Forum, 250 City Rd, London EC1V 8AF; ☎0207/250 3222; Minicom 0207/250 4119; *www.radar.org.uk.* Information on all aspects of travel.

Czech Republic

Prague Wheelchair Association, Pražská organizace vozíčkářů, Benediktská 6, Nové Město, Prague; ☎232 58 31, fax 24 81 62 31. Disabled-run organization that can provide limited assistance when you're in Prague, and which also produces the *Accessible Prague* (*Přístupná Praha*) guidebook.

Ireland

Irish Wheelchair Association, Blackheath Drive, Clontarf, Dublin 3 ☎01/833 8241. National voluntary organization working with people with disabilities, with related services for holidaymakers.

New Zealand

Disabled Persons Assembly, 173–175 Victoria St, Wellington ☎04/801 9100.

North America

Directions Unlimited, 720 N Bedford Rd, Bedford Hills, NY 10507; ☎1-800/533-5343. Tour operator specializing in custom tours for people with disabilities.

Mobility International USA, PO Box 10767, Eugene, OR 97440; Voice and TDD: ☎541/343-1284. Information and referral services, access guides, tours and exchange programs. Annual membership $25 (includes quarterly newsletter).

Society for the Advancement of Travel for the Handicapped (SATH), 347 5th Ave, Suite 610, New York, NY 10016 ☎212/447-7284; *www.sittravel.com.* Non-profit-making travel industry referral service that passes queries on to its members as appropriate; allow plenty of time for a response.

Twin Peaks Press, Box 129, Vancouver, WA 98666; ☎206/694-2462 or 1-800/637-2256. Publisher of the *Directory of Travel Agencies for the Disabled*, and a number of other useful publications loaded with personal tips.

Post and phones

Post

The **main post office** (*pošta*) in Prague is at Jindřišská 14 (☎23 13 14 45), just off Wenceslas Square. It is open daily 7am to 10pm, with a reduced service operating during the night. Designed in ornate neo-Renaissance style, the building has been undergoing a major overhaul for the last couple of years, during which 24-hour services have been curtailed. The chief problem, once inside, is making sure you queue at the right counter – look for the appropriate sign in order to buy *známky* (stamps); *telefonní karty* (phone cards) or send *balíky* (parcels). Each postal district in Prague has several post offices, though these have far less comprehensive hours and services.

Some foreign countries in Czech

Australia	*Austrálie*
Austria	*Rakousko*
Canada	*Kanada*
Eire	*Irsko*
Germany	*Německo*
Great Britain	*Velká Británie*
Hungary	*Maďarsko*
Netherlands	*Nizozemí*
New Zealand	*Nový Zéland*
USA	*Spojené státy americké*

Poste restante (pronounced as five syllables in Czech) letters to Prague will automatically arrive at the main post office mentioned above (the postcode is 110 00 PRAHA 1), though theoretically you may use any post office. Alternatively, American Express, at Václavské náměstí 56 (daily 9am–7pm), will hold mail for a month for credit card and/or cheque holders.

Outbound post is reasonably reliable, with letters or cards taking around five working days to Britain and Ireland, and one week to ten days to North America or Australasia. You can buy **stamps** from newsagents, tobacconists and some kiosks, as well as at the post offices. If you want to send an **email** or go on-line, head for one of Prague's Internet cafés (see p.217).

To send a **parcel over 2kg** (but below 15kg) you must go to the Pošta-Celnice customs parcel office at the junction of Plzeňská and Vrchlického in Prague 5 (tram #4, #7 or #9 from metro Anděl). After filling in two separate forms for shipping and customs, you then have a choice of sending your parcel by ship, air or express. Alternatively, you can save a lot of hassle, and get the parcel there in no time at all, by paying considerably more at a courier company like DHL, who are based at the airport (☎20 30 01 11), and downtown at Na poříčí 4, Nové Město (☎24 22 98 87).

Phones

Prague's **telephone system** is gradually being digitalized, but phone numbers can still vary in length from six (or even less) to eight digits. The majority of public phones in the centre of Prague take only **phone cards** (*telefonní karty*), currently available in 50, 100 and 150 units from post offices, tobacconists and some shops (prices vary). You can make international calls from all card phones (calls cost over 20Kč a minute to Britain and Ireland, over 30–40Kč to North America and a whopping 40–60Kč to Australasia). There are instructions in English, and if you press the appropriate button the language on the digital read-out will change to English. If you have any problems, ring ☎0149 to get through to international information.

DIALLING CODES

To Prague

From Britain & Ireland	☎ 00 420 2
From USA & Canada	☎ 011 420 2
From Australia & New Zealand	☎ 0011 420 2

Phoning from elsewhere in the Czech Republic, the Prague city code is ☎ 02

From Prague

UK	☎ 0044	New Zealand	☎ 0064
Eire	☎ 00353	USA and Canada	☎ 001
Australia	☎ 0061		

In **coin-operated phones**, you need to insert a minimum of 3Kč to make a local call, 5Kč for long-distance – if you stock up with enough coins, it is perfectly possible to make an international phone call. The **dialling tone** is a short followed by a long pulse; the **ringing tone** is long and regular; **engaged** is short and rapid (not to be confused with the connecting tone which is very short and rapid). The standard Czech response is *prosím*; the word for "extension" is *linka*.

You can also make phone calls from the 24-hour **telephone exchange** situated round the corner from the main post office at Politických vězňů 4. Write down the town and number you want, leave a deposit of around 200Kč and wait for your name to be called out. Calls from a telephone exchange cost slightly less, but avoid making any calls from hotels, where the surcharge is usually outrageous. To make a **collect call**, which will probably cost the recipient less than it costs you, you can either do it at the telephone exchange, or dial the international operator in the country you're phoning: ring ☎ 00 420 00 44 01 for the UK; ☎ 00 420 001 01 for the US; ☎ 00 420 001 51 for Canada; these calls are not free.

Opening hours, holidays and festivals

Closed for technical reasons

Don't be too surprised if one or two of Prague's museums and galleries are "closed for technical reasons", "closed due to illness", or, more permanently, "closed for reconstruction". Notices are rarely more specific than that, but the widespread shortage of staff and funds is often behind the closure. It's impossible to predict what will be closed when, but it's a good idea to make alternative plans when visiting galleries and museums, just in case.

Shops in Prague are generally open Monday to Friday from 9am to 5pm, though most supermarkets and tourist shops stay open later. Smaller shops may close for lunch for an hour some time between noon and 2pm. Some shops close by noon or 1pm on Saturday, and only a few open on Sunday. Most traditional pubs tend to close between 10 and 11pm, with food often difficult to obtain after 9pm. However, there are now plenty of late-night bars, where you can continue drinking, and restaurants that stay open much later.

Opening hours for **museums and galleries** are generally 9 or 10am to 5 or 6pm every day except Monday (when they are closed) all year round. Full opening hours are detailed in the text. Ticket prices to museums and galleries range between 50Kč and 100Kč, and are listed in the margins of the text – one or two major sights charge a great deal more, most notably the Jewish Museum.

Getting into **churches** can present more of a problem. Some of the more central ones operate in much the same way as museums and occasionally even have an entry charge, particularly for their crypts or cloisters. Most churches, however, are kept locked, with perhaps just the vestibule open, allowing you at least a glimpse of the interior, opening fully only for worship in the early morning (around 7 or 8am) and/or the evening (around 6 or 7pm). Synagogues in Josefov follow museum hours, except that they close on Saturdays rather than Mondays.

Outside Prague, in the high season, **castles and chateaux** open from 9am to noon, and again from 1 to 4pm. On Mondays and from the end of October to the beginning of April, apart from a few notable exceptions, most places are closed. In April and October, opening hours are often restricted to weekends and public holidays only. Whatever the time of year, if you want to see the interior of a castle or chateau, you're more than likely to have to go on a **guided tour** (nearly always in Czech) that usually lasts for an hour. Ask for an *anglický text*, an often unintentionally hilarious English resumé of the castle's history. Guided tours invariably set off on the hour, and the last one leaves an hour before the actual closing time: in practice, this means the last morning tour will usually set off at 11am, and the last afternoon tour will often be at 3pm. Again, ticket prices are relatively low, rarely exceeding 100Kč.

National holidays

National holidays were always a potential source of contention with the old regime, and they remain controversial even today. **May Day**,

National holidays

January 1
Easter Monday
May 1
May 8 (VE Day)
July 5 (Introduction of Christianity)
July 6 (Death of Jan Hus)
October 28 (Foundation of the Republic)
December 24
December 25
December 26

once a nationwide compulsory march under dull Commie slogans, remains a public holiday, though only the skinheads and anarchists bother to slug it out on the streets nowadays. Of the other *slavné májové dny* (Glorious May Days), as they used to be known, **May 5**, the beginning of the 1945 Prague Uprising, has been binned, and VE Day is now celebrated along with the western Allies on **May 8**, and not on May 9, as it was under the Communists, and still is in Russia. To scupper any celebration of the founding of the First Republic on **October 28**, the Communists hijacked the date for their very own Nationalization Day. Some Czechs argue that whichever way you look at it, this Czechoslovak/Communist holiday – which the extreme right-wing Republican Party regularly disrupts – should be ditched in favour of September 28, the feast day of the country's patron saint, St Wenceslas.

Festivals

Prague's **annual festive calendar** is light compared to most European capitals, with just a couple of cultural events in addition to the usual religious festivities. To find out what's going on, check out one of the listings magazines mentioned opposite.

The city's most famous festival is the **Pražské jaro** (Prague Spring), not to be confused with the political events of 1968. It begins every year on May 12, the anniversary of Smetana's death, with a procession from Smetana's grave in Vyšehrad to the Obecní dům, where the composer's *Má vlast* (My Country) is performed in the presence of the president. It ends three weeks later, on June 2, with Beethoven's Ninth Symphony, and generally attracts several top-class performers. Tickets can be extremely hard to come by (see p.233).

A new highlight in the city's cultural calendar is **Tanec Praha** (Dance Prague; *www.tanecpha.cz*), an international festival of modern dance which takes place throughout the city in June/July. One tradition that has returned to Prague with a vengeance, after a long absence, is the **ball season**, which apes that of the old imperial capital, Vienna. Each ball (*ples*) takes place in one of the city's many wonderful late nineteenth-century municipal halls and concert theatres from January to March. They're open to anyone, though it can be difficult to get hold of tickets.

The rest of Prague's stirrings are mostly of a religious nature. At **Easter** (*Velikonoce*), the age-old sexist ritual of whipping girls' calves with braided birch twigs tied together with ribbons (*pomlázky*) is still practised. To prevent such a fate, the girls are supposed to offer the boys a coloured easter egg and pour a bucket of cold water over them. What may once have been an innocent bucolic frolic has now become another excuse for Czech men to harass any woman who dares to venture onto the street during this period.

Halloween comes early to the Czech Republic, on April 30, when the "**Burning of the Witches**" (*pálení čarodějnic*) takes place. Bonfires are lit across the country, and old brooms thrown out and burned as everyone celebrates the end of the long winter. On December 4, the feast day of Saint Barbara, cherry tree branches are bought as decorations, the aim being to get them to blossom before Christmas.

On the evening of **December 5**, numerous trios, dressed up as *svaty Mikuláš* (Saint Nicholas), an angel and a devil, tour round the neighbourhoods, the angel handing out sweets and fruit to children who've been good, while the devil dishes out coal and potatoes to those who've been naughty. The Czech Saint Nicholas has white hair and a beard, and dresses not in red but in a white priest's outfit, with a bishop's mitre.

With a week or so to go, large barrels are set up in the streets from which huge quantities of live carp (*kapr*), the traditional Christmas dish, are sold. **Christmas Eve** (*štědrý večer*) is traditionally a day of fasting, broken only when the evening star appears, signalling the beginning of the Christmas feast of carp, potato salad, schnitzel and sweetbreads. Only after the meal are the children allowed to open their presents, which miraculously appear beneath the tree, thanks not to Santa Claus, but to *Ježíšek* (Baby Jesus).

Birthdays are much less important for the Czechs than **saints' name days**, which fall on the same day each year. Thus popular names like Jan or Anna are practically national celebrations, and an excuse for everyone to get drunk since you're bound to know at least one person with those names.

The media

It's a sign of the times that the most famous **Czech newspaper**, *Lidové noviny* (the best-known *samizdat* or underground publication under the Communists), is now owned by a Swiss company, Ringier. In fact over half the Czech press is now foreign-owned, including the country's most popular daily, *Blesk*, a sensationalist tabloid with lurid colour pictures, naked women and reactionary politics.

The most popular quality paper nowadays is *Mladá fronta dnes*, former mouthpiece of the Communist youth movement, now a centrist daily with solid coverage of local and international news. Next in the popularity stakes is *Právo* (formerly the official mouthpiece of the Communist Party *Rudé právo* or "Red Justice"), a surprisingly successful "left-wing daily". The other positive independent political voice is the weekly *Respekt*, which prides itself on its investigative journalism. If all you want, however, is yesterday's (or, more often than not, the day before yesterday's) international football results, pick up a copy of the daily *Sport*.

The **English-language** weekly to look out for is *The Prague Post*, a quality paper with strong business coverage and a useful pull-out **listings** section. More comprehensive listings are to be found in the monthly listings magazine *Culture in Prague*, the flimsy bilingual fortnightly listings handout, *Do města/Downtown*, and in *Přehled*, which is in Czech, but should be easily decipherable.

The entire range of **foreign newspapers** is available from the kiosks on Wenceslas Square and elsewhere. They're generally a day old, though one that you can buy on the day of issue is the European edition of *The Guardian*, printed in Frankfurt (it arrives on the streets of Prague around mid-morning).

In the **magazine** market, you'll find the best coverage of contemporary Czech politics in English in *The New Presence/Nová přítomnost*, a bilingual current affairs magazine, directly inspired by the Masaryk-funded *Přítomnost*, which was one of the leading periodicals of the First Republic. Various arty magazines run by ex-pats have come and gone over the years – the literary *Trafika* is probably the best-known of the genre – but it's still worth calling in at **The Globe** bookstore (see p.244) for the latest titles.

TV and radio

Česká televize's two state-owned channels, ІТ1 and ІТ2, have both been eclipsed as far as ratings go by the runaway success of the commercial channel, Nova. The latter features lots of American sitcoms dubbed into Czech, plenty of game shows and the most comprehensive coverage of Czech football. Prima, the other commercial channel, has yet to make any significant inroads into Nova's audience monopoly. ІТ2 is your best bet for foreign films with subtitles; it also shows news in English from the BBC on Monday to Friday at 8am, and on Saturday and Sunday at 7am.

On the **radio**, the BBC World Service now broadcasts loud and clear on 101.1FM, mostly in English, with occasional Czech news summaries. As far as domestic **radio** goes, the most popular station is still, as in Communist days, the state-run Český rozhlas news-orientated Radio Praha (92.6/102.7FM), on which Havel broadcasts his presidential Sunday evening chat; an English-language news summary goes out Monday to Friday at 5.30pm. The three top FM music channels are Evropa 2 (88.2FM), Radio Bonton (99.7FM) and Kiss FM (98FM), which dish out bland Euro-pop. More interesting is Radio 1 (91.9FM), which plays a wide range of indie rock from east and west, and broadcasts a brief news summary at 7am Monday to Friday.

Trouble and the police

Despite their change of name from *Veřejná bezpečnost* or *VB*, as the former Communist police were known, to **Policie**, the national police force are still hugely unpopular. Public confidence in their competence has suffered a severe blow due to the dramatic rise in the level of **crime** since 1989. However, you shouldn't be unduly paranoid: the crime rate is still very low compared with most European or North American cities. Pickpockets are the biggest hassle, especially in summer around the most popular tourist sights and on the trams and metro.

There are two main types of police nowadays: the aforementioned *Policie* and the municipal police (see below). The **Policie**, with white shirts, navy blue jackets and grey trousers, are the national force, with the power of arrest, and are under the control of the Ministry of Interior. If you do need the police, though – and above all if you're reporting a serious crime – you should always go to the **Městská policie** (municipal police), run by the Prague city authorities, distinguishable by their all-black uniforms.

In addition, there are various private security guards, who also dress in black – hence their nickname, *Cerné šerií* (Black Sheriffs) – employed mostly by hotels and banks. They are often very officious, incompetent and trigger-happy. They are allowed to carry guns, but have no powers of arrest, and you are not legally obliged to show them your ID.

The following is a list of the main police stations for each of Prague's ten postal districts.

Prague 1 – Bartolomějská 6
Prague 2 – Legerova 2
Prague 3 – Lupáčova 11
Prague 4 – U plynárny 2
Prague 5 – Nádražní 16a
Prague 6 – V. P. Čkalova 18
Prague 7 – Fr. Křížka 24
Prague 8 – Rosenbergových 1
Prague 9 – Jandova 1
Prague 10 – Přípotoční 300

Avoiding trouble

Almost all the problems encountered by tourists in Prague are to do with **petty crime** – mostly theft from cars and hotel rooms – rather than more serious physical confrontations. Sensible precautions include making photocopies of your passport, leaving passport and tickets in the hotel safe and noting down travellers' cheque and credit card numbers. If you have a car, don't leave anything in view when you park it, and take the cassette/radio with you if you can. Vehicles are rarely stolen, but luggage and valuables left in cars do make a tempting target and rental cars are easy to spot.

In theory, you're supposed to carry some form of **identification** at all times, and the police can stop you in the street and demand it. In practice, they're rarely bothered if you're clearly a foreigner (unless you're driving). In any case, the police are now so deferential that they tend to confine themselves to socially acceptable activities like traffic control and harassing Romanies.

What to do if you're robbed

If you are unlucky enough to have something stolen, you will need to **go to the police** to report it, not least because your insurance company will require a police report. It's unlikely that there'll be anyone there who speaks English, and even less likely that your belongings will be retrieved but, at the very least, you should get a statement detailing

Emergencies

Ambulance	☎155
Police	☎158
Fire	☎150

what you've lost for your insurance claim. Try the phrase *byl jsem oloupen* or (if you're a woman) *byla jsem oloupena* – "I have been robbed".

Sexual harassment

As far as **sexual harassment** is concerned, things are, if anything, marginally less intimidating than in western Europe, although without the familiar linguistic and cultural signs, it's easier to misinterpret situations. Specific places to avoid going after dark include Wenceslas Square, Uhelný trh, and the main train stations, Hlavní nádraží and nádraží Holešovice.

Part 2

The City

Chapter 1

Introducing the city

With a population of just one and a quarter million, **Prague** is one of the smallest capital cities in Europe. It originally developed as four separate self-governing towns and a Jewish ghetto, whose individual identities and medieval street plans have been preserved, more or less intact, to this day. Almost everything of any historical interest lies within these central districts, the majority of which are easy to master quickly on foot. Only in the last hundred years has Prague spread beyond its ancient perimeter, and its suburbs now stretch across the hills for miles on every side. There's a cheap and efficient transport system on which to explore them – a decent map is all you need to find your way around.

The castle district or **Hradčany** (Chapter Two) spreads across the hill on the left bank of the River Vltava where the first Slavs settled in the seventh or eighth century. At its eastern end is the Pražský hrad or Prague Castle (known simply as the Hrad in Czech), which contains a whole series of important historical buildings, including the city's cathedral, the seat of the president, and the old royal palace and gardens, as well as a host of museums and galleries. The rest of Hradčany lies to the west of the castle: a sleepy district ranging in scale from the miniature cottages of Nový Svět to the gargantuan facade of the Černínský palác.

Squeezed between the castle hill and the river are the Baroque palaces and houses of the "Little Quarter" or **Malá Strana** (Chapter Three) – around 150 acres of twisting cobbled streets and secret walled gardens – home to the Czech parliament and most of the city's embassies, and dominated by one of the landmarks of the left bank, the green dome and tower of the church of sv Mikuláš. At the southern end of Malá Strana, a funicular railway carries you out of the cramped streets to the top of Petřín hill, the city's most central leafy escape, with a wonderful view across the river.

The twisting matrix of streets is at its most confusing in the original medieval hub of the city, **Staré Město** (Chapter Four) – literally, the "Old Town" – on the right bank of the Vltava. The Karlův most, or **Charles Bridge**, its main link with the opposite bank, is easily the city's

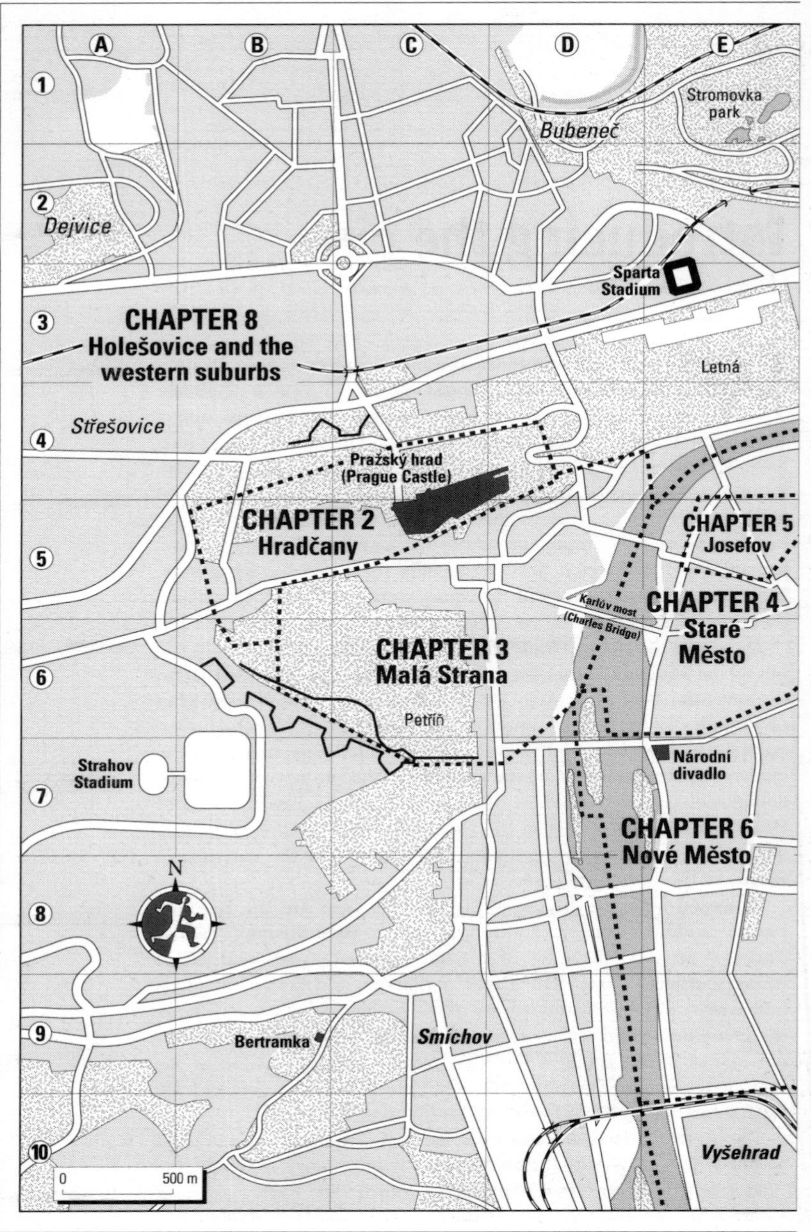
A
B
C
D
E
1
2
3
4
5
6
7
8
9
10
Stromovka park
Bubeneč
Dejvice
Sparta Stadium
CHAPTER 8
Holešovice and the western suburbs
Letná
Střešovice
Pražský hrad (Prague Castle)
CHAPTER 2
Hradčany
CHAPTER 5
Josefov
Karlův most (Charles Bridge)
CHAPTER 4
Staré Město
CHAPTER 3
Malá Strana
Petřín
Strahov Stadium
Národní divadlo
CHAPTER 6
Nové Město
N
Bertramka
Smíchov
Vyšehrad
0
500 m

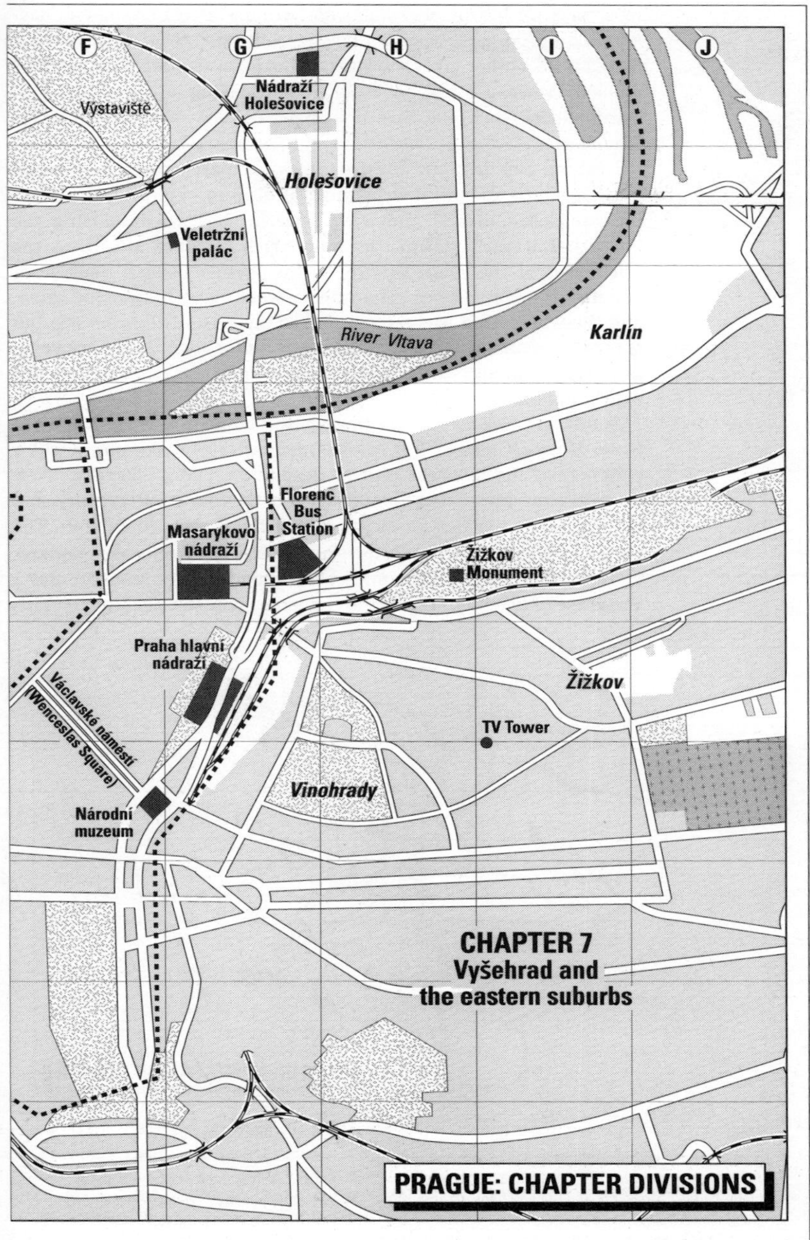
F
G
H
I
J
Nádraží Holešovice
Výstaviště
Holešovice
Veletržní palác
River Vltava
Karlín
Florenc Bus Station
Masarykovo nádraží
Žižkov Monument
Praha hlavní nádraží
Václavské náměstí (Wenceslas Square)
Žižkov
TV Tower
Vinohrady
Národní muzeum
CHAPTER 7
Vyšehrad and the eastern suburbs
PRAGUE: CHAPTER DIVISIONS

most popular historical monument, bristling with Baroque statuary and one of the most beautiful places from which to view the castle. Staré Město's other great showpiece is its main square, **Staroměstské náměstí**, where it's easy to sit for hours, soaking up the sights – the astronomical clock, the Hus monument and the spiky towers of the Týn church.

Nothing else in Staré Město can quite match these two spots, but it's worth spending at least an afternoon exploring the quarter's backstreets and alleyways, and in the process losing the crowds. Enclosed within the boundaries of Staré Město, to the northwest of the main square, is the former Jewish quarter or **Josefov** (Chapter Five). The ghetto walls have long since gone, and the whole area was remodelled at the turn of the century, but six synagogues, a medieval cemetery and a town hall survive as powerful reminders of a community which has existed here for over a millennium.

South and east of the old town is the large sprawling district of **Nové Město** (Chapter Six), whose main arteries make up the city's commercial and business centre. Despite its name – literally, "New Town" – Nové Město was founded back in the fourteenth century, and even its outer reaches are worth taking the trouble to explore. The nexus of Nové Město is Václavské náměstí or **Wenceslas Square**, focus of the political upheavals of the modern-day republic and a showcase of twentieth-century architecture. The district also contains

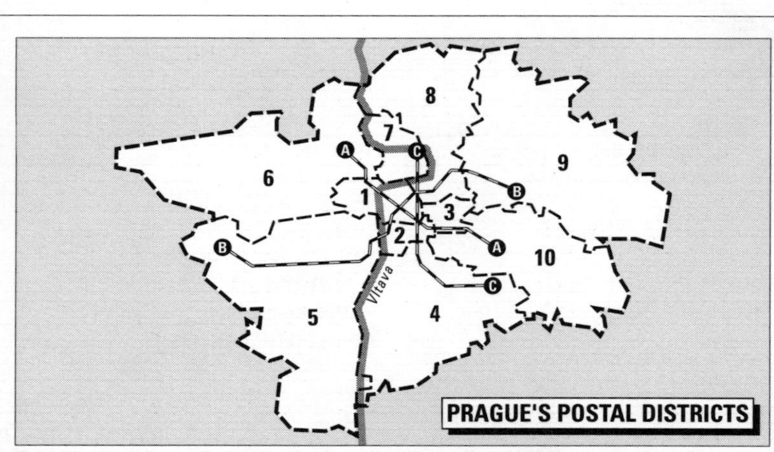

Addresses

The street name is always written before the number in Prague **addresses**. The word for street (*ulice*) is either abbreviated to *ul.* or missed out altogether – Celetná ulice, for instance, is commonly known as Celetná. Other terms often abbreviated are *náměstí* (square), *třída* (avenue), and *nábřeži* (embankment), which become *nám.*, *tř.* and *nábř.* respectively. Prague is divided into numbered **postal districts** (see map) – these are too large to be very much help in orientation, so in this guide, we have generally opted for the names of the smaller historic districts as they appear on street signs, for example Hradčany, Nové Město, Smíchov, etc.

numerous potent symbols of the Czech struggle for nationhood, such as the Národní muzeum (National Museum), Národní divadlo (National Theatre) and the Art Nouveau extravaganza of the Obecní dům (Municipal House).

Further afield lie various **suburbs**, most of which developed only in the last hundred years or so. The single exception is **Vyšehrad**, one of the original fortress settlements of the newly arrived Slavs in the last millennium. Nowadays, it's a peaceful escape from the city, and its cemetery is the final resting place for leading Czech artists of the modern age, including Smetana and Dvořák. To the east is the up-and-coming residential suburb of **Vinohrady**, peppered with parks and squares; and **Žižkov**, one of the city's poorer districts, whose two landmarks – the Žižkov monument and the futuristic TV tower – are visible for miles around. All of these areas are covered in Chapter Seven.

Nineteenth-century suburbs also sprang up to the north of the city centre in **Holešovice**, now home to the city's chief modern art museum, Veletržní palác. The area also boasts two huge swathes of greenery: the Letná plain, overlooking the city; and the Stromovka park, beyond which lie the city chateau of **Troja** and the zoo. Further west, leafy interwar suburbs like **Dejvice** and **Střešovice**, dotted with modernist family villas, give an entirely different angle on Prague. All these places are covered in Chapter eight.

If you're keen to head **out of the city** entirely, there's a wide choice of destinations within an hour or so's journey from Prague. The medieval mining town of **Kutná Hora**, east of Prague, boasts one of central Europe's most stunning pieces of ecclesiastical architecture, plus a host of other attractions. The royal hideaway of **Karlštejn**, 30km or so southwest of Prague, is an obvious day-trip, though the castle of **Konopiště**, some 40km southeast of the city, is perhaps more rewarding for those in search of period interiors. Last of all, the legacy of the war hangs over two places to the northwest: **Lidice**, which was razed to the ground by the Nazis; and the ghetto town of **Terezín** (Theresienstadt), through which most of the country's Jews passed, en route to the extermination camps. The above destinations are all covered in Chapter Nine.

Arrival in Prague

If you fly into Prague, you'll find yourself just over 10km northwest of the city centre, with only a bus link to get you into town. By contrast, both the international train stations and the main bus terminal are linked to the centre by the fast and efficient metro system. Driving into Prague is easy enough, though the city authorities, quite rightly, make it very awkward for drivers to enter the old town, and finding a parking space is also extremely difficult.

By Air

Prague's airport, **Ruzyně** (☎334 11 11), has been thoroughly revamped over the last decade and now has most of the facilities you'd expect of a European capital city airport, with shops, cafés, 24-hour exchange facilities and a variety of accommodation agencies (see p.199) and car rental outlets (see p.44).

The cheapest way to get into town is to take the **local bus #119** (daily: 5am–8pm every 10–15min, 8pm–5am every 30min; journey time 20–25min), which stops frequently and ends its journey outside Dejvická metro station; you must buy your ticket from the orange ticket machines or the newsagents in the airport. More convenient if you've a lot of luggage is to take the **express minibus service** (daily 5.30am–9.30pm every 30min), which stops first at Dejvická metro station, at the end of metro line A (journey time 20min) and ends up at náměstí Republiky (journey time 30min); the full journey currently costs 90Kč. The express minibuses will also take you straight to your hotel for around 350Kč per drop-off – a bargain if you're in a group. If you arrive after midnight, you can catch a night bus #510 to Divoká šárka, the terminus for night tram #51, which will take you to Národní in the centre of town; again, you'll need to buy a ticket in the airport.

Of course, it's easy enough to take a **taxi** from the airport into the centre, though Prague taxi drivers have a reputation for over-charging. If you do end up taking a taxi, make sure the driver turns on the meter, or, if in doubt, agree on a price before getting in; the correct fare to the centre should be around 350Kč.

By train and bus

International trains arrive either at the old Art-Nouveau **Praha hlavní nádraží**, on the edge of Nové Město and Vinohrady, or at **Praha-Holešovice**, which lies in an industrial suburb north of the city centre. At both stations you'll find exchange outlets (there's even a branch of the PIS tourist office at Hlavní nádraží), as well as a 24-hour left-luggage office (see p.248) and accommodation agencies (see p.199). Both stations are on metro lines, and Hlavní nádraží is only a five-minute walk from Václavské náměstí

(Wenceslas Square). Some **domestic train** services wind up at the central **Masarykovo nádraží** on Hybernská (metro náměstí Republiky) or in the suburban station of **Smíchovské nádraží** (metro Smíchovské nádraží).

If you're catching a **train out of Prague**, the easiest place to buy tickets is at Čedok's main office on Na příkopě 18, Nové Město; metro Můstek (Mon–Fri 8.30am–6pm, Sat 8.30am–1pm). Alternatively, you buy discounted tickets for under 26s from the Wasteels office inside Praha hlavní nádraží, and from the windows marked *mezinárodní jízdenky*. International tickets can also be bought at Praha Holešovice.

Prague's **main bus terminal** is **Praha-Florenc** (metro Florenc), on the eastern edge of Nové Město, where virtually all long-distance international and domestic services terminate. It's a confusing (and ugly) place to end up, but it has a 24-hour left luggage office and you can make a quick exit to the adjacent metro station.

Information and maps

Once in Prague, the main tourist office is the **Prague Information Service** or **PIS** (Pražská informační služba), whose main branch is at Na příkopě 20, Nové Město (Mon–Fri 8.30am–7pm, Sat & Sun 9am–5pm; ☎26 40 22). The staff speak at least four languages between them, including English, and will be able to answer most enquiries; they can organize private accommodation for you, sell maps and guides and they act as a general ticket agency, too. PIS also distributes some useful free publications, including *Culture in Prague*, a monthly English-language booklet listing the major events, concerts and exhibitions, and a fortnightly leaflet, *Do města/Downtown*, which concentrates on cinema, art exhibitions and club listings. There are additional PIS offices in the main train station, Praha hlavní nádraží, within the Staroměstská radnice on Staroměstské náměstí, plus a summer-only office in the Malá Strana bridge tower on the Charles Bridge.

The PIS should be able to furnish you with a quick reference **map** of central Prague, but to locate a specific street, or find your way round the suburbs, you'll need a detailed city map (*plán města)*. Kartografie Praha produces the cheapest and most comprehensive ones in a variety of scales. The 1:10,000 map covers the central districts in great detail and should be sufficient for most visitors. The 1:20,000 map covers many of the suburbs as well as the city centre, and has a full street index and the metro, tram and bus routes marked on; it's available in both booklet form (handier to carry about and leaf through) and the fold-out variety (better for the overall picture). You can buy most of the above maps from PIS offices, street kiosks, most bookshops (*knihkupectví*) and some hotels.

Information and maps

Another good source of information is the weekly **English-language paper**, *Prague Post*, which carries **listings** on the latest exhibitions, shows, gigs and events around the capital.

City transport

The centre of Prague, where most of the city's sights are concentrated, is reasonably small and best explored on foot. At some point, however, in order to cross the city quickly or reach some of the more widely dispersed attractions, you'll need to use the city's cheap and efficient public transport system (*dopravní podnik* or *DP*), comprised of the metro and a network of trams and buses. To get a clearer picture, it's essential to invest in a **city map** (see p.39), which marks all the tram, bus and metro lines.

Tickets and passes

Prague used to have a simple ticketing system for its public transport, but all that changed in 1996. Most Praguers simply buy monthly passes, and to avoid having to understand the complexities of the system, you too are best off buying a travel pass (for more on which, see opposite).

Probably the single most daunting aspect of buying a ticket is having to use the new ticket machines found inside all metro stations and at some bus and tram stops. The machines are covered in buttons, but only two are really relevant, since for a single **ticket** (*lístek* or *jízdenka*) in the two central zones (*2 pásma)*, there are just two basic choices. The 8Kč version (*zlevněná)* allows you to travel for up to fifteen minutes on the trams or buses, or up to four stops on the metro; it's known as a *nepřestupní jízdenka*, or "no change ticket", although you can in fact change metro lines (but not buses or trams). The 12Kč version (*plnocenná*) is valid for one hour at peak times (an hour and a half off-peak), during which you may change trams, buses or metro lines as many times as you like, hence its name, *přestupní jízdenka*, or "changing ticket". Half-price tickets are available for children aged 6 to 15, bikes and other large objects; under-6s travel free.

If you're buying a ticket from one of the new machines, you must press the appropriate button – press it once for one ticket, twice for two and so on – followed by the *výdej/enter* button, after which you put your money in. The machines do give change, but if you don't have enough coins, the person on duty in the metro office by the barriers will usually be able to give you change or sell you a ticket. Tickets can also be bought, en masse, and rather more easily, from a tobacconist (*tabák*), street kiosk, newsagent, PIS office or any place that displays the yellow *DP* sticker. When you enter the metro, or board a tram or bus, you must validate your ticket by placing it in one of the electronic machines to hand.

City transport

To save hassle, it's best to buy a **travel pass** (*denní jízdenka*). These are available for 24 hours (70Kč), three days (180Kč), seven days (250Kč) and fifteen days (280Kč); no photos or ID are needed, though you must write your name and date of birth on the reverse of the ticket, and punch it to validate when you first use it. All the passes are available from *DP* outlets, and the 24-hour pass is also available from ticket machines. Most Praguers buy a monthly, quarterly or yearly pass (*průkaz*), which is why you see so few of them punching tickets. To obtain one, simply present your ID and a passport-sized photo to the windows marked *DP* at major metro stations and ask for a *měsíční jízdenka*. Monthly passes currently cost around 380Kč. There's nothing to stop people from freeloading on the system, of course, since there are no barriers. However, plain-clothes **inspectors** (*revizoři*) make spot checks and will issue an on-the-spot fine of 200Kč to anyone caught without a valid ticket or pass; controllers should show you their ID (a small metal disc), and give you a receipt (*paragon*).

The metro

Prague's futuristic Soviet-built **metro** is fast, smooth and ultra-clean, running daily from 5am to midnight with trains every two minutes during peak hours, slowing down to every four to ten minutes by late in the evening. Its three lines (with a fourth planned) intersect at various points in the city centre and the route plans are easy to follow (see map below).

The stations are fairly discreetly marked above ground with the metro logo, in green (line A), yellow (line B) or red (line C). The constant bleeping at metro entrances is to enable blind people to locate the escalators, which are a free-for-all, with no fast lane. Once inside the metro, it's worth knowing that *výstup* means exit and *přestup*

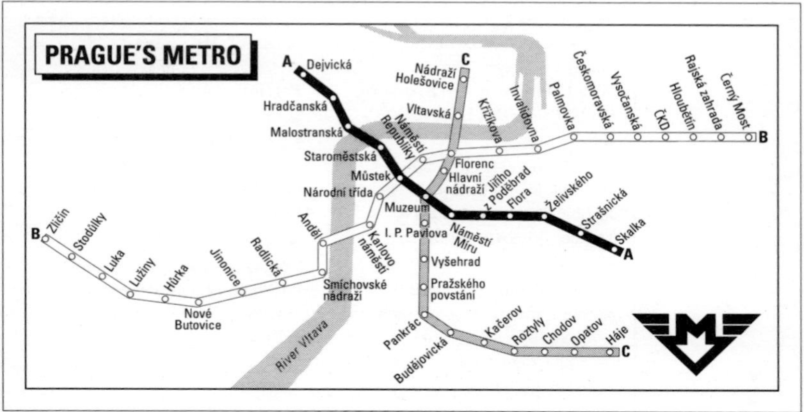

will lead you to one of the connecting lines at an interchange. The digital clock at the end of the platform tells you what time it is and how long it was since the last train.

Trams and buses

The electric **tram** (*tramvaj*) **system**, in operation since 1891, negogiates Prague's hills and cobbles with remarkable dexterity. Modern Škoda rolling stock is gradually being introduced, but many of Prague's trams (traditionally red, but often now plastered over with advertising) still date back to the 1950s. After the metro, trams are the fastest and most efficient way of getting around, running every six to eight minutes at peak times, and every five to fifteen minutes at other times – check the timetables posted at every stop (*zastávka*), which list the departure times from that specific stop.

Tram #22, which runs from Vinohrady to Hradčany via the centre of town and Malá Strana, is a good way to get to grips with the lie of the land, and a cheap way of sightseeing. From Easter to October, an interwar tram (#91) runs from Výstaviště to náměstí Republiky via Malá Strana (Sat & Sun hourly 1–7pm) and back again; the ride takes forty minutes and costs 15Kč. Trams run every six to eight minutes

Night trams

#51
Nádraží Strašnice, metro želivského, metro Flora, nám. Míru, nám. I. P. Pavlova, Lazarská, Národní, metro Staroměstská, nábř. kpt. Jaroše, metro Hradčanská, metro Dejvická, Evropská, **Divoká šárka**.

#52
Hlubočepy, metro Anděl, Lazarská, Masarykovo nádraží, metro Florenc, metro Křižíkova, metro Palmovka, **Lehovec**.

#53
Metro Pankrác, Lazarská, Masarykovo nádraží, nábř. kpt Jaroše, nádraží Holešovice, Trojská, **Vozovna Kobylisy**.

#54
Nádraží Braník, Lazarská, Národní, metro Staroměstská, nábř. kpt Jaroše, nádraží Holešovice, metro Palmovka, **sídliště Jáblice**.

#55
Ústřední dílny DP, metro Strašnická, Vršovická, Karlovo nám., Lazarská, Václavské nám., Masarykovo nádraží, metro Florenc, metro Křižíkova, metro Palmovka, **Lehovec**.

#56
Spořilov, Nuselská, Bělehradská, Lazarská, Masarykovo nádraží, metro Florenc, metro Hradčanská, **Petříny**.

#57
Nádraží Hostivař, Radošovická, nám. Míru, Lazarská, Národní, metro Malostranská, metro Hradčanská, **Bílá hora**.

#58
Spojovací, metro želivského, metro Flora, Olšanské nám., Lazarská, Národní, metro Anděl, **sídliště řepy**.

on the whole, while **night trams** (*noční tramvaje*) run roughly every thirty to forty minutes from around midnight to 4.30am; the routes are outlined in the box opposite, though each one passes along Lazarská and Spálená in Nové Město.

You'll rarely need to get on a Prague **bus** (*autobus*) – most of them keep well out of the centre of town. If you're intent upon visiting the zoo or staying in some of the city's more obscure suburbs, though, you may need to use them: their hours of operation are similar to those of the trams (though generally less frequent), and route numbers are given in the text where appropriate. **Night buses** (*noční autobusy*) run just once an hour between midnight and 5am.

Taxis

Taxis come in all shapes and sizes, and, theoretically at least, are extremely cheap. However, if they think they can, many Prague taxi drivers will attempt to rip you off; the worst offenders, needless to say, hang out at the taxi ranks closest to the tourist sights. Officially, the initial fare on the meter should be 25Kč, plus 17Kč per kilometre within Prague. The best advice is to hail a cab, rather than pick one up at the taxi ranks, and if the meter isn't switched on, ask the driver to do so – *zapněte taxametr, prosím*; if you suspect you've been overcharged, asking for a receipt – *prosím, dejte mi potrzení* – should have the desired effect. The following cab companies have fairly good reputations: *Profitaxi* ☎2213 5551; *AAA taxi* ☎312 2112.

Car rental

You really don't need a **car** in Prague, since much of the city centre is pedestrianized and the public transport system is so cheap and efficient. Should you want to drive out of Prague, however, **car rental** is easy to arrange, with all the major companies operating out of Ruzyně airport. If you book in advance with an international outfit you're looking at a whopping £60/$96 per day for a small car. You'll get a much cheaper deal, however, if you book your car through a local agent once you've arrived in Prague; prices can be as low as £10/$16 a day, though language may be a problem. In order to rent a car, you'll need to be at least 21 and have been driving for at least a year.

Driving in Prague

Rules and regulations on Czech roads are pretty stringent – a legacy of the police state – though less strictly adhered to by Czechs nowadays. On-the-spot fines are still regularly handed out, up to a maximum of 500Kč. The basic rules are driving on the right (introduced by the Nazis in 1939); compulsory wearing of seatbelts; and no alcohol at all in your blood when you're driving. Watch out for

Car rental firms in Prague

Avis
Klimentská 46,
Nové Město
☎21 85 12 25; fax 21 85 12 29

Budget
Hotel Intercontinental,
nám. Curieových,
Staré Město
☎24 88 99 95; fax 231 95 95

Hertz
Karlovo nám. 28,
Nové Město
☎29 18 51; fax 29 78 36

Car Lend
Hovorčovice
☎687 0519/0602 229 155

restricted streets, most notably Wenceslas Square, and give way to pedestrians crossing the road when turning left or right, even when you've been given a green light. You must give way to trams, and if there's no safety island at a tram stop, you must stop immediately and allow passengers to get on and off.

Speed limits are 130kph on motorways, 90kph on other roads and 50kph in all cities. In addition, there's a special limit of 30kph for level crossings (you'll soon realize why if you try ignoring it). If you want to use one of the motorways outside Prague, you must have a special tax disc (see p.8 for more details). As in other continental countries, a yellow diamond means you have right of way; a black line through it means you don't. If you have **car trouble**, dial ☎154 at the nearest phone and wait for assistance.

Petrol (*benzín*) comes in two types: *super* (96 octane) and *special* (90 octane); diesel (*nafta*) is also available, but two-stroke fuel (*mix*), which powers the old East German Trabants and Wartburgs, is being phased out. **Lead-free** petrol (*natural* or *bezolovnatý*) is available from most petrol stations in and around Prague, more and more of which are now open 24 hours, as in other European capitals.

Vehicle crime is on the increase and western cars are a favourite target – never leave anything visible or valuable in the car. The other big nightmare is **parking**. There are now three colour-coded parking zones, with pay-and-display meters: the orange zone (Mon–Sat 8am–6pm) allows you to park for up to two hours; the green zone (Mon–Fri & sometimes Sat 8am–6pm) allows you up to six hours; the blue zone is for locals only. Parking outside of the above times is free of charge. Illegally parked cars will either be clamped or towed away – if this happens, phone ☎158 to find out the worst. If you're staying in a private room outside the centre, you'll have no problems; if you're at a hotel in the centre, they'll probably have a few parking spaces reserved for guests, though whether you'll find one vacant is another matter. Otherwise, your best option is to park near one of the metro stations out of the centre, several of which have park-and-ride schemes: try Hradčanská, Opatov or Skalka.

Cycling

Cycling as a leisure activity is beginning to catch on in the Czech Republic, but only the brave (or foolish) use it as a form of transport in Prague. The combination of cobbled streets, tram lines and sulphurous air is enough to put most people off. Facilities for **bike rental** are still not that widespread, but if you're determined to give cycling a go, head for Landa, Numavská 33, Vinohrady (Mon–Fri 9am–6pm; ☎2425 6121; metro náměstí Míru), which rents out mountain bikes all year round. A bike (*kolo*) needs a half-price ticket to travel on the metro or the train (they're not allowed on trams and buses); they travel in the guard van on trains, and in the last carriage of the metro.

Chapter 2

Hradčany

HRADČANY's *raison d'être* is its castle, or **Hrad**, built on the site of one of the original hill settlements of the Slav tribes who migrated to the area in the seventh or eighth century AD. The Přemyslid prince, Bořivoj I, erected the first castle here sometime in the late ninth century, and, since then, whoever has had control of the

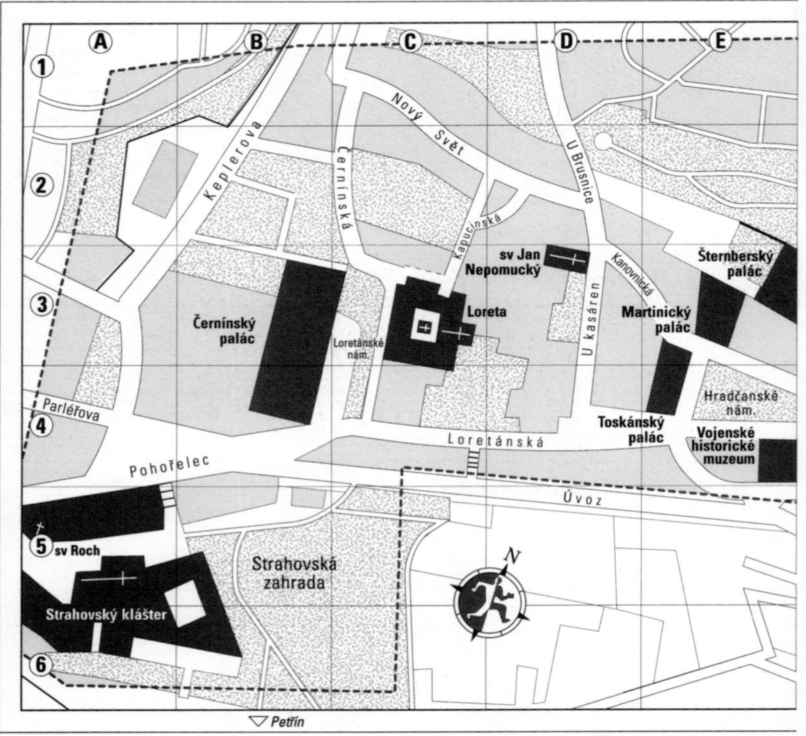

Hrad has exercised authority over the Czech Lands. Consequently, unlike the city's other districts, Hradčany has never had a real identity of its own, even after it became a royal town in 1598; it existed instead as a mere appendage, its inhabitants serving and working for their masters in the Hrad. The same is still true now. For although the odd café or *pivnice* (pub) survives in amongst the palaces (and even in the Hrad itself), there's very little real life here beyond the stream of tourists who trek through the castle and the civil servants who work either for the president or the government, whose departmental tentacles spread right across Hradčany and down into Malá Strana.

Stretched out along a high spur above the River Vltava, Hradčany shows a suitable disdain for the public transport system. There's a choice of **approaches** from Malá Strana, all of which involve at least some walking. From Malostranská metro station, most people take the steep short cut up the Staré zámecké schody, which brings you into the castle from its rear end. A better approach is up the stately Zámecké schody, where you can stop and admire the view, before entering the castle via the main gates. The alternative to all this

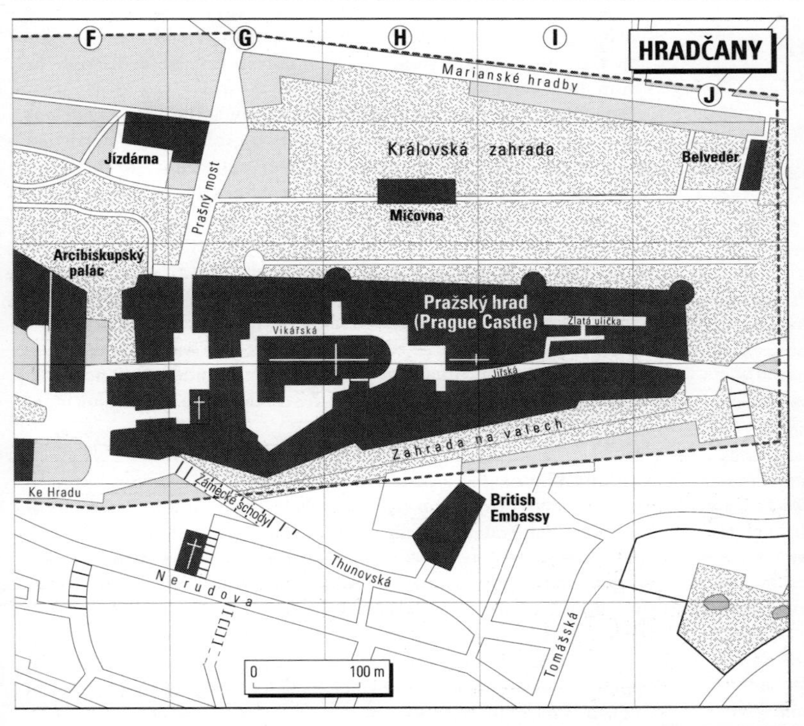

climbing is to take tram #22 from Malostranská metro, which tackles the hairpin bends of Chotkova with ease, and deposits you either outside the Královská zahrada (Royal Gardens) to the north of the Hrad, or, if you prefer, outside the gates of the Strahovský klášter (monastery), at the far western edge of Hradčany.

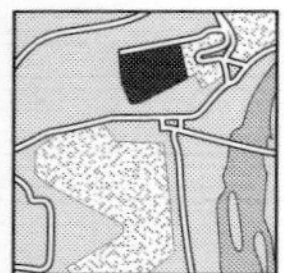

Pražský hrad (Prague Castle)

Viewed from the Charles Bridge, **Pražský hrad** (popularly known as the Hrad) stands aloof from the rest of the city, protected, not by bastions and castellated towers, but by its palatial Neoclassical facade – an "immense unbroken sheer blank wall", as Hilaire Belloc described it – breached only by the great Gothic mass of St Vitus Cathedral. It's *the* picture-postcard image of Prague, though for the Czechs the castle has been an object of disdain as much as admiration, its alternating fortunes mirroring the shifts in the nation's history. The golden age and the dark ages, interwar democracy and Stalinist terror – all have emanated from the Hrad. When the first posters appeared in December 1989 demanding "*HAVEL NA HRAD*" (Havel to the Castle), they weren't asking for his reincarceration. Havel's occupancy of the Hrad was the sign that the reins of government had finally been wrested from the Communist regime.

The site has been successively built on since the first castle was erected here in the ninth century, but two **architects** in particular bear responsibility for the present outward appearance of the Hrad. The first is **Nicolo Pacassi**, court architect to Empress Maria Theresa, whose austere restorations went hand in hand with the deliberate run-down of the Hrad until it was little more than an administrative barracks. For the Czechs, his grey-green eighteenth-century cover-up, which hides a variety of much older buildings, is unforgivable. Less apparent, though no less controversial, is the hand of **Josip Plečnik**, the Slovene architect who was commissioned by T. G. Masaryk, president of the newly founded Czechoslovak Republic, to restore and modernize the castle in the 1920s (for more on Plečnik, see box on p.50).

The grounds of Prague Castle are open daily: April–Oct 5am–midnight; Nov–March 6am–11pm; sights within the castle (unless otherwise stated) are open daily: April–Oct 9am–5pm; Nov–March 9am–4pm.

Visiting the castle

You can wander freely through the streets, courtyards and gardens of the castle and watch the changing of the guard without a ticket. A single ticket, costing 100kč and valid for three days, will give you entry to four sights within the castle: the choir, crypt and tower of the cathedral; the Starý královský palác (Old Royal Palace); the Basilica of sv Jiří; and the Prašná věž (Powder Tower). Tickets are available from the main information centre in the third courtyard, opposite the cathedral, where you can also pick up an audioguide (in English) for another 100Kč.

The art collections of the Jiřský klášter or the Obrazárna Pražského hradu, the toys at the Muzeum hraček, the museum in the Lobkovický palác, and the exhibitions held in Císařská konírna or Jízdárna, all have different opening hours and separate admission charges.

Within the castle precincts there are several cafés and restaurants, which are by no means as extortionate as you might expect from their location. If you simply want a quick cup of coffee and a place to write some postcards, head for the *Café Poet*, which has tables outside in the shade and is hidden away in the peaceful and little-visited Zahrada na baště.

The first and second courtyards

The **first courtyard** (první nádvoří), which opens onto Hradčanské náměstí, is guarded by Ignaz Platzer's blood-curdling *Battling Titans* – two gargantuan figures, one on each of the gate piers, wielding club and dagger and about to inflict fatal blows on their respective victims. Below them stand a couple of impassive presidential sentries, sporting blue uniforms that deliberately recall those of the First Republic. They were designed by the Oscar-winning costume designer for Miloš Forman's film *Amadeus*, and chosen by Havel himself. The hourly **Changing of the Guard** is a fairly subdued affair, but every day at noon there's a much more elaborate parade, accompanied by a brass ensemble which appears at the first-floor windows to play local rock star Michal Kocáb's gentle, slightly comical, modern fanfare.

The Changing of the Guard takes place in the first courtyard daily at noon.

To reach the **second courtyard** (druhé nádvoří), you must pass through the early Baroque Matyášova brána (Matthias Gate), originally a freestanding triumphal arch in the middle of the long-since defunct moat, now set into one of Pacassi's blank walls. Grand stairways on either side lead to the presidential apartments in the south wing, and to the **Španělský sál** (Spanish Hall) and **Rudofova galerie** (Rudolf Gallery) in the north wing – two of the most stunning rooms in the entire complex. Sadly, both are generally out of bounds, though concerts are occasionally held in the Španělský sál. The Rudofova galerie was decked out with gilded chandeliers and lined with mirrors for Emperor Franz-Josef I's coronation, though in the end he never turned up; under the Communists it was used for Politburo meetings; and more recently still it was discovered that behind the mirrors some eighteenth-century trompe l'oeil murals have been preserved.

Surrounded by monotonous Pacassi plasterwork, the courtyard itself is really just a through-route to the cathedral, with an early Baroque stone fountain, the **Kohlova kašna**, and a wrought-iron well grille the only distractions. The most visible intrusion is Anselmo Lurago's **chapel of sv Kříž**, which cowers in one corner. Its richly painted interior, dating mostly from the mid-nineteenth century,

Josip Plečnik: postmodernist in the making

Born in Ljubljana, **Josip Plečnik** (1872–1957) studied under the great Viennese architect Otto Wagner at the turn of the century, and was appointed chief architect to Prague Castle shortly after the foundation of the First Republic. Despite having the backing of the leading Czech architect Jan Kotěra, and of President Masaryk himself, controversy surrounded him as soon as the appointment was announced; his non-Czech background and, moreover, his quirky, eclectic style placed him at odds with the architectural establishment of the day. He remained so until his rediscovery in the 1980s by the newly ascendant postmodernist movement. Several leading postmodern architects, among them Richard Rogers, James Stirling, Robert Venturi and Denise Scott-Brown, made special trips to Prague to see Plečnik's work, which, like their own, borrows elements from any number of genres from classical to Assyrian architecture.

Plečnik's most conspicuous contributions to the castle are the fir-tree flag poles in the first courtyard and the granite obelisk in the third courtyard, but his light-hearted touch is to be seen throughout the castle grounds: check out the jokey palm tree with roped-on copper leaves outside the Jízdárna; the Bull Staircase, which leads down to the Zahrada na valech; or the impressive Sloupová síň (Hall of Columns), which contains the stairs going up to the Španělský sál, and can be peeked at through the glass doors between the first and second courtyards. Sadly, much of Plečnik's work – in particular the president's private apartments – remains hidden from public view, though thanks partly to Havel (a keen Plečnik fan), there are plans to increase public access wherever possible.

used to house the cathedral treasury, a macabre selection of medieval reliquaries. The striking gilded sculpture of a winged leopard by Bořek Šípek, at the entrance to the east wing, is clearly a postmodern homage to Plečnik. On the opposite side of the courtyard are the former **Císařská konírna** (Imperial Stables), which still boast their original, magnificent Renaissance vaulting dating from the reign of Rudolf II, and are now used to house temporary exhibitions (Tues–Sun 10am–6pm).

Obrazárna Pražského hradu

The Obrazárna is open daily 10am–6pm; 100Kč.

The remnants of the imperial collection, begun by the Habsburg Emperor Rudolf II (see p.61), are housed in the nearby **Obrazárna Pražského hradu** (Prague Castle Picture Gallery). However, the best of what Rudolf amassed was either taken as booty by the marauding Saxons and Swedes, or sold off by his successors. Most sorely missed are the works of Giuseppe Arcimboldo, whose surrealist portraits – such as the one of Rudolf himself as a collage of fruit, with his eyes as cherries, cheeks as apples and hair as grapes – now reside in Vienna and Madrid. The surviving collection is definitely patchy, and the lighting in the newly revamped gallery could be better, but it contains one or two masterpieces that are well worth seeing.

One of the collection's finest paintings is Rubens' richly coloured *Assembly of the Gods at Olympus*, featuring a typically voluptuous Venus and a slightly phased Zeus. The illusionist triple portrait of Rudolf (when viewed from the left), and his Habsburg predecessors (when viewed from the right), by Paulus Roy, is typical of the sort of tricksy work that appealed to the emperor. Elsewhere, there's an early, very beautiful *Young Woman at her Toilet* by Titian, and a superbly observed *Portrait of a Musician* by one of his pupils, Bordone. Veronese's best offering is his portrait of Jakob König, a German art dealer in Venice who worked for Rudolf II among others, and who was also a personal friend of the artist. Look out, too, for Tintoretto's *Flagellation of Christ*, a late work in which the artist makes very effective and dramatic use of light. Other works of note include a fragment of an altarpiece by Cranach the Elder and Holbein's portrait of Lady Vaux.

St Vitus Cathedral

St Vitus Cathedral (chram sv Víta) takes up so much of the third courtyard that it's difficult to get an overall impression of this chaotic Gothic edifice. Its asymmetrical appearance is the product of a long and chequered history, for although the foundation stone was laid in 1344, the cathedral was not completed until 1929 – exactly 1000 years after the death of Bohemia's most famous patron saint, Wenceslas.

Plečnik also built one of Prague's most unusual churches, in Vinohrady *(see p.157).*

The site of the present cathedral was originally a sacrificial altar to the heathen fertility god **Svantovit**, which partly explains why the first church, founded in 929 by Prince Václav, was dedicated to Saint Vitus (*svatý Vít* in Czech), who allegedly exorcized the Emperor Diocletian's son and was thereafter known as the patron saint of epilepsy and of the convulsive disorder, Sydenham's chorea (hence its popular name, St Vitus' Dance). The inspiration for the medieval cathedral came from Emperor Charles IV, who, while still only heir to the throne, not only wangled an independent archbishopric for Prague, but also managed to gather together the relics of Saint Vitus.

Inspired by the cathedral at Narbonne, Charles commissioned the Frenchman **Matthias of Arras** to start work on a similar structure. Matthias died eight years into the job in 1352, with the cathedral barely started, so Charles summoned **Peter Parler**, a precocious 23-year-old from a family of great German masons, to continue the work. For the next 46 years, Parler imprinted his slightly flashier, more inventive *SonderGotik* ("Unusual Gothic") style on the city, but the cathedral got no further than the construction of the choir and the south transept before his death in 1399.

Little significant work was carried out during the next four centuries and the half-built cathedral became a symbol of the Czechs' frustrated aspirations to nationhood. Not until the Czech national revival or *národní obrození* of the nineteenth century did building

Pražský hrad

begin again in earnest, with the foundation, in 1859, of the **Union for the Completion of the Cathedral**. A succession of architects, including Josef Mocker and Kamil Hilbert, oversaw the completion of the entire west end, and, with the help of countless other Czech artists and sculptors, the building was transformed into a treasure-house of Czech art. The cathedral was finally given an official opening ceremony in 1929, though work, in fact, continued right up to and beyond World War II.

The exterior

The sooty Prague air has made it hard now to differentiate between the two building periods. Close inspection, however, reveals that the **western facade**, including the twin spires, sports the rigorous if unimagi-

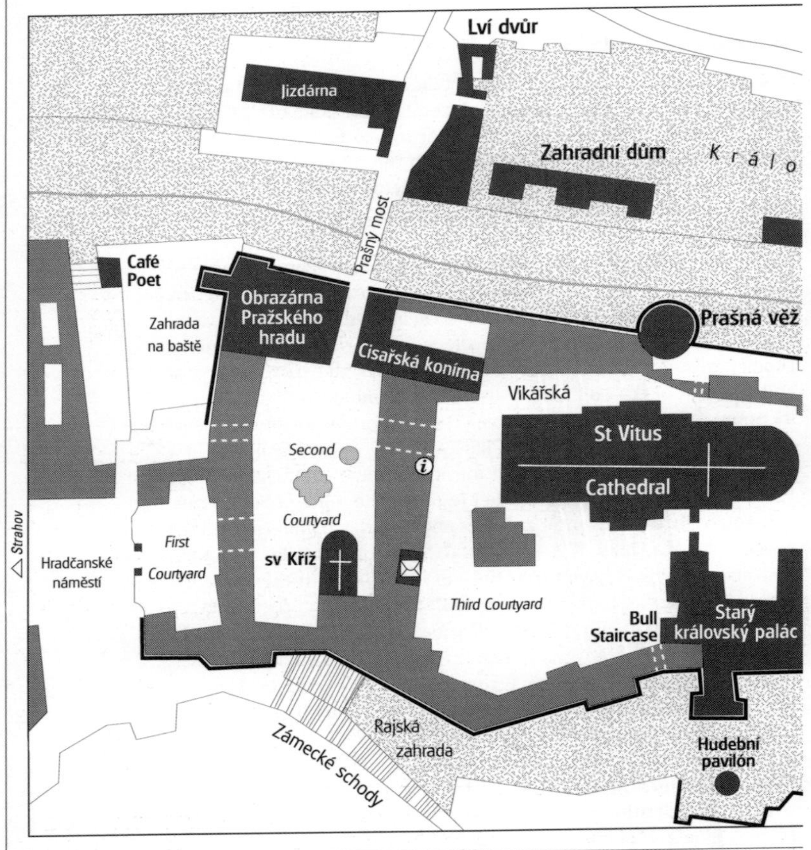

native work of the neo-Gothic restorers (their besuited portraits can be found below the rose window), while the **eastern section** – best viewed from the Belvedere – shows the building's authentic Gothic roots. The south door (see Zlatá brána on p.57) is also pure Parler. Oddly then, it's above the south door that the cathedral's tallest steeple reveals the most conspicuous stylistic join: Pacassi's Baroque topping resting absurdly on a Renaissance parapet of light stone, which is itself glued onto the blackened body of the original Gothic tower.

The nave

The cathedral is the country's largest, and once inside, it's difficult not to be impressed by the sheer height of the **nave**. This is the

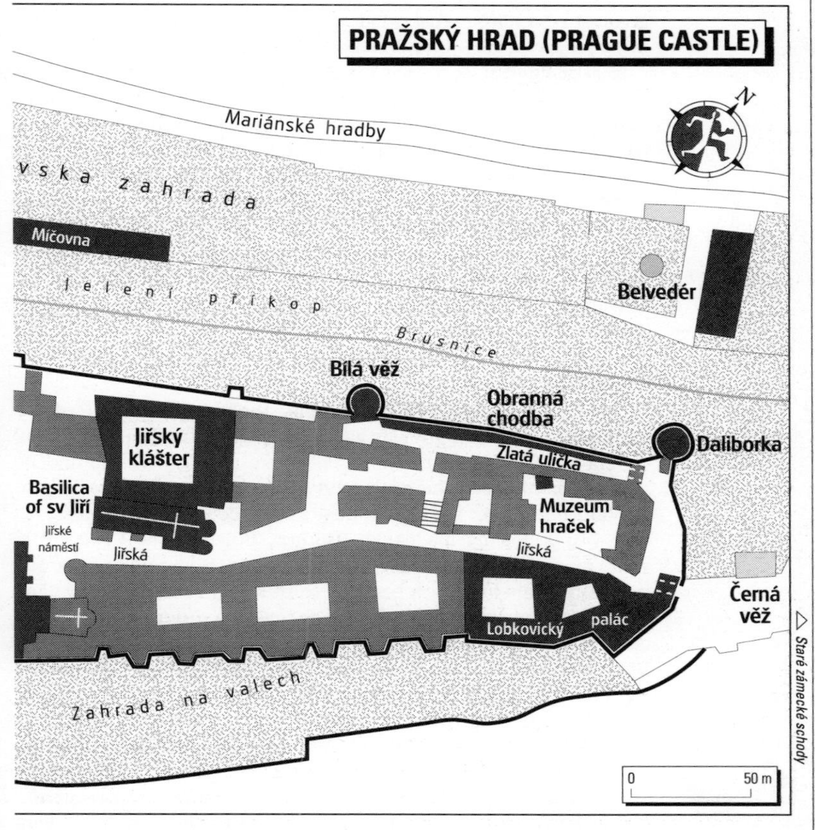

Entry to the main nave, the Chapel of sv Václav and to all services is free; the cathedral is open for services only on Sunday until noon. To enter the ambulatory, crypt or chancel, where the most interesting monuments are located, you must have a castle ticket, available from the box office in the south transept, or the information office opposite the cathedral.

newest part of the building, and, consequently, is decorated mostly with twentieth-century furnishings. The most arresting of these are the cathedral's modern **stained-glass** windows, which on sunny days send shafts of rainbow light into the nave. The effect is stunning, though entirely out of keeping with Parler's original concept, which was to have almost exclusively clear-glass windows. The most unusual windows are those by František Kysela, which look as though they have been shattered into hundreds of tiny pieces, a technique used to greatest effect in the rose window over the west door with its kaleidoscopic *Creation of the World* (1921).

In keeping with its secular nature, two of the works from the time of the First Republic were paid for by financial institutions. The *Cyril and Methodius* window, in the third chapel in the north wall, was commissioned from Art Nouveau artist Alfons Mucha by the Banka Slavie, while on the opposite side of the nave, the window on the theme *Those Who Sow in Tears Shall Reap in Joy* was sponsored by a Prague insurance company.

One of the most striking later additions to the church is František Bílek's **wooden altar**, in the north aisle, whose anguished portrait of Christ on the cross breaks free of the neo-Gothic strictures that hamper other contemporary works inside.

Chapel of sv Václav

Of the cathedral's 22 side chapels, the grand **Chapel of sv Václav**, by the south door, is easily the main attraction. Although officially dedicated to Saint Vitus, spiritually the cathedral belongs as much to the Přemyslid prince, Václav (Wenceslas, of "Good King" fame; see box opposite), the country's patron saint, who was killed by his pagan brother, Boleslav the Cruel. Ten years later, in 939, Boleslav repented, converted, and apparently transferred his brother's remains to this very spot. Charles, who was keen to promote the cult of Wenceslas in order to cement his own Luxembourgeois dynasty's rather tenuous claim to the Bohemian throne, had Peter Parler build the present chapel on top of the original grave; the lion's head **door-ring** set into the north door is said to be the one to which Václav clung before being killed. The chapel's rich, almost Byzantine decoration is like the inside of a jewel casket: the gilded walls are inlaid with approximately 1372 semiprecious Bohemian stones (corresponding to the year of its creation and symbolizing the New Jerusalem from Revelations), set around ethereal fourteenth-century frescoes of the Passion; meanwhile the tragedy of Wenceslas unfolds above the cornice in the later paintings of the Litoměřice school, dating from 1509.

Though a dazzling testament to the golden age of Charles IV's reign, it's not just the chapel's artistic merit which draws visitors. A door in the south wall gives access to a staircase leading to the coronation chamber (rarely open to the public), which houses the **Bohemian crown jewels**, including the gold crown of Saint Wenceslas, studded with some of the largest sapphires in the world. Closed to the public since 1867, the door is secured by seven different locks, the keys kept by seven different people, starting with the president himself – like the seven seals of the holy scroll from Revelations. The tight security is partly to prevent any pretenders to the throne trying on the headgear, an allegedly fatal act: the Nazi *Reichsprotektor* Reinhard Heydrich tried it, only to suffer the inevitable consequences (see pp.144–145). Replicas of the crown jewels are on display in the Lobkowicz Palace (see p.62).

The chancel

Having sated yourself on the Wenceslas Chapel, buy a ticket from the nearby box office, and head off to the north choir aisle – the only place where you can currently enter the **chancel**. Following the ambulatory round, make sure you check out the high-relief seventeenth-century wooden panelling between the arcading on the right, which glories in the flight of the "Winter King" (he's depicted crossing the Charles Bridge), following the disastrous Battle of Bílá hora. The remains of various early Czech rulers are scattered throughout the side chapels,

Good King Wenceslas

As it turns out, there's very little substance to the story related in the nineteenth-century English Christmas carol, *Good King Wenceslas*, by J.M. Neale, itself a reworking of the medieval carol *Tempus adest floridum*. For a start, **Václav** was only a duke and never a king (though he did become a saint); he wasn't even that "good", except in comparison with the rest of his family; the St Agnes fountain, by which "yonder peasant dwelt", wasn't built until the thirteenth century; and he was killed a good three months before the Feast of Stephen.

Born in 907, Václav inherited his title at the tender age of thirteen. His Christian grandmother, Ludmila, was appointed regent in preference to Drahomíra, his pagan mother, who had Ludmila murdered in a fit of jealousy the following year. On coming of age in 925, Václav became duke in his own right and took a vow of celibacy, intent on promoting Christianity throughout the dukedom. Even so, the local Christians didn't take to him, and when he began making conciliatory overtures to the neighbouring Germans, they persuaded his pagan younger brother, Boleslav the Cruel, to do away with him. On September 20, 929, Václav was stabbed to death by Boleslav at the entrance to a church just outside Prague.

most notably those of Přemysl Otakar I and II, in the Saxon Chapel (the fifth one along), whose limestone tombs are the work of Peter Parler and his workshop; you can also pay your respects to Rudolf II's internal organs buried in the chapel vault.

Slap bang in the middle of the ambulatory, close to the Saxon Chapel, is the perfect Baroque answer to the medieval chapel of sv Václav, the **Tomb of St John of Nepomuk**, plonked here in 1736. It's a work of grotesque excess, designed by Johann Bernhard Fischer von Erlach's son, Johann Michael, and sculpted in solid silver with free-flying angels holding up the heavy drapery of the baldachin. Where Charles sought to promote Wenceslas as the nation's preferred saint, the Jesuits, with Habsburg backing, replaced him with another Czech martyr, John of Nepomuk (Jan Nepomucký), who had been arrested, tortured, and then thrown – bound and gagged – off the Charles Bridge in 1393 on the orders of Václav IV, allegedly for refusing to divulge the secrets of the queen's confession. A cluster of stars was said to have appeared over the spot where he drowned, hence the halo of stars on every subsequent portrayal of the saint.

The Jesuits, in their efforts to get him canonized, exhumed his corpse and produced what they claimed to be his tongue – alive and licking, so to speak (it was in fact his very dead brain). In 1729, he duly became a saint, and, on the lid of the tomb, back-to-back with the martyr himself, a cherub points to his severed tongue, sadly no longer the "real" thing. The more prosaic reason for John of Nepomuk's death was simply that he was caught up in a dispute between the archbishop and the king over the appointment of the abbot of Kladruby, and backed the wrong side. John was tortured on the rack along with two other priests, who were then made to sign a document denying that they had been maltreated; John, however, died before he could sign, and his dead body was secretly dumped in the river. The Vatican finally admitted this in 1961, some 232 years after his canonization.

Between the tomb of St John of Nepomuk and the chapel of sv Václav, Bohemia's one and only Polish ruler, Vladislav Jagiello, built a **Royal Oratory**, connected to his bedroom in the royal palace by a covered bridge. The balustrade sports heraldic shields from Bohemia's (at the time) quite considerable lands, while the hanging vault is smothered in an unusual branch-like decoration, courtesy of Benedikt Ried. To the left, the statue of a miner is a reminder of just how important Kutná Hora's silver mines were in funding such artistic ventures.

The Imperial Mausoleum and the Royal Crypt

Before you leave the chancel, check out the sixteenth-century marble **Imperial Mausoleum**, situated in the centre of the choir, and surrounded by a fine Renaissance grille on which numerous cherubs are irreverently larking about. It was commissioned by Rudolf II and contains the remains of his grandfather Ferdinand I, his Polish grandmother, and his father Maximilian II, the first Habsburgs to wear the Bohemian crown. Rudolf himself rests beneath them, in one of the two pewter coffins in the somewhat cramped **Royal Crypt** (Královská hrobka), whose entrance is beside the Royal Oratory. Rudolf's coffin (at the back, in the centre) features yet more cherubs, brandishing quills, while the one to the right contains the remains of Maria Amelia, daughter of the Empress Maria Theresa. A good number of other Czech kings and queens are buried here, too, reinterred this century in incongruously modern 1930s sarcophagi, among them the Hussite King George of Poděbrady, Charles IV and, sharing a single sarcophagus, all four of his wives. The exit from the crypt brings you out in the centre of the nave.

The third courtyard and the Starý královský palác

There's a post office in the west wing of the third courtyard, open Mon–Fri 8am–7pm, Sat & Sun 10am–7pm.

The rest of the **third courtyard** (třetí nádvoří) reveals yet more of Pacassi's monotonous plasterwork. Plečnik's deliberately priapic granite **monolith** is a stunted and unfinished monument, originally designed to complement the granite bowl in the Jižní zahrady (South Gardens). Close by is a fourteenth-century **bronze statue**, executed by a couple of Transylvanian Saxon sculptors, and depicting a rather diminutive Saint George astride a disturbingly large horse (actually two hundred years younger than the rest of the ensemble), slaying an extremely puny dragon – the original is in the Convent of sv Jiří.

The other reason for hanging about in the third courtyard is to clock Parler's **Zlatá brána** (Golden Gate), decorated with a fourteenth-century mosaic of the *Last Judgement*, whose original, rich colouring has now been completely lost. Despite several attempts over the years, the secret of the mosaic's restoration has consistently eluded the experts; another attempt is scheduled to begin very soon, courtesy of the Getty Foundation. On the opposite side of the courtyard is Plečnik's **Bull Staircase**, which leads down to the Jižní zahrady (see p.63), and also to the newly opened **Tereziánské křídlo** (Theresian Wing), now used for temporary exhibitions.

Starý královský palác (Old Royal Palace)

Across the courtyard from the Zlatá brána, the **Starý královský palác** (Old Royal Palace) was home to the princes and kings of Bohemia from the eleventh to the sixteenth centuries. It's a sandwich of royal apartments, built one on top of the other by successive generations, but left largely unfurnished and unused for the last three hundred years. The original Romanesque palace of Soběslav I now forms the cellars of the present building, above which Charles IV built his own Gothic chambers; these days you enter at the third and top floor, built at the end of the fifteenth century.

Immediately past the antechamber is the bare expanse of the massive **Vladislavský sál** (Vladislav Hall), the work of Benedikt

Ried, the German mason appointed by Vladislav Jagiello as his court architect. It displays some remarkable, sweeping rib-vaulting which forms floral patterns on the ceiling, the petals reaching almost to the floor. It was here that the early Bohemian kings were elected, and since 1918 every president from Masaryk to Havel has been sworn into office in the hall. In medieval times, the hall was also used for banquets and jousting tournaments, which explains the ramp-like **Riders' Staircase** in the north wing (now the exit). At the far end of the hall, to the right, there's an outdoor **viewing platform**, from which you can enjoy a magnificent view of Prague (at its best in the late afternoon). You can also look down onto the chapel of **Všech svatých**, which Parler added to Charles IV's palace, but which had to be rebuilt after the 1541 fire, and has since been Baroquified. Its only point of interest is the remains of the Czech saint, Procopius, which are contained within an eighteenth-century wooden tomb along the north wall.

From a staircase in the southwest corner of the hall, you can gain access to the Ludvík Wing. The rooms themselves are pretty uninspiring, but the furthest one, the **Bohemian Chancellery**, was the scene of Prague's **second defenestration**. After almost two centuries of uneasy coexistence between Catholics and Protestants, matters came to a head over the succession to the throne of the Habsburg archduke Ferdinand, a notoriously intolerant Catholic. On May 23, 1618, a posse of more than one hundred Protestant nobles, led by Count Thurn, marched to the chancellery for a showdown with Jaroslav Bořita z Martinic and Vilém Slavata, the two Catholic governors appointed by Ferdinand I. After a "stormy discussion", the two councillors (and their personal secretary, Filip Fabricius) were thrown out of the window. As a contemporary historian recounted: "No mercy was granted them and they were both thrown dressed in their cloaks with their rapiers and decoration head first out of the western window into a moat beneath the palace. They loudly screamed *ach, ach, oweh!* and attempted to hold on to the narrow window-ledge, but Thurn beat their knuckles with the hilt of his sword until they were both obliged to let go." There's some controversy about the exact window from which they were ejected, although it's agreed that they survived to tell the tale, landing in a medieval dung heap below, and – so the story goes – precipitating the Thirty Years' War.

Back down in the Vladislavský sál, to the right of the Riders' Staircase, a door leads into the vaulted room of the **Diet**, whose (purely decorative) ribs imitate those of the Vladislav Hall. The room is laid out as if for a seventeenth-century session of the Diet: the king on his throne, the archbishop to his right, the judiciary to his left, the nobility facing him, and representatives from towns across Bohemia (with just one collective vote) confined to the gallery by the window.

A staircase to the left of the Riders' Staircase will take you up to the sparsely furnished rooms of the New Land Rolls, whose walls are tattooed with coats-of-arms. More rewarding, though, is the quick canter down the Riders' Staircase to the **Gothic and Romanesque chambers** of the palace, equally bare, but containing a couple of interesting models showing the castle at various stages in its development. Also on display are copies of busts by Peter Parler's workshop, which are virtually hidden from view in the triforium of the cathedral. As well as the architect's remarkable self-portrait, there are portraits of Charles IV and his four wives, including his formidable fourth spouse, Elizabeth of Pomerania, who used to bend horseshoes and tear chained mail to shreds with her bare hands.

The Basilica and Convent of sv Jiří

The only exit from the Royal Palace is via the Riders' Staircase, which deposits you in Jiřské náměstí. Don't be fooled by the russet-red Baroque facade of the **Basilica of sv Jiří** (St George) which dominates the square; inside is Prague's most beautiful Romanesque building, meticulously scrubbed clean and restored to re-create something like the honey-coloured stone basilica that replaced the original tenth-century church in 1173. The double staircase to the chancel is a remarkably harmonious late Baroque addition and now provides a perfect stage for chamber music concerts. The choir vault contains a rare early thirteenth-century painting of the New Jerusalem from Revelations – not to be confused with the very patchy sixteenth-century painting on the apse – while to the right of the chancel, only partially visible, are sixteenth-century frescoes of the **burial chapel of sv Ludmila**, grandmother of Saint Wenceslas, who was murdered by her own daughter-in-law in 921 (see box on p.55), thus becoming Bohemia's first Christian martyr and saint. There's a replica of the recumbent Ludmila, which you can inspect at close quarters, in the south aisle. Also worth a quick peek is the Romanesque crypt, situated beneath the choir, which contains a macabre sixteenth-century statue of Vanity, whose shrouded, skeletal body is crawling with snakes and lizards.

Jiřský klášter (the old Bohemian art collection)

Next door is Bohemia's first monastery, the **Jiřský klášter** (St George's Convent) founded in 973 by Mlada, sister of the Přemyslid prince Boleslav the Pious, who became its first abbess. Like most of the country's religious institutions, it was closed down and turned into a barracks by Joseph II in 1782, and now houses the Národní galerie's **old Bohemian art collection** (Staré české umění), which spans the Gothic and Baroque period. The exhibition is arranged chronologically, starting in the crypt with a remarkable collection of Gothic art, which first flourished here under the patronage of Charles IV.

The Jiřský klášter is open Tues–Sun 10am–6pm; 70Kč.

The **earliest works** are almost exclusively symbolical depictions of the Madonna and Child, the artists known only by their works and locations, not by name. Here you'll find – among other things – the monumental tympanum from the church of Panna Maria Sněžná in Prague and nine panels from the altarpiece of the Cistercian monastery at Vyšší Brod. The first named artist is **Master Theodoric**, who painted over one hundred panels for Charles IV's castle at Karlštejn (see p.193); just six are on display here, their larger-than-life portraits overflowing onto the edges of the panels.

On the next floor are paintings by the **Master of Třeboň**, whose work shows even greater variety of balance and depth, moving ever closer to realistic portraiture. The following room contains the stone-carved tympanum from the Týn church (see p.101) – originally coloured and gilded – with high-relief figures by Peter Parler's workshop, whose mastery of composition and depth heralded a new stage in the development of Bohemian art. The last room on this floor is devoted to a series of superb sixteenth-century woodcuts by **Master I. P.**, including an incredibly detailed scene, *Christ the Redeemer before Death*, showing a skeleton whose entrails are in the process of being devoured by a frog.

The transition from this to the next floor, where you are immediately thrown into the overtly sensual and erotic **Mannerist paintings** of Rudolf II's reign, is something of a shock. The majority of the works that survive from Rudolf's superlative collection are now displayed in the Obrazárna Pražského hradu (see p.50). Of the few that remain here, make sure you check out Bartolomeus Spranger's colourfully erotic works and Josef Heintz's riotous orgy in his *Last Judgement*. The rest of the gallery is given over to Czech **Baroque art**, as pursued by the likes of Bohemia's Karel Škréta and Petr Brandl, whose paintings and sculptures fill chapels and churches across the Czech Lands. Michael Leopold Willmann's portrait of St Bartholomew being skinned alive is disturbingly gruesome, but aside from the works of Jan Kupecký and the statues of Matthias Bernhard Braun and Ferdinand Maximilian Brokof, this section is unlikely to hold your attention for long.

Zlatá ulička and the castle towers

Around the corner from the convent is the **Zlatá ulička** (Golden Lane), a seemingly blind alley of miniature cottages in dolly-mixture colours. The contrast in scale with the rest of the Hrad makes this by far the most popular sight in the entire complex, and during the day, at least, the whole street is mobbed, so if you want to try and recapture some of the original atmosphere, you really need to come back in the late evening. Originally built in the sixteenth century for the 24 members of Rudolf II's castle guard, the lane allegedly takes its name from the goldsmiths who followed (and modified the buildings) a century later, though the only house which survives from the sixteenth century is no. 13, the least cute of the lot. By the nineteenth century,

Rudolf II (1576–1612)

In 1583 Emperor **Rudolf II** switched the imperial court from Vienna to Prague. This was to be the first and last occasion in which Prague would hold centre-stage in the Habsburg Empire, and as such is seen as something of a second golden age for the city (the first being under Holy Roman Emperor Charles IV, for more on whom, see p.93). Bad-tempered, paranoid and probably insane, Rudolf had little interest in the affairs of state – instead, he holed up in the Hrad and indulged his own personal passions of alchemy, astrology and art. Thus, Rudolfine Prague played host to an impressive array of international artists, including the idiosyncratic Giuseppe Arcimboldo, whose surrealist portraits were composed entirely of fruit and vegetables. The astrologers, Johannes Kepler and Tycho Brahe, were summoned to Rudolf's court to chart the planetary movements and assuage Rudolf's superstitions, and the English alchemists, Edward Kelley and John Dee, were employed in order to discover the secret of the philosopher's stone, the mythical substance that would transmute base metal into gold.

Accompanied by his pet African lion, Otakar, Rudolf spent less and less time in public, hiding out in the Hrad, where he "loved to paint, weave and dabble in inlaying and watchmaking", according to modern novelist Angelo Maria Ripellino. With the Turks rapidly approaching the gates of Vienna, Rudolf spent his days amassing exotic curios for his strange and vast *Kunst- und Wunderkammer*, which contained such items as "two nails from Noah's Ark...a lump of clay out of which God formed Adam...and large mandrake roots in the shape of little men reclining on soft velvet cushions in small cases resembling doll beds". He refused to marry, though he sired numerous bastards, since he had been warned in a horoscope that a legitimate heir would rob him of the throne. He was also especially wary of the numerous religious orders which inhabited Prague at the time, having been warned in another horoscope that he would be killed by a monk. In the end, he was relieved of his throne by his younger brother, Matthias, in 1611, and died the following year, the day after the death of his beloved pet lion.

the whole street had become a kind of palace slum, attracting artists and craftsmen, its two most famous inhabitants being Jaroslav Seifert, the Czech Nobel prize-winning poet, and Franz Kafka. Kafka's youngest sister, Ottla, rented no. 22, and during a creative period in the winter of 1916 he came here in the evenings to write short stories. Finally, in 1951, the Communists kicked out the last residents and turned most of the houses into souvenir shops for tourists.

At no. 12, at the eastern end of Zlatá ulička, is a throughway to the **Černá věž** (Black Tower), standing at the top of the Staré zamecké schody, which leads down to Malostranská metro. There's no access to the Černá věž but at the other end of the lane, at no. 24, you can climb a flight of stairs to the **Obranná chodba** (defence corridor), which is lined with wooden shields, suits of armour and period costumes. The **Bílá věž** (White Tower), at the western end of the corridor, was the city's main prison from Rudolf's reign onwards. Edward Kelley, the English alchemist, was locked up here by Rudolf for failing to turn base metal into gold, while the emperor's treasurer hanged himself by his gold cord on the treasury keys, after being accused of embezzlement. There's a reconstructed torture chamber on the first floor, and in the shop on the floor above you can kit yourself out as a medieval knight with replica swords and maces, not to mention chastity belts and various torture instruments.

In the opposite direction, the corridor leads to a shooting range, where for a small fee you can have a few shots with a crossbow. The tower which lies beyond is the **Daliborka**, dedicated to its first prisoner, the young Czech noble, Dalibor, accused of supporting a peasants' revolt at the beginning of the fifteenth century. According to Prague legend, he learnt to play the violin while imprisoned here, and his playing could be heard all over the castle until his execution in 1498 – a tale that provided material for Smetana's opera *Dalibor*.

To get inside the castle's other tower, the **Prašná věž** (Powder Tower) or Mihulka, which once served as the workshop of gunsmith and bell-founder Tomáš Jaroš, you'll have to backtrack to Vikářská, the street which runs along the north side of the cathedral. The powder tower's name comes from the lamprey (*mihule*), an eel-like fish supposedly bred here for royal consumption, though it's actually more noteworthy as the place where Rudolf's team of alchemists (including Kelley) were put to work trying to discover the secret of the philosopher's stone (see box on p.61). Despite its colourful history, the exhibition currently on display within the tower is dull, with just a pair of furry slippers and hat belonging to Emperor Ferdinand I to get excited about.

Muzeum hraček (Toy Museum)

The Muzeum hraček is open daily 9.30am–5.30pm; 40Kč.

If you continue east down Jiřská, which runs parallel with Zlatá ulička, you'll come to the courtyard of the former Purkrabství (Burgrave's House) on the left, which hides a café, exhibition space and **Muzeum hraček** (Toy Museum). With brief, Czech-only captions and unimaginative displays, the museum is a disappointing venture, which fails to live up to its potential. The succession of glass cabinets contains everything from toy cars and motorbikes to robots and even Barbie dolls, but there are only a few buttons for younger kids to press, and unless you're really lost for something to do, you could happily skip the whole enterprise.

Lobkovický palác

The Lobkovický palác is open Tues–Sun 9am–5pm; 40Kč.

The hotchpotch historical collection in the **Lobkovický palác** (Lobkowicz Palace), on the opposite side of Jiřská, is marginally more rewarding, despite the ropey English text provided. The exhibition actually begins on the top floor, though by no means all the objects on display deserve attention; the following is a quick rundown of some of the more memorable exhibits. The first cabinet worth more than a passing nod is in the second room, and contains copies of the Bohemian crown jewels (the originals are hidden away above the Chapel of sv Václav in the cathedral and are very rarely on view). Next door, in the Hussite room, there's an interesting sixteenth-century carving of *The Last Supper*, originally an altarpiece from the Betlémská kaple, while, further on, Petr Vok's splendid funereal shield, constructed out of wood covered with cloth shot through with gold, hangs on the wall.

Pražský hrad

All things post-1620 and pre-1848 are displayed in the six rooms downstairs, starting with the sword of the famous Prague executioner, Jan Mydlář, who could lop a man's head off with just one chop, a skill he demonstrated on 24 of the 27 Protestant leaders who were executed on Staroměstské náměstí in 1621; Mydlář's invoice covering labour and expenses is displayed beside the sword. Several rooms on are some more unusual exhibits – three contemporary scaled-down models of eighteenth-century altars, and further on still, three carved marionettes from later that century, among the oldest surviving in Bohemia.

The Castle Gardens

The Hrad boasts some of the city's loveliest **gardens**, particularly in terms of views. The Jižní zahrady (South Gardens) enjoy wonderful vistas over the city and link up the terraced gardens of Malá Strana, while the Královska zahrada (Royal Gardens) allow a better view of the cathedral and the Vltava's many bridges.

The gardens are open May–Oct daily 10am–6pm.

Jižní zahrady

For recuperation and a superlative view over the rest of Prague – not to mention a chance to inspect some of Plečnik's quirky additions to the castle – head for the **Jižní zahrady** (South Gardens), accessible via Plečnik's copper-canopied Bull Staircase on the south side of the third courtyard. Originally laid out in the sixteenth century, but thoroughly remodelled in the 1920s by Josip Plečnik, the first garden you come to from the Bull Staircase, the **Zahrada na valech** (Garden on the Ramparts), features an observation terrace and colonnaded pavilion, below which is an earlier eighteenth-century **Hudební pavilón** (Music pavilion). Two sandstone obelisks further east record the arrival of Slavata and Martinic after their defenestration from the royal palace above (see p.58); beyond them lies yet another of Plečnik's observation pavilions. In the opposite direction, beyond the Baroque fountain lies the smaller **Rajská zahrada** (Paradise Garden), on whose lawn Plečnik plonked a forty-ton granite basin suspended on two small blocks. From here, a quick slog up the monumental staircase will bring you out onto Hradčanské náměstí.

The Královská zahrada and Belvedér

Before exploring the rest of Hradčany, it's worth taking a stroll through the north gate of the second courtyard and across the

Prašný most (Powder Bridge), erected in the sixteenth century to connect the newly established royal gardens (see below) with the Hrad (the original wooden structure has long since been replaced). Below lies the wooded **Jelení příkop** (Stag Ditch), once used by the Habsburgs for growing figs and lemons, and storing game for the royal hunts, but now populated only by bored castle guards.

The Jízdárna is open Tues–Sun 10am–6pm.

Beyond the bridge, opposite the former riding school or **Jízdárna** (now used for temporary art exhibitions) is the entrance to the most verdant of all the castle's gardens, the **Královská zahrada** (Royal Gardens), founded by Emperor Ferdinand I in the 1530s on the site of a former vineyard. Burned down by the Saxons and Swedes during the Thirty Years' War, and blown up by the Prussians, the gardens were only saved from French attack in 1741 by the payment of thirty pineapples. Today, these are some of the best-kept gardens in the capital, with fully functioning fountains and immaculately cropped lawns. Consequently, it's a very popular spot, though more a place for admiring the azaleas and almond trees than lounging around on the grass. It was here that tulips brought from Turkey were first acclimatized to Europe, before being exported to the Netherlands, and every spring there's an impressive, disciplined crop.

The gardens are open May–Oct Tues–Sun 10am–5.45pm.

At the entrance to the gardens is the **Lví dvůr** (Lion's Court), now a restaurant but originally built by Rudolf II to house his private zoo, which included leopards, lynxes, bears, wolves and lions, all of whom lived in heated cages to protect them from the Prague winter. Rudolf was also responsible for the Renaissance ball-game court, known as the **Míčovna** (occasionally open to the public for concerts and exhibitions), built into the south terrace and tattooed with sgraffito by his court architect Bonifaz Wolmut. If you look carefully at the top row of allegorical figures on either side of the sandstone half-columns, you can see that the figure of Industry, between Justice and Peace, is holding a hammer and sickle and a copy of the Five-Year Plan, thoughtfully added by restorers in the 1950s. Incidentally the guarded ochre building to the right of the Míčovna, the **Zahradní dům**, is one of Havel's presidential pads, built as a summer house by Dientzenhofer only to be destroyed during the Prussian bombardment of 1757. It was later restored by Pavel Janák who added the building's two modern wings on a postwar whim of the ill-fated President Beneš.

The Belvedér is open Tues–Sun 10am–6pm.

The Chotkovy sady and the Bílkova vila are both within easy walking distance of the Belvedér; see p.162 for details.

At the end of the gardens is Prague's most celebrated Renaissance legacy, Letohrádek královny Anny (Queen Anne's Summer Palace), popularly known as the **Belvedér**, a delicately arcaded summerhouse topped by an inverted copper ship's hull, built by Ferdinand I for his wife, Anne (though she didn't live long enough to see it completed). It was designed by the Genoese architect Paolo della Stella, one of a number of Italian masons who settled in Prague in the sixteenth century, and is decorated by a series of lovely figural reliefs depicting scenes from mythology. Unlike the gardens, the Belvedér is open for most of the year and is mostly used for exhibitions by contemporary artists; if the gardens are closed you'll have to leave the Královská zahrada and head down Mariánské hradby. At the centre of the palace's miniature formal garden is the **Zpívající fontána** (Singing Fountain), built shortly after the palace and named for the musical sound of the drops of water falling in the metal bowls below – you have to stick your ears up close to the underneath of the bowl to get the full effect. From the garden terrace, you also have an unrivalled view of the castle's finest treasure – the cathedral.

Pražský hrad

From Hradčanské náměstí to the Strahovský klášter

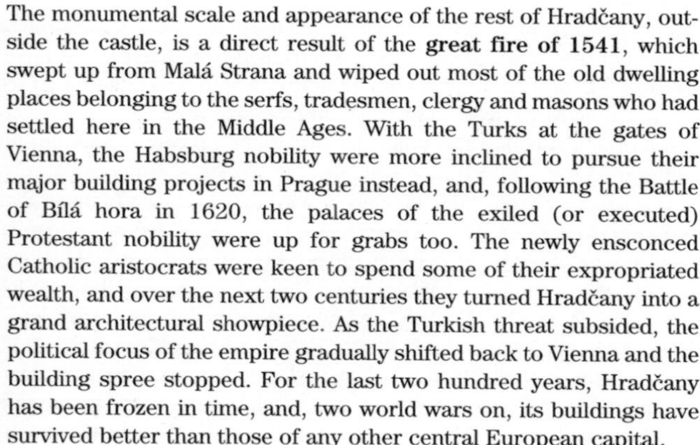

The monumental scale and appearance of the rest of Hradčany, outside the castle, is a direct result of the **great fire of 1541**, which swept up from Malá Strana and wiped out most of the old dwelling places belonging to the serfs, tradesmen, clergy and masons who had settled here in the Middle Ages. With the Turks at the gates of Vienna, the Habsburg nobility were more inclined to pursue their major building projects in Prague instead, and, following the Battle of Bílá hora in 1620, the palaces of the exiled (or executed) Protestant nobility were up for grabs too. The newly ensconced Catholic aristocrats were keen to spend some of their expropriated wealth, and over the next two centuries they turned Hradčany into a grand architectural showpiece. As the Turkish threat subsided, the political focus of the empire gradually shifted back to Vienna and the building spree stopped. For the last two hundred years, Hradčany has been frozen in time, and, two world wars on, its buildings have survived better than those of any other central European capital.

Hradčanské náměstí

Hradčanské náměstí fans out from the castle gates, surrounded by the oversized palaces of the old Catholic nobility. For the most part, it's a tranquil space that's overlooked by the tour groups marching through, intent on the Hrad. The one spot everyone heads for is the ramparts in the southeastern corner, by the top of the Zámecké schody, which allow an unrivalled view over the red rooftops of Malá Strana, past the famous green dome and tower of the church of sv Mikuláš and beyond, to the spires of Staré Město. Only the occasional bookish Praguer or tired traveller makes use of the square's central green patch, which is marked by a giant green wrought-iron lamppost decked with eight separate lamps – one of the few that have survived from the 1860s.

Until the great fire of 1541, the square was the hub of Hradčany, lined with medieval shops and stalls but with no real market as such. After the fire, the developers moved in; the **Martinický palác** at no.

8 was one of the more modest newcomers, built in 1620 by one of the councillors who survived the second defenestration. Its rich sgraffito decoration, which continues in the inner courtyard, was only discovered during restoration work in the 1970s, and was part of the reason it was featured as Mozart's house in the film *Amadeus*. Mathey's rather cold, formal **Toskánský palác** (now in the hands of the Foreign Ministry) was built on a more ambitious scale, replacing the row of butchers' shops that once filled the west end of the square.

The powerful Lobkowicz family replaced seven houses on the south side of the square with the over-the-top sgraffitoed pile at no. 2, known as the **Schwarzenberský palác** after its last aristocratic owners (the present-day Count Schwarzenberg, Karl, is one of the republic's leading capitalists). For a brief period, it belonged to the Rožmberk family, whose last in line, Petr Vok, held the infamous banquet which proved fatal to the Danish astronomer Tycho Brahe. So as not to offend his host, Tycho refrained from leaving the table before Vok, only to burst his bladder, after which he staggered off to his house in Nový Svět, where he died five days later.

The museum is open May–Oct Tues–Sun 10am–5.30pm.

All of which makes the **Vojenské historické muzeum** (Museum of Military History), which now occupies the palace, seem considerably less gruesome. Predictably enough, it was the Nazis who founded the museum, though the Czechs themselves have a long history of manufacturing top-class weaponry to world powers (Semtex is probably their best-known export). It's no coincidence that of the two Czech words to have made it into the English language, one is pistol (from *pišťale*, a Hussite weapon); the other is robot (from Karel Čapek's play *R.U.R.*). The museum is currently desperately underfunded, yet, somewhat surprisingly, many of the captions are in English. Among the ostentatious Habsburg uniforms and finely crafted instruments of death, all of which are pre-1914, you'll find the first Colt 45 produced outside the USA, manufactured in 1849 for the Austrian Navy, a field altar donated by Prince Eugène of Savoy, and a mannekin of General Windischgrätz surveying Prague, as he did before bombing it into submission in 1848. Prague's post-1914 military collections are housed at the Armádní muzeum on Žižkov Hill (see p.160).

The Archbishop's Palace is open to the public only on Maundy Thursday – the Thursday before Easter.

The adjacent **Salmovský palác**, at no. 1, was another Schwarzenberg pile, which served as the Swedish Embassy until the 1970s when the dissident writer Pavel Kohout took refuge there. Frustrated in their attempts to force him out, the Communists closed the embassy down and left it to rot, though it looks likely, eventually, to be turned into a hotel. On the opposite side of the square, just outside the castle gates, stands the sumptuous **Arcibiskupský palác** (Archbishop's Palace), seat of the archbishop of Prague since the beginning of the Roman Catholic church's suzerainty over the Czechs, following the Battle of Bílá hora. The Rococo exterior only hints at the even more extravagant furnishings inside.

Šternberský palác – the old European art collection

From Hradčanské náměstí to the Strahovský klášter

A passage down the side of the archbishop's palace leads to the early eighteenth-century **Šternberský palác**, which houses the Národní's galerie's **old European art collection** (Staré evropské umění), mostly ranging from the fourteenth to the eighteenth century, but excluding works by Czech artists of the period (you'll find them in the Jiřský klášter in the Hrad). It would be fair to say that the collection is relatively modest in comparison with those of other major European capitals, though the handful of masterpieces makes a visit here worthwhile. To see the late nineteenth- and twentieth-century European art which used to be housed here, you need to pay a visit to the Národní Galerie's modern and contemporary art collection in the Veletržní palác (see p.166).

The Šternberský palác is open Tues–Sun 10am–6pm; 70Kč. Tickets for the gallery allow free entry into the Jiřský klášter, Anežský klášter and Jízdárna.

The **first floor** kicks off with Florentine religious art, most notably a series of exquisite miniature triptychs by Bernardo Daddi, plus several gilded polyptychs by the Venetian artist Antonio Vivarini. Moving swiftly into the gallery's large Flemish contingent, it's worth checking out Dieric Bouts' *Lamentation*, a complex composition crowded with figures in medieval garb, and the bizarre *Well of Life*, painted around 1500 by an unknown artist. The latter features a squatting Christ depicted as a Gothic fountain issuing forth blood which angels in turn serve in goblets to passing punters. One of the most eye-catching works is Jan Gossaert's *St Luke Drawing the Virgin*, an exercise in architectural geometry and perspective which used to hang in the cathedral. The section ends with a series of canvases by the Brueghel family; before you head upstairs, though, don't miss the side rooms containing Orthodox icons from Venice, the Balkans and Russia.

The **second floor** contains one of the most prized paintings in the whole collection, the *Feast of the Rosary* by Albrecht Dürer, depicting, among others, the Virgin Mary, the Pope, the Holy Roman Emperor, and even a self-portrait of Dürer himself (top right). This was one of Rudolf II's most prized aquisitions (he was an avid Dürer fan), and was transported on foot across the Alps to Prague (he didn't trust wheeled transport with such a precious object). There are other outstanding works here, too: two richly coloured Bronzino portraits, a Rembrandt, a Canaletto of the Thames, a whole series by the Saxon master, Lucas Cranach – including the striking, almost minimalist *Portrait of an Old Man* – and a mesmerizing *Praying Christ* by El Greco. Rubens' colossal *Murder of St Thomas* is difficult to miss, with its pink-buttocked cherubs hovering over the bloody scene. Nearby, in the hugely expanded (and uneven) Dutch section, there's a wonderful portrait of an arrogant "young gun" named Jasper by Frans Hals. A few of the rooms in the gallery have preserved their original decor, the best of which is the chinoiserie of the Čínský kabinet.

From Hradčanské náměstí to the Strahovský klášter

Nový Svět to Loreta

At the other end of Hradčanské náměstí, Kanovnická heads off towards the northwest corner of Hradčany. Nestling in this shallow dip, **Nový Svět** (meaning "New World", though not Dvořák's) provides a glimpse of life on a totally different scale from Hradčanské náměstí. Similar in many ways to the Zlatá ulička in the Hrad, this cluster of brightly coloured cottages, which curls around the corner into Černínská, is all that's left of Hradčany's medieval slums, painted up and sanitized in the eighteenth and nineteenth centuries. Despite having all the same ingredients for mass tourist appeal as Zlatá ulička, it remains remarkably undisturbed, save for a few swish wine bars, and Gambra, a surrealist art gallery at Černínská 5 (Wed–Sun noon–6pm), which sells works by, among others, the renowned Czech animator, Jan Švankmajer, and his wife Eva, who live nearby.

The Černínský palác is not open to the public.

Up the hill from Nový Svět, Loretánské náměstí is dominated by the phenomenal 135-metre-long facade of the **Černínský palác**, decorated with thirty Palladian half-columns and supported by a swathe of diamond-pointed rustication. For all its grandeur – it's the largest palace in Prague, for the sake of which two whole streets were demolished – it's a pretty brutal building, commissioned in the 1660s by Count Humprecht Jan Černín, one-time imperial ambassador to Venice and a man of monumental self-importance. After quarrelling with the master of Italian Baroque, Giovanni Bernini, and disagreeing with Prague's own Carlo Lurago, Count Černín settled on Francesco Caratti as his architect, only to have the finished building panned by critics as a tasteless mass of stone. The grandiose plans, which were nowhere near completion when the count died, nearly bankrupted future generations of Černíns, who were eventually forced to sell the palace in 1851 to the Austrian state, which converted it into military barracks.

Since the First Republic, the palace has housed the Ministry of Foreign Affairs, and during the war it was, for a while, the Nazi *Reichsprotektor*'s residence. On March 10, 1948, it was the scene of Prague's third – and most widely mourned – defenestration. Only days after the Communist coup, **Jan Masaryk**, the only son of the founder of the Republic, and the last non-Communist in Gottwald's cabinet, plunged 45 feet to his death from the top-floor bathroom window of the palace. Whether it was suicide (he had been suffering from bouts of depression, partly induced by the country's political path) or murder will probably never be satisfactorily resolved, but for most people Masaryk's death cast a dark shadow over the newly established regime.

The Loreta is open Tues–Sun 9am–12.15pm & 1–4.30pm; 80Kč.

Loreta

The facade of the **Loreta**, immediately opposite the Černínský palác, was built by the Dientzenhofers, a Bavarian family of architects, in the early part of the eighteenth century, and is the perfect antidote to Caratti's humourless monster. It's all hot flourishes and twirls, topped by a tower which lights up like a Chinese lantern at night, and by day clanks out the hymn *We Greet Thee a Thousand Times* on its 27 Dutch bells (it also does special performances of other tunes from time to time).

The facade and the cloisters, which were provided a century earlier to shelter pilgrims from the elements, are, in fact, just the outer casing for the focus of the complex, the **Santa Casa**, founded by Kateřina Lobkowicz in 1626 and smothered in a rich mantle of stucco depicting the building's miraculous transportation from the Holy Land. Legend has it that the Santa Casa (Mary's home in Nazareth), under threat from the heathen Turks, was transported by a host of angels to a small village in Dalmatia and from there, via a number of brief stopoffs, to a small laurel grove (*lauretum* in Latin, hence Loreta) in northern Italy. News of the miracle spread across the Catholic lands, prompting a spate of copy-cat shrines, and during the Counter-Reformation, the cult was actively encouraged in an attempt to broaden the popular appeal of Catholicism. The Prague Loreta is one of fifty to be built in the Czech Lands, each of the shrines following an identical design, with pride of place given to a lime-wood statue of the *Black Madonna and Child*, encased in silver.

The Lobkowicz family gave Prague its other famous pilgrimage shrine, the Pražské Jezulátko (see p.83).

Behind the Santa Casa, the Dientzenhofers built the much larger **Church of Narození Páně** (Church of the Nativity), which is like a mini version of sv Mikulaš, down in Malá Strana. There's a high cherub count, plenty of gilding and a lovely organ replete with music-making angels and putti. On either side of the main altar are glass cabinets containing the fully clothed and wax-headed skeletons of Saint Felicissimus and Saint Marcia, and next to them, paintings of Saint Apolena – who had her teeth smashed in during her martyrdom and is now invoked for toothache – and Saint Agatha, carrying her severed breasts on a dish. As in the church, most of the saints honoured in the cloisters are women. Without doubt, the weirdest of the lot is Saint Wilgefortis (aka Starosta), whose statue stands in the final chapel of the cloisters. Daughter of the King of Portugal, she was due to marry the King of Sicily, despite having taken a vow of virginity. God intervened and she grew a beard, whereupon the King of Sicily broke off the marriage and her father had her crucified. Wilgefortis thus became the patron saint of unhappily married women, and is depicted bearded on the cross (and easily mistaken for Christ in drag).

You can get some idea of the Santa Casa's serious financial backing in the **treasury** (situated on the first floor of the west wing), much ransacked over the years but still stuffed full of gold. The padded ceilings and low lighting create a kind of giant jewellery box for the master exhibit, a tasteless Viennese silver monstrance designed by Fischer von Erlach in 1699, and studded with diamonds taken from the wedding dress of Countess Kolovrat, who had made the Loreta sole heir to her fortune.

From Hradčanské náměstí to the Strahovský klášter

Strahovský klášter

Continuing westwards from Loretánské náměstí, Pohořelec, an arcaded street-cum-square, leads to the chunky remnants of the zigzag eighteenth-century fortifications that mark the edge of the old city, as defined by Charles IV back in the fourteenth century. Close by, to the left, is the **Strahovský klášter** (Strahov Monastery), founded in 1140 by the Premonstratensian order. Strahov was one of the lucky few to escape Joseph II's 1783 dissolution of the monasteries, a feat it managed by declaring itself a scholarly institution – the monks had, in fact, amassed one of the finest libraries in Bohemia. It continued to function until shortly after the Communists took power, when, along with all other religious establishments, it was closed down and most of its inmates thrown into prison; following the happy events of 1989, the monks have returned.

The Baroque entrance to the monastery is topped by a statue of Saint Norbert, founder of the Premonstratensian order, whose relics were brought here in 1627. Just inside the cobbled outer courtyard is a tiny deconsecrated church built by Rudolf II and dedicated to **sv Roch**, protector against plagues, one of which had very nearly rampaged through Prague in 1599; it's now an art gallery. The other church in this peaceful little courtyard is the still functioning twelfth-century monastery church of **Nanebezvetí Panny Marie**, which was given its last remodelling in Baroque times by Jean-Baptiste Mathey. It has undergone extensive work to restore it to its former glory, with lots of colourful frescoes relating to Saint Norbert's life, making it well worth a quick peek.

The libraries are open daily 9am–noon & 1–5pm; 40Kč.

It's the monastery's two **libraries**, though, that are the real reason for visiting Strahov; the entrance for both is to the right as you enter the outer courtyard. The first library you come to is the later and larger of the two, the **Filosofický sál** (Philosophical Hall), built in some haste in the 1780s, in order to accommodate the books and bookcases from Louka, a Premonstratensian monastery in Moravia that failed to escape Joseph's decree. The walnut bookcases are so tall they touch the library's lofty ceiling, which is busily decorated with frescoes by the Viennese painter Franz Maulbertsch on the theme of the search for truth. Don't, whatever you do, miss the collection of curios exhibited in the glass cabinets outside the library, which features shells, turtles, crabs, lobsters, dried-up sea monsters, butterflies, beetles, plastic fruit and moths. There's even a pair of whale's penises set amidst a narwhal horn, several harpoons and a model ship. The other main room is the low-ceilinged **Teologický sál** (Theological Hall), studded with ancient globes, its wedding-cake stucco framing frescoes on a similar theme, executed by one of the monks seventy years earlier. Outside the hall the library's oldest book, the ninth-century gem-studded *Strahov Gospel*, is displayed. Look out, too, for the cabinet of books documenting Czech trees, each of which has the bark of the tree on its spine.

An archway on the far side of the church contains the ticket office for the **Strahovská obrazárna** (Strahov Gallery), situated above the cloisters, and accessible from the door on the right, beyond the ticket office. The gallery's collection of religious art, church plate and reliquaries – a mere fraction of the monastery's total – may not be to everyone's taste, but it does contain the odd gem from Rudolf II's collection, including a portrait of the emperor himself by his court painter, Hans von Aachen, plus a superb portrait of Rembrandt's elderly mother by Gerrit Dou.

If you leave the monastery through the narrow doorway in the eastern wall, you enter the gardens and orchards of the **Strahovská zahrada**, from where you can see the whole city in perspective. The gardens form part of a wooded hill known as Petřín, and the path to the right contours round to the Stations of the Cross that lead up to the miniature Eiffel Tower known as the Rozhledna (see p.85). Alternatively, you can catch tram #22 from outside Strahov's main entrance to Malostranská metro or the centre of town.

The Strahovská obrazárna is open Tues–Sun 9am–noon & 12.30–5pm; 40Kč.

Chapter 3

Malá Strana

More than anywhere else, **MALÁ STRANA**, the "Little Quarter", conforms to the image of Prague as the ultimate Baroque city. It was here that film director Miloš Forman chose to shoot many of the street scenes in *Amadeus*, judging that its picturesque alleyways resembled Mozart's Vienna more than Vienna itself. And it's true; the streets have changed very little since Mozart walked them, as he often did on his frequent visits to Prague between 1787 and 1791. Unlike Hradčany, its main square is filled with city life during the day; while around practically every corner, narrow cobbled streets lead to some quiet walled garden, the perfect inner-city escape.

Foolishly, many visitors never stray from the well-trodden paths that link the Charles Bridge with Hradčany, thus bypassing most of Malá Strana. This is easy to do given that the whole town takes up a mere 600 square metres of land squeezed in between the river and the Hrad, but it means missing out on one of the greatest pleasures of Malá Strana – casually exploring its hilly eighteenth-century backstreets.

Some of the city's best restaurants and jazz clubs are located within Malá Strana; see Chapters 11 and 12 for details.

Long before the Přemyslid king, Otakar II, decided to establish a German community here in 1257, a mixture of Jews, merchants and monks had settled on the slopes below the castle. But, as with Hradčany, it was the fire of 1541 – which devastated the entire left bank of the Vltava – and the expulsion of the Protestants after 1620, that together had the greatest impact on the visual and social make-up of the quarter. In place of the old Gothic town, the newly ascendant Catholic nobility built numerous palaces here, though generally without quite the same destructive glee as up in Hradčany.

In 1918, the majority of these buildings became home to the foreign embassies of the newly established First Republic, and after 1948 the rest of the real estate was turned into flats to alleviate the postwar housing shortage. The cycle has come full circle again since 1989, and property in Malá Strana – much of it still in need of repair – is now among the most sought-after in Prague. The restitution law has brought back many former owners, while many of the old tenants have been forced out by rent increases – the face of Malá Strana is beginning to change once more.

Malostranské náměstí and around

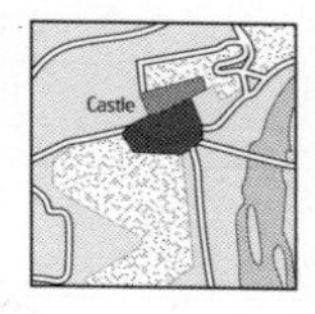

The main focus of Malá Strana has always been the sloping, cobbled **Malostranské náměstí**, which is dominated and divided into two by the church of sv Mikuláš (see p.76). Trams and cars hurtle across it, regularly dodged by a procession of people – some heading up the hill to the Hrad, others pausing for coffee and cakes at the numerous bars and restaurants hidden in the square's arcades and Gothic vaults. The most famous (and the most central) of the cafés is the **Malostranská kavárna**, established in 1874, and an occasional haunt of Kafka, Brod, Werfel and friends in the 1920s.

On every side, Neoclassical facades line the square, imitating the colour and grandeur of those of Hradčanské and Staroměstské náměstí. The largest Baroque re-development, the **Lichtenštejnský palác**, takes up the square's entire west side and is home to the university music faculty, as well as being a concert venue, art gallery and café. Its pleasing frontage hides a history linked to repression: first as the home of Karl von Liechtenstein, the man who pronounced the death sentence on the 27 Protestant leaders in 1621; then as headquarters for the Swedes during the 1648 siege; and later as the base of the Austrian General Windischgrätz, scourge of the 1848 revolution.

On the north side, distinguished by its two little turrets and rather shocking pistachio and vanilla colour scheme, is the **dům Smiřických** (no. 18), where the Protestant posse met up in 1618 to decide how to get rid of Emperor Ferdinand's Catholic governors:

Mozart in Prague

Mozart made the first of several visits to Prague with his wife Constanze in 1787, staying with his friend and patron Count Thun in what is now the British Embassy (Thunovská 14). A year earlier, his opera *The Marriage of Figaro*, which had failed to please the opera snobs in Vienna, had been given a rapturous reception at Prague's Nostitz Theater (now the Stavovské divadlo; see p.105); and on his arrival in 1787, Mozart was already flavour of the month, as he wrote in his diary: "Here they talk about nothing but Figaro. Nothing is played, sung or whistled but Figaro. Nothing, nothing but Figaro. Certainly a great honour for me!" Encouraged by this, he chose to premiere his next opera, *Don Giovanni*, later that year, in Prague rather than Vienna. He arrived with an incomplete score in hand, and wrote the overture at the Dušeks' Bertramka villa in Smíchov (see p.178), dedicating it to the "good people of Prague". Apart from a brief sojourn whilst on a concert tour, Mozart's fourth and final visit to Prague took place in 1791, the year of his death. The climax of the stay was the première of Mozart's final opera, *La Clemenza di Tito*, commissioned for the coronation of Leopold II as King of Bohemia (and according to tradition written on the coach from Vienna to Prague). The opera didn't go down quite as well as previous ones – according to tradition it sent the queen to sleep. Nevertheless, four thousand people turned out for his memorial service, held in Malá Strana's church of sv Mikuláš to the strains of his *Requiem Mass*.

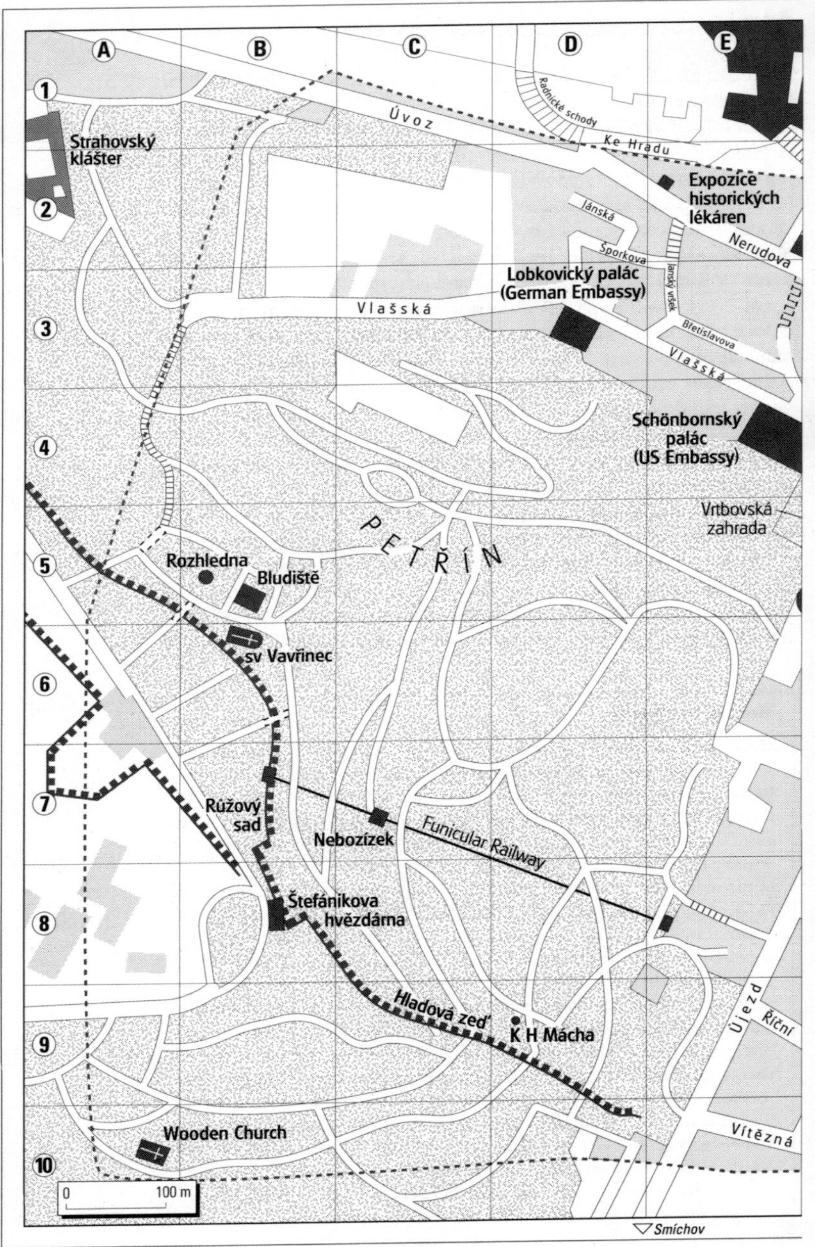
A
B
C
D
E
1
2
3
4
5
6
7
8
9
10
Strahovský klášter
Úvoz
Radnické schody
Ke Hradu
Expozice historických lékáren
Jánská
Šporkova
Nerudova
Lobkovický palác (German Embassy)
Jánský vršek
Vlašská
Břetislavova
Vlašská
Schönbornský palác (US Embassy)
Vrtbovská zahrada
PETŘÍN
Rozhledna
Bludiště
sv Vavřinec
Růžový sad
Nebozízek
Funicular Railway
Štefánikova hvězdárna
Hladová zeď
K H Mácha
Újezd
Říční
Wooden Church
Vítězná
0
100 m
Smíchov

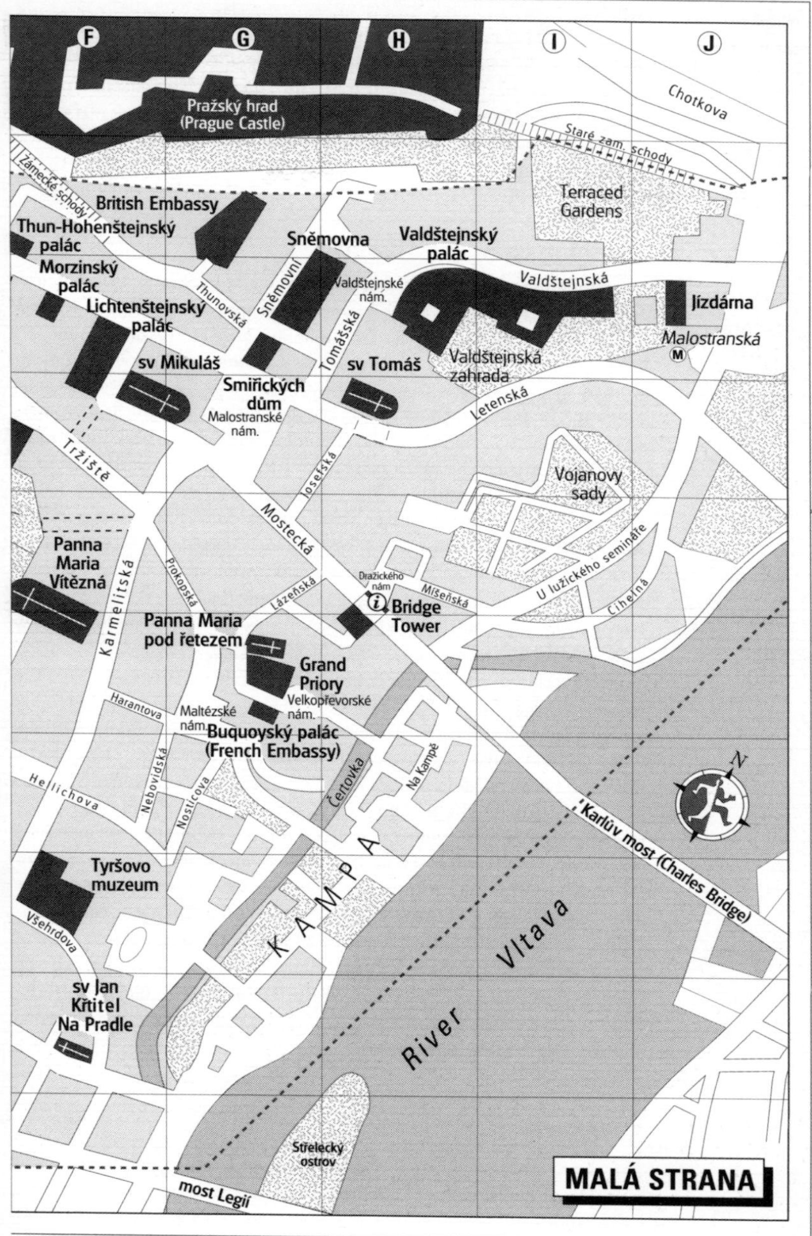
F
G
H
I
J
Pražský hrad
(Prague Castle)
Chotkova
Staré zam. schody
Zámecké schody
Terraced Gardens
British Embassy
Thun-Hohenštejnský palác
Sněmovna
Valdštejnský palác
Valdštejnská
Jízdárna
Malostranská
M
Morzinský palác
Thunovská
Sněmovní
Valdštejnské nám.
Lichtenštejnský palác
Tomášská
sv Mikuláš
sv Tomáš
Valdštejnská zahrada
Smiřických dům
Malostranské nám.
Letenská
Tržiště
Josefská
Vojanovy sady
Mostecká
U lužického semináře
Panna Maria Vítězná
Karmelitská
Prokopská
Lázeňská
Dražického nám
Míšeňská
Cihelná
Bridge Tower
Panna Maria pod řetezem
Grand Priory
Velkopřevorské nám.
Harantova
Maltézské nám.
Buquoyský palác
(French Embassy)
N
Nebovidská
Hellichova
Nosticova
Čertovka
Na Kampě
Karlův most (Charles Bridge)
Tyršovo muzeum
KAMPA
Všehrdova
Vltava
sv Jan Křtitel Na Pradle
River
Střelecký ostrov
most Legií
MALÁ STRANA

whether to attack them with daggers, or, as they eventually attempted to do, kill them by chucking them out of the window (see p.58). Sněmovní, the side street which runs alongside the palace's western facade, takes its name from the **Sněmovna**, the Neoclassical palace at no. 4, which served as the provincial Diet in the nineteenth century, the National Assembly of the First Republic in 1918, the Czech National Council after 1968, and finally, since 1993, as home to the lower house of the Czech parliament, as the Chamber of Deputies.

The church of sv Mikuláš

The church is open daily 9am–4pm; 40Kč.

Towering above the square, and the whole of Malá Strana, is the church of **sv Mikuláš** (St Nicholas), easily the most magnificent Baroque building in the city, and one of the last great structures to be built on the left bank, begun in 1702. For Christoph Dientzenhofer, a German immigrant from a dynasty of Bavarian architects, this was his most prestigious commission and is, without doubt, his finest work. For the Jesuits, who were already ensconced in the adjoining college, it was their most ambitious project yet in Bohemia, and the ultimate symbol of their stranglehold on the country. When Christoph died in 1722, it was left to his son Kilian Ignaz Dientzenhofer, along with Kilian's son-in-law, Anselmo Lurago, to finish the project, which they did with a masterful flourish, adding the giant green dome and tower – now among the most characteristic landmarks on Prague's left bank. Sadly for the Jesuits, they were able to enjoy the finished product for just twenty years, before they were banished from the Habsburg Empire in 1773.

Nothing about the relatively plain west facade prepares you for the overwhelming High Baroque **interior**. The vast fresco in the nave, by Johann Lukas Kracker, portrays some of the more fanciful miraculous feats of Saint Nicholas. Apart from his role as Santa Claus, he is depicted here rescuing sailors in distress, saving women from prostitution by throwing them bags of gold, and reprieving from death three unjustly condemned men. Even given the overwhelming proportions of the nave, the dome at the far end of the church, built by the younger Dientzenhofer, remains impressive, thanks, more than anything, to its sheer height. Leering over you as you gaze up at the dome are Ignaz Platzer's four terrifyingly oversized and stern Church Fathers, one of whom brandishes a gilded thunderbolt, leaving no doubt as to the gravity of the Jesuit message. Before you leave, check out the church's superb organ, its white case and gilded musical cherubs nicely offsetting the grey pipes.

Nerudova

The most important of the various streets leading up to the Hrad from Malostranské náměstí is **Nerudova**, named after the Czech journalist and writer Jan Neruda (1834–91), who was born at *U dvou*

House Signs

As well as preserving their Gothic or Romanesque foundations, many houses throughout Prague retain their ancient **house signs**, which you'll see carved into the gables, on hanging wooden signs, or inscribed on the facade. The system originated in medieval times, and still survives today, though it's now used predominantly by *pivnice* (pubs), restaurants and *vinárny* (wine bars).

Some signs were deliberately chosen to draw custom to the business of the house, like *U zeleného hroznu* (The Green Bunch of Grapes), a wine shop in the Malá Strana; others, like *U železných dveří* (The Iron Door), simply referred to some distinguishing feature of the house, often long since disappeared. The pervasive use of *zlatý* (gold) in the house names derives from the city's popular epithet, *Zlatá Praha* (Golden Prague), which could either refer to the halcyon days of Charles IV, when the new Gothic copper roofing shone like gold, or to the period of alchemy under Rudolf II. Religious names, like *U černé Matky boží* (The Black Madonna), were popular, too, especially during the Counter-Reformation.

In the 1770s, the Habsburgs, in their rationalizing fashion, introduced a numerical system, with each house in the city entered onto a register according to a strict chronology. Later, however, the conventional system of progressive street numbering was introduced, so don't be surprised if seventeenth-century pubs like *U medvídků* (The Little Bears) have two numbers, in addition to a house sign, in this case 7 and 345. The former, Habsburg number is written on a red background, the latter, modern number, on blue.

Malostranské náměstí and around

slunců (The Two Suns), at no. 47, an inn at the top of the street. His tales of Malá Strana immortalized bohemian life on Prague's left bank, though he's perhaps best-known in the West via the Chilean Nobel prize-winner, Pablo Neruda, who took his pen name from the lesser-known Czech. Historically, this is Prague's **artists' quarter**, and although few of the present inhabitants are names to conjure with, the various private galleries and craft shops that have sprouted up over the last few years continue the tradition.

Nerudova was once famous for its pubs, though sadly only a few remain; see p.219 for details.

The houses that line the steep climb up to the Hrad are typically restrained, many retaining their medieval barn doors, and most adorned with their own peculiar house signs (see box above). A short way up the hill, you'll pass two of the street's fancier buildings: at no. 5 is the **Morzinský palác**, now the Romanian Embassy, its doorway designed by Giovanni Santini and supported by two Moors (a pun on the owner's name) sculpted by Brokof; diagonally opposite, at no. 20, two giant eagles by Braun hold up the portal of the **Thun-Hohenštejnský palác**, now the Italian Embassy (also by Santini). Further up the street, according to Prague legend, Casanova and Mozart are thought to have met up at a ball given by the aristocrat owners of no. 33, the Bretfeldský palác, in 1791, while the latter was in town for the première of *La Clemenza di Tito* (see box on p.73). On the opposite side of the street, at no. 32, the former Dittrich pharmacy, dating from 1821, has been restored to its former glory and now houses a small and mildly diverting **Expozice**

The pharmacy is open April–Sept Tues–Fri noon–6pm, Sat & Sun 10am–6pm; Oct–March Thurs–Sun 10am–5pm; 20Kč.

historických lékáren, whose prize exhibits are its leech bottles and a large dried fruit fish.

Halfway up the hill, Nerudova halts at a crossroads where it meets the cobbled hairpin of Ke Hradu, which the royal coronation procession used to ascend; continuing west along **Úvoz** (The Cutting) takes you to the Strahovský klášter (see p.70). On the south side of Úvoz, the houses come to an end, and a view opens up over the picturesque jumble of Malá Strana's red-tiled roofs, while to the north, narrow stairways squeeze between the towering buildings of Hradčany, emerging on the path to the Loreta.

Tržiště and Vlašská

Running (very) roughly parallel to Nerudova – and linked to it by several side streets and steps – is **Tržiště**, which sets off from the south side of Malostranské náměstí. Halfway up on the left is the **Schönbornský palác**, now the US Embassy. The entrance, and the renowned gardens, are nowadays watched over by closed-circuit TV and twitchy Czech policemen – a far cry from the dilapidated palace in which Kafka rented an apartment in March 1917, and where he suffered his first bout of tuberculosis.

As Tržiště swings to the right, bear left up **Vlašská**, home to yet another **Lobkovický palác**, now the German Embassy. In the summer of 1989, several thousand East Germans climbed over the garden wall and entered the embassy compound to demand West German citizenship, which had been every German's right since partition. The neighbouring streets were soon jam-packed with abandoned Trabants, as the beautiful palace gardens became a muddy home to the refugees. Finally, the Czechoslovak government gave in and organized special trains to take the East Germans – cheered on their way by thousands of Praguers – over the federal border, thus prompting the exodus that eventually brought the Berlin Wall down.

The palace itself is a particularly refined building, best viewed from the rear – you'll have to approach it from Petřín (see p.84). The gardens, laid out in the early nineteenth century by Václav Skalník (who went on to landscape the spa at Mariánské Lázně), are no longer open to the public, but you should be able to see David Černý's sculpture, *Quo Vadis?*, a gold Trabant on legs, erected in memory of the fleeing East Germans.

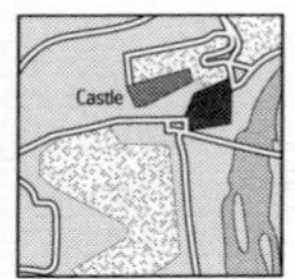

Valdštejnské náměstí and around

To the north of Malostranské náměstí, up Tomášská, lies the **Valdštejnský palác**, which takes up the whole of the eastern side of **Valdštejnské náměstí** and Valdštejnská. As early as 1621, Albrecht von Waldstein started to build a palace which would reflect his status as commander of the Imperial Catholic armies of the Thirty Years' War. By buying, confiscating, and then destroying 26 houses, three

Waldstein

Albrecht von Waldstein (known to the Czechs as Albrecht z Valdštejna, and to the English as Wallenstein – the name given to him by the German playwright Schiller in his tragic trilogy) was the most notorious warlord of the Thirty Years' War. If the imperial astrologer Johannes Kepler is to be believed, this is all because he was born at four in the afternoon on September 14, 1583. According to Kepler's horoscope Waldstein was destined to be greedy, deceitful, unloved and unloving. Sure enough, at an early age he tried to kill a servant, for which he was expelled from his Lutheran school. Recuperating in Italy, he converted to Catholicism (an astute career move) and married a wealthy widow who conveniently died shortly after the marriage. Waldstein used his new fortune to cultivate a friendship with Prince Ferdinand, heir to the Habsburg Empire, who in turn thought that a tame Bohemian noble could come in handy.

Within five years of the Battle of Bílá hora in 1620 (see p.175), Waldstein owned a quarter of Bohemia, either by compulsory purchase or in return for money or troops loaned to Ferdinand. It was a good time to go into property as Ferdinand's imperial armies, who were busy restoring Catholicism throughout Europe, provided a ready-made market for agricultural produce. And as a rising general, Waldstein could get away with a certain amount of insider trading, marching armies with as many as 125,000 men over enemy territory or land owned by rivals, laying fields waste and then selling his troops supplies from his own pristine Bohemian estates.

As Waldstein ranged further afield in Germany, conquering Jutland, Pomerania, Alsace and most of Brandenburg on Ferdinand's behalf, his demands for reward grew ever more outrageous. Already Duke of Friedland and Governor of Prague, Waldstein was appointed Duke of Mecklenburg in 1628. This upset not only the existing duke, who had backed Ferdinand's opponents, but even the Emperor's loyalist supporters. If Ferdinand thought fit to hand one of the greatest German titles to this Czech upstart, what family's inheritance could be secure? By 1630, Waldstein had earned himself the right to keep his hat on in the imperial presence as well as the dubious honour of handing the Emperor a napkin after he had used his fingerbowl. However, at this point Waldstein's services became too expensive for Ferdinand, so the duke was relieved of his command.

The following year, the Saxons occupied Prague, and the Emperor was forced to reinstate Waldstein. Ferdinand couldn't afford to do without the supplies from Waldstein's estates, but knew he was mortgaging large chunks of the empire to pay for his services. More alarmingly, there were persistent rumours that Waldstein was about to declare himself King of Bohemia and defect to the French enemy. In 1634, Waldstein openly rebelled against Ferdinand, who immediately hatched a plot to murder him, sending a motley posse including English, Irish and Scottish mercenaries to the border town of Cheb (Eger), where they cut the general down in his nightshirt as he tried to rise from his sickbed. Some see him as the first man to unify Germany since Charlemagne, others see him as a wily Czech hero. In reality he was probably just another ambitious, violent man, as his stars had predicted.

gardens and a brick factory, he succeeded in ripping apart a densely populated area of Malá Strana to make way for one of the first, largest and, quite frankly, most unappealing (at least from the outside) Baroque palaces in the city.

The Pedagogické muzeum is open Tues–Sun 10am–12.30pm & 1–5pm; 10Kč.

The Czech upper house, or Senát, is now housed in the palace, and only the former stables, housing the **Pedagogické muzeum**, are accessible to the public. This is a small and none too exciting exhibition on Czech education and, in particular, the influential teachings of Jan Amos Komenský (1592–1670) – often anglicized to John Comenius – who was forced to leave his homeland after the victory of Waldstein's Catholic armies, eventually settling in Protestant England. To get to the exhibition, go through the main gateway and continue straight across the first courtyard; the museum is on your right. The only way to get to see the palace's magnificent main hall – used in the filming of *Amadeus* – is to go to one of the concerts occasionally held there.

The Valdštejnská zahrada is open daily: mid-March to April & Oct 10am–6pm; May–Sept 9am–7pm.

If you've no interest in pedagogical matters, the palace's formal gardens, the **Valdštejnská zahrada** – accessible only from a doorway in the palace walls along Letenská – are a good place to take a breather from the city streets. The focus of the gardens is the gigantic Italianate *sala terrena*, a monumental loggia decorated with frescoes of the Trojan Wars, which stands at the end of an avenue of sculptures by Adriaen de Vries. The originals, which were intended to form a fountain, were taken off as booty by the Swedes in 1648 and now adorn the royal gardens in Drottningholm. In addition, there's a café, a pseudo grotto along the south wall, with quasi-stalactites, a door that once led to Waldstein's observatory, and a small aviary, home to the gardens' peacock population.

The Valdštejnská jízdárna is open Tues–Sun 10am– 6pm.

On the opposite side of the gardens, the palace's former riding school, **Valdštejnská jízdárna**, has been converted into a gallery, which puts on temporary exhibitions of fine art and photography organized by the Národní galerie. The riding school is accessible only from the courtyard of the nearby Malostranská metro station.

Letenská and sv Tomáš

Walking southwest along **Letenská** from the gardens back towards Malostranské náměstí, takes you past **U svatého Tomáše**, the oldest *pivnice* in Prague, established in 1352 by Augustinian monks who brewed their own lethal dark beer on the premises. Unfortunately, the Communists succeeded in kicking out the monks and closing down the brewery – the surviving pub is now shamelessly touristy and overpriced.

Better preserved are the neighbouring cloisters and priory church of **sv Tomáš** (St Thomas), which bear few traces of their Gothic origins since Kilian Ignaz Dientzenhofer's rebuilding in the 1720s. The rich burghers of Malá Strana spared no expense, as is clear from the ornate pink and white plasterwork, the glorious dome, and the fantastically colourful frescoes by Václav Vavřinec Reiner. They also bought a couple of Rubens for the altarpiece (the originals now belong to the Národní galerie) and two dead saints, St Just and St Boniface, whose gruesome clothed skeletons lie in glass coffins on either side of the nave, by the second pillar.

Malá Strana's terraced gardens

One of the chief joys of Malá Strana is its **terraced gardens**, hidden away behind the Baroque palaces on Valdštejnská, on the slopes below the castle, where the royal vineyards used to be, and commanding superb views over Prague. After lengthy restoration, all the gardens, except the Polish Embassy's Fürstenberská zahrada, are once more open to the public. In fact, now you can climb all the way up through the gardens to the Zahrada na valech beneath the Hrad itself.

The best-loved of the three adjoining gardens is the **Kolovratská** or **Černínská zahrada**, which makes the most of its cramped site with a jumble of balustrades and terraces which culminate in a small *sala terrena* by Giovanni Alliprandi – as does the **Ledeburská zahrada** to the west. The largest of the gardens is the central **Pálffyovská zahrada**, made up of two older plots, joined together and renovated in Rococo style in 1751.

Another option is to seek out the **Vojanovy sady**, securely concealed behind a ring of high walls off U lužického semináře. Originally a monastic garden belonging to the Carmelites, it's now an informal public park, with sleeping babies, weeping willows, and lots of grass on which to lounge about; outdoor art exhibitions and occasional concerts also take place here. One final Malá Strana Baroque garden worth exploring is the Vrtbovská zahrada, off Karmelitská (see p.83).

The Vojanovy sady are open May–Sept daily 9am–7pm.

Southern Malá Strana

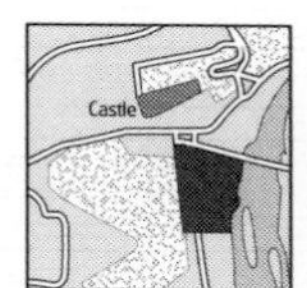

Karmelitská is the busy cobbled street that runs south from Malostranské náměstí along the base of Petřín towards the industrial suburb of Smíchov, becoming Újezd at roughly its halfway point. Between here and the River Vltava are some of Malá Strana's most picturesque and secluded streets. Although there are no major sights around here, the island of **Kampa**, in particular, makes up one of the most peaceful stretches of riverfront in Prague.

Maltézské náměstí and around

From the trams and traffic fumes of Karmelitská, it's a relief to cut across to the calm restraint of **Maltézské náměstí**, one of a number of delightful little squares between here and the river. At its centre is a plague column, topped by at statue of St John the Baptist, but the square takes its name from the Order of the Knights of St John of Jerusalem (better-known by their later title, the Maltese Knights), who in 1160 founded the nearby church of **Panna Maria pod řetězem** (Saint Mary below-the-chain), so called because it was the Knights' job to guard the Judith Bridge. The original Romanesque church was pulled down by the Knights themselves in the fourteenth century, but only the chancel and towers were successfully rebuilt by the time of the Hussite Wars. The two bulky Gothic towers are still standing and the apse is now thoroughly Baroque, but the nave remains unfinished and open to the elements.

The Knights have now reclaimed (and restored) the church and the adjacent Grand Priory, which backs onto **Velkopřevorské náměstí**, another pretty little square to the south, which echoes to the sound of music from the nearby Prague conservatoire. Following the violent death of John Lennon in 1980, Prague's youth established an ad hoc shrine smothered in graffiti tributes to the ex-Beatle along the Grand Priory's garden wall. The running battle between police and graffiti artists continued well into the 1990s, with the Maltese Knights taking an equally dim view of the mural, but a compromise has now been reached and the wall's scribblings legalized. On the opposite side of the square from the wall, sitting pretty in pink behind a row of chestnut trees, is the Rococo **Buquoyský palác**, built for a French family and appropriately enough now the French Embassy.

Kampa

The two or three streets that make up **Kampa**, the largest of the Vltava's islands, contain no notable palaces or museums; just a couple of old mills, an exquisite main square, and a serene riverside park – in other words, plenty enough diversion for a lazy summer afternoon. The island is separated from the left bank by Prague's "Little Venice", a thin strip of water called **Čertovka** (Devil's Stream), which used to power several mill-wheels until the last one ceased to function in 1936. In contrast to the rest of the left bank, the fire of 1541 had a positive effect on Kampa, since the flotsam from the blaze effectively stabilized the island's shifting shoreline. Nevertheless, Kampa was still subject to frequent flooding right up until the Vltava was dammed in the 1950s.

For much of its history, the island was the city's main wash house, a fact commemorated by the church of sv Jan Křtitel Na Prádle (St John-the-Baptist at the Cleaners) on Říční, near the southernmost tip of the island. It wasn't until the sixteenth and seventeenth centuries that the Nostitz family, who owned Kampa, began to develop the northern half of the island; the southern half was left untouched, and today is laid out as a public park, with riverside views across to Staré Město. To the north, the oval main square, **Na Kampě**, once a pottery market, is studded with slender acacia trees and cut through by the Charles Bridge, to which it is connected by a double flight of steps.

Karmelitská and Újezd

Southern Malá Strana

On the corner of Karmelitská and Tržiště, at no. 25, is the entrance to one of the most elusive of Malá Strana's many Baroque gardens, the **Vrtbovská zahrada**, founded on the site of the former vineyards of the **Vrtbovský palác**. Laid out on Tuscan-style terraces, dotted with ornamental urns and statues of the gods by Matthias Bernhard Braun, the gardens twist their way up the lower slopes of Petřín Hill to an observation terrace, from where there's a spectacular rooftop perspective on the city.

Panna Maria Vítězná and the Pražské Jezulátko

Further down, on the same side of the street, is the rather plain church of **Panna Maria Vítězná**, which was begun in early Baroque style by German Lutherans in 1611, and later handed over to the Carmelites after the Battle of Bílá hora. The main reason for coming here is to see the **Pražské Jezulátko** or *Bambino di Praga*, a high-kitsch wax effigy of the infant Jesus as a precocious three-year old, enthroned in a glass case illuminated with strip-lights, which was donated by one of the Lobkowicz family's Spanish brides in 1628. Attributed with miraculous powers, the *pražské Jezulátko* became an object of international pilgrimage equal in stature to the Santa Casa in Loreta, similarly inspiring a whole series of replicas. It continues to attract visitors (as the multilingual prayer cards attest) and boasts a vast personal wardrobe of expensive swaddling clothes – approaching a hundred separate outfits at the last count – regularly changed by the Carmelite nuns. If you're keen to see some of the infant's outfits, there's a small museum, up the spiral staircase in the south aisle. Here, you get to see his lacy camisoles, as well as a selection of his velvet and satin overgarments sent from all over the world. There are also chalices, monstrances and a Rococo crown studded with diamonds and pearls to admire.

The church is open Mon–Sat 10am–5.30pm, Sun 1–5pm; entry to the museum is 40Kč.

Michnův palác: Tyršovo muzeum

A block or so further south, Karmelitská becomes Újezd, on the east side of which is the **Michnův palác**, at no. 40, built on the site of another former nunnery, this time Dominican. The facade and gateway still incorporates elements of the Renaissance summer palace built by the Kinský family around 1580. From 1787 the building was used as an armoury and fell into disrepair until the Czech nationalist sports movement *Sokol* bought it in 1921. Nowadays, it is home to the university's sports faculty and the **Tyršovo muzeum**, which focuses on the history of Czech sport. **Sport** played an important part in the Czech national revival (*národní obrození*) through *Sokol*, the extremely popular nationalist organization set up in 1862, in direct response to the German *Turnverband* physical education movement. The Communists outlawed *Sokol* (as the Nazis had also done) and, in its place, established a tradition of *Spartakiáda*, extravaganzas of synchronized gymnastics held every five years in the Strahov stadium, behind Petřín. Even the *Spartakiáda* were popular, but, indelibly tainted by their political past, the last one, due to have been held in 1990, was cancelled. The museum, named after one of *Sokol*'s founders, Miroslav Tyrš, is currently closed until further notice.

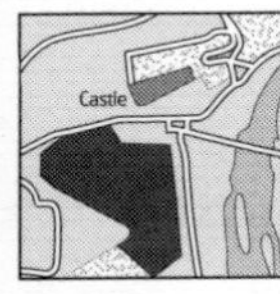

Petřín

The scaled-down version of the Eiffel Tower is the most obvious landmark on the wooded hill of **Petřín**, the largest green space in the city centre. The tower is just one of the exhibits built for the 1891 Prague Exhibition, whose modest legacy includes the **funicular railway** (lanová dráha) which climbs up from a station just off Újezd. The original funicular was powered by a simple but ingenious system whereby two carriages, one at either end of the steep track, were fitted with large watertanks that were alternately filled at the top and emptied at the bottom; it was replaced in the 1960s by the current electric system. As the carriages pass each other at the halfway station of Nebozízek, you can get out and soak in the view from the restaurant of the same name.

The funicular runs every 10–15 minutes, 9.15am–8.45pm. Tickets are the same as for the rest of the public transport system and travel passes are valid.

Along the Hunger Wall

At the top of the hill, it's possible to trace the southernmost perimeter wall of the old city – popularly known as the **Hladová zeď** (Hunger Wall) – as it creeps eastwards back down to Újezd, and northwestwards to the Strahovský klášter. Instigated in the 1460s by Charles IV, it was much lauded at the time (and later by the Communists) as a great public work which provided employment for the burgeoning ranks of the city's destitute (hence its name); in fact, much of the wall's construction was paid for by the expropriation of Jewish property.

The observatory is open April–Aug Tues–Fri 2–7pm & 9–11pm, Sat & Sun 10am–noon, 2–7pm & 9–11pm; shorter hours in winter.

Follow the wall southeast and you come to the aromatic **Růžový sad** (Rose Garden), whose colour-coordinated rose beds are laid out in front of Petřín's observatory, the **Štefánikova hvězdárna**, run by star-gazing enthusiasts. The small astrological exhibition inside is hardly worth bothering with, but if it's a clear night, a quick peek through the observatory's two powerful telescopes is a treat. A little further down the hill, on the other side of the wall from the observatory, stands a bust of the leading Czech Romantic poet **Karel Hynek Mácha**, who penned the poem *Maj* (May), on the subject of unrequited love. In spring, and in particular on the first of May, the statue remains a popular place of pilgrimage for courting couples.

Another curiosity, hidden in the trees on the southern side of the Hladová zeď, is a **wooden church** that was brought here, log by log, from an Orthodox village in Carpatho-Ruthenia (now part of

Ukraine) in 1929. Churches like this are still common in eastern Slovakia, and this is a particularly ornate example from the eighteenth century, with multiple domes like piles of giant acorns.

Petřín

Back at the Růžový sad, follow the wall northwest and you'll come to Palliardi's twin-towered church of **sv Vavřinec** (St Lawrence), from which derives the German name for Petřín – Laurenziberg. Dotted along the path that leads to Strahov are the Stations of the Cross, culminating in the sgraffitoed Calvary Chapel, just beyond the church. Opposite the church are a series of buildings from the 1891 Exhibition, starting with the diminutive **Rozhledna**, an octagonal interpretation – though a mere fifth of the size – of the Eiffel Tower which shocked Paris in 1889, and a tribute to the city's strong cultural and political links with Paris at the time; the view from the public gallery is terrific in fine weather.

The Rozhledna is open April–Oct daily 9.30am–7pm; Nov–March Sat & Sun 9.30am–5pm; 25Kč.

The next building along is the **Bludiště**, a mini neo-Gothic castle complete with mock drawbridge. The first section of the interior features a **mirror maze**, a stroke of infantile genius by the exhibition organizers. This is followed by an action-packed, life-sized diorama of the Prague students' and Jews' victory over the Swedes on the Charles Bridge in 1648. The humour of the convex and concave mirrors that lie beyond the diorama is so simple, it has both adults and kids giggling away. From the tower and maze, the path with the Stations of the Cross will eventually lead you to the perimeter wall of the Strahovský klášter (see p.70), giving great views over Petřín's palatial orchards and the sea of red tiles below.

The Mirror Maze is open April–Oct daily 10am–7pm; Nov–March Sat & Sun 10am–5pm; 30Kč.

Chapter 4

Staré Město

STARÉ MĚSTO, literally the "Old Town", is Prague's most central, vital ingredient. Most of the capital's busiest markets, shops, restaurants and pubs are in this area, and during the day a gaggle of shoppers and tourists fills its complex web of narrow streets. Yet despite all the commercial activity, there are still plenty of residential streets, giving the area a lived-in feel that is rarely found in European city centres. The district is bounded on one side by the river, on the other by the arc of Národní, Na příkopě and Revoluční, and at its heart is **Staroměstské náměstí**, Prague's showpiece main square, easily the most magnificent in central Europe.

Merchants and craftsmen began settling in what is now Staré Město as early as the tenth century, and in the mid-thirteenth century it was granted town status, with jurisdiction over its own affairs. The fire of 1541, which ripped through the quarters on the other side of the river, never reached Staré Město, though the 1689 conflagration made up for it. Nevertheless, the victorious Catholic nobles built fewer large palaces here than on the left bank, leaving the medieval street plan intact with the exception of the Klementinum (the Jesuits' powerhouse) and the Jewish Quarter, Josefov, which was largely reconstructed in the late nineteenth century (see p.112). Like so much of Prague, however, Staré Město is still, on the surface, overwhelmingly Baroque, built literally on top of its Gothic predecessor to guard against the floods which plagued the town.

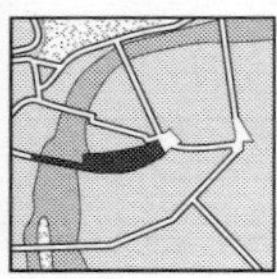

From the Karlův most to Malé náměstí

In their explorations of Staré Město, most people unknowingly retrace the **královácesta**, the traditional route of the coronation procession from the medieval gateway, the Prašná brána (see p.137), to the Hrad. Established by the Přemyslids, the route was followed, with a few minor variations, by every king until the Emperor Ferdinand IV in 1836, the last of the Habsburgs to bother having himself crowned in Prague. It's also the most direct route from the Charles Bridge to Prague's main square, Staroměstské náměstí, and therefore a natural choice. However, many of the real treasures of Staré Město lie away from the *králová cesta*, so if you want to escape the crowds, it's worth heading off into the quarter's silent, twisted matrix of streets, then simply following your nose – for details of specific sights to the south of Karlova, see p.94.

From the Karlův most to Malé náměstí

The Karlův most (Charles Bridge)

The **Karlův most**, or Charles Bridge – which for over four hundred years was the only link between the two halves of Prague – is by far the city's most familiar monument. It's an impressive piece of medieval engineering, aligned slightly askew between two mighty Gothic gateways, but its fame is due almost entirely to the magnificent, mostly Baroque statues, additions to the original structure, that punctuate its length. Individually, only a few of the works are outstanding, but taken collectively, set against the backdrop of the Hrad, the effect is breathtaking.

The bridge was begun in 1357 to replace an earlier structure which had been swept away by one of the Vltava's frequent floods in 1342. Charles IV commissioned his young German court architect, Peter Parler, to carry out the work, which was finally completed in the early fifteenth century. Given its strategic significance, it comes as no surprise that the bridge has played an important part in Prague's history: in 1648, it was the site of the last battle of the Thirty Years' War, fought between the besieging Swedes and an ad hoc army of Prague's students and Jews; in 1744, the invading Prussians were defeated at the same spot; and in 1848, it formed the front line between the revolutionaries on the Staré Město side, and the reactionary forces on the left bank. For the first four hundred years it was known simply as the Prague or Stone Bridge – only in 1870 was it officially named after its patron. Since 1950, the bridge has been closed to vehicles, and is now one of the most popular places to hang out, day and night; apart from the steady stream of sightseers, the niches created by the bridge-piers are keenly fought over by souvenir hawkers and buskers.

Building the bridge

There are countless legends regarding the bridge's initial construction: the most persistent is that the builders mixed eggs (and, in some versions, wine) with the mortar to strengthen it. Having quickly depleted the city's egg supply, orders were sent out for contributions from the surrounding villages: the villagers of Velvary, who were worried that raw eggs wouldn't have quite the right consistency, hard-boiled theirs, and from Unhošt curd, cheese and whey were sent to bond the bricks even harder.

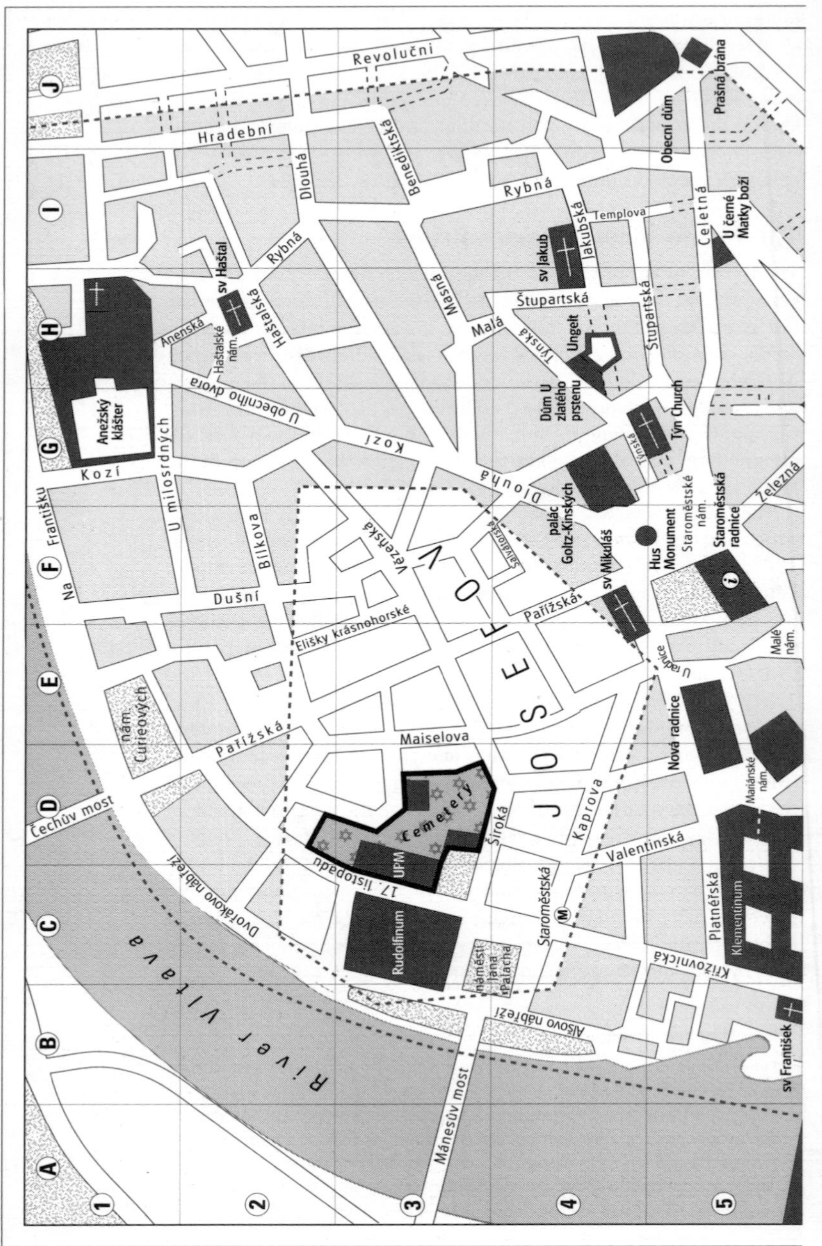
River Vltava
Čechův most
Mánesův most
Dvořákovo nábřeží
Alšovo nábřeží
nám. Curieových
Rudolfinum
UPM
Cemetery
17. listopadu
náměstí Jana Palacha
Staroměstská
Široká
Kaprova
Valentinská
Platnéřská
Křižovnická
Klementinum
sv František
Mariánské nám.
Nová radnice
U radnice
Malé nám.
Staroměstská radnice
Železná
Staroměstské nám.
Hus Monument
sv Mikuláš
Pařížská
Maiselova
Elišky Krásnohorské
JOSEFOV
Salvátorská
Vězeňská
Dušní
Bílkova
U milosrdných
Kozí
Na Františku
Anežský klášter
Anenská
Haštalské nám.
sv Haštal
Haštalská
U obecního dvora
Rybná
Dlouhá
Hradební
Benediktská
Revoluční
Masná
Malá
Týnská
Štupartská
Ungelt
Dům U zlatého prstenu
Týn Church
palác Golz-Kinských
sv Jakub
Jakubská
Templova
Celetná
U černé Matky boží
Obecní dům
Prašná brána
A
B
C
D
E
F
G
H
I
J
1
2
3
4
5

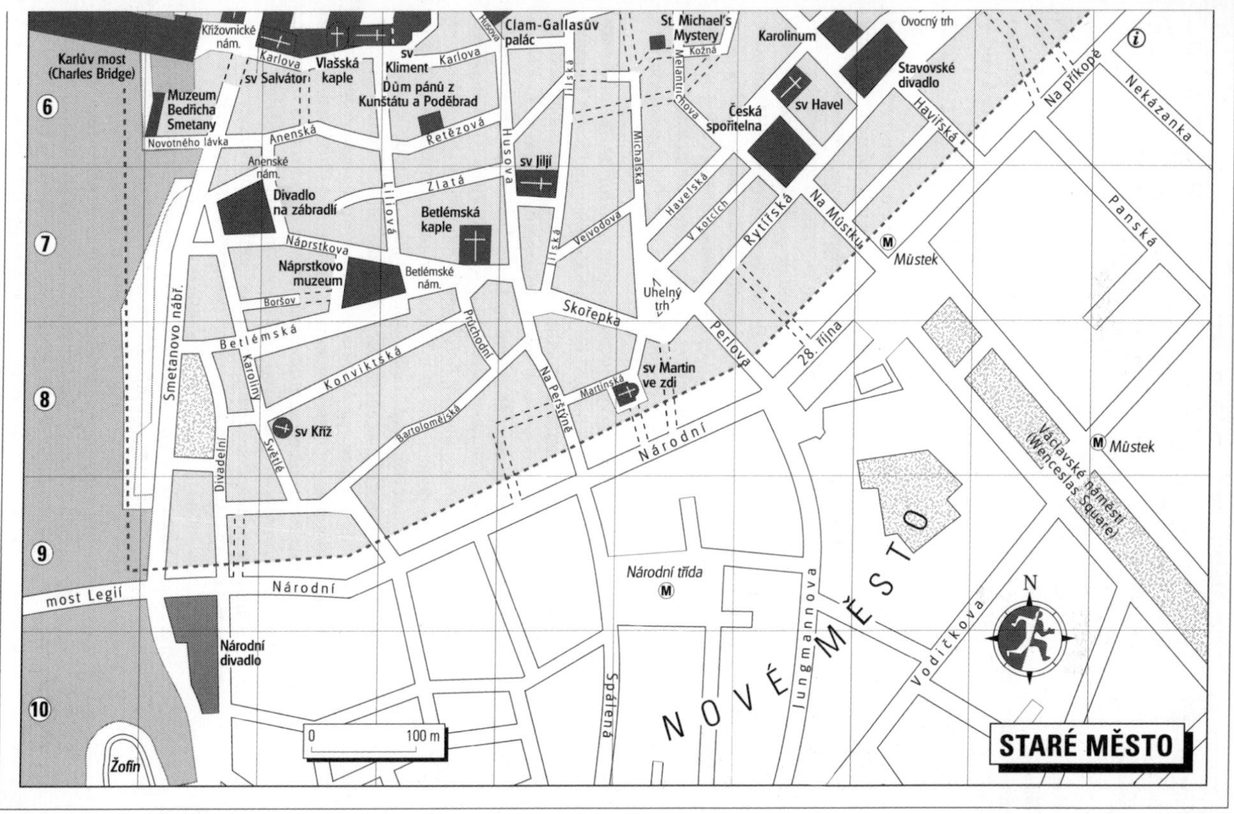

Křižovnické nám.
Clam-Gallasův palác
St. Michael's Mystery
Karolinum
Ovocný trh
Na příkopě
Nekázanka
Karlův most
(Charles Bridge)
Karlova
Vlašská kaple
sv Salvátor
sv Kliment
Dům pánů z Kunštátu a Poděbrad
Husova
Jilská
Kožná
Melantrichova
sv Havel
Stavovské divadlo
Česká spořitelna
Havířská
Muzeum Bedřicha Smetany
Novotného lávka
Anenská
Řetězová
sv Jiljí
Michalská
Anenské nám.
Zlatá
Divadlo na zábradlí
Liliová
Betlémská kaple
Havelská
V kotcích
Rytířská
Na Můstku
Vejvodova
Panská
Náprstkova
Náprstkovo muzeum
Betlémské nám.
Můstek
Uhelný trh
Boršov
Skořepka
Smetanovo nábř.
Betlémská
Průchodní
Perlova
28. října
Karoliny
Konviktská
sv Martin ve zdi
Martinská
Na Perštýně
sv Kříž
Bartolomějská
Národní
Světlé
Divadelní
Václavské náměstí
(Wenceslas Square)
Národní třída
most Legií
Národní divadlo
Jungmannova
Vodičkova
N
NOVÉ MĚSTO
Spálená
0
100 m
STARÉ MĚSTO
Žofín
6
7
8
9
10

From the Karlův most to Malé náměstí

The bridge tower is open daily April–Oct 9am–5.30pm.

The Malá Strana bridge towers

The following account of the statuary starts from the Malá Strana side, where two unequal **bridge towers**, connected by a castellated arch, form the entrance to the bridge. The smaller, stumpy tower was once part of the original Judith Bridge (named after the wife of Vladislav I, who built the twelfth-century original); the taller of the two, crowned by one of the pinnacled wedge-spires more commonly associated with Prague's right bank, contains an exhibition relaying the history of the towers, the bridge itself, and the story of St John of Nepomuk (see p.56). You can also walk out onto the balcony that connects the two towers for a bird's-eye view of the seething masses pouring across the bridge.

The statues

A bronze crucifix has stood on the bridge since its construction, but the first sculpture wasn't added until 1683, when St John of Nepomuk appeared. His statue was such a propaganda success with the Catholic church authorities that another 21 were added between 1706 and 1714. These included works by Prague's leading Baroque sculptors, led by Matthias Bernhard Braun and Ferdinand Maximilian Brokof; the Max brothers unimaginatively filled in the remaining piers in the mid-nineteenth century. The sculptures, mostly crafted in sandstone, have weathered badly over the years and are gradually being replaced by copies; to see the originals you can visit the Lapidárium (see p.171).

In the first statue group on the north side, paid for by the university medical faculty, Jesus is flanked by **Saint Cosmas and Saint Damian** (1), both dressed in medieval doctors' garb – they were renowned for offering their medical services free of charge to the poor. Opposite stands **Saint Wenceslas** (2), added by Czech nationalists in the nineteenth century. On the next pier, Brokof's **Saint Vitus** (3) is depicted as a Roman legionary, his foot being gently nibbled by one of the lions that went on to devour him in a Roman amphitheatre. Facing him is one of the most striking sculptural groups, the founders of the **Trinitarian Order** (4), again by Brokof: Saints John of Matha, Felix of Valois and his pet stag (plus, for some unknown reason, Saint Ivan), whose good works included ransoming persecuted Christians – three petrified souls can be seen through the prison bars below – from the infidels, represented by a bored Turkish jailor and his rabid dog.

Amid all the blackened sandstone, the lightly coloured figure of the (at the time) only recently canonized Servite friar, **Saint Philip Benizi** (5), stands out as the only marble statue on the bridge. At his feet sits the papal crown, which he refused to accept when it was offered to him in 1268. Opposite stands Prague's second bishop, the youthful **Saint Adalbert** (6), who was hounded out of the city on more than one occasion by the blissfully pagan citizens of Prague. Another (at the time) recently canonized saint is **Cajetan** (7), founder of the Theatine Order (and of a whole chain of non-profit-making pawnshops in Naples), who stands in front of a column of cherubs sporting a sacred heart.

One of the most successful statues is that of the blind Cistercian nun, **Saint Lutgard (8)**, sculpted by Braun when he was just 26 years old. She is depicted here in the middle of her celebrated vision, in which Christ appeared so that she could kiss his wounds. The Augustinians sponsored the next duo, on the other side of the steps leading down to Kampa Island: **Saint Augustine (9)**, and one of his later followers, **Saint Nicholas of Tolentino (10)**, who is depicted dishing out bread to the poor. On the top-floor balcony of the house immediately behind Saint Nicholas of Tolentino is a strange collection of objects – a Madonna, a mangle and a lantern. The story goes that the Madonna was retrieved from the river during a particularly bad flood, and saved the house from further inundation. She then went on to save a washerwoman whose sleeves got caught in the mangle; as for the lantern, if it goes out while you're passing by, it means you'll die within the year.

Next pier along, the apostle **Saint Jude Thaddaeus (11)**, patron saint of those in dire straits, holds the club with which the pagans beat him to death. On the opposite side, the Dominican friar **Saint Vincent Ferrer (12)** stands over one of his converts to self-flagellation, while the inscription below lists his miraculous achievements, including the conversion of 2500 Jews, some forty resurrections and the exorcism of seventy demons. He is joined on his pedestal, somewhat inexplicably, by Bohemia's best-loved hermit, **Saint Procopius**. If you look over the side of the bridge at this point, you'll see a nineteenth-century sculpture of **Roland (13)** – known as *Bruncvík* in Czech – brandishing his miraculous golden sword (the real thing is said to be embedded in the bridge, to be used in case of municipal emergency). The original, erected to protect the rights of the Staré Město over the full extent of the bridge, was destroyed in 1648.

The Franciscan pier – **Saint Anthony of Padua (14)**, and a lifeless nineteenth-century figure of **Saint Francis of Assisi**, accompanied

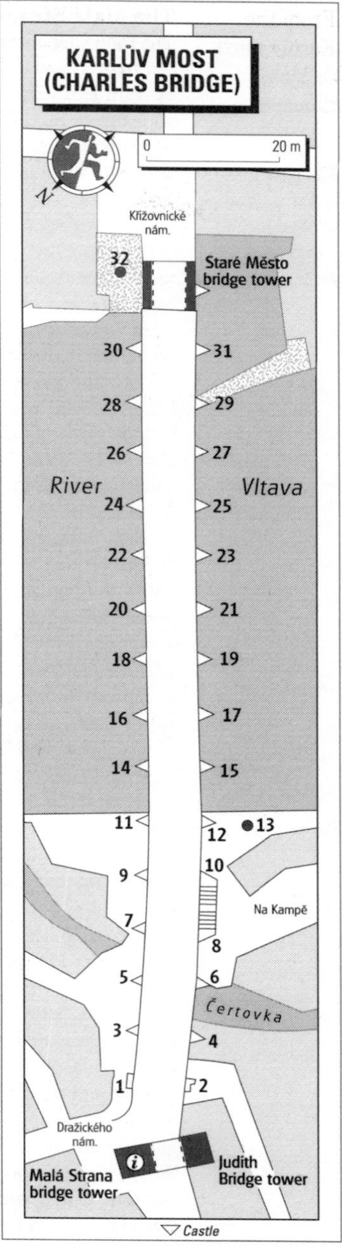

From the Karlův most to Malé náměstí

For the story of Saint John of Nepomuk's martyrdom, see p.56.

by two angels (15) – is worth passing over to reach the bridge's earliest and most popular sculpture, **Saint John of Nepomuk (16)**. The only bronze statue on the bridge, it's now green with age, the gold-leaf halo of stars and palm branch gently blowing in the breeze. Saint John's appearance in 1683, on the bridge from which he was thrown to his death, was part of the Jesuits' persistent campaign to have him canonized; the statue later inspired hundreds of copies, which adorn bridges throughout central Europe. On the base, there's a bronze relief depicting his martyrdom, the figure of John now extremely worn through years of being touched for good luck. Facing Saint John is Bohemia's first martyr, a rather androgynous version of **Saint Ludmilla (17)**, holding the veil with which she was strangled and standing alongside her grandson, Saint Wenceslas, here depicted as a young child; his future martyrdom is recounted in the base-relief (for more on Wenceslas and co, see p.55).

With the exception of the Jesuit general **Saint Francis Borgia (19)**, the next two piers are glum nineteenth-century space-fillers: a trio of Bohemian saints – **Norbert**, **Sigismund** and, for the third time, **Wenceslas (18)** – followed by **John the Baptist (20)** and **Saint Christopher** (21). Between the piers (18 & 20), on the north side, a small bronze cross is set into the wall marking the spot where John of Nepomuk was dumped in the river (see above); touch it and, according to the locals, you're guaranteed to return to the city. In 1890, the two Jesuit statues on the next pier were swept away by a flood: the statue of the founder of the order, Saint Ignatius Loyola, was replaced with the most recent additions to the bridge (completed in 1938), **saints Cyril and Methodius** (22), the ninth-century missionaries who first introduced Christianity to the Slavs; the other, the Jesuit missionary **Saint Francis Xavier** (23), survived the order's unpopularity and was replaced by a copy. This is one of the more unusual sculptural groups on the bridge: the saint, who worked in India and the Far East, is held aloft by three Moorish and two "Oriental" converts; Brokof placed himself on the saint's left side.

Next in line are Jesus, Mary, and Mary's mother, **Saint Anne** (24) and, facing them, with a slightly older Jesus at his feet, **Joseph** (25), a nineteenth-century replacement for another Brokof, this time destroyed by gunfire during the 1848 revolution. The **Crucifixion** scene (26) is where the original fourteenth-century crucifix stood alone on the bridge for two hundred years. The gold-leaf, Hebrew inscription, "Holy, Holy, Holy" was added in 1696, paid for by a Prague Jew who was ordered to do so by the city court, having been found guilty of blasphemy before the cross. Apart from Christ himself, all the figures, and the **Pietà** opposite (27), were added by the Max brothers.

On the penultimate pier, the Dominicans placed their founder, **Saint Dominic**, and their other leading light, **Saint Thomas Aquinas**, beside the **Madonna** (28); in amongst the cherubs is the order's emblem, a dog with a burning torch in his mouth. Opposite, **Saint Barbara**, the patron saint of miners, whose beautifully sculpted hands so impressed Kafka, is accompanied by **Saint Margaret** and **Saint Elizabeth (29)**. There's one final Madonna (**30**), this time presiding over the kneeling figure of Saint Bernard, and a bubbling mass of cherubs mucking about with the instruments of the Passion – the cock, the dice and the centurion's gauntlet. Lastly, **Saint Ivo (31)**, patron saint of lawyers, flanked by Justice and a prospective client, stands with an outstretched hand, into which Prague law students traditionally place a glass of beer after their finals.

From the Karlův most to Malé náměstí

The Staré Město bridge tower

On the Staré Město side is arguably the finest **bridge tower** of the lot: the western facade was trashed in the battle of 1648 but the eastern facade is still encrusted in Gothic cake-like decorations from Peter Parler's

The bridge tower is open daily April–Oct 9am–5.30pm.

Charles IV (1346–78)

There may be more legends and intrigue associated with the reign of Rudolf II (see p.61), but it was under **Emperor Charles IV** (Karel IV to the Czechs) that Prague enjoyed its true golden age. In just over thirty years, Charles transformed Prague into the effective capital of the Holy Roman Empire, establishing the city's archbishopric, its university, a host of monasteries and churches, an entire new town (Nové Město), plus several monuments which survive to this day, most notably St Vitus Cathedral, and, of course, the Charles Bridge (**Karlův most**).

Born in 1316 (and christened Václav), Charles was the only son of King John of Luxembourg and Queen Eliška, daughter of Přemysl King Václav II. Suspecting his wife of plotting to dethrone him, King John imprisoned her and Charles, keeping his three-year-old son in a dungeon with only "a little light coming in from a hole in the ceiling". In 1323, the young Charles was despatched to the fashionable French court to keep him out of any further trouble and complete his education – he never saw his mother again. In France he was given the name Charles (after Charlemagne) by the French king and married off to Blanche de Valois, the first of his four wives.

In 1346, his father (by then totally blind) was killed at the Battle of Crécy, and Charles, who escaped with just a wound, inherited the Czech crown. He immediately busied himself with building up his Bohemian power base, and within two years had got himself elected Holy Roman Emperor. Fluent in Czech, French, German, Latin and Italian, Charles used his international contacts to gather together a whole host of foreign artists to his new capital, most famously persuading the Italian man of letters, Petrarch, to pay a visit.

Though later chroniclers tried to paint Charles as chaste and pure, even he admitted in his autobiography that he had strayed in his youth; "seduced by the perverted people, we were perverted by the perverts", he wrote of his Italian sojourn. And just as Rudolf II created his *Kunst- und Wunderkammer*, Charles also spent much of his spare time amassing a bizarre collection of relics to ensure a smooth passage into the after-life. He cajoled and blackmailed his way into obtaining part of the whip used in the Passion, two thorns from Christ's crown, a few drops of milk from the Virgin Mary and one of Mary Magdalene's breasts, all beautifully encased in reliquaries designed by Prague's finest goldsmiths.

workshop, plus a series of mini-sculptures. The central figures are Saint Vitus, flanked by Charles IV on the right and his son, Václav IV, on the left; above stand two of Bohemia's patron saints, Adalbert and Sigismund. The severed heads of twelve of the Protestant leaders were suspended from the tower in iron baskets following their execution on Staroměstské náměstí in 1621, and all but one remained there until the Saxons passed through the capital ten years later. The tower now contains a small display of antique musical instruments, and allows you access onto the roof for another aerial perspective on the bridge.

Křižovnické náměstí

Pass under the Staré Město bridge tower and you're in **Křižovnické náměstí**, an awkward space hemmed in by its constituent buildings, and, with traffic hurtling across the square, a dangerous spot for unwary pedestrians. Hard by the bridge tower is a nineteenth-century cast-iron statue of **Charles IV (32)**, erected on the 500th anniversary of his founding of the university, and designed by a German, Ernst Julius Hähnel, in the days before the reawakening of Czech sculpture. To his left is an unusual plaque commemorating a Czech who was shot by mistake by the Red Army during the liberation on May 9, 1945.

The two churches facing onto the square are both quite striking and definitely worth exploring. The half-brick church of **sv František z Assisi** (St Francis of Assisi) was built in the 1680s to a design by Jean-Baptiste Mathey for the Czech Order of Knights of the Cross with a Red Star, the original gatekeepers of the old Judith Bridge. The order was founded by Saint Anežka in the thirteenth century, and reached the zenith of its power in the seventeenth century, during which its monks supplied most of the archbishops of Prague. The design of the church's interior, dominated by its huge dome, decorated with a fresco of *The Last Judgement* by Václav Vavřinec Reiner, and rich marble furnishings, served as a blueprint for numerous subsequent Baroque churches in Prague.

The **Galerie Křižovníků** (Tues–Sun: May–Oct 10am–5pm; Nov–April 10am–5pm; closed Jan; 40Kč), next door, houses a fairly indifferent Baroque art collection, various robes and mitres relating to the order, and a very bad copy of the altar from the Chapel of sv Kříž in Karlštejn (see p.194). Better are the panels from the fifteenth-century altarpiece by Nicholas Puchner depicting the foundation of the order. However, the best section by far is the treasury, which contains a stunning collection of silver and gold chalices, monstrances and reliquaries purporting to harbour, among other things, a thorn from Christ's crown. The gallery also hosts fairly dreadful commercial art exhibitions. On your way out, though, don't miss the subterranean chapel, whose unusual stalactite décor was completed in 1683.

Over the road is the church of **sv Salvátor**, its facade prickling with saintly statues which are lit up enticingly at night. Founded in 1593, but not completed until 1714, sv Salvátor marks the beginning of the Jesuits' rise to power and, like many of their churches, its design copies that of the Gesù church in Rome. It's worth a quick look, if only for the frothy stucco plasterwork and delicate ironwork in its triple-naved interior.

From the Karlův most to Malé náměstí

Karlova

Running from Křižovnické náměstí all the way to Malé náměstí is the narrow street of **Karlova**, packed with people winding their way towards Staroměstské náměstí, their attention divided between checking out the souvenir shops, and not losing their way. With Europop blaring from several shops, jesters hats and puppets in abundance, and a strip club for good measure, the whole atmosphere can be oppressive in the height of summer, and is, in many ways, better savoured at night.

While much of what's on offer in Karlova is eminently missable, there is one sight worth seeking out, and that's the **Muzeum loutkářských kultur** (Puppet Museum), in the cool Gothic cellars of Karlova 12. Despite the appalling lack of information in either Czech or English, the museum, run by the international puppetry organization UNIMA, which has its headquarters here, has an impressive display of historic Czech puppets, both string and rod, mostly dating from the late nineteenth and the early twentieth centuries. Some of the most appealing figures are the wonderfully malevolent devils, and there's a great miniature theatre from 1933, complete with backcloth scenery changes.

The Muzeum loutkářských kultur is open daily 9am–8pm in summer, and Sat & Sun only in winter; 50Kč.

At the first wiggle in Karlova, you come to the **Vlašská kaple** (Italian Chapel), which served the community of Italian masons, sculptors and painters who settled in Prague during the Renaissance period, and is still, strictly speaking, the property of the Italian state. The present Vlašská kaple is a tiny oval Baroque chapel completed in 1600, though sadly it's rarely open except for services.

You may have more luck with the adjacent church of **sv Kliment**, accessible from the same portal. It's a minor gem of Prague Baroque by Dientzenhofer with statues by Braun, a spectacular set of frescoes depicting the life of Saint Clement (whose fate was to be lashed to an anchor and hurled into the Black Sea), and an unusual spiky golden iconostasis added in the 1980s by its new owners, the Greek-Catholic church, who observe Orthodox rites but, confusingly, belong to the Roman Catholic church.

On the opposite side of Karlova, at the junction with Liliová, is **U zlatého hada** (The Golden Serpent), where the Armenian Deomatus Damajan opened the city's first coffee house in 1708. According to legend, the café was always full, not least because Damajan had a red-wine fountain inside. It is now a Chinese restaurant, though sadly minus the fountain and its original furnishings.

Klementinum

As they stroll down Karlova, few people notice the **Klementinum**, the former Jesuit College on the north side of the street, which covers an area second in size only to the Hrad. In 1556, Ferdinand I summoned the

Jesuits to Prague to help bolster the Catholic cause in Bohemia, giving them the church of sv Kliment (see above), which Dientzenhofer later rebuilt for them. Initially, the Jesuits proceeded with caution, but once the Counter-Reformation set in, they were put in control of the entire university and provincial education system. From their secure base at sv Kliment, they began to establish space for a great Catholic seat of learning in the city by buying up the surrounding land, demolishing more than thirty old town houses, and, over the next two hundred years, gradually building themselves a palatial headquarters. In 1773, soon after the Klementinum was completed, the Jesuits were turfed out of the country and the building handed over to the university authorities.

Nowadays the Klementinum houses the National Library's collection of over five million volumes, but much of the original building has been left intact. The **entrance**, inconspicuously placed just past the church of sv Kliment, lets you into a series of rather plain courtyards. The entrance to the **Zrcadlová kaple** (Mirrored Chapel) is immediately to the left after passing through the archway on the far side of the first courtyard; its interior of fake marble, gilded stucco and mirror panels boasts fine acoustics and is regularly used for concerts.

The Zrcadlová kaple is open only for concerts and special exhibitions.

The Klementinum hides several other attractions inside, but the authorities are none too keen to let the public inside. The most spectacular sight – not officially open to the public – is the **Hudební oddělení** (Music Library) on the first floor to the west of the chapel, a stunning Rococo reading room filled with leather tomes, ancient globes and frescoes. In the same wing there are temporary exhibitions (Mon–Fri 9am–9pm) of some of the library's prize possessions, which include the world's largest collection of works by the early English reformer, Yorkshireman John Wycliffe, whose writings had an enormous impact on the fourteenth-century Czech religious community, inspiring preachers like Hus to speak out against the social conditions of the time.

At roughly the centre of the Klementinum complex is the Jesuits' **observatory tower**, which is the only place in the world that has being monitoring and recording meteorological data since 1775 – too late, though, for Prague's most illustrious visiting scientist, Johannes Kepler, who did his planet-gazing in the Belvedér. A religious exile from his native Germany, Kepler succeeded Tycho Brahe as court astronomer to Rudolf II, and lived at no. 4 Karlova for a number of years, during which time he drew up the first heliocentric laws on the movement of the planets.

Mariánské náměstí and around

Where the Klementinum ends, the Renaissance corner house **U zlaté studně** (The Golden Well), now a wine bar and *pension* (see p.203), stands out like a wedge of cheese; its thick stucco reliefs of assorted saints were commissioned in 1701 by the owner in gratitude for having been spared the plague.

From the Karlův most to Malé náměstí

A short diversion here, down Seminářská, brings you out onto **Mariánské náměstí**, generally fairly deserted compared to Karlova. It's hard to believe that the rather severe **Nová radnice** (New Town Hall), on the east side of the square, was built by Osvald Polívka, architect of the exuberant Art-Nouveau Obecní dům (see p.137). Its most striking features are the two gargantuan figures which stand guard at either corner, by the sculptor of the Hus Monument, Ladislav Šaloun. The one on the left, looking like Darth Vader, is the "Iron Knight", mascot of the armourers' guild; to the right is the somewhat grotesquely caricatured sixteenth-century Jewish sage and scholar, Rabbi Löw, who was visited by Death on several occasions, but allowed to live to the ripe old age of 96, provided he did not stray from his religious studies – here, a naked woman tries unsuccessfully to attract his attentions.

For the full story of Rabbi Löw, see p.117.

To get back to Karlova, head down Husova, past the Baroque **Clam-Gallasův palác** (not open to the public), which, despite its size – it takes up a good five or six old houses – is easy to overlook in this narrow space. It's a typically lavish affair by the Viennese architect Fischer von Erlach, with big and burly *Atlantes* supporting the portals.

Malé náměstí

After a couple more shops, boutiques, hole-in-the-wall bars and a final twist in Karlova, you emerge onto **Malé náměstí**, a square originally settled by French merchants in the twelfth century. The square was also home to the first apothecary in Prague, opened by a Florentine in 1353, and the tradition is continued today by the pharmacy **U zlaté koruny** (The Golden Crown), at no. 13, which boasts chandeliers and a restored Baroque interior. The square's best-known building, though, is the russet-red, neo-Renaissance **Rott Haus**, originally an ironmongers' shop founded by V. J. Rott in 1840, whose facade is smothered in agricultural scenes and motifs inspired by the Czech artist Mikuláš Aleš. The building is currently home to Prague's largest delicatessen, Dům lahůdek (see p.244). At the centre of the square stands a fountain dating from 1560, which retains its beautiful, original wrought-iron canopy, though it's no longer functioning.

Staroměstské náměstí

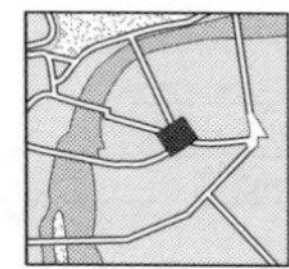

East of Malé náměstí is **Staroměstské náměstí** (Old Town Square), easily the most spectacular square in Prague, and the traditional heart of the city. Most of the brightly coloured houses look solidly eighteenth-century, but their Baroque facades hide considerably older buildings. From the eleventh century onwards, this was the city's main marketplace, known simply as Velké náměstí (Great Square), to which all roads in Bohemia led, and where merchants from all over Europe gathered. When the five towns that made up Prague were united in 1784, it was the Old Town Square's town hall that was made the seat of the new city council, and for the next two hundred years the square was the scene of the country's most violent demonstrations and battles. For a long time now, the whole place has been closed to traffic, and the cafés spread out their tables in summer, while tourists pour in to watch the town hall clock chime, to sit on the steps of the Hus Monument, and to drink in this historic showpiece.

The Hus Monument

For a brief biography of Jan Hus, see p.109.

The most recent arrival in the square is the colossal **Jan Hus Monument**, a turbulent sea of blackened bodies – the oppressed to his right, the defiant to his left – out of which rises the majestic moral authority of Hus himself, gazing into the horizon. For the sculptor Ladislav Šaloun, a maverick who received no formal training, the monument was his life's work, commissioned in 1900 when the Art Nouveau style, Viennese Secession, was at its peak, but strangely old-fashioned by the time it was completed in 1915. It would be difficult to claim that it blends in with its Baroque surroundings, yet this has never mattered to the Czechs, for whom its significance goes far beyond aesthetic merit.

The Austrians refused to hold an official unveiling of the statue; in protest, on July 6, 1915, the 500th anniversary of the death of Hus, Praguers smothered the monument in flowers. Since then it has been a powerful symbol of Czech nationalism: in March 1939, it was draped in swastikas by the invading Nazis, and in August 1968, it was shrouded in funereal black by Praguers, protesting at the Soviet invasion. The inscription along the base is a quote from the will of Comenius, one of Hus's later followers, and includes Hus's most famous dictum, *Pravda vítězí* (Truth Prevails), which has been the motto of just about every Czech revolution since then.

Staroměstská radnice

The Staroměstská radnice is open Mon 11am–5pm & Tues–Sun 9am–5pm; 30Kč.

It wasn't until the reign of King John of Luxembourg (1310–46) that Staré Město was allowed to build its own town hall, the **Staroměstská radnice**. Short of funds, the citizens decided against an entirely new structure, buying a corner house on the square instead and simply adding an extra floor; later on, they added the east wing, with its graceful Gothic oriel and obligatory wedge-tower. Gradually, over the centuries, the neighbouring merchants' houses to the west were incorporated into the building, so that now it stretches all the way across to the richly sgraffitoed **Dům U minuty**, which juts out into the square.

On May 8, 1945, on the final day of the Prague Uprising, the Nazis still held on to Staroměstské náměstí, and in a last desperate act set fire to the town hall – one of the few buildings to be irrevocably damaged in the old town. The tower and oriel chapel were rebuilt immediately, but of the neo-Gothic **east wing**, which stretched almost to the church of sv Mikuláš, only a crumbling fragment remains; the rest of it is marked by the stretch of grass to the north. Embedded in the wall of the tower is a plaque marked "Dukla", and a case containing a handful of earth from the Slovak pass where some 80,000 Soviet and Czechoslovak soldiers lost their lives in the first (and most costly) battle to liberate the country in October 1944.

Staroměstské náměstí

Below, set into the paving, are 27 **white crosses** commemorating the Protestant leaders who were condemned to death on the orders of the Emperor Ferdinand II, following the Battle of Bílá hora. They were publicly executed in the square on June 21, 1621 by the Prague executioner, Jan Mlydář: 24 enjoyed the nobleman's privilege and had their heads lopped off; the three remaining commoners were hung, drawn and quartered. Mlydář also chopped off the right hand of three of the nobles, and hacked off the tongue of the rector of Prague University, Johannes Jessenius, which he then nailed to their respective severed heads for public display on the Charles Bridge.

The Astronomical Clock

Today, the town hall's most popular feature is its *orloj* or **Astronomical Clock** – on the hour, a crowd of tourists and Praguers gather in front of the tower to watch a mechanical dumbshow by the clock's assorted figures. The Apostles shuffle past the top two windows, bowing to the audience, while perched on pinnacles below are the four threats to the city as perceived by the medieval mind: Death carrying his hourglass and tolling his bell, the Jew with his moneybags (since 1945 minus his stereotypical beard), Vanity admiring his reflection, and a turbaned Turk shaking his head. Beneath the moving figures, four characters representing Philosophy, Religion, Astronomy and History, stand motionless throughout the performance. Finally, a cockerel pops out and flaps its wings to signal that the show's over; the clock then chimes the hour. The clock itself has been here since the beginning of the fifteenth century; the working figures were added in 1490 by a **Master Hanuš** who, legend has it, was then blinded with a red-hot poker by the town councillors, to make sure he couldn't repeat the job for anyone else. In retaliation, he groped his way around the clock, succeeded in stopping it, and then promptly died of a heart attack – the clock stayed broken for over eighty years.

The astronomical clock chimes daily 8am–8pm.

The complex clock face tells three different sets of time: the golden hand points to a double set of Roman numerals from I to XII, and when the hand points to the top XII, it's noon (Central European Time); it also points to the outer ring of Gothic numbers from 1 to 24, which can rotate independently, and when the hand points to 24 it is sunset (Old Bohemian Time); finally, the numbers from 1 to 12 immediately below the Roman numerals divide the day into twelve hours, however many normal hours of daylight there are, and the golden sun tells you what time of day it is (Babylonian Time). The clock also charts – as the medieval astrologer saw it – the movements of the sun and planets around the earth, and the movement of the sun and moon through the signs of the zodiac; therefore, if you know how, you can determine the date. The revolving dial below the clock face is decorated with bucolic paintings of the "cycle of twelve idylls from the life of the Bohemian peasant", plus the signs of the zodiac, by Josef Mánes, a leading light in the Czech national revival. Around the edge, yet another pointer shows what day of the month and week it is, and, more importantly, what saint's day it is (and therefore when it's a holiday).

The interior of the radnice

The powder-pink facade on the south side of the town hall now forms the **entrance** to the whole complex. Apart from getting married, you can also sign up for a twenty-minute guided tour of the few rooms that survived the last war. It was in these rooms that the Bohemian kings were elected until the Habsburgs established hereditary rule, and in 1422 Jan Želivský, the fiery Hussite preacher and inspiration behind Prague's first defenestration (see p.143), was executed here. Despite being steeped in history, there's not much of interest here, apart from a few pretty decorated ceilings, striped with chunky beams, and a couple of Renaissance portals. You'll probably get more enjoyment from climbing the tower, which has access for the disabled, for the panoramic sweep across Prague's spires. You can also visit the chapel, designed by Peter Parler, which has patches of medieval wall painting, and wonderful grimacing corbels at the foot of the ribbed vaulting. If you get there just before the clock strikes the hour, you can watch the apostles going out on their parade; the figures all had to be re-carved by a local puppeteer after the war.

The church of sv Mikuláš

The destruction of the east wing of the town hall in 1945 rudely exposed Kilian Ignaz Dientzenhofer's church of **sv Mikuláš**, built in just three years between 1732 and 1735. The original church was founded by German merchants in the thirteenth century, and served as Staré Město's parish church until the Týn Church (see opposite) was completed. Later, it was handed over to the Benedictines, who commissioned Dientzenhofer to replace it with the present building. His hand is obvious: the south front is decidedly luscious – painted creamy white, with Braun's blackened statuary popping up at every cornice – promising an interior to surpass even its sister church of sv Mikuláš in Malá Strana, which Dientzenhofer built with his father immediately afterwards (see p.76). Inside, however, it's a curious mixture. Although caked in the usual mixture of stucco and fresco and boasting an impressive dome, the church has been stripped over the years of much of its ornament and lacks the sumptuousness of its namesake on the left bank. This is partly due to the fact that Joseph II closed down the monastery and turned the church into a storehouse, and partly because it's now owned by the very "low", modern, Czech Hussite Church.

Palác Goltz-Kinských and around

Staroměstské náměstí

The largest secular building on the square is the Rococo **palác Goltz-Kinských**, designed by Kilian Ignaz Dientzenhofer and built by his son-in-law Anselmo Lurago. In the nineteenth century it became a German *Gymnasium*, which was attended by, among others, Franz Kafka (whose father ran a haberdashery shop on the ground floor). The palace is perhaps most notorious, however, as the venue for the fateful speech by the Communist prime minister, Klement Gottwald, who walked out on to the grey stone balcony one snowy February morning in 1948, flanked by his Party henchmen, to address the thousands of enthusiastic supporters who packed the square below. It was the beginning of *Vítězná února* (Victorious February), the bloodless coup which brought the Communists to power and sealed the fate of the country for the next 41 years. The top floor now hosts top-flight exhibitions of graphic art put on by the National Gallery.

The palace is open Tues–Sun 10am–6pm.

Gottwald's appearance forms the opening to Milan Kundera's novel The Book of Laughter and Forgetting; *see Books, p.277.*

Until relatively recently, the adjacent **Dům U kamenného zvonu** (House at the Stone Bell) was much like any other of the merchant houses that line Staroměstské náměstí – covered in a thick icing of Baroque plasterwork and topped by an undistinguished roof gable. In the process of restoration in the 1970s, however, it was controversially stripped down to its Gothic core, uncovering the original honey-coloured stonework and simple wedge roof, and it now serves as a central venue for cutting-edge modern art exhibitions, lectures and concerts, organized by the City of Prague Gallery.

Dům U kamenného zvonu is open Tues–Sun 10am–6pm.

The south side of the square boasts a fine array of facades, mostly Baroque, with the notable exception of the neo-Renaissance **Štorchův dům**, adorned with a late nineteenth-century sgraffito painting of Saint Wenceslas by Mikuláš Aleš. Next door, **U bílého jednorožce** (The White Unicorn) – the sixteenth-century house sign actually depicts a one-horned ram – was Prague's one and only *salon*, run by Berta Fanta. An illustrious membership, including Kafka, Max Brod and Franz Werfel, came here to attend talks given by, among others, Albert Einstein and Rudolf Steiner.

The Týn church and Ungelt

Staré Město's most impressive Gothic structure, the mighty **Týn church** (Matka boží před Týnem), whose two irregular towers, bristling with baubles, spires and pinnacles, rise like giant antennae above the arcaded houses which otherwise obscure its facade, is a far more imposing building than sv Mikuláš. Like the nearby Hus monument, the Týn church, begun in the fourteenth century, is a source of Czech national pride. In an act of defiance, George of Poděbrady, the last Czech and the only Hussite King of Bohemia, adorned the high stone gable with a statue of himself and a giant gilded *kalich* (chalice), the mascot of all Hussite sects. The church remained a hotbed of Hussitism until the Protestants' crushing defeat at the Battle of Bílá hora, after which the chalice was melted down to provide the newly ensconced statue of the Virgin Mary with a golden halo, sceptre and crown.

Despite being one of the main landmarks of Staré Město, it's well-nigh impossible to appreciate the church from anything but a considerable distance, since it's boxed in by the houses around it, some of which are actually built right against the walls. To reach the entrance, take the third arch on the left, which passes under the Venetian gables of the former Týn School. The church's **interior** has been undergoing a very lengthy, thorough restoration, but should be open to the public again by the time you read this; otherwise you'll have to visit just before services (Mon–Fri 5.30pm, Sat 1pm & Sun 11.30am & 9pm). The rather appealing gloom of the place has been swept away by the repainting, leaving a lofty, thin nave, dominated at ground level by the dark morass of black and gold Baroque altarpieces. One or two original Gothic furnishings survive, most notably the fifteenth-century pulpit, whose panels are enhanced by some sensitive nineteenth-century icons. To view the north portal and canopy, which bears the hallmark of Peter Parler's workshop, you must go outside into Týnská.

The pillar on the right of the chancel steps contains the red marble **tomb of Tycho Brahe**, the famous Danish astronomer who arrived in Prague wearing a silver and gold false nose, having lost his own in a duel over a woman in Rostock. Court astronomer to Rudolf II for just two years, Brahe laid much of the groundwork for Johannes Kepler's later discoveries – Kepler getting his chance of employment when Brahe died of a burst bladder after one of Petr Vok's notorious binges in 1601 – hence the colloquial expression *nechci umřít jako Tycho Brahe* ("I don't want to die like Tycho Brahe", in other words, I need to go to the toilet).

Behind the Týn Church lies the Týn courtyard, better known by its German name, **Ungelt** (meaning "No Money", a pseudonym used to deter marauding invaders), which, as the trading base of German merchants, was one of the first settlements on the Vltava. A hospice, church and hostel were built for the use of the merchants, and by the fourteenth century the area had become an extremely successful international marketplace; soon afterwards the traders moved up to the Hrad, and the court was transformed into a palace. The whole complex has now been restored, and the Dominicans have reclaimed one section, while the rest houses various shops, restaurants, and a luxury hotel.

Dům U zlatého prstenů

The Dům U zlatého prstenů is open daily 10am–6pm; 100Kč.

Back on Týnská itself, the City of Prague Gallery has renovated the handsome Gothic townhouse of **Dům U zlatého prstenů** (House of the Golden Key), and converted it into a fascinating new art gallery, dedicated to twentieth-century Czech art. The permanent collection is spread out over three floors, and arranged thematically rather than chronologically, while the cellars provides space for installations by up-and-coming contemporary artists; there's also a nice café across the courtyard.

Staroměstské náměstí

On the first floor, symbolism looms large, with *Destitute Land*, Max Švabinský's none-too-subtle view of life under the Habsburg yoke, and works by two of Bohemia's best-loved eccentrics, Josef Váchal and František Bílek. There's a decent selection of grim 1920s paintings, too, typified by *Slagheaps in the Evening* by Jan Zrzavý, plus the usual Czech Surrealist suspects. More refreshing is the sight of Eduard Stavinoha's cartoon-like *Striking Demonstrator*, an ideological painting from 1948 that appears almost like Pop Art. Antonín Slavíček's easy-on-the-eye Impressionist views of Prague kick off proceedings on the second floor, along with works by Cubist Emil Filla, and abstract artist Mikuláš Medek. Also on this floor, there's the chance to see a lot of 1980s works that don't often see the light of day nowadays, such as Michael Rittstein's political allegory *Slumber beneath a Large Hand*. Highlights on the third floor include an excellent collection of mad collages by Jiří Kolář, made up of cut-up pieces of reproductions of other artists' works; abstract Vorticist works by Zdeněk Sýkora; and studies for kinetic-light sculptures by Zdeněk Pešanek.

From Celetná to the Anežský klášter

Celetná, whose name comes from the bakers who used to bake a particular type of small loaf (*calty*) here in the Middle Ages, leads east from Staroměstské náměstí direct to the Prašná brána, one of the original gateways of the old town. It's one of the oldest streets in Prague, lying along the former trade route from the old town market square, as well as on the *králová cesta*. Its buildings were smartly re-faced in the Baroque period, and their pastel shades are now crisply maintained. Most of Celetná's shops veer towards the chic end of the Czech market, making it a popular place for a bit of window-shopping. Dive down one of the covered passages to the left and into the backstreets, however, and you'll soon lose the crowds, and eventually end up at the atmospheric ruins of **Anežsky klášter**, now home to the National Gallery's nineteenth-century Czech art collection.

Dům U černé Matky boží

Two-thirds of the way along Celetná, at the junction with Ovocný trh, is the **Dům U černé Matky boží** (House at the Black Madonna), built as a department store in 1911–12 by Josef Gočár and one of the best examples of Czech Cubist architecture in Prague. It was a short-lived style, whose most surprising attribute, in this instance, is its ability to adapt existing Baroque motifs: Gočár's house sits much more happily amongst its eighteenth-century neighbours than, for example, the functionalist shop opposite – one of Gočár's later designs from the 1930s.

The museum is open Tues–Sun 10am–6pm; 35Kč.

Happily, the building has recently been renovated and now houses, among other things, a small, but excellent permanent exhibition of

Český Kubismus (Czech Cubism), on the top two floors. There's a little bit of everything from sofas and sideboards by Gočár himself, to porcelain and paintings, plus some wonderful sculptures by Otto Gutfreund. To whet your appetite further, there are photographs of the Cubist villas in Vyšehrad (covered on p.155) and of the Cubist café which originally graced the first floor, and which the curators hope one day to rebuild. In the meantime, the first, second and third floors are currently given over to temporary exhibitions of twentieth-century art, while the basement has been converted into a cheap café/restaurant.

The church of sv Jakub

The church is open Mon–Fri 9am–1pm & 2.30–4pm, Sat 9.30am–12.30pm & 2–4pm, Sun 2–4pm.

Celetná ends at the fourteenth-century Prašná brána (see p.137), beyond which is náměstí Republiky, at which point, strictly speaking, you've left Staré Město behind. Back in the old town, head north from Celetná into the backstreets which conceal the Franciscan church of **sv Jakub**, with its distinctive bubbling, stucco portal on Malá Štupartská. The church's massive Gothic proportions – it has the longest nave in Prague after the cathedral – make it a favourite venue for organ recitals, Mozart masses and other concerts. After the great fire of 1689, Prague's Baroque artists remodelled the entire interior, adding huge pillasters, a series of colourful frescoes and over twenty side altars. The most famous of these is the tomb of the Count of Mitrovice, in the northern aisle, designed by Fischer von Erlach and Prague's own Maximilian Brokof.

The church has close historical links with the butchers of Prague, who were given a chapel in gratitude for their defence of the city in 1611 and 1648. Hanging high up on the west wall, on the right as you enter, is a thoroughly decomposed human forearm. It has been there for over four hundred years now, ever since a thief tried to steal the jewels of the Madonna from the high altar. As the thief reached out, the Virgin supposedly grabbed his arm and refused to let go. The next day the congregation of butchers had no option but to lop it off, and it has hung there as a warning ever since.

Anežský klášter

The Anežský klášter is open Tues–Sun 10am–6pm; 70Kč.

Further north through the backstreets, the **Anežský klášter** (Convent of St Agnes), Prague's oldest surviving Gothic building, stands within a stone's throw of the river as it loops around to the east. It was founded in 1233 as a Franciscan convent for the Order of the Poor Clares, and takes its name from Agnes (Anežka), youngest daughter of Přemysl Otakar I, who left her life of regal privilege to become the convent's first abbess. Agnes took her vows seriously, living on a diet of raw onions and fruit with long periods of fasting, and in 1874 she was beatified to try and combat the spread of Hussitism amongst the Czechs. There was much speculation about the wonders that would occur when she was officially canonized, an event which finally took place on November 12, 1989, when Czech Catholics were invited to a special mass at St Peter's in Rome. Four days later the Velvet Revolution began: a happy coincidence, even for agnostic Czechs.

The convent itself was turned into an arsenal under the Hussites, and eventually closed down in 1782 by Joseph II, who turned it into a place where the Prague poor could live and set up their own workshops. The whole neighbourhood remained a slum area until well into this century, and its restoration only finally took place in the 1980s. The convent now houses the Národní galerie's **nineteenth-century Czech art collection**, which has recently been attractively rehung, with fulsome descriptions in Czech and English. Even if the art inside is not always of the highest quality, the collection is at least interesting in terms of the Czech national revival. The building itself is also worth inspecting, and the gallery's temporary exhibitions are now among the best in the capital.

The National Gallery's modern art collection (both foreign and Czech) can be found in the Veletržní palác *(see p.166).*

The well-preserved cloisters and the three remaining chapels on the ground floor are used for special exhibitions; for the permanent collection, you need to go up to the first floor. The collection kicks off in room 1 with Ludvík Kohl's fantasy paintings: the one of Vienna's Stephansdom shows the cathedral with two complete towers (instead of one); his imaginary completion of Prague's St Vitus Cathedral was eventually fulfilled more or less to the letter by nineteenth-century architects. Rooms 2 and 3 focus on the work of the **Mánes family**: father Antonín gave birth to romantic Czech landscape painting, and three of his offspring – Quido, Josef and Amálie – took up the brush. Josef Mánes was the most successful of the trio, much in demand as a portrait artist among the newly emerging Czech bourgeoisie, and one of the leading exponents of patriotically uplifting depictions of events of national significance (Mánes himself took part in the 1848 disturbances in Prague). Favourite themes – on display in several works in rooms 3 and 5 – range from legendary figures such as Břetislav and Jitka to the real-life tragedy of the Battle of Bílá hora.

The first six rooms can be taken at a steady canter, for the cream of the collection's late nineteenth-century works are reserved for the gallery's final double room (7 & 8). Some of the most eye-catching works are **Jaroslav Čermák**'s paintings of Yugoslavia, where he was decorated for his bravery by the Montenegran prince Nicholas I. With a dark, treacle-brown palette and an eye for drama, Čermák displays an unhealthy obsession with the depiction of white Slav women being captured by swarthy Ottoman Turks. **Antonín Chittussi**'s Corot-esque landscapes proved very popular in the Parisian salons of the 1880s; not so his most influential and uncharacteristic work, *Paris seen from Montmartre*, whose flat colours and precise lines were deemed beyond the pale.

Mikuláš Aleš, whose designs can be seen in the sgraffito on many of the city's nineteenth-century buildings, provides a few wonderfully decorative historical moments, such as the meeting between George of Poděbrady and Matthias Corvinus. Prize for most striking portrait goes to Václav Brožík's portrayal of his wife, the daughter of a wealthy

Parisian art dealer. There are several other crowd pleasers, including Josef Schusser's *Lady with a Red Parasol* and G. C. Max's *Saint Julia*, which features a woman being crucified. And the collection ends with a bevy of decadent Art Nouveau nudes by Maximilián Pirner, and several of Jakub Schikaneder's misty, moody streetscapes.

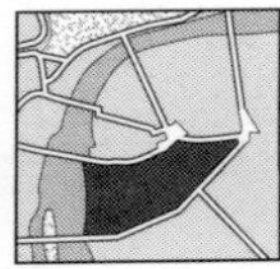

Southern Staré Město

The southern half of Staré Město is bounded by the *králová cesta* (the coronation route; see p.86) to the north, and the curve of Národní and Na příkopě, which follow the course of the old fortifications, to the south. There are no showpiece squares like Staroměstské náměstí here, but the complex web of narrow lanes and hidden passageways, many of which have changed little since medieval times, make this an intriguing quarter to explore, and one where it's easy to lose the worst of the crowds.

Ovocný trh

Heading southwest from the Dům U černé Matky boží (see p.103), you enter **Ovocný trh**, site of the old fruit market, its cobbles fanning out towards the back of the lime-green and white **Stavovské divadlo** (Estates Theatre). Built in the early 1780s by Count Nostitz (after whom the theatre was originally named) for the entertainment of Prague's large and powerful German community, the theatre is one of the finest Neoclassical buildings in Prague, reflecting the enormous self-confidence of its patrons. The Stavovské divadlo has a place in Czech history too, for it was here that the Czech national anthem, *Kde domov můj* (Where is My Home), was first performed, as part of the comic opera *Fidlovačka*, by J. K. Tyl (after whom the theatre was later renamed). It is also something of a mecca for Mozart fans, since it was here, rather than in the hostile climate of Vienna, that the composer chose to première both *Don Giovanni* and *La Clemenza di Tito*. This is, in fact, one of the few opera houses in Europe which remains intact from Mozart's time (though it underwent major refurbishment during the nineteenth century), and it was used by Miloš Forman to film the concert scenes for his Oscar-laden *Amadeus*.

For more on Mozart's time in Prague, see p.73.

On the north side of the Stavovské divadlo is the home base of the **Karolinum** or Charles University, named after its founder Charles IV, who established it in 1348 as the first university in this part of Europe. Although it was open to all nationalities, with instruction in Latin, it wasn't long before disputes between the various "nations" came to a head. In 1408, Václav IV issued the Decree of Kutná Hora, which gave the Bohemian "nation" – both Czech- and German-speaking – a majority vote in the university. In protest, the other "nations" upped and left for Leipzig, the first of many ethnic problems which continued to bubble away throughout the university's six-hundred-year history until the forced and extremely violent expulsion of all German-speakers after World War II.

To begin with, the university had no fixed abode; it wasn't until 1383 that Václav IV bought the present site. All that's left of the original fourteenth-century building is the Gothic oriel window which emerges from the south wall; the rest was trashed by the Nazis in 1945. The new main entrance is a peculiarly ugly red-brick curtain wall building by Jaroslav Fragner, set back from the street and inscribed with the original Latin name *Universitas Karolina*. Only a couple of small departments and the chancellor's office and administration are now housed here, with the rest spread over the length and breadth of the city. The heavily restored Gothic vaults, on the ground floor of the south wing, are now used as a contemporary **art gallery**.

Sv Havel and around

The junction of Melantrichova and Rytířská is always teeming with people pouring out of Staroměstské náměstí and heading for Wenceslas Square. Clearly visible from Melantrichova is Santini's undulating Baroque facade of the church of **sv Havel**, sadly no relation to the playwright-president but named after the Irish monk, Saint Gall. It was built in the thirteenth century to serve the local German community who had been invited to Prague partly to replace the Jewish traders killed in the city's 1096 pogrom. After the expulsion of the Protestants, the church was handed over to the Carmelites who redesigned the interior, now only visible through an iron grille.

Straight ahead of you as you leave sv Havel is Prague's last surviving **open-air market** – a poor relation of its Germanic predecessor, which

The former Gottwald Museum

One block west of the Stavovské divadlo, at Rytířská 29, is the former Prague Savings Bank, a large, pompous neo-Renaissance building designed in the 1890s by Osvald Polívka, before he went on to erect some of Prague's most flamboyant Art Nouveau structures. The building currently serves as a branch of Česká spořitelna (Mon–Fri 8am–6pm), and is definitely worth a quick peek inside; go up the monumental staircase and check out the main banking hall on the first floor, which now houses a café.

For over thirty years it housed the museum all Praguers loved to hate – dedicated to Klement Gottwald, the country's first Communist president. A joiner by trade, a notorious drunkard and womanizer by repute, he led the Party with unswerving faith from the beginnings of Stalinism in 1929 right through to the show trials of the early 1950s. He died shortly after attending Stalin's funeral in 1953 – either from grief or, more plausibly, from drink.

Remarkably, his reputation survived longer than that of any other East European leader. While those whom he had wrongfully sent to their deaths were posthumously rehabilitated, and the figure of Stalin denigrated, Gottwald remained sacred, his statue gracing every town in the country. As late as October 1989, the Communists were happily issuing brand new 100kčs notes emblazoned with his bloated face, only to have them withdrawn from circulation a month later, when the regime toppled.

stretched all the way from Ovocný trh to Uhelný trh. Traditionally a flower and vegetable market, it runs the full length of the arcaded Havelská, and sells everything from celery to CDs, with plenty of souvenirs and wooden toys in between; the stalls on V kotcích, the narrow street parallel to Havelská, sell mainly clothes.

St Michael's Mystery

St Michael's Mystery is open daily 10am–8pm; 250Kč.

Prague's most crude, out-and-out tourist trap is **St Michael's Mystery** (Tajemství u sv. Michala), which occupies the Baroque church of sv Michal, tucked away down a passageway connecting Melantrichova with Michalská. Impressionistic is probably the kindest term you could use to describe this very expensive multi-media assault on the senses. Led round by folk dressed as monks, you walk through a labyrinth of wacky stage sets inspired in the vaguest possible way by Prague's history, and interspersed by random quotes from Kafka. The special effects reach a crescendo as you eventually make your way into the main body of the church, where you get to sit in a pew and watch a multi-media film lasting twenty minutes or so, and surprisingly – given the average clientele – in Czech.

Uhelný trh, sv Martin ve zdi and Bartolomějská

Both markets run west into **Uhelný trh**, which gets its name from the *uhlí* (coal) that was sold here in medieval times. Nowadays, however, it's Prague red-light district – particularly along Perlová and Na Perštýně – and although you'll see little evidence during the day, it can get busy at night, as a result of which the local authorities are constantly drawing up plans to move the trade elsewhere.

South of Uhelný trh, down Martinská, the street miraculously opens out to make room for the twelfth-century church of **sv Martin ve zdi** (St Martin-in-the-Walls), originally built to serve the Czech community of the village of sv Martin, until it found itself the wrong side of the Gothic fortifications when they were erected in the fourteenth century. It's still essentially a Romanesque structure, adapted to suit Gothic tastes a century later; it was, however, closed down in 1784 by Joseph II and turned into a warehouse, shops and flats. The city bought the church in 1904 and thoroughly restored it, adding the creamy neo-Renaissance tower, and eventually handing it over to the Czech Brethren. For them, it has a special significance as the place where communion "in both kinds" (ie bread and wine), one of the fundamental demands of the Hussites, was first administered to the whole congregation, in 1414. To be honest, there's very little to see inside, which is just as well as it's only open for concerts nowadays.

It's possible to stay the night in Havel's old cell; see p.203 for details.

Around the corner from sv Martin ve zdi is the gloomy lifeless street of **Bartolomějská**, dominated by a tall, grim-looking building on its south side, which served as the main interrogation centre of the universally detested Communist secret police, the *Státní bezpečnost*, or *StB*. Although now officially disbanded, the *StB* continues to be one of the most controversial issues of the post-revolutionary period. As in the rest of Eastern Europe, the accusations (often unproven) and revelations of who exactly collaborated with the *StB* have caused the downfall of a number of leading politicians right across the political spectrum. The building is now back in the hands of the Franciscan nuns who occupied the place prior to 1948, and its former police cells now serve as rooms for a small *pension*.

Betlémské náměstí

The Betlémská kaple is open daily 9am–6pm; 30Kč.

After leaving the dark shadows of Bartoloměјská, the brighter aspect of **Betlémské náměstí** comes as a welcome relief. The square is named after the **Betlémská kaple** (Bethlehem Chapel), whose high wooden gables face on to the square. This was founded in 1391 by religious reformists, who, denied the right to build a church, proceeded instead to build the largest chapel in Bohemia, with a total capacity of 3000. Sermons were delivered not in the customary Latin, but in the language of the masses – Czech. From 1402 to 1413, **Jan Hus** preached here (see box opposite), regularly pulling in more than enough commoners to fill the chapel. Hus was eventually excommunicated for his outspokenness, found guilty of heresy and burnt at the stake at the Council of Constance in 1415.

The chapel continued to attract reformists from all over Europe for another two centuries – the leader of the German Peasants' Revolt, **Thomas Müntzer**, preached here in the sixteenth century – until the advent of the Counter-Reformation in Bohemia. Inevitably, the chapel was handed over to the Jesuits, who completely altered the original building, only for it to be demolished after they were expelled by the Habsburgs in 1773. Of the original building, only the three outer walls remain, with patches of their original decoration – biblical scenes which were used to get the message across to the illiterate congregation. The rest is a scrupulous reconstruction of the fourteenth-century building by Jaroslav Fragner, using the original plans and a fair amount of imaginative guesswork. The initial reconstruction work was carried out after the war by the Communists, who were keen to portray Hus as a Czech nationalist and social critic as much as a religious reformer, and, of course, to dwell on the revolutionary Müntzer's later appearances here.

Náprstkovo muzeum

The Náprstkovo muzeum is open Tues–Sun 9am–noon & 12.45–5.30pm; 30Kč.

At the western end of the square stands the **Náprstkovo muzeum**, whose founder, Czech nationalist Vojta Náprstek, was inspired by the great Victorian museums of London while in exile following the 1848 revolution. On his return, he turned the family brewery into a museum, initially intending it to concentrate on the virtues of industrial progress. Náprstek's interests gradually shifted towards anthropology, however, and it is his ethnographic collections that are now displayed in the museum; the original technological exhibits are housed in Prague's Národné technické muzeum (see p.165).

Jan Hus

The legendary preacher – and Czech national hero – **Jan Hus** (often anglicized to John Huss) was born in the small village of Husinec in South Bohemia around 1372. From a childhood of poverty, he enjoyed a steady rise through the Czech education system, taking his degree at the Karolinum in the 1390s, and eventually being ordained as a deacon and priest around 1400. Although without doubt an admirer of the English religious reformer, John Wycliffe, Hus was by no means as radical as many of his colleagues who preached at the Betlémská kaple. Nor did he actually advocate many of the more famous tenets of the heretical religious movement that took his name: Hussitism. In particular, he never advocated giving communion "in both kinds" (bread and wine) to the general congregation.

In the end, it wasn't the disputes over Wycliffe, whose books were burned on the orders of the archbishop in 1414, that proved Hus's downfall, but an argument over the sale of indulgences to fund the papal wars that prompted his unofficial trial at the Council of Constance in 1415. Having been guaranteed safe conduct by Emperor Sigismund himself, Hus naïvely went to Constance to defend his views, and was burnt at the stake as a heretic. The Czechs were outraged, and Hus became a national hero overnight, inspiring thousands to rebel against the authorities of the day. In 1965, the Vatican finally overturned the sentence, and the anniversary of his death is now a national holiday.

The museum is open daily except Tues 10am–5pm; 40Kč.

Despite the fact that the museum could clearly do with an injection of cash, it still manages to put on some really excellent temporary ethnographic exhibitions on the ground floor, and also does a useful job of promoting tolerance of different cultures. The permanent collection begins on the first floor, where you'll find the skeleton of a fin-whale over 20m long suspended from the ceiling. Underneath it there's a range of exhibits from the Americas, with everything from Inuit furs and Apache smoking pipes, decorated with porcupine quills and beads, to toy skeletons on bicycles from Mexico and Amazonian shrunken heads. Upstairs, there's a much smaller display of stuff from Australia and Oceania including some remarkable sculptures, but sadly the labelling is pretty minimal.

Husova

Between Betlémské náměstí and Karlova lies a confusing maze of streets, passageways and backyards, containing few sights as such, but nevertheless a joy to explore. One building that might catch your eye is the church of **sv Jiljí** (St Giles), on Husova, whose outward appearance suggests another Gothic masterpiece, but whose interior is decked out in the familiar black excess of the eighteenth century, with huge gilded acanthus leaf capitals and barley-sugar columns galore. The frescoes by Václav Vavřinec Reiner (who is buried in the church) are full of praise for his patrons, the Dominicans, who took over the church after the Protestant defeat of 1620. They were expelled, in turn, after the Communists took power, only to return following the events of 1989.

Reiner's paintings also depict the unhappy story of Giles himself, a ninth-century hermit who is thought to have lived somewhere in Provence. Out one day with his pet deer, Giles and his companion were chased by the hounds of King Wanda of the Visigoths. The hounds were rooted to the spot by an invisible power, while the arrow from the hunters struck Giles in the foot as he defended his pet – the hermit was later looked upon as the patron saint of cripples.

A short step away, just off Husova on Řetězová, is the **Dům pánů z Kunštátu a Poděbrad** (House of the Lords of Kunštát and Poděbrady), the home of George of Poděbrady before he became the Czechs' first and last Hussite king in 1458. It's not exactly gripping, but it does give you a clear impression of the antiquity of the houses in this area, and illustrates the way in which the new Gothic town was built on top of the old Romanesque one. Thus the floor on which you enter was originally the first floor of a twelfth-century palace, whose ground floor has been excavated in the cellars.

The house is open May–Sept Tues–Sun 10am–6pm; 20Kč.

To the waterfront

Continuing west along Řetězová and Anenská brings you eventually to the waterfront. On Anenské náměstí, just before you reach the river, is the **Divadlo na zábradlí** (Theatre on the Balustrade). This was at the centre of Prague's absurdist theatre scene in the 1960s, with Havel himself working first as a stagehand and later as resident playwright, and is currently enjoying something of a renaissance.

The gaily decorated neo-Renaissance building at the very end of Novotného lávka, on the riverfront itself, was once the city's waterworks. It now houses, among other things, the newly revamped **Muzeum Bedřicha Smetany**, on the first floor. Bedřich Smetana (1824–84), despite having German as his mother tongue, was without doubt the most nationalist of all the great Czech composers, taking an active part in the 1848 revolution and the later national revival movement. He enjoyed his greatest success as a composer with *The Bartered Bride*, which marked the birth of Czech opera, but he was forced to give up conducting in 1874 with the onset of deafness, and eventually died of syphilis in a mental asylum. Unfortunately, the museum fails to capture much of the spirit of the man, concentrating instead on items such as his spectacles, and the garnet jewellery of his first wife. Still, the views across to the castle are good, and you get to wave a laser baton around in order to listen to his music. Outside, beneath the large weeping willow that droops over the embankment, the statue of the seated Smetana is rather unfortunately placed, with his back towards one of his most famous sources of inspiration, the River Vltava (Moldau in German).

Chapter 5

Josefov

It is crowded with horses; traversed by narrow streets not remarkable for cleanliness, and has altogether an uninviting aspect. Your sanitary reformer would here find a strong case of overcrowding.

Walter White,

"A July Holiday in Saxony, Bohemia and Silesia" (1857)

Less than half a century after Walter White's comments, all that was left of the former ghetto of **JOSEFOV** were six synagogues, the town hall and the medieval cemetery. At the end of the nineteenth century, a period of great economic growth for the Habsburg Empire, it was decided that Prague should be turned into a beautiful bourgeois city, modelled on Paris. The key to this transformation was the "sanitization" of the ghetto, a process, begun in 1893, which reduced the notorious malodorous backstreets and alleyways of Josefov to rubble and replaced them with block after block of luxurious five-storey mansions. The Jews, the poor, the gypsies and the prostitutes were cleared out so that the area could become a desirable residential quarter, rich in Art Nouveau buildings festooned with decorative murals, doorways and sculpturing. This building frenzy marked the beginning of the end for a community which had existed in Prague for almost a millennium.

In any other European city occupied by the Nazis in World War II, what little was left of the old ghetto would have been demolished. But although Prague's Jews were transported to the new ghetto in Terezín, by a grotesque twist of fate the ghetto itself was preserved by Hitler himself in order to provide a site for his planned "Exotic Museum of an Extinct Race". With this in mind, Jewish artefacts from all over central Europe were gathered here, and now make up one of the richest collections of Judaica in Europe, and one of the most fascinating sights in Prague. Also included in this chapter, at the end, are the sights around náměstí Jana Palacha, adjacent to, but strictly speaking outside of, the Jewish quarter, most notably the city's excellent Decorative Arts Museum (or UPM).

A brief history of Jewish settlement in Prague

Jews probably settled in Prague as early as the tenth century and, initially at least, are thought to have settled on both sides of the river. In 1096, at the time of the first crusade, the first recorded pogrom took place, an event which may have hastened the formation of a much more closely knit "Jewish town" within Staré Město during the twelfth century. It wasn't until much later that Jews were actually herded into a **walled ghetto** (and several centuries before the word "ghetto" was actually first coined in Venice), sealed off from the rest of the town and subject to a curfew. Jews were also subject to laws restricting their choice of profession to usury and the rag trade; in addition, some form of visible identification, a cap or badge, remained a more or less constant feature of Jewish life until the Enlightenment.

In 1262, Přemysl King Otakar II issued a *Statuta Judaeorum*, which granted the Jews their own religious and civil self-administration. In effect, however, the Jews were little more than the personal property of the king, and though Otakar himself appears to have been genuine in his motives, later rulers used the *Statuta* as a form of blackmail, extorting money whenever they saw fit. During one of the worst pogroms, in 1389, 3000 Jews were massacred over Easter, some while sheltering in the Old-New Synagogue – an event commemorated every year thereafter on Yom Kippur. In 1541, a fire ripped through Hradcany and Malá

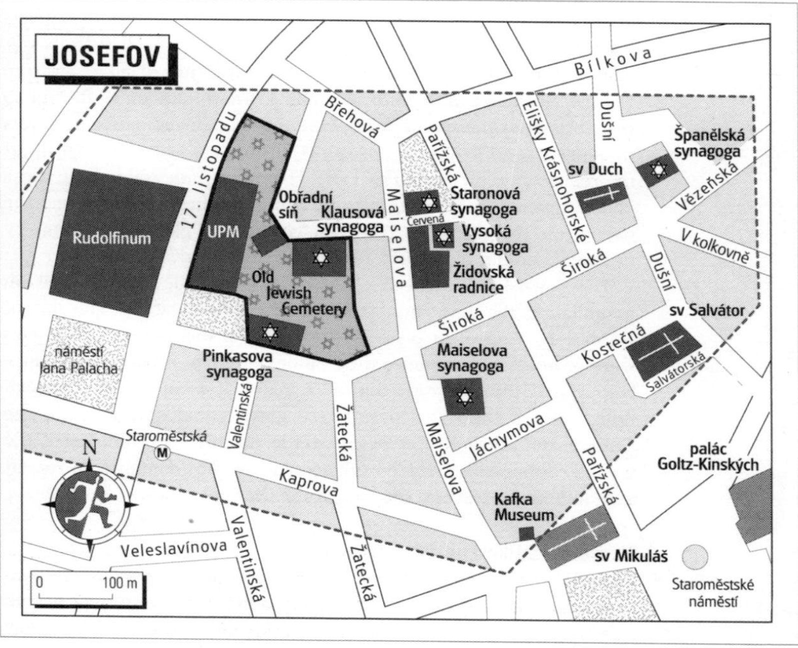

Strana and a Jew was tortured into confessing the crime. The Bohemian Estates immediately persuaded the Emperor Ferdinand I to expel the Jews from Prague. In the end, however, a small number of families were allowed to remain.

By contrast, the reign of Rudolf II (1576–1612) was a time of economic and cultural prosperity for the community, which is thought to have numbered up to 10,000, making it by far the largest Jewish community in the Diaspora. The Jewish mayor, **Mordecai Maisel**, Rudolf's minister of finance, became one of the richest men in Bohemia and the success symbol of a generation; his money bought and built the Jewish quarter, its town hall, a bath house, pavements and several synagogues. This was the "golden age" of the ghetto: the time of **Rabbi Löw**, the severe and conservative chief rabbi of Prague, who is now best-known as the legendary creator of the Jewish Frankenstein's monster or "golem", though, in fact, the story of Rabbi Löw and the golem first appeared only in the nineteenth century (see box on p.117).

Amidst the violence of the Thirty Years' War, the Jews enjoyed an unusual degree of protection from the emperor, who was heavily dependent on their financial acumen. In 1648, the Jews, along with the city's students, repaid their imperial bosses by repelling the marauding Swedes on the Charles Bridge, for which they won the lasting respect of Ferdinand III (1637–57). Things went into reverse again during the eighteenth century, until in 1744, Empress Maria Theresa used the community as a scapegoat for her disastrous war against the Prussians, and ordered the expulsion of all Jews from Prague. She allowed them to return in 1748, though only after much pressure from the guilds, who were missing Jewish custom. It was the enlightened **Emperor Joseph II** (1780–90) who did most to lift the restrictions on Jews. His 1781 Toleration Edict ended the dress codes, opened up education to all non-Catholics, and removed the gates from the ghetto. In 1850, the community paid him homage by officially naming the ghetto Josefov, or Josefstadt.

The downside to Joseph's reforms was that he was hellbent on assimilating the Jews into the rest of the population. The use of Hebrew or Yiddish in business transactions was banned, and Jews were ordered to Germanize their names (the list of permitted names comprised 109 male ones and 35 female). It wasn't until the social upheavals of 1848 that Jews were given equal status within the Empire and allowed officially to settle outside the confines of the ghetto – concessions which were accompanied by a number of violent anti-Semitic protests on the part of the Czechs.

From 1848 to the present day

From 1848, the ghetto went into terminal decline. The more prosperous Jewish families began to move to other districts of Prague, leaving behind only the poorest Jews and strictly Orthodox families, who were rapidly joined by the underprivileged ranks of Prague society: gypsies, beggars, prostitutes and alcoholics. By 1890, only twenty percent of Josefov's population was Jewish, yet it was still the most densely populated area in Prague, with a staggering 186,000 people crammed into its streets. The ghetto had become a carbuncle in the centre of bourgeois Prague, a source of disease and vice: in the words of Gustav Meyrink, a "demonic underworld, a place of anguish, a beggarly and phantasmagorical quarter whose eeriness seemed to have spread and led to paralysis".

The ending of restrictions, and the destruction of most of the old ghetto, increased the pressure on Jews to assimilate, a process which brought with it its own set of problems. Prague's Jews were split roughly half and half between predominantly German- or Yiddish-speakers and Czech-speakers. Yet since some two-thirds of Prague's German population were Jewish, and all Jews had been forced to take German names by Josef II, all Jews were seen by Czech nationalists as a Germanizing influence. Tensions between the country's German-speaking minority and the Czechs grew steadily worse in the run-up to World War I, and the Jewish community found itself caught in the firing line – "like powerless stowaways attempting to steer a course through the storms of embattled nationalities", as one Prague Jew put it.

Despite several anti-Semitic riots in the first few years following the war, the foundation of the new republic in 1918, and, in particular, its founder and first president, T. G. Masaryk, whose liberal credentials were impeccable, were welcomed by most Jews. For the first time in their history, Jews were given equal rights as a recognized ethnic minority, though only a small number opted to be registered as Jewish. The interwar period was probably the nearest Prague's Jewish community came to a second "golden age", a time most clearly expressed in the now famous flowering of its *Deutsche Prager Literatur*, led by German-Jewish writers such as Franz Werfel, Franz Kafka, Max Brod and Egon Erwin Kisch.

After Nazi troops occupied Prague on March 15, 1939, the city's Jews were subject to an increasingly harsh set of regulations, which saw them barred from most professions, placed under curfew, and compelled to wear a yellow Star of David. In November 1941, the first transport of Prague Jews set off for the new ghetto in Terezín, 60km northwest of Prague. Of the estimated 55,000 Jews in Prague at the time of the Nazi invasion, over 36,000 died in the camps. Many survivors emigrated to Israel and the USA. Of the 8000 who registered as Jewish in the Prague census of 1947, a significant number joined the Communist Party, only to find themselves victims of Stalinist anti-Semitic wrath during the 1950s.

It's difficult to calculate exactly how many Jews now live in Prague – around a thousand were officially registered as such prior to 1989 – though their numbers have undoubtedly been bolstered by a new generation of Czech Jews who have rediscovered their roots, and by the new influx of Jewish Americans and Israelis. The controversy over Jewish property – most of which was seized by the Nazis, and therefore not covered by the original restitution law – has finally been resolved, allowing the community to reclaim at least some of its buildings, most importantly the six synagogues, town hall and cemetery of Josefov itself.

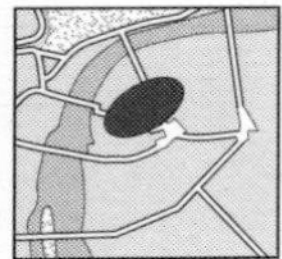

The former ghetto

Geographically, Josefov lies to the northwest of Staroměstské náměstí, between the main square and the Vltava river. The warren-like street plan of the old ghetto has long since disappeared, and through the heart of Josefov the ultimate bourgeois avenue, **Pařížská**, now runs, a riot of turn-of-the-century sculpturing, spikes and turrets, its ground floor premises home to a parade of international airline offices, boutiques and cafés. If Josefov can still be said to have a main street, it is really the parallel street of **Maiselova**, named after the community's sixteenth-century leader. The sheer volume of tourists – over a million a year – that visit Josefov has brought with it the inevitable rash of souvenir stalls, flogging dubious "Jewish" souvenirs, and, it has to be said, the whole area is now something of a tourist trap. Yet to skip this part of the old town is to miss out on a whole slice of the city's cultural history.

All the "sights" of Josefov, bar the Staronová synagoga, are covered by an all-in-one 450Kč ticket, available from any of the quarter's ticket offices. Opening hours vary but are basically daily except Sat: April–Oct 9.30am–6pm; Nov–March 9.30am–4.30pm. In order to try and regulate the flow of visitors, the authorities have introduced a timed entry system, giving you around twenty minutes at each sight, though don't worry if you don't adhere rigidly to your timetable.

Staronová synagoga and Židovská radnice

The synagogue is open April–Oct Mon–Thurs & Sun 9am–6pm, Fri 9am–5pm; Nov–March Mon–Thurs & Sun 9am–5pm, Fri 9am–2pm; 200Kč.

Walking down Maiselova, it's impossible to miss the steep, sawtooth brick gables of the **Staronová synagoga** or Altneuschul (Old-New Synagogue), so called because when it was built it was indeed very new, though it eventually became the oldest synagogue in Josefov. Begun in the second half of the thirteenth century, it is, in fact, the oldest functioning synagogue in Europe, one of the earliest Gothic buildings in Prague and still the religious centre for Prague's Orthodox Jews. Since Jews were prevented by law from becoming architects, the synagogue is thought to have been constructed by the Franciscan builders working on the convent of sv Anežka. Its five-ribbed vaulting is unique for Bohemia; the extra, purely decorative rib was added to avoid any hint of a cross.

The former ghetto

The Golem

Legends concerning the animation of unformed matter (which is what the Hebrew word **golem** means), using the mystical texts of the Kabbala, were around long before Frankenstein started playing around with corpses. Two hungry fifth-century rabbis may have made the most practical golem when they sculpted a clay calf, brought it to life and then ate it; but the most famous is undoubtedly **Rabbi Löw**'s giant servant made from the mud of the Vltava, who was brought to life when the rabbi placed a *shem* in its mouth, a tablet with a magic Hebrew inscription.

There are numerous versions of the tale, though the earliest invoking Rabbi Löw only appeared in the nineteenth century. In some, Yossel, the golem, is a figure of fun, flooding the rabbi's kitchen rather in the manner of Disney's *Sorcerer's Apprentice*; others portray him as the guardian of the ghetto, helping Rabbi Löw in his struggle with the anti-Semites at Rudolf II's court. In almost all versions, however, the golem finally runs amok. One particularly appealing tale is that the golem's rebellion was because Löw forgot to allow his creature to rest on the Sabbath. He was conducting the service when news of its frenzy arrived, and he immediately ran out to deal with it. The congregation, reluctant to continue without him, merely repeated the verse in the psalm the rabbi had been reciting until Löw returned. This explains the peculiarity at the Staronová synagoga where a line in the Sabbath service is repeated even today. In all the stories, the end finally comes when Löw removes the *shem* once and for all, and carries the remains of his creature to the attic of the Old-New Synagogue, where they have supposedly resided ever since (a fact disputed by the pedantic journalist Egon Erwin Kisch, who climbed in to check).

The legends are amended at each telling, and have proved an enduringly popular theme for generations of artists and writers. Paul Wegener's German expressionist film version and the dark psychological novel of Gustav Meyrink are probably two of the most powerful treatments. Meyrink's golem lives in a room which has no windows and no doors, emerging to haunt the streets of Prague every 33 years – by which reckoning, it's slightly overdue to make a reappearance.

To enter the synagogue, you must buy a separate ticket (200Kč) from the ticket office opposite the synagogue's entrance on Červená (or from one of the other ticket offices). Men are asked to cover their heads out of respect – paper *kippahs* are handed out at the ticket office, though a handkerchief will do. To get to the **main hall**, you must pass through one of the two low vestibules from which women watch the proceedings through narrow slits. Above the entrance is an elaborate tympanum covered in the twisting branches of a vine tree, its twelve bunches of grapes representing the tribes of Israel. The low glow from the chandeliers is the only light in the hall, which is mostly taken up with the elaborate wrought-iron cage enclosing the *bimah* in the centre. In 1357, Charles IV allowed the Jews to fly their own municipal standard, a moth-eaten remnant of which is still on show, bearing the Star of David (Prague's Jewish community were the first to adopt the Star as their official symbol). The other flag – a tattered red banner

– was a gift to the community from Emperor Ferdinand III for helping fend off the Swedes in 1648. On the west wall a glass cabinet, shaped like Moses' two tablets of stone, is filled with tiny personalized light bulbs, which are paid for by grieving relatives and light up on the anniversary of the person's death (there's even one for Kafka).

Just south of the synagogue is the **Židovská radnice** (Jewish Town Hall), one of the few such buildings to survive the Holocaust. Founded and funded by Maisel in the sixteenth century, it was later rebuilt as the creamy-pink Baroque house you now see, housing an overpriced kosher restaurant. The belfry, permission for which was granted by Ferdinand III, has a clock on each of its four sides, plus a Hebrew one stuck on the north gable which, like the Hebrew script, goes "backwards". On the other side of the synagogue is one of the many statues in Prague that were hidden from the Nazis for the duration of the war: an anguished statue of Moses by František Bílek, himself a committed Protestant.

On Kafka's trail

Prague never lets go of you . . . this little mother has claws. We ought to set fire to it at both ends, on Vyšehrad and Hradčany, and maybe then it might be possible to escape.

Franz Kafka "Letter to Oskar Polak" (December 2, 1902)

Franz Kafka was born on July 3, 1883, above the *Batalion* Schnapps bar on the corner of Maiselova and Kaprova (the original building has long since been torn down, but a gaunt-looking modern bust now commemorates the site). He spent most of his life in and around Josefov. His father was an upwardly mobile small businessman from a Czech-Jewish family of kosher butchers (Kafka himself was a vegetarian), his mother from a wealthy German-Jewish family of merchants. The family owned a haberdashery shop, located at various premises on or near Staroměstské náměstí. In 1889, they moved out of Josefov and lived for the next seven years in the beautiful Renaissance Dům U minuty, next door to the Staroměstská radnice, during which time Kafka attended the *Volksschule* on Masná (now a Czech primary school), followed by a spell at an exceptionally strict German *Gymnasium*, located on the third floor of the palác Goltz-Kinských.

At 18, he began a law degree at the German half of the Karolinum, which was where he met his lifelong friend and posthumous biographer and editor, Max Brod. Kafka spent most of his working life as an accident insurance clerk, until he was forced to retire through ill health in 1922. Illness plagued him throughout his life and he spent many months as a patient at the innumerable spas in *Mitteleuropa*. He was engaged three times, twice to the same woman, but never married, finally leaving home at the age of 31 for bachelor digs on the corner of Dlouhá and Masná, where he wrote the bulk of his most famous work, *The Trial*. He died of tuberculosis at the age of 40 in a sanatorium just outside Vienna, on June 3, 1924, and is buried in the Nový Gidovský hřbitov in Pižkov (see p.159).

Pinkasova synagoga

Jutting out at an angle on the south side of the cemetery, with its entrance on Široká, the **Pinkasova synagoga** was built in the 1530s for the powerful Pinkas family, and has undergone countless restorations over the centuries. In 1958, the synagogue was transformed into a chilling memorial to the 77,297 Czech Jews killed during the Holocaust. The memorial was closed shortly after the 1967 Six Day War – due to damp, according to the Communists – and remained so, allegedly due to problems with the masonry, until it was finally, painstakingly restored in the 1990s. All that remains of the synagogue's original decor today is the ornate *bimah* surrounded by a beautiful wrought-iron grille, supported by barley-sugar columns.

Prague's other working synagogue is in Nové Město (see p.139).

Of all the sights of the Jewish quarter, the Holocaust memorial is perhaps the most moving, with every bit of wall space taken up with

As a German among Czechs, a Jew among Germans, and an agnostic among believers, Kafka had good reason to live in a constant state of fear, or *Angst*. Life was precarious for Prague's Jews, and the destruction of the Jewish quarter throughout his childhood – the so-called "sanitization" – had a profound effect on his psyche, as he himself admitted. It comes as a surprise to many Kafka readers that anyone immersed in so beautiful a city could write such claustrophobic and paranoid texts; and that as a member of the café society of the time, he could write in a style so completely at odds with his verbose, artistic friends. It's also hard to accept that Kafka could find no publisher for *The Castle* or *The Trial* during his lifetime.

After his death, Kafka's works were published in Czech and German and enjoyed brief critical acclaim, before the Nazis banned them, first within Germany, then across Nazi-occupied Europe. Even after the war, Kafka, along with most German-Czech authors, was deliberately overlooked in his native country, since he belonged to a community and a culture which had been exiled. In addition, his account of the terrifying brutality and power of bureaucracy over the individual, though not in fact directed at totalitarian systems as such, was too close to the bone for the Communists. The 1962 Writers' Union conference at Liblice finally broke the official silence on Kafka, and, for many people, marked the beginning of the Prague Spring. In the immediate aftermath of the 1968 Soviet invasion, the Kafka bust was removed from Josefov, and his books remained unpublished in Czechoslovakia until 1990.

Having been *persona non grata* in his homeland for most of the last century, Kafka now suffers from over-exposure, due to his popularity with western tourists. The term "Kafkaesque", denoting some strange unfathomable, bureaucratic nightmare, has now entered the English language, and his image is plastered across T-shirts, mugs and postcards all over the city centre. Thankfully, the small **Expozice Franze Kafky** (Tues–Fri 10am–6pm, Sat 10am–5pm), next door to the church of sv Mikuláš, retells Kafka's life simply but effectively with pictures and quotes (in Czech, German and English), and flogs souvenirs. It's run by the Kafka Society, as is the Franz Kafka bookshop and *Café Milena*, situated opposite the town hall on Staroměstské náměstí.

The former ghetto

the carved stone list of victims, stating simply their name, date of birth and date of death or transportation to the camps. It is the longest epitaph in the world, yet it represents a mere fraction of those who died in the Nazi concentration camps. Upstairs in a room beside the women's gallery, there's also a harrowing exhibition of drawings by children from the Jewish ghetto in Terezín, most of whom later perished in the camps.

For a full account of Terezín see p.183.

Starý židovský hřbitov (Old Jewish Cemetery)

At the heart of Josefov is the **Starý židovský hřbitov**, known as *beit hayyim* in Hebrew, meaning "House of Life". Established in the fifteenth century, it was in use until 1787, by which time there were an estimated 100,000 buried here, one on top of the other, six palms apart, and as many as twelve layers deep. The enormous numbers of visitors has meant that the graves themselves have been roped off to protect them, and a one-way system introduced: you enter from the Pinkasova synagoga, on Široká, and leave by the Klausová synagoga. The oldest grave, dating from 1439, belongs to the poet Avigdor Karo, who lived to tell the tale of the 1389 pogrom. Get there before the crowds – a difficult task for much of the year – and the cemetery can be a poignant reminder of the ghetto, its inhabitants subjected to inhuman overcrowding even in death. The rest of Prague recedes beyond the sombre lime trees and cramped perimeter walls, the haphazard headstones and Hebrew inscriptions casting a powerful spell.

A single ticket to the Old Jewish Cemetery costs 250Kč; alternatively, you can buy an all-in-one ticket for 450Kč.

Each headstone bears a symbol denoting the profession or tribe of the deceased: a pair of hands for the Cohens; a pitcher and basin for the Levites; scissors for a tailor; a violin for a musician, etc. On many graves you'll see pebbles, some holding down *kvittleh* or small messages of supplication. The greatest number of these sits on the grave of Rabbi Löw, creator of the "golem", who is buried by the wall directly opposite the entrance; followed closely by the rich Renaissance tomb of Mordecai Maisel, some ten metres to the southeast.

The Nový židovský hřbitov (New Jewish Cemetery), where Kafka, among others, is buried, is in Žižkov (see p.159).

Obřadní síň and Klausová synagoga

Immediately on your left as you leave the cemetery is the **Obřadní síň**, a lugubrious neo-Renaissance house built in 1906 as a ceremonial hall by the Jewish Burial Society. Appropriately enough, it's now devoted to an exhibition on Jewish traditions of burial and death, which you can peruse before you head off into the cemetery.

Close to the entrance to the cemetery is the **Klausová synagóga**, a late seventeenth-century building, founded in the 1690s by Mordecai Maisel on the site of several small buildings (*klausen*), in what was then a notorious red-light district of Josefov. The ornate Baroque interior contains a rich display of religious objects from embroidered *kippah* to *Kiddush* cups, and explains the very basics of Jewish religious practice, and the chief festivals or High Holidays.

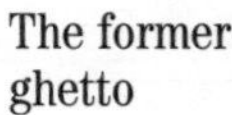

Vysoká and Maiselova synagóga

Adjacent to the town hall it was once part of is the **Vysoká synagóga** (High Synagogue), whose rich interior stands in complete contrast to its dour, grey facade. The huge vaulted hall was, until recently, used to display a selection of the hundreds of Jewish textiles, dating from the sixteenth to the early twentieth century, which were gathered here by the Nazis for their infamous museum. The building has now been restored as a working, non-Orthodox synagogue, and is closed to the general public.

Founded and paid for entirely by Mordecai Maisel, the neo-Gothic **Maiselova synagoga**, set back from the neighbouring houses on Maiselova, was, in its day, one of the most ornate synagogues in Josefov. Nowadays, its whitewashed interior is almost entirely bare apart from the rich offerings of its glass cabinets, which contain gold and silverwork, *hanukkah* candlesticks, *torah* scrolls and other religious artefacts.

Španělská synagoga

East of Pařížská, up Niroká, stands the **Španělská synagoga** (Spanish Synagogue), built on the spot once occupied by Prague's Alt Schul or Old Synagogue. The current building, begun in 1868, is by far the most ornate synagogue in Josefov, its stunning, gilded Moorish interior deliberately imitating the Alhambra (hence its name). Every available surface is smothered with a profusion of floral motifs and geometric patterns, in vibrant reds, greens and blues, which are repeated in the synagogue's huge stained-glass windows. The synagogue now houses an interesting exhibition on the history of Prague's Jews from the time of the 1848 emancipation. Lovely, slender, painted cast-iron columns hold up the women's gallery, where the displays contain a fascinating set of photos depicting the old ghetto at the time of its demolition. There's a section on Prague's German-Jewish writers, including Kafka, and information on the planned Nazi museum and the Holocaust.

Around náměstí Jana Palacha

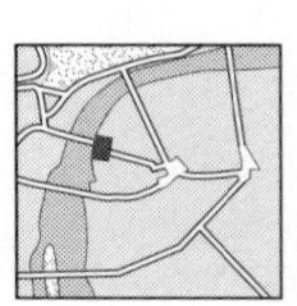

As Kaprova and Široká emerge from Josefov, they meet at **náměstí Jana Palacha**, previously called náměstí Krasnoarmejců (Red Army Square) and embellished with a flowerbed in the shape of a red star (now replaced by the circular vent of an underground car park), in memory of the Soviet dead who were temporarily buried here in May 1945. It was probably this, as much as the fact that the building on the east side of the square is the Faculty of Philosophy, where Palach was a student, that prompted the new authorities to make the first of the street name changes here in 1989 (there's a bust of Palach on the corner of the building). By a happy coincidence, the road which intersects the square from the north is called 17 listopadu (17 November),

Palach is also honoured at the memorial to victims of Communism on Wenceslas Square (see p.130).

Around náměstí Jana Palacha

originally commemorating the day in 1939 when the Nazis closed down all Czech institutions of higher education, but now equally good for the 1989 march (see p.135).

The north side of the square is taken up by the **Rudolfinum** or Dům umělců (House of Artists), designed by Josef Zítek and Josef Schulz. One of the proud civic buildings of the nineteenth-century Czech national revival, it was originally built to house an art gallery, museum and concert hall for the Czech-speaking community. In 1918, however, it became the seat of the new Czechoslovak parliament, until 1938 when it was closed down by the Nazis. According to Jiří Weil, the Germans were keen to rid the building's balustrade of its statue of the Jewish composer Mendelssohn. However, since none of the statues was actually named, they decided to remove the one with the largest nose; unfortunately for the Nazis, this turned out to be Wagner, Hitler's favourite composer. In 1946, the building returned to its original artistic purpose and it's since been sandblasted back to its original woody-brown hue. Now one of the capital's main exhibition and concert venues (it's home to the Czech Philharmonic), it boasts a wonderfully grand café (see p.216), open to the general public on the first floor.

UPM (Decorative Arts Museum)

The UPM is open Tues–Sun 10am–6pm; 40Kč.

A short way down 17 listopadu from the square is the **UPM** (Umělecko-průmyslové muzeum), installed in another of Schulz's worthy nineteenth-century creations, richly decorated in mosaics, stained glass and sculptures. Literally translated, this is a "Museum of Decorative Arts", though the translation hardly does justice to what is one of the most fascinating museums in the capital. From its foundation in 1885 through to the end of the First Republic, the UPM received the best that the Czech modern movement had to offer – from Art Nouveau to the avant-garde – and judging from previous catalogues and the various short-term exhibitions mounted in the past, its collection is unrivalled.

The public library is open Mon noon–6pm, Tues–Fri 10am–6pm; closed July & Aug.

Unfortunately, the permanent exhibition consists of just a sample from each of the main artistic periods from the Renaissance to the 1930s, giving only the vaguest hints at the wealth of exhibits stored away in the museum's vaults. Worse still, the top floor, which covers the period from the 1880s to the 1930s, has been closed for years. As a consolation, the museum's ground and first floors (and occasionally the nearby Rudolfinum) are used for some of the best temporary exhibitions in Prague, mostly taken from its turn-of-the-century and early twentieth-century collections. There's also a **public library** in the building, specializing in catalogues and material from previous exhibitions, and an excellent café on the ground floor (see p.216).

Chapter 6

Nové Město

Although it comes over as a sprawling late nineteenth-century bourgeois quarter, **NOVÉ MĚSTO** was actually founded way back in 1348 by Charles IV as an entirely new town – three times as big as Staré Město – intended to link the southern fortress of Vyšehrad with Staré Město to the north. Large market squares, wide streets, and a level of town-planning far ahead of its time were employed to transform Prague into the new capital city of the Holy Roman Empire. Instead, however, Nové Město remained incomplete when Charles died, and quickly became the city's poorest quarter after Josefov, fertile ground for Hussites and radicals throughout the centuries. In the second half of the nineteenth century, the authorities set about a campaign of slum clearance similar to that inflicted on the Jewish quarter; only the churches and a few important historical buildings were left standing, but Charles' street layout survives pretty much intact. The leading architects of the day began to line the wide boulevards with ostentatious examples of their work, which were eagerly snapped up by the new class of status-conscious businessman – a process that has continued into this century, making Nové Město the most architecturally varied part of Prague.

Today, Nové Město remains the city's main commercial and business district, housing most of its hotels, nightclubs, cafés, fast-food outlets and department stores. The obvious starting point, and probably the

An Art Nouveau hit list

Prague's Art Nouveau (the term is *secesní* in Czech) ranges from the vivacious floral motifs of the Paris metro to the more restrained style of the Viennese Secession. The following are some of the more striking examples covered in this chapter:

Grand Hotel Evropa	p.129	Pojišťovna Praha	p.134
Hlahol	p.146	Praha hlavní nádraží	p.132
Hotel Central	p.138	Topičův dům	p.134
Obecní dům	p.137	U Dorflerů	p.136
Peterkův dům	p.128	U Nováků	p.141

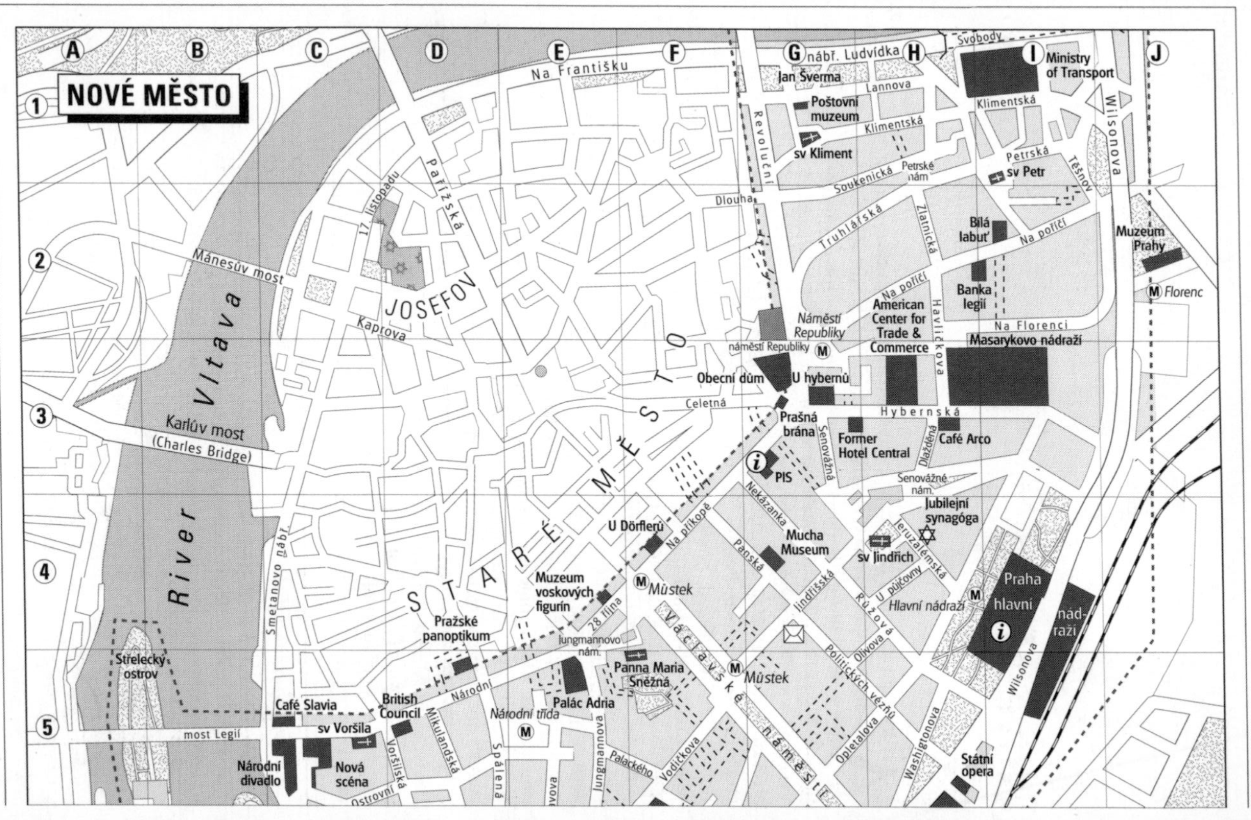

NOVÉ MĚSTO
A
B
C
D
E
F
G
H
I
J
1
2
3
4
5
Na Františku
nábř. Ludvíka
Svobody
Ministry of Transport
Jan Šverma
Lannova
Klimentská
Poštovní muzeum
Revoluční
sv Kliment
Petrská
Těšnov
Wilsonova
sv Petr
Soukenická
Petrské nám
Dlouha
Pařížská
17 listopadu
Truhlářská
Zlatnická
Bílá labuť
Na poříčí
Muzeum Prahy
Florenc
Mánesův most
Vltava
JOSEFOV
Kaprova
Náměstí Republiky
Banka legií
American Center for Trade & Commerce
Havlíčkova
Na Florenci
Masarykovo nádraží
náměstí Republiky
Obecní dům
U hybernů
Celetná
Hybernská
Karlův most (Charles Bridge)
Prašná brána
Senovážná
Former Hotel Central
Dlážděná
Café Arco
PIS
Senovážné nám.
Jubilejní synagóga
STARÉ MĚSTO
Nekázanka
U Dörflerů
Na příkopě
Mucha Museum
Panská
sv Jindřich
Jeruzalémská
River
Smetanovo nábř.
Muzeum voskových figurín
Můstek
Jindřišská
Růžová
U půjčovny
Hlavní nádraží
Praha hlavní nádraží
Pražské panoptikum
28 října
Jungmannovo nám.
Panna Maria Sněžná
Václavské náměstí
Politických vězňů
Olivova
Wilsonova
Střelecký ostrov
Café Slavia
British Council
Národní
Národní třída
Palác Adria
most Legií
sv Voršila
Mikulandská
Spálená
Jungmannova
Palackého
Vodičkova
Opletalova
Washingtonova
Státní opera
Národní divadlo
Nová scéna
Voršilská
Ostrovní

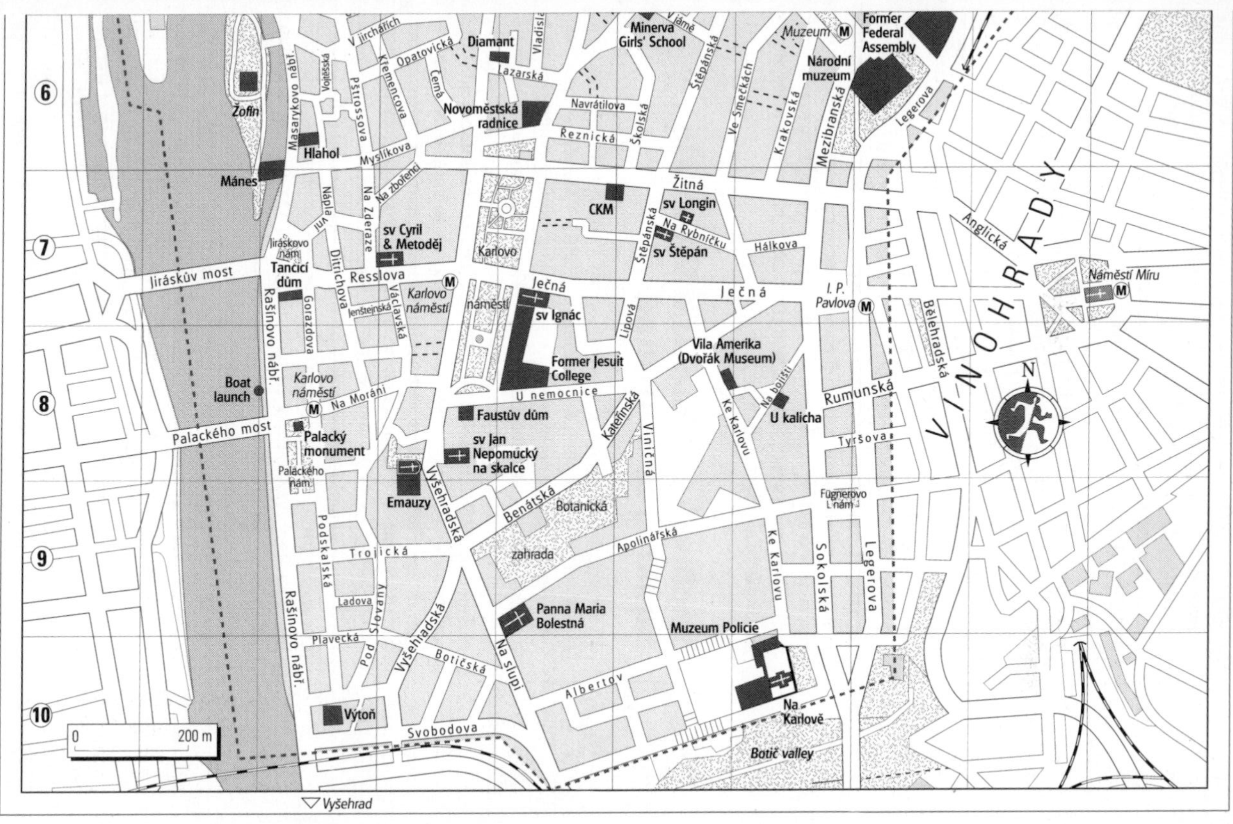
VINOHRADY
Náměstí Míru
Anglická
Bělehradská
Legerova
Former Federal Assembly
Národní muzeum
Muzeum
Mezibranská
Rumunská
I.P. Pavlova
Tyršova
Fügnerovo nám.
Sokolská
U kalicha
Na bojišti
Ke Karlovu
Krakovská
Ve Smečkách
Hálkova
Ječná
Vila Amerika (Dvořák Museum)
Muzeum Policie
Na Karlově
Botič valley
Štěpánská
V jámě
Minerva Girls' School
Žitná
sv Longin
Na Rybníčku
sv Štěpán
Viničná
Apolinářská
Školská
Kateřinská
Lipová
Navrátilova
CKM
Řeznická
Former Jesuit College
sv Ignác
U nemocnice
Botanická
Albertov
Panna Maria Bolestná
Vladislavova
Lazarská
Novoměstská radnice
Diamant
Karlovo náměstí
Faustův dům
sv Jan Nepomucký na skalce
Benátská
zahrada
Na slupi
Opatovická
Černá
Vyšehradská
Botičská
Svobodova
Emauzy
sv Cyril & Metoděj
Resslova
Václavská
Na zbořenci
Myslíkova
Křemencova
V jirchářích
Pštrossova
Na Zderaze
Jenštejnská
Na Moráni
Trojická
Pod Slovany
Ditrichova
Vojtěšská
Hlahol
Náplavní
Gorazdova
Palacký monument
Palackého nám.
Podskalská
Ladova
Plavecká
Vytoň
Vyšehrad
Masarykovo nábř.
Jiráskovo nám.
Tančící dům
Rašínovo nábř.
Žofín
Mánes
Boat launch
Jiráskův most
Palackého most
N
0
200 m
6
7
8
9
10

only place in Prague most visitors can put a name to, is Wenceslas Square or **Václavské náměstí**, hub of the modern city, and somewhere you're bound to find yourself passing through again and again. The two principal partially pedestrianized streets which lead off it are **Národní třída** and **Na příkopě**, which together form the *zlatý kříž* or golden cross, Prague's commercial centre and for over a century the most expensive slice of real estate in the capital. The *zlatý kříž* and the surrounding streets also contain some of Prague's finest late nineteenth-century, Art Nouveau and early twentieth-century architecture.

The rest of Nové Město, which spreads out northeast and southwest of Wenceslas Square, is much less explored, and for the most part heavily residential; unusually for Prague, using the tram and metro systems to get around here will save some unnecessary legwork. A few specific sights are worth singling out for attention – the museum devoted to **Dvořák** on Ke Karlovu, the **Mánes** art gallery on the waterfront, and the memorial to the Czechoslovak parachutists off Karlovo náměstí, for example – but the rest is decidedly less exciting than all that's gone before. However, if your ultimate destination is Vyšehrad, you can easily take in some of the more enjoyable bits of southern Nové Město en route.

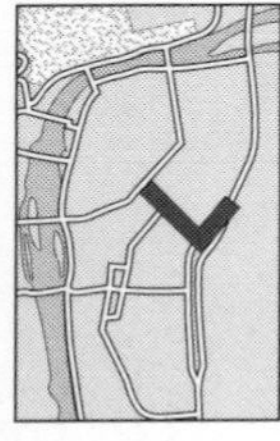

Václavské náměstí (Wenceslas Square) and around

The natural pivot around which modern Prague revolves, and the focus of the events of November 1989, **Václavské náměstí** (Wenceslas Square) is more of a wide, gently sloping boulevard than a square as such. It's scarcely a conventional – or even convenient – space in which to hold mass demonstrations, yet night after night in November 1989, more than 250,000 people crammed into the square, often enduring subzero temperatures, to call for the resignation of the Party leaders and demand free elections. On November 27, the whole of Prague came to a standstill, a bigger crowd than ever converging on the square to show their support for the two-hour nationwide general strike called by the opposition umbrella group, Občanské fórum (Civic Forum), who led the revolution. It was this last mass mobilization that proved decisive – by noon the next day, the Communist old guard had thrown in the towel.

The square's **history of protest** goes back to the 1848 revolution, whose violent denouement began here on June 12 with a peaceful open-air mass organized by the Prague students. On the crest of the nationalist disturbances, the square – which had been known as Koňský trh (Horse Market) since its foundation as such by Charles IV – was given its present name. Naturally enough, it was one of the rallying points for the jubilant crowds on October 28, 1918, when Czechoslovakia's independence was declared. Thirty years later, in 1948, the square was filled to capacity once more, this time with

Communist demonstrators enthusiastically supporting the February coup. Then in August 1968, it was the scene of some of the most violent confrontations between the Soviet invaders and the local Czechs, during which the Národní muzeum came under fire – according to the Czechs, the Soviet officer in charge mistook it for the Parliament building, though they were most probably aiming for the nearby Radio Prague building, which was transmitting news of the Soviet invasion out to the West. And, of course, it was at the top of the square, on January 16, 1969, that Jan Palach set fire to himself in protest at the continuing occupation of the country by Russian troops.

Despite the square's medieval origins, its oldest building dates only from the eighteenth century, and the vast majority are much younger. As the city's money moved south of Staré Město during the industrial revolution, so the square became the architectural showpiece of the nation, and it is now lined with self-important six- or seven-storey buildings, representing every artistic trend of the last hundred years, from neo-Renaissance to Socialist Realism. Even if you've no interest in modern architecture, there's plenty to keep you occupied in the swanky shops, time-piece arcades or *pasáže*, cinemas, theatres and general hubbub of the square.

Wenceslas Square has always been the place to be seen, and, at its bottom end, to participate in the Prague version of the *passeggiata*. This is also the one place in the city where streetlife and nightlife continue long after midnight – the hotels and tacky nightclubs buzzing with tourists and mafiosi, while the police, the pimps and the prostitutes patrol the pavements. Access to the square by car is restricted to those who are staying at one of the square's hotels, so this has traditionally been the place to inspect the latest flash cars. However, the days when unfamiliarity with western vehicles meant that even a Vespa was looked on as if it were a recently landed intergalactic spaceship have long since gone.

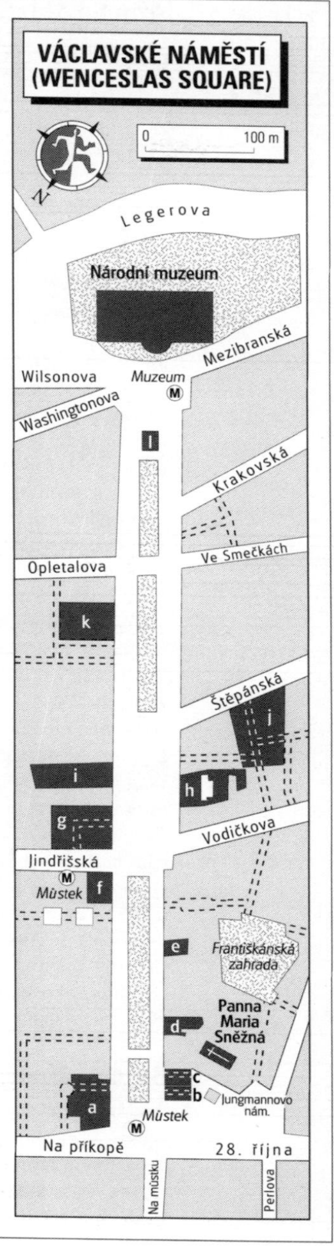

Václavské náměstí (Wenceslas Square) and around

Around Můstek

The busiest part of Wenceslas Square and a popular place to meet up before hitting town is around **Můstek**, the city's most central metro station, at the northern end of the square. The area is dominated by the **Palác Koruna (a)**, a hulking wedge of sculptured concrete and gold, built for an insurance company in 1914 by Antonín Pfeiffer, one of Jan Kotěra's many pupils. The building is a rare mixture of heavy constructivism and gilded Secession-style ornamentation, but the *pièce de résistance* is the palace's bejewelled crown which lights up at night.

Opposite Palác Koruna, adjacent to one another, are two functionalist buildings designed by Ludvík Kysela in the late 1920s, billed at the time as the first glass curtain-wall buildings. Along with the *Hotel Juliš* (see below), they represent the perfect expression of the optimistic mood of progress and modernism that permeated the interwar republic. The building on the right as you face them (**b**), built for the chocolate firm, Lindt, was the first to be erected; the **Baťa** store (**c**), on the left, followed a few years later. The latter was built for the Czech shoe magnate, Tomáš Baťa, one of the greatest patrons of avant-garde Czech art, who fled the country in 1948, when the Communists nationalized the shoe industry; the store was returned to the family, along with a number of their shoe factories, after 1989. Even if you've no intention of buying a pair of Baťa boots, it's worth taking the lift to the top floor for a bird's-eye view onto the square.

Twenty-five years earlier, Czech architecture was in the throes of its own version of Art Nouveau, one of whose earliest practitioners was Jan Kotěra. The **Peterkův dům (d)**, a slender essay in the new style, was his first work, undertaken at the tender age of 28. Kotěra, a pupil of the great architect of the Viennese Secession, Otto Wagner, eventually moved on to a much more brutal constructivism. Another supreme example of Czech functionalism, a few doors further up at no. 22, is the **Hotel Juliš (e)**, designed by Pavel Janák, who had already made his name as one of the leading lights of the short-lived Czech Cubist (and later Rondo-Cubist) movement (see p.155). Another point of interest, on the corner of Jindřišská, is the neo-Baroque **Assicurazione Generali (f)** – now home to the Polish Cultural Institute. It was designed by Osvald Polívka and Bedřich Ohmann, and was where the young Kafka worked for a couple of years as an insurance clerk.

Beyond Jindřišská

One of the Communists' most miserable attempts to continue the square's tradition of grand architecture was the Družba (Friendship) department store, now **Krone (g)**, which stands like a 1970s reject on the other side of Jindřišská, its only redeeming feature the view from its rooftop disco *Fromin*. Diagonally opposite is the

Prague's pasáže

Prague has an impressive array of old **shopping arcades** or *pasáže*, as they're known in Czech, the majority of which are located in and around Wenceslas Square and date from the first half of this century. Compared with the chic *passages* off the Champs-Élysées, Prague's *pasáže* offer more modest pleasures: a few shops, the odd café and, more often than not, a cinema. The king of the lot is the lavishly decorated Lucerna *pasáž*, which stretches all the way from Štěpánská to Vodičkova and contains an equally ornate cinema, café and vast concert hall. You can continue your indoor stroll on the other side of Vodičkova through the Světozor *pasáž*, which boasts another cinema, and a wonderful stained-glass mosaic advertising the old state electronics company Tesla. The first of the *pasáže* to receive a 1990s' facelift was the marble-clad Koruna *pasáž*, on the corner of Na příkopě, now lined with upmarket shops including Prague's largest music store, Bonton Megastore. There have also been renewed attempts to continue the tradition, but judging by the limply modern Myslbek *pasáž*, fronted by a Marks & Spencer store and situated on the other side of Na příkopě, the glory days are over.

Václavské náměstí (Wenceslas Square) and around

Melantrich publishing house (**h**), whose first floor is occupied by the offices of the former Socialist Party newspaper, *Svobodné slovo* (The Free Word). For forty years, the Socialist Party was a loyal puppet of the Communist government, but on the second night of the November 1989 demonstrations, the newspaper handed over its well-placed balcony to the opposition speakers of Občanské fórum (Civic Forum), and later witnessed the historic appearance of Havel and Dubček.

Melantrich House faces probably the most famous and the two most ornate buildings on the entire square, the Art Nouveau **Grand Hotel Evropa** (**i**), and its slim neighbour, the *Hotel Meran*, both built in 1903–05 by two of Ohmann's disciples, Bendelmayer and Dryák. They represent everything the Czech modern movement stood against: chiefly, ornament for ornament's sake, not that this has in any way dented the *Evropa*'s popularity. The café terrace has always had a reputation for low-key cruising and a great deal of posing, but it's worth forgoing the sunlight for the sumptuous interior, with its symbolist art and elaborate brass fittings and light fixtures, unchanged since the hotel first opened.

Opposite the hotel is the vast **Palác Lucerna** (**j**), one of the more appealing of the square's numerous dimly lit shopping arcades (see box). Designed in the early part of this century in Moorish style by, among others, Havel's own grandfather, it was returned to Havel and his brother after 1989, and has been the focus of much family squabbling ever since. Apart from a brief glance at the **Hotel Jalta** (**k**), built in the Stalinist aesthetic of the 1950s, there's nothing more to stop for, architecturally speaking, until you get to the Wenceslas Monument.

Václavské náměstí (Wenceslas Square) and around

For a brief biography of Wenceslas, see p.55.

The Wenceslas Monument

A statue of Saint Wenceslas (sv Václav) has stood at the top of the square since 1680, but the present **Wenceslas Monument** (1), by the father of Czech sculpture, Josef Václav Myslbek, was not finally unveiled until 1912, after thirty years on the drawing board. The Czech patron saint sits astride his mighty steed, surrounded by smaller-scale representations of four other Bohemian saints – his mother Ludmilla, Procopius, Adalbert and Agnes – added in the 1920s. In 1918, 1948, 1968, and again in 1989, the monument was used as a national political notice board, festooned in posters, flags and slogans and even now, it remains the city's favourite soapbox venue.

Two of Prague's most famous martyrs were fatally wounded close by. On October 28, 1939, during the demonstrations against the Nazi occupation, the medical student Jan Opletal was fatally wounded when troops opened fire on protesters. And on January 16, 1969, the 21-year-old philosophy student Jan Palach set himself alight in protest against the continuing occupation of his country by the Soviets; he died from his wounds three days later. Several others followed Palach's example, including Jan Zajíc, who set fire to himself on the same spot on February 25, the anniversary of the Communist coup. Attempts to lay flowers on this spot on the anniversary of Palach's protest provided an annual source of confrontation; Václav Havel received the last of his many prison sentences for just such an action in January 1989. An impromptu martyrs' shrine of candles and messages, set up in the aftermath of the November 1989 revolution, has now been formalized as a simple memorial to *obětem komunismu* (the victims of Communism), adorned with flowers and photos of Palach and Zajíc.

Národní muzeum (National Museum)

The Národní muzeum is open daily: May–Sept 10am–6pm; Oct–April 9am–5pm; closed first Tuesday of the month; 70Kč.

At the top, southern, end of Wenceslas Square sits the broad, brooding hulk of the **Národní muzeum**, built by Josef Schulz in 1890. Deliberately modelled on the great European museums of Paris and Vienna, it dominates the view up the square like a giant golden eagle with outstretched wings. Along with the National Theatre (see p.135), this is one of the great landmarks of the nineteenth-century Czech *národní obrození*, sporting a monumental gilt-framed glass cupola, worthy clumps of sculptural decoration and narrative frescoes from Czech history.

The museum is old-fashioned and underfunded, but it's worth taking at least a quick look at the ornate marble entrance hall and splendid monumental staircase leading to the **Pantheon** of Czech notables at the top of the main staircase. Arranged under the glass-domed hall are 48 busts and statues of distinguished bewhiskered Czech men (plus a couple of token women and Slovaks), including the universally adored

T.G. Masaryk, the country's founding president, whose statue was removed by the Communists from every other public place.

The rest of the museum is dowdy and badly labelled, though numismatists will enjoy the exhibition of medals and orders belonging to Václav Měřička, from the Order of the Bath to the French Légion d'Honneur, and geologists can admire rocks and minerals in tasteful mahogany cases. Those with children might like to head upstairs for the fossils and stuffed animals, where you can also view the smallest and the largest butterfly in the world, a range of lovely shells and some frighteningly large and lethal-looking beetles. The museum's temporary exhibitions, displayed on the ground floor, can be very good indeed, so it's always worth checking to see what's on.

Wilsonova

At the southern end of Wenceslas Square is some of the worst blight that Communist planners inflicted on Prague, above all, the six-lane highway that now separates Nové Město from the residential suburb of Vinohrady to the east and south, and effectively cuts off the Národní muzeum from Wenceslas Square. Previously known as Vítězného února (Victorious February) after the 1948 Communist coup, the road was renamed **Wilsonova** in honour of US President Woodrow Wilson (a personal friend of the Masaryk family), who effectively gave the country its independence from Austria-Hungary in 1918.

The Prague stock exchange building alongside the Národní muzeum, only completed in the 1930s but rendered entirely redundant by the 1948 coup, was another victim of postwar "reconstruction". The architect Karel Prager was given the task of designing a new "socialist" **Federal Assembly** building on the same site, without destroying the old bourse: he opted for a supremely unappealing bronze-tinted plate-glass structure, supported by concrete stilts and sitting uncomfortably on top of its diminutive predecessor. Since the break-up of the country, the building has lost its *raison d'être* once more, and now provides a home for, among other things, Radio Free Europe's headquarters.

Next to the Parliament building, the grandiose **Státní opera** (State Opera), built by the Viennese duo Helmer and Fellner, looks stunted and deeply affronted by the traffic which now tears past its front entrance. It was opened in 1888 as the *Neues Deutsches Theater*, shortly after the Czechs had built their own national theatre on the waterfront. Always second fiddle to the Stavovské divadlo, though equally ornate inside, it was one of the last great building projects of Prague's once all-powerful German minority. The velvet and gold interior is still as fresh as it was when the Bohemian-born composer Gustav Mahler brought the traffic to a standstill, conducting the première of his *Seventh Symphony*.

The last building on this deafening freeway is **Praha hlavní nádraží**, Prague's main railway station, and one of the final glories of the dying Empire, designed by Josef Fanta and officially opened in 1909 as the *Franz-Josefs Bahnhof*. Trapped in the over-polished subterranean modern section, it's easy to miss the station's surviving Art Nouveau parts. The original entrance on Wilsonova still exudes imperial confidence, with its wrought-iron canopy and naked figurines clinging to the sides of the towers; on the other side of the road, two great glass protrusions signal the new entrance that opens out into the seedy green space of the Vrchlického sady.

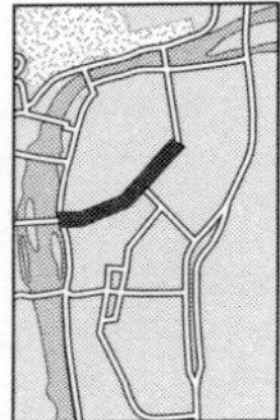

Národní třída and Na příkopě

Národní třída and **Na příkopě** trace the course of the old Staré Město moat, which was finally filled in in 1760. Their boomerang curve still marks the border between Staré Město and Nové Město, though strictly speaking, the dividing line runs down the middle of the street. At the turn of the century, these two partly pedestrianized streets formed the chief venue for the weekend *passeggiata*, and even today they are among the most crowded expanses of pavement in Prague. Along with a variety of stylish shops, banks, restaurants and clubs, you'll also discover some of the city's most flamboyant Art Nouveau buildings.

Jungmannovo náměstí and around

Before you hit Národní třída proper, you must pass through **Jungmannovo náměstí**, named for Josef Jungmann (1772–1847), a prolific writer, translator and leading light of the Czech national revival, whose pensive, seated statue was erected here in 1878. This small, ill-proportioned square boasts an unrivalled panoply of Czech architectural curiosities, ranging from Emil Králíček and Matěj Blecha's unique **Cubist streetlamp** (and seat) from 1912, crumbling away beyond the Jungmann statue in the far eastern corner of the square to the gleaming, functionalist facade of the ARA department store (now the Investiční banka), built in the late 1920s on the corner of Perlova and ulica 28 října (October 28 Street, commemorating the foundation of the First Republic).

There's an earlier, purer example of Rondo-Cubism at Jungmannovo náměstí 4, decorated in the Czech national colours of red and white, and you'll find another example of the style on p.139.

Palác Adria

Diagonally opposite the ARA department store is the square's most imposing building, the chunky, vigorously sculptured **Palác Adria**, on the south side of the square. It was designed in the early 1920s by Pavel Janák and Josef Zasche, with sculptural extras by Otto Gutfreund and a central *Seafaring* group by Jan Ntursa. Janák was a pioneering figure in the short-lived, prewar Czech Cubist movement; after the war, he and Josef Gočár attempted to create a national style of architecture appropriate for the newly founded republic. The style was dubbed "Rondo-Cubism" – semi-circular motifs are a recurrent theme – though the Palác Adria owes as much to the Italian Renaissance as it does to the new national style.

Originally constructed for the Italian insurance company Reunione Adriatica di Sicurità – hence its current name – the building's *pasáž* still retains its wonderful original portal featuring sculptures by Bohumil Kafka, depicting the twelve signs of the zodiac. The theatre in the basement of the building was once a studio for the multimedia **Laterna magika** (Magic Lantern) company. In 1989, it became the underground nerve centre of the Velvet Revolution, when Civic Forum found temporary shelter here shortly after their inaugural meeting on the Sunday following the November 17 demonstration. Against a stage backdrop for Dürenmatt's *Minotaurus*, the Forum thrashed out tactics in the dressing rooms and gave daily press conferences in the auditorium during the crucial fortnight before the Communists relinquished power.

The Church of Panna Maria Sněžná

Right beside the Cubist streetlamp is the medieval gateway of the church of **Panna Maria Sněžná** (St Mary-of-the-Snows), once one of the great landmarks of Wenceslas Square, but now barely visible from any of the surrounding streets. To enter the church, go through the unpromising courtyard back near the Jungmann statue. Like most of Nové Město's churches, the Panna Maria Sněžná was founded by Charles IV, who envisaged a vast coronation church on a scale comparable with the St Vitus Cathedral, on which work had just begun. Unfortunately, the money ran out shortly after completion of the chancel; the result is curious – a church which is short in length, but equal to the cathedral in height. The 100ft-high, prettily painted vaulting – which collapsed on the Franciscans who inherited the half-completed building in the seventeenth century – is awesome, as is the gold and black Baroque altar which touches the ceiling. To get an idea of the intended scale of the finished structure, take a stroll through the **Františkanská zahrada**, to the south of the church; these gardens make a lovely hideaway from Nové Mesto's bustle, marred only by the intrusive modern garden furniture.

Prague's wax museums

Both wax museums are open daily 10am–8pm.

A short walk down ulica 28 října, which connects Jungmannovo náměstí with Wenceslas Square, is one of Prague's new commercial museums, the **Muzeum voskových figurín** (Wax Museum), laid out on the ground floor of the Art Nouveau palác Rapid at no. 13. The current entrance fee of 120Kč is steep for most Czechs, yet the museum is aimed primarily at a domestic audience. For anyone familiar with London's Madame Tussaud's, the formula is predictable enough, but unless your grasp of Czech history is pretty good, many of the wax tableaux will remain slightly baffling. The most popular section with the locals is the podium of Commie stooges ranging from Lenin to the Czechs' home-grown Stalinist, Klement Gottwald, followed by today's generation of Czech politicians dressed in bad suits, sat amidst naff office furniture.

Within a few months of the Muzeum voskových figurín opening, a second wax museum, the **Pražské panoptikum**, opened up just down the street at Národní 25, in the *pasáž* of the palác Metro. It's equally professional and slick, with similar ticket prices (99Kč), and follows pretty much the same formula, with many of the same historical characters, from Hus to Havel, appearing again. If anything, you'll need an even better knowledge of Czech history and culture to enjoy the *panoptikum*, though you do get the added extra of a short miniature dance show cleverly projected onto a three-dimensional stage.

Národní třída

The eastern end of **Národní** is taken up with shops, galleries and clubs, all of which begin to peter out as you near the river. At the last crossroads before the waterfront is the new **British Council** building, which used to belong to the East German cultural institute. On the outside, the original constructivist facade, designed in the 1930s by Osvald Polívka, has been kept intact, while the light interior has been thoroughly and imaginatively modernized in an interesting synthesis of central European and British architectural styles, using ample helpings of the country's surplus glass. There's a window gallery on the ground floor overlooking Národní, which is run by the British Council, and you're free to walk in and take a peek at the lobby – the entrance is up Voršilská – where you can pick up information on the latest cultural offerings sponsored by the BC.

Further down Národní, on the right-hand side, is an eye-catching duo of much earlier Art Nouveau buildings, designed by Polívka in 1907–08. The first, at no. 7, was built for the **pojišťovna Praha** (Prague Savings Bank), hence the beautiful mosaic lettering above the windows advertizing *život* (life insurance) and *kapital* (loans), as well as help with your *důchod* (pension) and *věno* (dowry). Next door, the slightly more ostentatious **Topičův dům**, headquarters of Československý spisovatel, the official state publishers, provides the perfect accompaniment, with a similarly ornate wrought-iron and glass canopy.

Opposite, the convent and church of **sv Voršila** (St Ursula) are distinguished by the rare sight (in this part of town) of a tree sticking out of its white facade. When it was completed in 1678, this was one of the first truly flamboyant Baroque buildings in Prague, and its white stucco and frescoed interior have recently been restored to their original state. The Ursuline nuns were booted out by the Communists, but returned post-1989 to found one of the first ecclesiastical schools in the country.

The masakr – November 17, 1989

On the night of Friday, November 17, 1989, a 50,000-strong, officially sanctioned student demonstration, organized by the students' union, SSM (League of Young Socialists), worked its way down Národní with the intention of reaching Wenceslas Square. Halfway down the street they were confronted by the *bílé přílby* (white helmets) and *červené barety* (red berets) of the hated riot-police. For what must have seemed like hours, there was a stalemate as the students sat down and refused to disperse, some of them handing flowers out to the police. Suddenly, without any warning, the police attacked and what became known as the **masakr** (massacre) began. In the end, no one was actually killed, though it wasn't for want of trying by the police. Under the arches of the Kaňkův dům, Národní 16, there's a small symbolic bronze relief of eight hands reaching out for help, a permanent shrine in memory of the hundreds who were hospitalized in the violence.

Národní divadlo and Café Slavia

See p.234 for details of Prague's theatres and box offices.

At the western end of Národní, overlooking the Vltava, is the gold-crested **Národní divadlo** (National Theatre), proud symbol of the Czech nation. Refused money from the Habsburg state coffers, Czechs of all classes dug deep into their pockets to raise funds for the venture themselves. The foundation stones, gathered from various historically significant sites in Bohemia and Moravia, were laid in 1868 by the historian and politician, František Palacký, and the composer, Bedřich Smetana; the architect, Josef Zítek, spent the next thirteen years on the project. In June 1881, the theatre opened with a première of Smetana's *Libuše*. In August of the same year, fire ripped through the building, destroying everything except the outer walls. Within two years the whole thing was rebuilt – even the emperor contributed this time – under the supervision of Josef Schulz (who went on to design the National Museum), and it opened once more to the strains of Smetana's opera *Libuše*. The grand portal on the north side of the theatre is embellished with suitably triumphant allegorical figures, and, inside, every square inch is taken up with paintings and sculptures by leading artists of the Czech national revival. Tickets are relatively cheap but most productions are in Czech, so unless there's an opera or ballet on, content yourself with a quick peek at the decor prior to a performance.

Standing behind the Národní divadlo, and in dramatic contrast with it, is the theatre's state-of-the-art extension, the ultra-modern glass box of the **Nová scéna**, designed by Karel Prager, the leading architect of the Communist era, and completed in 1983. It's one of those buildings most Praguers love to hate – it was described by one Czech as looking like "frozen piss" – though compared to much of Prague's Communist-era architecture, it's not that bad. Just for the record, the lump of molten rock in the courtyard is a symbolic evocation of *My Socialist Country*, by Malejovský.

For more on Jaroslav Seifert, see p.160.

The **Café Slavia**, opposite the theatre, has been a favourite haunt of the city's writers, dissidents and artists (and, inevitably, actors) since the days of the First Republic. The Czech avant-garde movement, *Devětsil*, led by Karel Teige, used to hold its meetings here in the 1920s; the meetings are recorded for posterity by another of its members, the Nobel prize-winner Jaroslav Seifert, in his *Slavia Poems*. The café has been carelessly modernized since those arcadian days, but it still has a great riverside view and Manet's famous *Absinthe Drinker* canvas on the wall.

Na příkopě

Heading northeastwards from Můstek at the bottom end of Wenceslas Square, you can join the crush of bodies ambling down **Na příkopě** (literally "On the moat"). The big multinational franchises have staked their claim on this stretch of Prague with the **Pasáž Myslbek**, fronted by Marks & Spencer, which is one of the few contemporary works of architecture in central Prague. The street has, of course, been an architectural showcase for more than a century. On the opposite side of the street, there are grandiose buildings, like the former Haas department store at no. 4, built in 1869–71 by Theophil Hansen, the Danish architect responsible for much of the redevelopment of the Ringstrasse in Vienna. Many of the finest turn-of-the-century buildings, though – like the *Café Corso* and the *Café Français*, once the favourite haunts of Prague's German-Jewish literary set – were torn down and replaced during the enthusiastic construction boom of the interwar republic. The Art Nouveau **U Dörflerů**, at no. 7, from 1905, is one of the few survivors along this stretch, its gilded floral curlicues gleaming in the midday sun.

Prague's main tourist office is at no. 22.

There are another couple of interesting buildings on the opposite side of the street, at nos. 18 and 20, designed by Polívka over the course of a twenty-year period for the Zemská banka and connected by a kind of Bridge of Sighs suspended over Nekázanka. The style veers between 1890s neo-Renaissance and later Art Nouveau elements, such as Jan Preisler's gilded mosaics and Ladislav Saloun's attic sculptures. It's worth nipping upstairs to the main banking hall of what is now the **Živnostenka banka**, at no. 20, to appreciate the financial might of the Czech capital in the last decades of the Austro-Hungarian Empire. Yet more financial institutions, this time from the dour 1930s, line the far end of Na příkopě, as it opens up into náměstí Republiky, including the palatial Národní banka (National Bank), which has recently undergone a controversial and very expensive makeover.

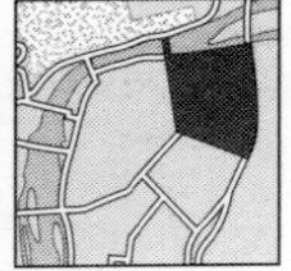

Northern Nové Město

Náměstí Republiky is worth pausing at, if only to admire the Obecní dům – Prague's most alluring Art Nouveau structure – but this aside, there's nothing in the northern or eastern part of Nové Město that merits a special trip. Nevertheless, you may find yourself in this part of town by dint of its shops, restaurants and hotels, or perhaps en route to Prague's main domestic train station, Masarykovo nádraží. Tourists rarely venture this far east, and for that reason alone, it makes an interesting diversion, revealing a side to central Prague that few visitors see.

Náměstí Republiky

Náměstí Republiky is an unruly space, made more so since the construction of its metro station and the ugly brown Kotva department store, built by Swedish architects in the 1970s. The oldest structure on the square is the **Prašná brána** (Powder Gate), one of the eight medieval gate-towers that once guarded Staré Město. The present tower was begun by King Vladislav Jagiello in 1475, shortly after he'd moved into the royal court, which was situated next door at the time. Work stopped when he retreated to the Hrad to avoid the wrath of his subjects; later on, it was used to store gunpowder – hence the name and the reason for the damage incurred in 1757. The small historical exhibition inside traces the tower's architectural metamorphosis over the centuries, up to its present remodelling courtesy of the nineteenth-century restorer, Josef Mocker. Most people, though, ignore the displays, and climb straight up for the modest view from the top.

The Prašná brána is open daily 10am–6pm; 20Kč.

Obecní dům

Attached to the tower, and built on the ruins of the old royal court, the **Obecní dům** (Municipal House) is by far the most exciting Art Nouveau building in Prague, one of the few places that still manages to conjure up the atmosphere of Prague's turn-of-the-century café society. Conceived as a cultural centre for the Czech community, it's probably the finest architectural achievement of the Czech national revival, designed by Osvald Polívka and Antonín Balšánek, and extravagantly decorated inside and out with the help of almost every artist connected with the Czech Secession. From the lifts to the cloakrooms, just about all the furnishings remain as they were when the building was completed in 1911, and every square inch of the interior and exterior has recently been lovingly renovated. Appropriately enough, it was here that Czechoslovakia's independence was declared on October 28, 1918.

The ticket office and information centre at the Obecní dům are open daily 10am–6pm.

The simplest way of soaking up the interior – peppered with mosaics and pendulous brass chandeliers – is to have a coffee in the cavernous café, or a full meal in the equally spacious *Francouská restaurace* or the *Plzenská restaurace* in the basement. For a more detailed inspection of the building's spectacular interior (which includes paintings by Alfons Mucha, Jan Preisler and Max Švabinský, among others), you can sign up for a **guided tour**; tickets are available from the new information and ticket centre on the ground floor, beyond the main foyer. Several

A new museum dedicated to Alfons Mucha has opened on Panská, see p.139.

rooms on the second floor are given over to temporary art exhibitions, while the building's **Smetanova síň**, Prague's largest concert hall, stages numerous concerts, including the opening salvo of the *Pražské jaro* (Prague Spring Festival) – traditionally a rendition of Smetana's *Má vlast* (My Country) – which takes place in the presence of the president.

Hybernská and Senovážné náměstí

Directly opposite the Obecní dům stands a haughty Neoclassical building, **U hybernů** (The Hibernians), built as a customs office in the Napoleonic period, on the site of a Baroque church which belonged to the order of Irish Franciscans who fled Tudor England (hence its name). If you walk down **Hybernská** from here, you'll pass the Art Nouveau **Hotel Central** on the right. Designed by Dryák and Bendelmayer (who built the *Grand Hotel Evropa*) and dating from 1900, its gilded decoration stands out amidst its dour nineteenth-century neighbours.

Opposite the hotel is the **American Center for Culture and Commerce**, formerly the headquarters of the Social Democratic Party, which was forcibly amalgamated with the Communist Party shortly after the 1948 coup. The party regained its independence in 1989, and, after a shaky start, looks set to be the next party in government when Václav Klaus finally falls from power. In January 1912, a small backroom in the building was given over to a congress of the Russian Social Democratic Labour Party. The party was deeply divided, and the meeting poorly attended, with only fourteen voting delegates present (all but two of them Bolsheviks), and **Lenin** himself in the chair. It was this meeting which pushed through the formal takeover of the party by the Bolsheviks, to the exclusion of the Mensheviks and others, and gave the Czech Communists the perfect excuse for turning the whole place into a vast museum dedicated to Lenin, of which there is now, not surprisingly, absolutely no trace.

Around Masarykovo nádraží and Senovážné náměstí

A little further down Hybernská, a wrought-iron canopy marks the entrance to Prague's first railway station, **Masarykovo nádraží**, opened in 1845 and still much as it was then – a modest, almost provincial affair compared to the Art Nouveau Praha hlavní nádraží. On the opposite side of Hybernská is the **Café Arco**, once a favourite of Kafka (who worked nearby), and the circle of Prague-German writers known as the Arconauts. The current incumbents make nothing of its literary associations, and have filled the place with slot machines and pool tables.

South of Masarykovo nádraží, down Dlážděná, is the old hay market, **Senovážné náměstí**, packed out with parked cars and a couple of market stalls. Its most distinguished feature is the free-standing fifteenth-century belfry of the church of **sv Jindřich** (St Henry); both have undergone several facelifts, most recently by the ubiquitous Gothic restorer, Josef Mocker.

A short way up Jeruzalémská, you'll find the **Jubilejní synagoga**, named in honour of the sixtieth year of the Emperor Franz-Josef I's reign in 1908. Built in a colourful Moorish style similar to that of the Španělská synagoga in Josefov, the Hebrew inscription on the facade strikes a note of liberal optimism: "Do we not have one father? Were we not created by the same God?" The synagogue holds regular Sabbath services; at all other times, it's usually closed.

Prague's other synagogues are covered in Chapter 5.

Mucha Museum

Dedicated to **Alfons Mucha** (1860–1939), probably the most famous of all Czech artists in the West, the **Mucha Museum**, which opened in 1998 in the Kaunicky palác on Panská, southwest of Senovážné náměstí, has proved very popular indeed. Mucha made his name in *fin-de-siècle* Paris, where he shot to fame after designing the Art Nouveau poster *Gismonda* for the actress Sarah Bernhardt. "Le Style Mucha" became all the rage, but the artist himself came to despise this "commercial" period of his work, and in 1910, Mucha moved back to his homeland and threw himself into the national cause, designing patriotic stamps, banknotes and posters for the new republic.

The Mucha Museum is open daily 10am–6pm; 120Kč.

The whole of Mucha's career is covered in the permanent exhibition, and there's a good selection of informal photos taken by the artist himself of his models, and of Paul Gauguin (with whom he shared a studio) playing the harmonium with his trousers down. The only work not represented here is his massive *Slav Epic*, but the excellent video (in English) covers the decade of his life he devoted to this cycle of nationalist paintings. In the end, Mucha paid for his Czech nationalism with his life; dragged in for questioning by the Gestapo after the 1939 Nazi invasion, he died shortly after being released.

North of Masarykovo nádraží

Running roughly parallel with Hybernská, to the north of Masarykovo nádraží, is the much busier street of **Na poříčí**, an area that, like sv Havel in Staré Město, was originally settled by German merchants. Kafka spent most of his working life as a frustrated and unhappy clerk for the *Arbeiter-Unfall-Versicherungs-Anstalt* (Workers' Accident Insurance Company), in the grand nineteenth-century building at no. 7. Further along on the right is a much more unusual piece of corporate architecture, the **Banka legií**, one of Pavel Janák's rare Rondo-Cubist efforts from the early 1920s. Set into the bold smoky-red moulding is a striking white marble frieze by Otto Gutfreund, depicting the epic march across Siberia undertaken by the Czechoslovak Legion and their embroilment in the Russian Revolution. You're free to wander into the main banking hall on the ground floor, which, though marred by the current bank fittings, retains its curved glass roof and distinctive red-and-white marble patterning. The glass curtain-walled **Bílá labuť** (White Swan) department store, opposite, is a good example of the functionalist style which Janák and others went on to embrace in the late 1920s and 1930s.

The Banka legií is open Mon–Fri 8am–5pm; for more on Janák and the Cubists, see p.155.

Northern Nové Město

The museum is open Tues–Sun 10am–6pm; 30Kč .

As a lively shopping street, Na poříčí seems very much out on a limb, as do the cluster of hotels at the end of the street, and around the corner in **Těšnov**. The reason behind this is the now defunct Těšnov train station, which was demolished in the 1960s to make way for the monstrous Wilsonova flyover. Antonín Balšánek's purpose-built neo-Renaissance mansion, housing the **Muzeum Prahy** (Prague Museum), on the other side of the flyover, is the lone survivor of this redevelopment. Inside, there's an ad hoc collection of the city's art, a number of antique bicycles, and usually an intriguing temporary exhibition on some aspect of the city. The museum's prize possession, though, is Antonín Langweil's paper model of Prague which he completed after eleven years in 1837. It's a fascinating insight into early nineteenth-century Prague – predominantly Baroque, with the cathedral incomplete and the Jewish quarter "unsanitized" – and, consequently, has served as one of the most useful records for the city's restorers. The most surprising thing, of course, is that so little has changed.

Nábřeží Ludvika Svobody and around

The Poštovní muzeum is open Tues–Sun 9am–5pm; 25Kč.

North of Na poříčí, close to the river bank, nábřeží Ludvika Svobody, there's another museum which might appeal to some: the **Poštovní muzeum** (Postage Museum), housed in the Vávra mill on Nové mlýny, near one of Prague's many water towers. The first floor contains a series of jolly nineteenth-century wall paintings of Romantic Austrian landscapes, and a collection of drawings on postman themes. The real philately is on the ground floor – a vast international collection of stamps arranged in vertical pull-out drawers. The Czechoslovak issues are historically and artistically interesting, as well as of appeal to collectors. Stamps became a useful tool in the propaganda wars of this century; even such short-lived ventures as the Hungarian-backed Slovak Socialist Republic of 1918–19 and the Slovak National Uprising of autumn 1944 managed to print special issues. Under the First Republic, the country's leading artists, notably Alfons Mucha and Max Švabinský, were commissioned to design stamps, some of which are exceptionally beautiful.

As you leave the museum, look across to your left towards Revoluční: the statue of **Jan Šverma** is one of the few Communist-era monuments to have survived the post-1989 iconoclasm that brought countless statues tumbling down. Šverma, who joined the Communist Party shortly after it was formed in 1921 and died fighting against the Nazis in 1944, has been targeted by anti-Communists who want him removed from his pedestal, and the nearby bridge (Švermův most) renamed. Further east along the embankment is another monument of the Communist era, the former headquarters of the Party's Central Committee, now the **Ministry of Transport**, where Dubček and his fellow reformers were arrested in August 1968, before being spirited away to Moscow for "frank and fraternal" discussions.

Southern Nové Město

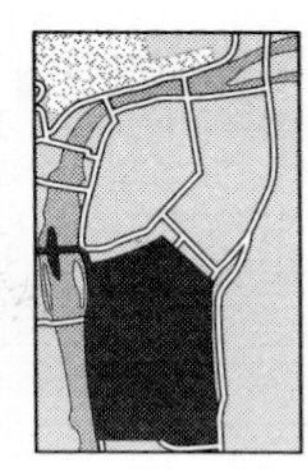

The streets south of Národní and Wenceslas Square still run along the medieval lines of Charles IV's town plan, though they're now lined with grand, late nineteenth- and twentieth-century buildings. Such is their scale, however, that some of these broad boulevards – like Žitná and Ječná – have become the main arteries for Prague's steadily increasing traffic. Together with the large distances involved, this makes southern Nové Město one part of the city where hopping on a tram can be a good way of getting about. Three tram routes worth knowing about are: tram #24, which goes along Vodičkova, up the side of Karlovo náměstí and past the Botanická zahrada; tram #3, which follows a similar route but heads off to Palackého náměstí and south along the riverfront; and tram #18, which heads south from Národní down Spálená, up the side of Karlovo náměstí and past the Botanická zahrada.

South to Karlovo náměstí

Of the many roads which head down towards Karlovo náměstí, **Vodičkova** is probably the most impressive, running southwest for half a kilometre from Wenceslas Square. You can catch several trams along this route, though there are a handful of buildings worth checking out on the way, so you may choose to walk. The first, **U Nováků**, is impossible to miss, thanks to Jan Preisler's mosaic of bucolic frolicking (its actual subject, *Trade and Industry*, is confined to the edges of the picture), and Polívka's curvilinear window frames and delicate, ivy-like ironwork – look out for the frog-prince holding up a windowsill. Originally built for the Novák department store in the early 1900s, for the last sixty years it has been a cabaret hall, restaurant and café all rolled into one; however, the original fittings have long since been destroyed.

Halfway down the street, at no. 15, the *McDonald's* "restaurant" – the first to open in the Czech Republic in 1992 – must qualify as a landmark of sorts. It occupies the site of the *Akademická kavárna*, one of the many lost literary cafés of turn-of-the-century Prague. Directly opposite stands the imposing neo-Renaissance **Minerva girls' school**, covered in bright-red sgraffito. Founded in 1866, it was the first such institution in Prague, and was notorious for the antics of its pupils, the "Minervans", who shocked bourgeois Czech society with their experimentations with fashion, drugs and sexual freedom (see box p.142). As Vodičkova curves left towards Karlovo náměstí, Lazarská, meeting point of the city's night trams, leads off to the right. At the bottom of this street is **Diamant**, another of Prague's Cubist buildings, completed in 1912 by Emil Králíček. It's grubby with pollution now, but the geometric sculptural reliefs on the facade, the main portal and the frame enclosing a Baroque statue of St John of Nepomuk on Spálená, remain worth viewing nonetheless.

Milena Jesenská

The most famous "Minervan" was **Milena Jesenská**, born in 1896 into a Czech family whose ancestry stretched back to the sixteenth century. Shortly after leaving school, she was confined to a mental asylum by her father when he discovered that she was having an affair with a Jew. On her release, she married the Jew, Ernst Polak, and moved to Vienna, where she took a job as a railway porter to support the two of them. While living in Vienna, she sent a Czech translation of one of Kafka's short stories to his publisher; Kafka wrote back himself, and so began their platonic, mostly epistolary, relationship. Kafka described her later as "the only woman who ever understood me", and with his encouragement she took up writing professionally. Tragically, by the time Milena had extricated herself from her disastrous marriage, Kafka, still smarting from three failed engagements with other women, had decided never to commit himself to anyone else; his letters alone survived the war, as a moving testament to their love.

Milena returned to Prague in 1925, and moved on from writing exclusively fashion articles to critiques of avant-garde architecture, becoming one of the city's leading journalists. She married again, this time to the prominent functionalist architect Jaromír Krejcar, but later, a difficult pregnancy and childbirth left her addicted to morphine. She overcame her dependency only after joining the Communist Party, but was to quit after the first of Stalin's show trials in 1936. She continued to work as a journalist in the late 1930s, and wrote a series of articles condemning the rise of Fascism in the Sudetenland.

When the Nazis rolled into Prague in 1939, Milena's Vinohrady flat had already become a centre for resistance. For a while, she managed to hang on to her job, but her independent intellectual stance and provocative gestures – like wearing a yellow star as a mark of solidarity with her Jewish friends – soon attracted the attentions of the Gestapo, and after a brief spell in the notorious Pankrác prison, she was sent to Ravensbrück, the women's concentration camp near Berlin, where she died of nephritis (inflammation of the kidneys) in May 1944.

Karlovo náměstí

Once Prague's biggest square, **Karlovo náměstí**'s impressive proportions are no longer so easy to appreciate, obscured by a tree-planted public garden and cut in two by the busy thoroughfare of Ječná. It was created by Charles IV as Nové Město's cattle market (Dobytčí trh) and used by him for the grisly annual public display of his impressive collection of saintly relics (see p.93), though now it actually signals the southern limit of the city's main commercial district and the beginning of residential Nové Město.

The **Novoměstská radnice** (New Town Hall), at the northeastern corner of the square, sports three impressive triangular gables embellished with intricate blind tracery. It was built, like the one on Staroměstské náměstí, during the reign of King John of Luxembourg, though it has survived rather better, and thanks to its recent facelift, is now one of the finest Gothic buildings in the city. After the amalgamation of Prague's separate towns in 1784, however, it was used solely as a criminal court and prison, and even today the public are only allowed to visit the building's small art gallery, which puts on temporary art exhibitions (Tues–Sun 10am–6pm). It was here that Prague's **first defenestration** took place on July 30, 1419, when the radical Hussite preacher Jan Želivský and his penniless religious followers stormed the building, mobbed the councillors and burghers and threw twelve or thirteen of them (including the mayor) out of the town hall windows onto the pikes of the Hussite mob below, who clubbed any survivors to death. Václav IV, on hearing the news, suffered a stroke and died just two weeks later. So began the long and bloody Hussite Wars.

Southern Nové Město

For details of Prague's second defenestration, see p.58.

Following the defeat of Protestantism two centuries later, the Jesuits were allowed to demolish 23 houses on the east side of the square to make way for their college (now one of the city's main hospitals) and the accompanying church of **sv Ignác** (St Ignatius), begun in 1665 by Carlo Lurago and Paul Ignaz Bayer. The latter looks quite remarkable now it's been restored, and is modelled, like so many Jesuit churches, on the Gesù in Rome; it's worth looking in if only for the wedding-cake stucco on the ceiling.

Nos. 40–41, at the southern end of the square, is the so-called **Faustův dům** (Faust House), a late Baroque building with a long and diabolical history of alchemy. An occult priest from Opava owned the house in the fourteenth century, and, two hundred years later, the English alchemist and international con-man Edward Kelley was summoned here by the eccentric Emperor Rudolf II to turn base metal into gold. The building is also the traditional setting for the Czech version of the Faust legend, with the arrival one rainy night of a penniless and homeless student, Jan Šťastný (meaning lucky, or *Faustus* in German). Finding money in the house, he decided to keep it – only to discover that it was put there by the Devil, who then claims his soul in return. Seemingly unperturbed by the historical fate of the site, a new pharmacy now plies its trade on the ground floor.

The Orthodox cathedral of sv Cyril and Metoděj

West off Karlovo náměstí, down Resslova, the noisy extension of Ječná, is the Orthodox cathedral of **sv Cyril and Metoděj**, originally constructed for the Roman Catholics by Bayer and Dientzenhofer in the eighteenth century, but since the 1930s, the main base of the Orthodox church in the Czech Republic. Amid all the traffic, it's extremely difficult to imagine the scene here on June 18, 1942, when seven of the Czechoslovak secret agents involved in the most dramatic assassination of World War II (see box on pp.144–145) were besieged in the church by over seven hundred members of the Waffen SS. Acting on the basis of a tip-off by one of the Czech resistance who turned himself in, the Nazis surrounded the church just after 4am and fought a pitched battle for over six hours, trying explo-

The church crypt is open Tues–Sun 10am–4pm; 30Kč.

sives, flooding and any other method they could think of to drive the men out of their stronghold in the crypt. Eventually, all seven agents committed suicide rather than give themselves up. There's a plaque at street level on the south wall commemorating those who died, and an exhibition on the whole affair situated in the crypt itself, which has been left pretty much as it was; the entrance is underneath the church steps on Na ýderaze.

Along the embankment

Magnificent turn-of-the-century mansions line the Vltava's right bank, almost without interruption, for some two kilometres from the Charles Bridge south to the rocky outcrop of Vyšehrad. It's a long walk, even just along the length of **Masarykovo** and **Rašínovo nábřeží**, though there's no need to do the whole lot in one go: you can hop on a tram (#17 or #21) at various points, drop down from the embankments to the waterfront itself, or escape to one of the two islands connected to them, Střelecký ostrov, or Slovanský ostrov, better known as Pofín.

Access to either of the two islands in the central section of the Vltava is from close to the Národní divadlo. The first, **Střelecký ostrov**, or

The Assassination of Reinhard Heydrich

The assassination of Reinhard Heydrich in 1942 was the only attempt the Allies ever made on the life of a leading Nazi. It's an incident which the Allies have always billed as a great success in the otherwise rather dismal seven-year history of the Czech resistance. But, as with all acts of brave resistance during the war, there was a price to be paid. Given that the reprisals meted out to the Czech population were entirely predictable, it remains a controversial, if not suicidal, decision to have made.

The target, **Reinhard Tristan Eugen Heydrich**, was a talented and upwardly mobile anti-Semite (despite rumours that he was partly Jewish himself), a great organizer and a skilful concert violinist. He was a late recruit to the Nazi Party, signing up in 1931, after having been dismissed from the German Navy for dishonourable conduct towards a woman. However, he swiftly rose through the ranks of the SS to become second in command after Himmler, and in the autumn of 1941, he was appointed *Reichsprotektor* of the puppet state of *Böhmen und Mähren* – effectively, the most powerful man in the Czech Lands. Although his rule began with brutality, it soon settled into the tried and tested policy which Heydrich liked to call *Peitsche und Zucker* (literally, "whip and sugar").

On the morning of May 27, 1942, as Heydrich was being driven by his personal bodyguard, *Oberscharführer* Klein, in his open-top Mercedes from his manor house north of Prague to his office in Hradčany, three Czechoslovak agents (parachuted in from England) were taking up positions in the northeastern suburb of Libeň. As the car pulled into Kirchmayer Boulevard (now V Holešovičkách), one of them, a Slovak called Gabčík, pulled out a Sten gun and tried to shoot. The gun jammed,

Shooters' Island, is where the army held their shooting practice, on and off, from the fifteenth until the nineteenth century. Closer to the other bank, and accessible via most Legií (Legion's Bridge), it became a favourite spot for a Sunday promenade, and is still popular, especially in summer. The first *Sokol* festival took place here in 1882 (see p.83), and the first May Day demonstrations in 1890.

The second island, Slovanský ostrov, more commonly known as **Žofín** (after the island's concert hall, itself named for Sophie, the mother of the Emperor Franz-Josef I), came about as a result of the natural silting of the river in the eighteenth century. By the late nineteenth century it had become one of the city's foremost pleasure gardens, where, as the composer Berlioz remarked, "bad musicians shamelessly make abominable music in the open air and immodest young males and females indulge in brazen dancing, while idlers and wasters . . . lounge about smoking foul tobacco and drinking beer". On a good day, things seem pretty much unchanged from those heady times. Concerts, balls and other social gatherings take place here in the newly renovated and very yellow cultural centre, built in 1835, and there are rowing boats for hire from May to October.

at which Heydrich, rather than driving out of the situation, ordered Klein to stop the car and attempted to shoot back. At this point, another agent, Kubiš, threw a bomb at the car. The blast injured Kubiš and Heydrich, who immediately leapt out and began firing at Kubiš. Kubiš, with blood pouring down his face, jumped on his bicycle and fled downhill. Gabčík meanwhile pulled out a second gun and exchanged shots with Heydrich, until the latter collapsed from his wounds. Gabčík fled into a butcher's, shot Klein – who was in hot pursuit – in the legs and escaped down the backstreets.

Meanwhile back at the Mercedes, a baker's van was flagged down by a passer-by, but refused to get involved. Eventually, a small truck carrying floor polish was commandeered and Heydrich taken to the Bulovka hospital. Heydrich died eight days later from shrapnel wounds and was given full Nazi honours at his Prague funeral; the cortège passed down Wenceslas Square, in front of a crowd of thousands. As the home resistance had forewarned, revenge was quick to follow. The day after Heydrich's funeral, the village of **Lidice** (see p.195) was burnt to the ground and its male inhabitants murdered; two weeks later the village of Ležáky suffered a similar fate.

The plan to assassinate Heydrich had been formulated in the early months of 1942 by the Czechoslovak government-in-exile in London, without consultation with the Czech Communist leadership in Moscow, and despite fierce opposition from the resistance within Czechoslovakia. Since it was clear that the reprisals would be horrific – thousands were executed in the aftermath – the only logical explanation for the plan is that this was precisely the aim of the government-in-exile's operation – to forge a solid wedge of resentment between the Germans and Czechs. In this respect, if in no other, the operation was ultimately successful.

Southern Nové Město

The Mánes art gallery is open Tues–Sun 10am–6pm.

At the southern tip of Slovanský ostrov stands the onion-domed Šítek water tower, which provided a convenient look-out post for the Czech secret police, whose job it was to watch over Havel's Prague flat (see below). Close by, spanning the narrow channel between the island and the river bank, is the striking white functionalist box of the **Mánes** art gallery. Designed in open-plan style by Otakar Novotný in 1930, the gallery is named after Josef Mánes, a traditional nineteenth-century landscape painter and Czech nationalist, and puts on consistently interesting exhibitions; in addition there's a café and an upstairs restaurant, suspended above the channel. Most of the ornate apartment buildings along the waterfront itself are private, and therefore inaccessible. One exception is the Art Nouveau concert hall, **Hlahol**, at Masarykovo nábřeží 16, built for the Hlahol men's choir in 1903–06, and designed by the architect of the main railway station, Josef Fanta, with a pediment mural by Mucha and statues by Šaloun – check the listings magazines or the posters outside the hall for details of forthcoming concerts.

Tančící dům, Havel and Palackého náměstí

If the Mánes gallery seems at odds with the turn-of-the-century architecture along the embankment, it is as nothing to what stands at the beginning of **Rašínovo nábřeží** (named after the interwar Minister of Finance, Alois Rašín, who was assassinated by a non-card-carrying Communist in the 1920s). Designed by the Canadian-born Frank O. Gehry and the Yugoslav-born Vlado Milunić, the building is known as the **Tančící dům** (Dancing House) or "Fred and Ginger", after the shape of building's two towers, which look vaguely like a couple ballroom dancing. The site is all the more controversial as it stands next door to an apartment block built at the turn of the century by Havel's grandfather, where, until the early 1990s, Havel and his first wife, Olga, lived in the top-floor flat.

Further along the embankment, at **Palackého náměstí**, the buildings retreat for a moment to reveal an Art Nouveau sculpture to rival Šaloun's monument in Staroměstské náměstí (see p.97): the **Monument to František Palacký**, the great nineteenth-century Czech historian, politician and nationalist, by Stanislav Sucharda. Like the Hus Monument, which was unveiled three years later, this mammoth project – fifteen years in the making – had missed its moment by the time it was finally completed in 1912, and found universal disfavour. The critics have mellowed over the years, and nowadays it's appreciated for what it is – an energetic and inspirational piece of work. Ethereal bronze bodies, representing the world of the imagination, shoot out at all angles, contrasting sharply with the plain stone mass of the plinth, and below, the giant seated figure of Palacký himself, representing the real world.

Vyšehradská and Ke Karlovu

Behind Palackého náměstí, on **Vyšehradská**, the twisted concrete spires of the **Emauzy monastery** are an unusual modern addition to the Prague skyline. The monastery was one of the few important historical buildings to be damaged in the last war, in this case by a stray Anglo-American bomb. Charles IV founded the monastery for Croatian Benedictines, who used the Old Slavonic liturgy (hence its Czech name, na Slovanech, or "at the Slavs"), but after the Battle of Bílá hora it was handed over to the more mainstream Spanish Benedictines. The cloisters contain some extremely valuable Gothic frescoes, but since the return of the monks from their forty-year exile, access has become unpredictable.

Rising up behind Emauzy, is one of Kilian Ignaz Dientzenhofer's little gems, the church of **sv Jan Nepomucký na skalce** (St John of Nepomuk-on-the-rock), perched high above Vyšehradská, with a facade that displays the plasticity of the Bavarian's Baroque style in all its glory. Heading south, Vyšehradská descends to a junction, where you'll find the entrance to the university's **Botanická zahrada** (Botanical gardens), laid out in 1897 on a series of terraces up the other side of the hill. Though far from spectacular – the 1930s' greenhouses are a bit sad – they're one of the few patches of green in this part of town.

The Botanical gardens are open daily April–Oct 9am–6pm, Nov–March 10am–4pm.

On the far side of the gardens, Apolinářská runs along the south wall and past a grimly Gothic red-brick maternity hospital with steeply sided stepped gables, before joining up with **Ke Karlovu**. Head left up here and the first street off to the right is Na bojišti, which is usually packed with tour coaches. The reason for this is the **U kalicha** pub, on the right, which was immortalized in the opening passages of the consistently popular comic novel *The Good Soldier Švejk*, by Jaroslav Hašek. In the story, on the eve of the Great War, Švejk (*Schweik* to the Germans) walks into *U kalicha*, where a plain-clothes officer of the Austrian constabulary is sitting drinking and, after a brief conversation, finds himself arrested in connection with the assassination of Archduke Ferdinand. Whatever the pub may have been like in Hašek's day (and even then, it wasn't his local), it's now unashamedly oriented towards reaping in the Deutschmarks, and about the only authentic thing you'll find inside – albeit at a price – is the beer.

Vila Amerika (Muzeum Antonína Dvořáka)

Further north along Ke Karlovu, set back from the road behind wrought-iron gates, is a more rewarding place of pilgrimage, the russet-coloured **Vila Amerika** (named after the local pub), now a museum devoted to Czech composer, **Antonín Dvořák** (1841–1904), who lived for a time on nearby Pitná. Even if you've no interest in Dvořák, the house itself is a delight, built as a Baroque summer palace around 1720 and one of Kilian Ignaz Dientzenhofer's most successful secular works.

The Dvořák Museum is open Tues–Sun 10am–5pm; 30Kč.

Dvořák, easily the most famous of all Czech composers, for many years had to play second fiddle to Smetana in the orchestra at the Národní divadlo, where Smetana was the conductor. In his forties, Dvořák received an honorary degree from Cambridge before leaving for the "New World", and his gown is one of the very few items of memorabilia to have found its way into the museum, along with the programme of a concert given at London's Guildhall in 1891. However, the tasteful period rooms with the composer's music wafting in and out and the tiny garden dotted with Baroque sculptures compensate for what the display cabinets may lack.

Muzeum Policie and Na Karlově church

I. P. Pavlova metro station is not far from Vila Amerika, but if you've got a few hundred more metres left in you, head south down Ke Karlovu. At the end of the street, the former Augustinian monastery of Karlov is now the **Muzeum Policie** (Police Museum), formerly the Museum of the Security Forces – and, in the heyday of "normalization" in the 1970s, one of the most fascinating museums in the city. Works by Trotsky, photos of Bob Dylan, plays by Havel and contraband goods were all displayed in the grand room of dissidence; closed-circuit TV watched over your every move; and the first thing you saw on entry were two hundred pistols confiscated from western secret agents pointing at you from the wall. But the most famous exhibit was undoubtedly a stuffed German shepherd dog called Brek, who saw twelve years' service on border patrols, intercepted sixty "law-breakers", was twice shot in action and eventually retired to an old dogs' home.

The Muzeum Policie is open Tues–Sun 10am–5pm; 20Kč.

With the barbed wire and border patrols all but disappeared, and the police at the nadir of their popularity, the new exhibition concentrates on road and traffic offences, and the force's latest challenges: forgery, drugs and murder. It's not what it used to be, but it's still mildly diverting, with several participatory displays, including a quiz on the Highway Code (in Czech) and a particularly gruesome section on forensic science.

Na Karlově is open Sundays 2–5.15pm.

Attached to the museum is **Na Karlově** church, founded by Charles IV (of course), designed in imitation of Charlemagne's tomb in Aachen, and quite unlike any other church in Prague. If it's open, you should take a look at the dark interior, which was remodelled in the sixteenth century by Bonifaz Wohlmut. The stellar vault has no central supporting pillars – a remarkable feat of engineering for its time, and one which gave rise to numerous legends about the architect being in league with the devil.

From outside the church, there's a great view south across the Botič valley, to the twin delights of the skyscraper *Hotel Forum* and the low-lying **Palác kultury** (Palace of Culture), originally used for party congresses and now the country's biggest concert venue; to the right of the Palác kultury is Vyšehrad (see opposite). Vyšehrad metro is on the other side of the Nuselské most; alternatively, you can walk down to the bottom of the valley and catch a tram (#7, #18 or #24).

Chapter 7

Vyšehrad and the eastern suburbs

By the end of his reign in 1378, Charles IV had laid out his city on such a grand scale that it wasn't until the industrial revolution hit Bohemia in the mid-nineteenth century that Prague began to spread beyond the boundaries of the medieval town. The first of the suburbs, industrial Karlín, was rigidly planned, with public parks and grid street plans strictly laid out to the east of the old town; twentieth-century suburbs have tended to grow with less grace, trailing their tenements across the hills, and swallowing up existing villages on the way. **Vinohrady** and **Žižkov**, which are covered in this chapter, still retain their individual late nineteenth-century identities, which makes them worth checking out on even a short visit to the city; they also contain one or two specific sights to guide your wandering. **Vyšehrad**, which was actually one of the earliest points of settlement in Prague, is something of an exception to all the above, and is by far the most enticing of the outlying areas. Its cemetery contains the remains of Bohemia's artistic elite; the ramparts afford superb views over the river; and below its fortress, there are several examples of Czech Cubist architecture.

Vyšehrad

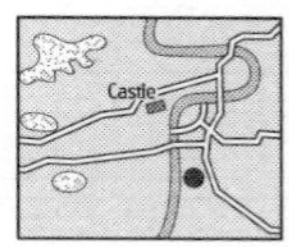

At the southern tip of Nové Město, around 3km south of the city centre, the rocky red-brick fortress of **VYŠEHRAD** (literally "High Castle") has more myths attached to it per square inch than any other place in Bohemia. According to Czech legend, this is the place where the Slav tribes first settled in Prague, where the "wise and tireless chieftain" Krok built a castle, and whence his youngest daughter Libuše went on to found *Praha* itself. Alas, the archeological evidence doesn't bear this claim out, but it's clear that Přemyslid Vratislav II (1061–92), the first Bohemian ruler to bear the title "king", built a royal palace here to get away from his younger brother who was lording it in the Hrad. Within half a century the royals had moved back to Hradčany, into a new palace, and from then on Vyšehrad began to lose its political significance.

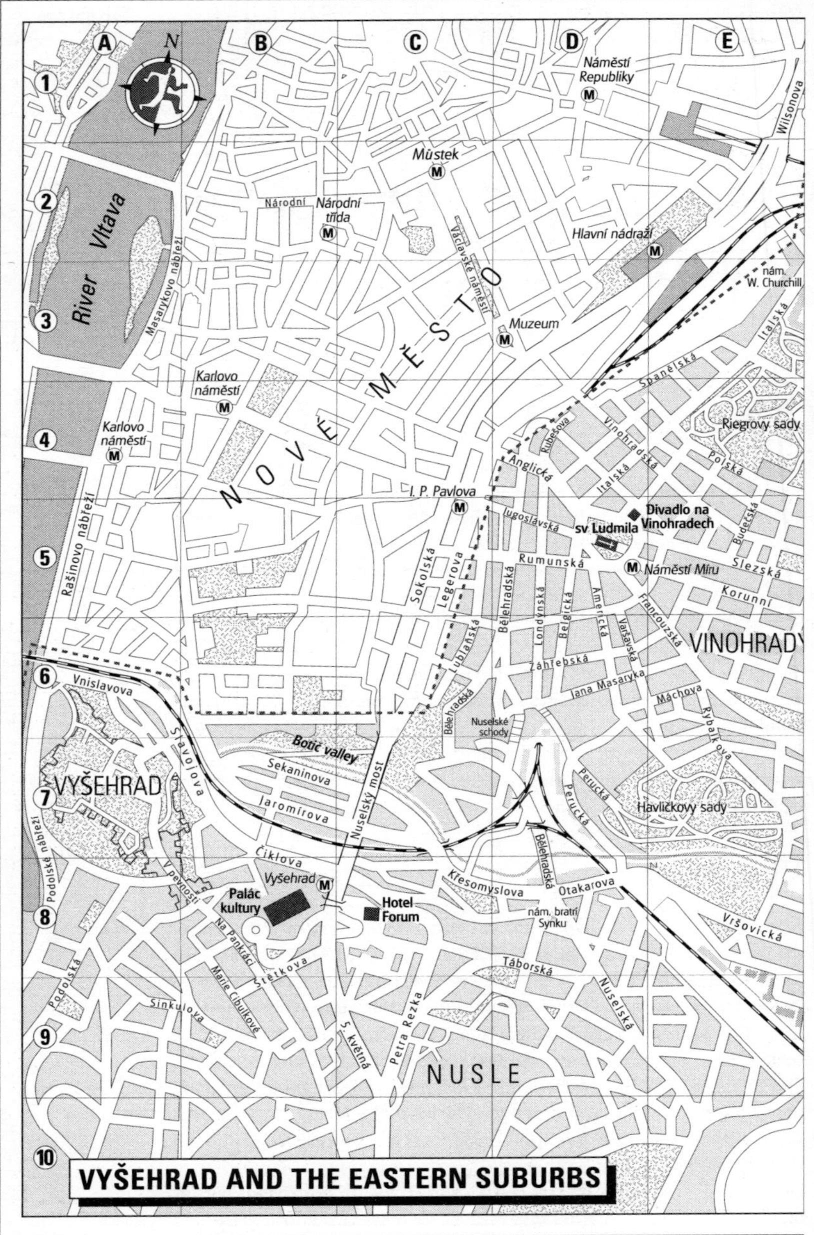
VYŠEHRAD AND THE EASTERN SUBURBS
N
River Vltava
Masarykovo nábřeží
Rašínovo nábřeží
Podolské nábřeží
Náměstí Republiky
Můstek
Národní
Národní třída
Václavské náměstí
Hlavní nádraží
nám. W. Churchill
Muzeum
NOVÉ MĚSTO
Karlovo náměstí
Karlovo náměstí
I. P. Pavlova
Wilsonova
Italská
Španělská
Riegrovy sady
Rubešova
Vinohradská
Anglická
Polská
Italská
Divadlo na Vinohradech
sv Ludmila
Jugoslávská
Budečská
Rumunská
Náměstí Míru
Slezská
Korunní
Sokolská
Legerova
Bělehradská
Londýnská
Belgická
Americká
Varšavská
Francouzská
VINOHRADY
Lublaňská
Záhřebská
Jana Masaryka
Máchova
Rybalkova
Bělehradská
Nuselské schody
Vnislavova
Slavojova
Botič valley
Sekaninova
Jaromírova
Nuselský most
VYŠEHRAD
Perucká
Perucká
Havlíčkovy sady
Bělehradská
Čiklova
Vyšehrad
Palác kultury
Hotel Forum
Křesomyslova
Otakarova
nám. bratří Synků
Vršovická
V pevnosti
Na Pankráci
Táborská
Nuselská
Štětkova
Marie Cibulkové
Podolská
Sinkulova
5. května
Petra Rezka
NUSLE

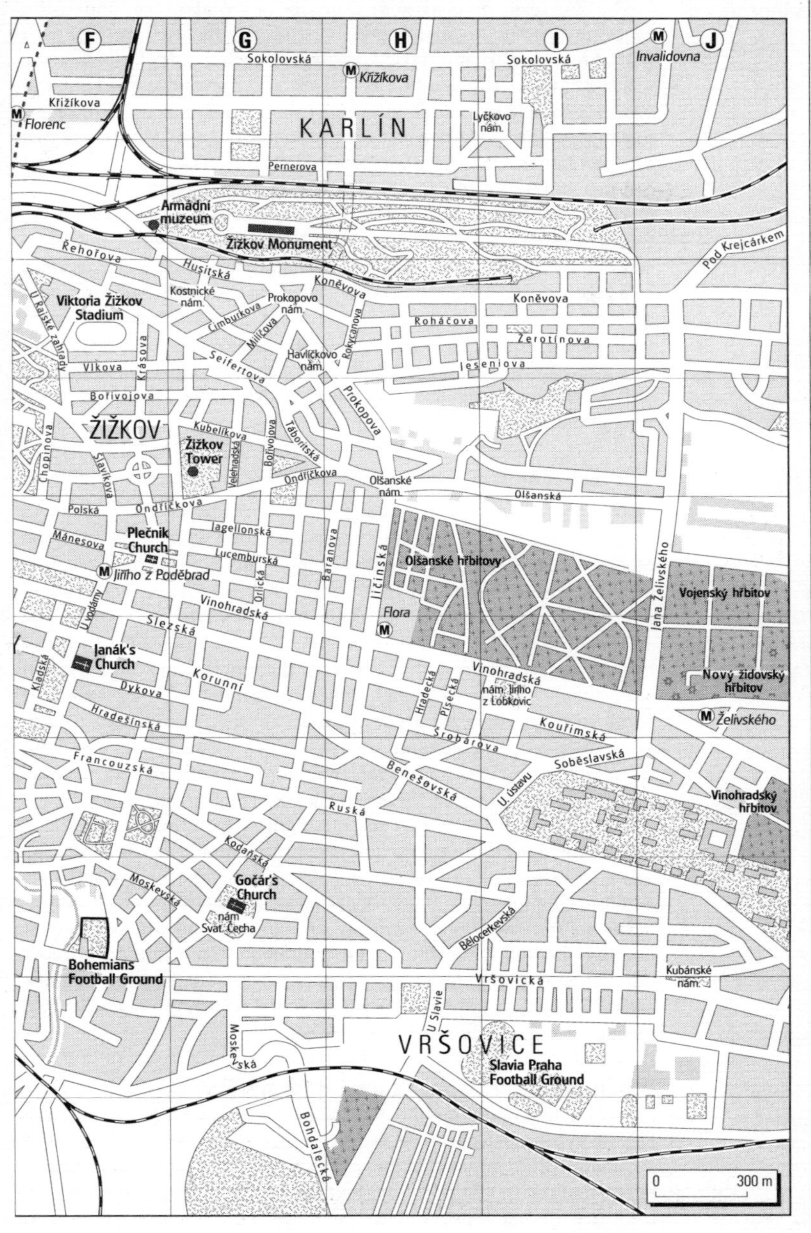
KARLÍN
ŽIŽKOV
VRŠOVICE
Armádní muzeum
Žižkov Monument
Viktoria Žižkov Stadium
Žižkov Tower
Plečnik Church
Janák's Church
Gočár's Church
Bohemians Football Ground
Slavia Praha Football Ground
Olšanské hřbitovy
Vojenský hřbitov
Nový židovský hřbitov
Vinohradský hřbitov
Florenc
Křižíkova
Invalidovna
Jiřího z Poděbrad
Flora
Želivského
0 300 m

The fortress enjoyed something of a renaissance under the Emperor Charles IV, who wished to associate his own dynasty with that of the early Přemyslids. A system of walls was built to link the fortress to the newly founded Nové Město, and it was decreed that the *králová cesta* (the coronation route) should begin from here. These fortifications were destroyed by the Hussites in 1420, but the hill was settled again over the next two hundred years. In the mid-seventeenth century, the Habsburgs turfed everyone out and rebuilt the place as a fortified barracks, only to tear it down in 1866 to create a public park. By the time the Czech national revival movement became interested in Vyšehrad, only the red-brick fortifications were left as a reminder of its former strategic importance; they rediscovered its history and its legends, and gradually transformed it into a symbol of Czech nationhood. Today, Vyšehrad makes for one of the most rewarding trips away from the human congestion of the city, a perfect afternoon escape and a great place from which to watch the evening sun set behind the Hrad.

The fortress

The nearest metro is Vyšehrad.

There are several **approaches to the fortress** (see map on pp.150–151): from Vyšehrad metro station, walk west past the modern Palác kultury, and enter through the Leopoldova brána (**a**); if you've come by tram #3, #7, #16, #17 or #21, which trundle along the waterfront, you can either wind your way up Vratislavova and enter through the Cihelná brána (**b**), or take the steep stairway from Rašínovo nábřeží that leads up through the trees to a small side entrance in the west wall. Vyšehrad is perfect for a picnic, but **food and drink** can also be had at *Na Vyšehradě* (daily 10am–10pm), a reasonably priced *vinárna* (wine bar) opposite the church of sv Petr and Pavel. In addition, there are several good pubs and restaurants in the streets below the fortress (see p.221).

The last approach brings you out right in front of the blackened sandstone church of **sv Petr and Pavel** (**c**), rebuilt in the 1880s by Josef Mocker in neo-Gothic style (with further, even more ruthless, additions completed in the 1900s) on the site of an eleventh-century basilica. The twin open-work spires are now the fortress's most familiar landmark; however, the church's polychrome interior is often closed to the public to protect against vandalism and to allow archeologists to search for the remains of the eleventh-century royal palace, discovered here some time ago.

Vyšehradský hřbitov (Vyšehrad Cemetery)

One of the first initiatives of the national revival movement was to establish the **Vyšehradský hřbitov**, which spreads out to the north and east of the church. It's a measure of the part that artists and intellectuals played in the foundation of the nation, and the regard in which they are still held, that the most prestigious graveyard in the city is given over to them: no soldiers, no politicians, not even the Communists managed to muscle their way in here (except on artistic merit). Sheltered from the wind by its high walls, lined on two sides by delicate arcades, it's a tiny cemetery (reflecting, as it were, the size of the nation) filled with well-kept graves, many of them designed by the country's leading sculptors.

Vyšehrad

To the uninitiated only a handful of figures are well-known, but for the Czechs the place is alive with great names (there's a useful plan of the most notable graves at the entrance nearest the church). Ladislav Šaloun's grave for **Dvořák**, situated under the arches, is one of the more showy ones, with a mosaic inscription, studded with gold stones, glistening behind wrought-iron railings. **Smetana**, who died twenty years earlier, is buried in comparatively modest surroundings near the Slavín monument (see p.154). The *Pražské jaro* festival begins with a procession from his grave to the Obecní dům, on the anniversary of his death (May 12).

The cemetery is open daily: March, April & Oct 8am–6pm; May–Sept 8am–7pm; Nov–Feb 9am–4pm.

Other graves that attract (mostly Czech) pilgrims are those of the nineteenth-century writer Božena Němcová, by the east end of the church; and playwright Karel Čapek, whose grave faces the arcades – he coined one of the two Czech words to have entered the English language, "robot" (the other is "pistol"). Several graves of lesser-known individuals stand out artistically, too: in particular, František

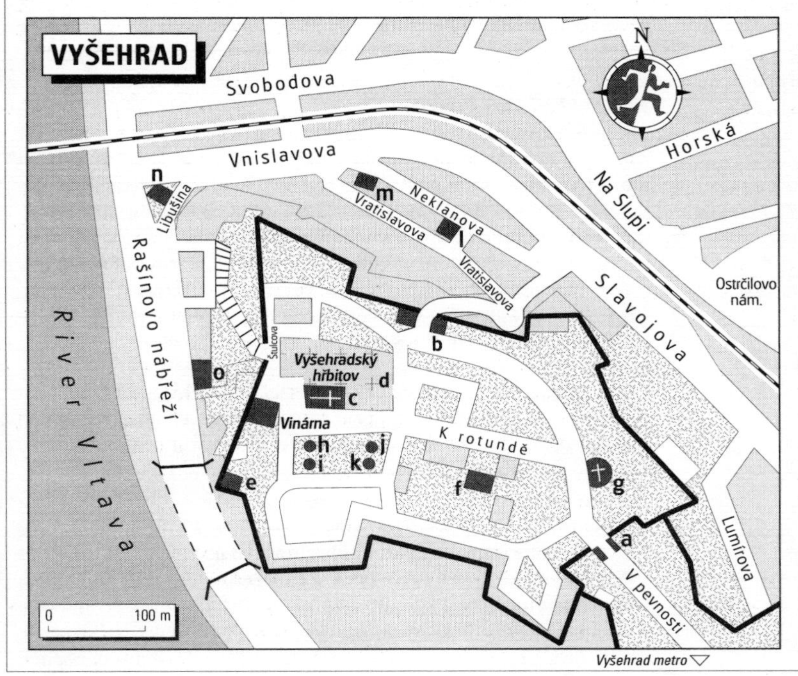

Bílek's towering statue of *Sorrow* on the grave of the writer Václav Beneš Třebízský, which aroused a storm of protest when it was first unveiled; Bohumil Kafka's headstone for Dr Josef Kaizl, with a woman's face peeping out from the grave; and Karel Hladík's modern *Cathedral* sculpture, which sits above his own grave.

The focus of the cemetery, though, is the **Slavín monument (d)**, a big, bulky stele built in 1893 to a design by Antonín Wiehl, covered in commemorative plaques and topped by a sarcophagus and a statue representing Genius. It's the communal resting place of more than fifty Czech artists, including the painter Alfons Mucha, the sculptors Josef Václav Myslbek and Ladislav Šaloun, the architect Josef Gočár, and the opera singer Ema Destinová.

Mácha's remains were brought here from a cemetery in Litoměřice in 1938, when the Nazis took over the Sudetenland.

The grave of the Romantic poet **Karel Hynek Mácha** was the assembly point for the demonstration on November 17, 1989, which triggered the Velvet Revolution. This was organized to commemorate the 50th anniversary of the Nazi attack on Czech higher education institutions in 1939. Student protests against the German occupation reached a peak on October 28, 1939, when violent clashes resulted in the death of medical student, **Jan Opletal**; his funeral, on November 11, was accompanied by more violent disturbances. On November 17, the Nazis took the initiative, executing various student leaders, packing thousands off to the camps and shutting down all Czech higher education institutes. Fifty years later, in 1989, the cemetery was the gathering point for a 50,000-strong crowd who attempted to march from here to Wenceslas Square.

The rest of the fortress

The next best thing to do after a stroll around the cemetery is to head off and explore the **Kasematy** (dungeons), which you enter via the **Cihelná brána (b)**. After a short guided tour of a section of the underground passageways underneath the ramparts, you enter a vast storage hall, which shelters several of the original statues from the Charles Bridge, and, when the lights are switched off, reveals a camera obscura image of a tree.

The Cihelná brána is open daily 9.30am–4.30 pm; 20Kč.

The rest of the deserted fortress makes for a pleasant afternoon stroll; you can walk almost the entire length of the ramparts, which give some superb views out across the city. The small museum of historical drawings in the hradební věž (e) and the exhibition in the neo-Gothic Nové děkanství (f) are both pretty dull. The heavily restored rotunda of **sv Martin (g)** – one of a number of Romanesque rotundas scattered across Prague – is the sole survivor of the medieval fortress built by Vratislav II in the eleventh century; it's only open for services.

If the weather's good, though, time is probably better spent lounging on the patch of grass to the south of the church, where you'll come across the gargantuan statues by Myslbek that used to grace the city's Palackého most. Four couples are dotted across the green, all taken from Prague legends: *Přemysl and Libuše* (h), the husband and wife team who founded Prague and started Bohemia's first royal dynasty, the Přemyslids; *Lumír and Píseň* (i), the legendary Czech singer and his muse, Song; *Záboj and Slavoj* (**j**), two mythical Czech warriors; and *Ctirad and Nárka* (**k**), for whose story, see p.174.

Czech Cubism in Vyšehrad

Even if you harbour only a passing interest in modern architecture, it's worth seeking out the cluster of **Cubist villas** below the fortress in Vyšehrad. Whereas Czech Art Nouveau was heavily influenced by the Viennese Secession, it was Paris rather than the imperial capital that provided the stimulus for the short-lived but extremely productive Czech Cubist movement. In 1911, the *Skupina výtvarných umělců* or SVU (Group of Fine Artists) was founded in Prague, and quickly became the movement's organizing force. **Pavel Janák** was the SVU's chief theorist, **Josef Gočár** its most illustrious exponent, but **Josef Chochol** was the most successful practitioner of the style in Prague.

Cubism is associated mostly with painting, and the unique contribution of its Czech offshoot was to apply the theory to **furniture** (some of which is now on permanent display at the Dům U Černé Matky boží; see p.103) and **architecture**. In Vyšehrad alone, Chochol completed three buildings, close to one another below the fortress, using prismatic shapes and angular lines to produce the sharp geometric contrasts of light and dark shadows characteristic of Cubist painting. Outside the Czech Republic, only the preparatory drawings by the French architect Duchamp-Villon for his *Maison Cubiste* (never realized), can be considered remotely similar.

The SVU's plans were cut short by World War I, after which Janák and Gočár attempted to establish a specifically Czechoslovak style of architecture incorporating prewar Cubism. The style was dubbed **Rondo-Cubism** since the prismatic moulding had been replaced by semicircular motifs, but only a few projects got off the ground before Czech architects turned to the functionalist ideals of the international modernist movement.

Cubist and Rondo-Cubist buildings in Prague

Prague's unique Cubist and Rondo-Cubist buildings, most of which are covered in the text, are scattered right across the city. Here is a checklist of where to find the best examples of the style.

Staré Město

Gočár's Dům U černé Matky boží	p.103

Nové Město

Janák & Zasche's Palác Adria	p.132
Blecha & Králíček's lamppost	p.132
Gočár's Banka legií	p.139
Králíček's Diamant	p.141

Vyšehrad

Chochol's nájemný obytný dům	p.156
Belada's nájemný obytný dům	p.156
Chochol's Kovařovicova vila	p.156
Chochol's Rodinný trojdům	p.156

The suburbs

Gočár's Rodinný dvojdům	p.162

The buildings

The most impressive example of Czech Cubist architecture, brilliantly exploiting its angular location, is Chochol's **nájemný obytný dům** (l), an apartment block at Neklanova 30, begun in 1913 for František Hodek and now housing a restaurant on its ground floor. Further along Neklanova at no. 2, there's Antonín Belada's **nájemný obytný dům** (m), with its Cubist facade, and around the corner is the most ambitious project of the lot – Chochol's **Kovařovicova vila** (n), which backs onto Libušina. The front, on Rašínovo nábřeží, is presently concealed behind some overenthusiastic shrubs, but it's still possible to appreciate the clever, slightly askew layout of the garden, designed right down to its zigzag garden railings. Further along the embankment is Chochol's largest commission, the **Rodinný trojdům** (o), a large building complex with a heavy mansard roof, a central "Baroque" gable with a pedimental frieze, and room enough for three families.

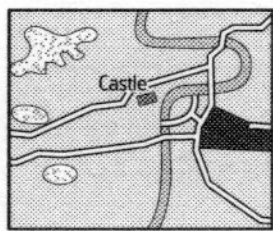

Vinohrady

Southeast of Nové Město is the well-to-do late nineteenth-century suburb of **VINOHRADY**, home over the years to many of the country's most notable personages. Under the Communists, the suburb became decidedly run-down, but with the re-emergence of the property market, Vinohrady has once more become a desirable part of town to live in, with two spacious parks – **Riegrovy sady**, to the north, and **Havlíčkovy sady**, to the south – and a fabulous array of turn-of-the-century apartment buildings. In terms of conventional sightseeing, however, the area is definitely low priority, but there are a few places here (and in neighbouring Žižkov) worth a visit, most of them quick and easy to reach by metro.

For details of cafés, pubs and restaurants in Vinohrady, see p.218, p.222 and p.227.

If Vinohrady has a centre, it's the leafy square of **náměstí Míru**, a good introduction to the aspirations of this confident, bourgeois neighbourhood. At its centre stands the brick-built basilica of **sv Ludmila**, designed by Josef Mocker in the late 1880s in a severe neo-Gothic style, though the interior furnishings have the odd flourish of Art Nouveau. In front of the church is a statue commemorating the **Čapek brothers**, writer Karel and painter Josef, who together symbolized the golden era of the interwar republic. Karel died in 1938, shortly after the Nazi invasion, while Josef perished in Belsen seven years later; their influence was deliberately underplayed by the Communists, and the memorial was only erected in the 1990s. Two more buildings on the square deserve attention, the most flamboyant being the **Divadlo na Vinohradech**, built in 1907, using Art Nouveau and neo-Baroque elements in equal measure. More subdued, but equally ornate inside and out, is the district's former **Národní dům**, a grandiose neo-Renaissance edifice from the 1890s housing a ballroom/concert hall and restaurant.

From náměstí Míru, block after block of decaying tenements, each clothed in its own individual garment of sculptural decoration, form a grid plan of grand bourgeois avenues stretching eastwards to the city's great cemeteries (see p.158). If the weather's nice, you could stroll your way to Plečnik's church (see below), dropping in at U knihomola (The Bookworm), Mánesova 79, one of Prague's best foreign-language **bookshops** (see p.244). However, distances are deceptive, and you may prefer to take the metro.

Plečník's church

Vinohrady's other main square, **náměstí Jiřího z Poděbrad**, halfway between náměstí Míru and the cemeteries, contains Prague's most celebrated modern church, **Nejsvětější Srdce Páně** (Most Sacred Heart of Our Lord), built in 1928 by Josip Plečník, the Slovene architect responsible for much of the remodelling of the Hrad (see box on p.50). It's a marvellously eclectic and individualistic work, employing a sophisticated potpourri of architectural styles: a Neoclassical pediment and a great slab of a clock tower with a giant transparent face in imitation of a Gothic rose window, as well as the bricks and mortar of contemporary constructivism. Plečník also had a sharp eye for detail; look out for the little gold crosses inset into the brickwork like stars, inside and out, and the celestial orbs of light suspended above the heads of the congregation. If you can collar the priest, it may be possible to climb the clock tower.

Janák and Gočár's functionalist churches

Further afield are two more uncompromisingly modernist churches. The first is the **Husův sbor** (Hussite Church), three blocks south of Plečník's church down U vodárny, on the corner of Dykova. Built in the early 1930s by Pavel Janák, the church's most salient feature is its freestanding hollow tower, which encloses a corkscrew spiral staircase and is topped by a giant copper chalice, symbol of the Hussite faith. A memorial on the wall commemorates the church's pioneering role in the Prague Uprising against the Nazis in May 1945, when it served as a clandestine Czech resistance headquarters.

Josef Gočár's equally severe, functionalist church of **sv Václav**, built around the same time, lies a kilometre or so southeast on náměstí Svatopluka Čecha; take tram #4 or #22 from náměstí Miru or the bottom of U vodárny. Here it forms the centrepiece of a sloping green square, with a distinctive stepped roof rising up from a slender, smoothly rendered 80m-high tower.

Žižkov

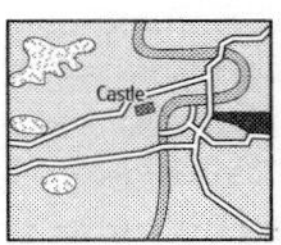

Though they share much the same architectural heritage, **ŽIŽKOV**, unlike Vinohrady, is a traditionally working-class area, and was a Communist Party stronghold even before the war, earning it the nickname "Red Žižkov". Nowadays its peeling turn-of-the-century tenements are home to a large proportion of Prague's Romany community, and it boasts more pubs per head than any other district in Prague, and some of its roughest nightlife. The main reason for venturing into Žižkov is to visit its two landmarks – ancient (Žižkov hill) and modern (the television tower) – and the city's main cemeteries, at the eastern end of Vinohradská.

The Žižkov TV tower

The TV Tower is open daily 10am–11pm; 30Kč.

At over 100m in height, the **Žižkov TV tower** (Televizní vysílač), is the tallest (and the most unpopular) building in Prague. Close up, though, it's difficult not to be impressed by this truly intimidating piece of futuristic architecture, its smooth grey exterior giving no hint of humanity. Begun in the 1970s in a desperate bid to jam West German television transmission, the tower only become fully operational in the 1990s. In the course of its construction, however, the Communists saw fit to demolish part of a nearby Jewish cemetery, that had served the community between 1787 and 1891; a small section survives to the northwest of the tower. From the fifth-floor café or the viewing platform on the eighth floor, you can enjoy a spectacular view across Prague. To get to the tower, take the metro to Jiřího z Poděbrad and walk northeast a couple of blocks – it's difficult to miss.

The cemeteries

The cemeteries are open daily dawn to dusk. The nearest metro to the Olšany cemeteries is Flora; the nearest metro to the war cemetery is Želivského.

There's a memorial to Palach and other victims of the Communist era on Wenceslas Square (see p.130), and a box on Gottwald on p.107.

Approaching from the west, the first and the largest of Prague's vast cemeteries – each of which is bigger than the entire Jewish quarter – are the **Olšanské hřbitovy**, originally created for the victims of the great plague epidemic of 1680. The perimeter walls are lined with glass cabinets, stacked like shoe-boxes, containing funereal urns and mementoes, while the graves themselves are a mixed bag of artistic achievements, reflecting the funereal fashions of the day as much as the character of the deceased. The cemeteries are divided into districts and crisscrossed with cobbled streets; at each gate there's a map, and an aged janitor ready to point you in the right direction.

The cemeteries' two most famous incumbents are an ill-fitting couple: Klement Gottwald, the country's first Communist president, whose ashes were removed from the mausoleum on Žižkov hill after 1989 and reinterred here, and Jan Palach, the philosophy student who set light to himself in January 1969 in protest at the Soviet occupation. More than 750,000 people attended Palach's funeral in January 1969, and in an attempt to put a stop to the annual vigils at his graveside, the secret police removed his body in 1973 and reburied him in his home town, 60km outside Prague. His place was taken by an unknown woman, Maria Jedličková, who for the next seventeen years had her grave covered in flowers instead. Finally, in 1990, Palach's body was returned to Olšany; you'll find it just to the east of the main entrance on Vinohradská.

To the east of Olšany cemeteries, and usually totally deserted, is the **Vojenský hřbitov** (Military Cemetery); the entrance is 200m up Jana Želivského, on the right. Its centrepiece is the monument to the 436 Soviet soldiers who lost their lives on May 9, 1945 in the liberation of Prague, surrounded by a small, tufty meadow dotted with simple white crosses. Nearby, the graves of Czechs who died fighting for the Habsburgs on the Italian front in World War I are laid out in a semicircle.

Nový Židovský hřbitov (New Jewish Cemetery)

Immediately south of the war cemetery is the **Nový Židovský hřbitov**, founded in the 1890s, when the one by the Žižkov TV tower was full (see opposite); it was designed to last for a century, with room for 100,000 graves. It's a melancholy spot, particularly so in the east of the cemetery, where large empty allotments wait in vain to be filled by the generation who perished in the Holocaust. In fact, the community is now so small that it's unlikely the graveyard will ever be full. Most people come here to visit **Franz Kafka**'s grave, 400m east along the south wall and signposted from the entrance. He is buried, along with his mother and father (both of whom outlived him), beneath a plain headstone; the plaque below commemorates his three sisters who died in the camps.

The cemetery is open daily except Sat: April–Aug 8am–5pm; Sept–March 8am–4pm. For more on Kafka's associations with Prague, see pp.118–119.

Žižkov hill

Žižkov hill (also known as Vítkov) is the thin green wedge of land that separates Žižkov from Karlín, the grid-plan industrial district to the north. From its westernmost point, which juts out almost to the edge of Nové Město, is the definitive panoramic view over the city centre. It was here, on July 14, 1420, that the Hussites enjoyed their first and finest victory at the **Battle of Vítkov**, under the inspired leadership of the one-eyed general, Jan Žižka (hence the name of the district). Ludicrously outnumbered by more than ten to one, Žižka and his fanatically motivated troops thoroughly trounced Emperor Sigismund and his papal forces.

Despite its overblown totalitarian aesthetics, the giant concrete **Žižkov monument** which graces the crest of the hill, was actually built between the wars as a memorial to the Czechoslovak Legion who fought against the Habsburgs – the gargantuan equestrian statue of the mace-wielding Žižka, which fronts the monument, is reputedly the world's largest. The building was later used by the Nazis as an arsenal, and eventually became a Communist mausoleum: presidents Gottwald, Zápotocký and Svoboda were all buried here, along with the Unknown Soldier and various other Party hacks. Žižkov was an ideal resting place, lying as it does in the heart of "Red Žižkov", from where the Communists drew so much of their pre-1948 working-class support. Gottwald himself was originally pickled and embalmed (à la Lenin), but a fire damaged his corpse so badly that the leader had to be cremated in 1963. In 1990, the remaining bodies were cremated and quietly reinterred in Olšany, and at present there's an ongoing legal battle over what should happen next with the monument.

Jaroslav Seifert of Žižkov

The Czech Nobel prize-winning poet **Jaroslav Seifert** (1901–86) was born and bred in the Žižkov district. He was one of the founding members of the Czechoslovak Communist Party, and in 1920 helped found Devětsil, the most daring and provocative avant-garde movement of the interwar republic. Always accused of harbouring bourgeois sentiments, Seifert and eight other Communist writers were expelled from the Party when Gottwald and the Stalinists hijacked the Party at the Fifth Congress in 1929. After the 1948 coup, he became a *persona non grata*, though he rose to prominence briefly during the 1956 Writers' Union congress, when he attempted to lead a rebellion against the Stalinists. Later on, he became involved in Charter 77, and in 1984, amidst much controversy, he became the one and only Czech to win the Nobel Prize for Literature.

The Armádní muzeum is open April–Oct Tues–Sun 10am–6pm; Nov–April Mon–Fri 9am–5pm; 20Kč. For the pre-1914 military museum, see p.66.

To get to the monument, take the metro to Florenc, walk under the railway lines, and then up the steep lane U památníku. On the right as you climb the hill is the **Armádní muzeum** (Army Museum), guarded by a handful of unmanned tanks, howitzers and armoured vehicles. Before 1989, this museum was a glorification of the Warsaw Pact, pure and simple; its recent overhaul has produced a much more evenly balanced account of both world wars, particularly in its treatment of the previously controversial subjects of the Czechoslovak Legion, the Heydrich assassination (see pp.144–145) and the Prague Uprising. The collection now covers only the period from 1914 to 1945.

Chapter 8

Holešovice and the western suburbs

The northern and western **suburbs** on the left bank of the Vltava are spread over a much larger area than those to the east of the river. They are also far more varied: some, like Holešovice and parts of Smíchov, date from the nineteenth century, whereas Dejvice and Střešovice were laid out between the wars as well-to-do garden suburbs. The left bank also boasts a great deal more greenery, including the city's largest public park, Stromovka. All this goes to make up

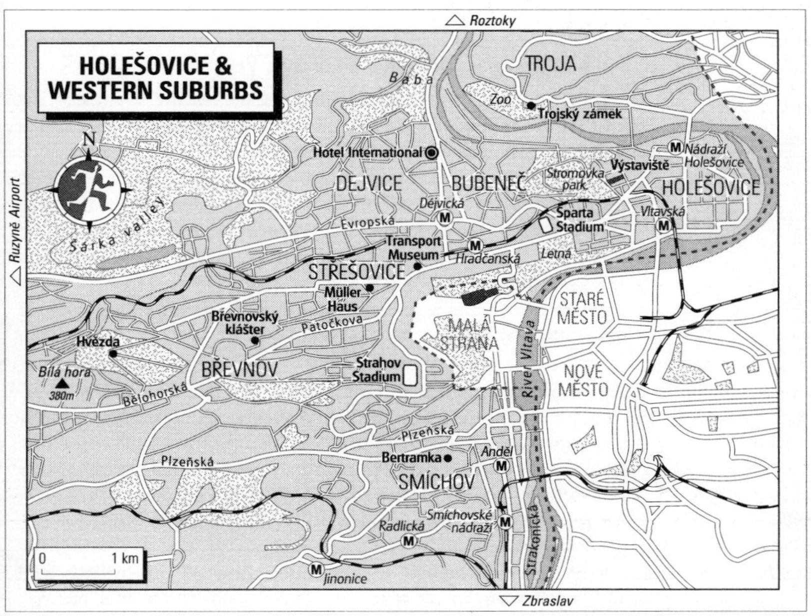

a fascinating patchwork of communities, which few tourists bother to see. It's worth the effort, though, if only to remind yourself that Prague doesn't begin and end at the Charles Bridge.

There are several specific sights in each suburb that can lend structure to your meanderings. The single most important sight is the **Veletržní palác** in **Holešovice**, the long-awaited home for the nation's modern art collection. Another popular destination is the **Bertramka** (Mozart Museum) in **Smíchov**. Other sights – like the functionalist villas in **Dejvice** and **Střešovice** – are of more specialized interest; and some are simply unknown to most visitors, like the exquisite Renaissance chateau of **Hvězda**.

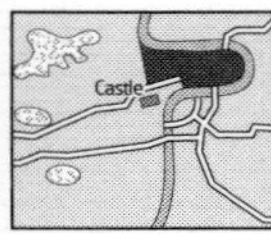

Holešovice and Bubeneč

The late nineteenth- and early twentieth-century districts of **HOLEŠOVICE** and **BUBENEČ**, tucked into a huge U-bend in the Vltava, have little in the way of truly magnificent architecture, but they make up for it with two huge splodges of green: to the south, **Letná**, overlooking the city centre, and to the north, **Stromovka**, bordering the Výstaviště funfair and international trade fair grounds. Holešovice also has a couple of excellent museums: the city's **Národní technické muzeum**, which shows off the Czechs' past scientific and industrial achievements, and the aforementioned **Veletržní palác**, Prague's impressive new modern art museum.

Chotkovy sady and the Bílkova vila

These first two sights are strictly speaking part of the Hradčany that lies to the northeast of the castle, but, for convenience, they begin this chapter. The easiest way to this part of town is to take tram #22 one stop from Malostranská metro to the Belvedér, or the metro to Hradčanská metro and head up Tychonova, a street flanked on one side by a military barracks and training ground, and on the other by a series of semi-detached houses. These include **Josef Gočár**'s rodinný dvojdům at nos. 4 & 6, built with a traditional mansard roof in a restrained Cubist style, similar to that employed on the Dům U černé Matky boží in Staré Město (see p.103).

Chotkovy sady

The Belvedér and the Královská zahrada are both covered in Chapter 1 (see p.64)

At the top of Tychonova, the leafy avenue of Marianské hradby slopes down to the left, past the Belvedér, to the **Chotkovy sady**, Prague's first public park, founded in 1833 by the ecologically minded city governor, Count Chotek. The atmosphere here is a lot more relaxed than in the nearby Královská zahrada, and you can happily stretch out on the grass and soak up the sun, or head for the south wall, which enjoys an unrivalled view of the bridges and islands of the Vltava. At the centre of the park there's a bizarre,

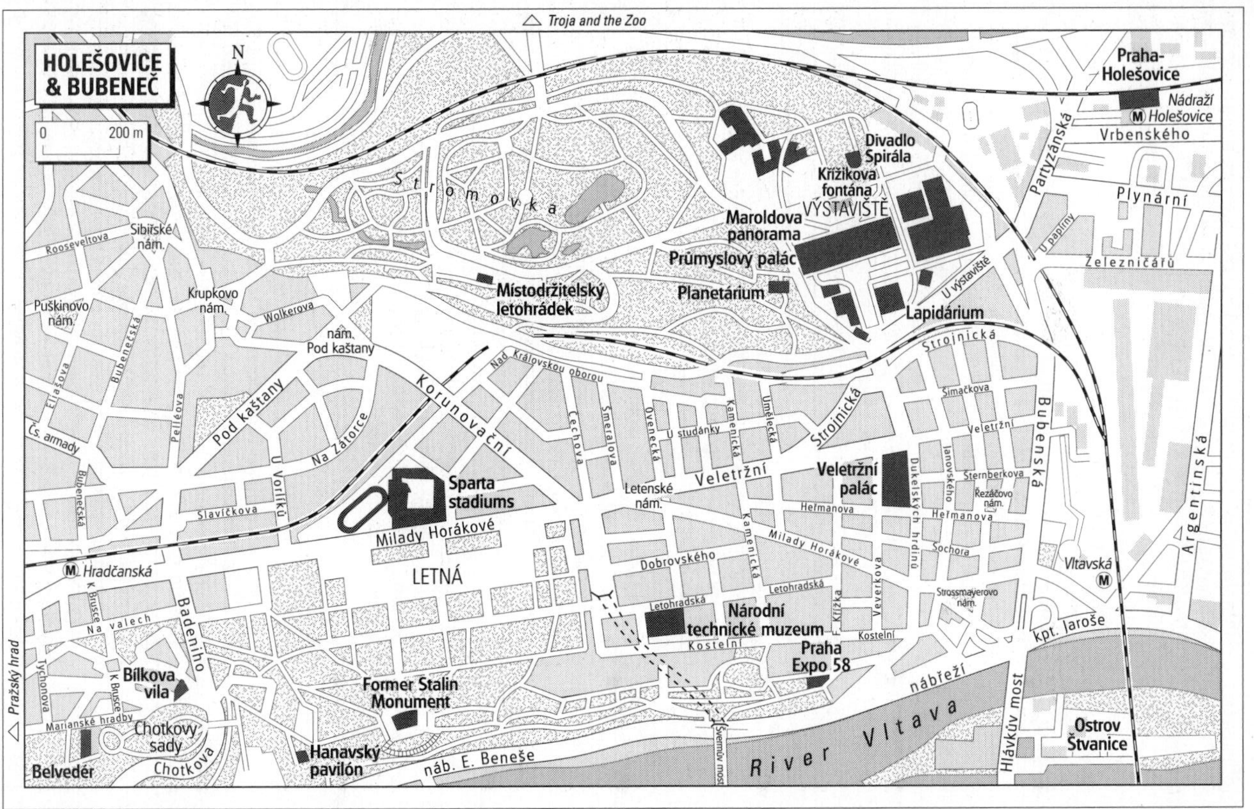
HOLEŠOVICE & BUBENEČ
N
0
200 m
Troja and the Zoo
Pražský hrad
Praha-Holešovice
Nádraží
Holešovice
Vrbenského
Plynární
Železničářů
Argentinská
Partyzánská
U papírny
Bubenská
Vltavská
kpt. Jaroše
Ostrov Štvanice
Hlávkův most
Divadlo Spirála
Křižíkova fontána
VÝSTAVIŠTĚ
Maroldova panorama
Průmyslový palác
Planetárium
Lapidárium
U výstaviště
Stromovka
Místodržitelský letohrádek
Strojnická
Šimáčkova
Veletržní
Šternberkova
Řezáčovo nám.
Heřmanova
Janovského
Sochora
Strossmayerovo nám.
Dukelských hrdinů
Veletržní palác
Veverkova
Kostelní
Praha Expo 58
Národní technické muzeum
F. Křížka
nábřeží
River Vltava
Švermův most
Umělecká
Kamenická
U studánky
Letenské nám.
Ovenecká
Šmeralova
Čechova
Nad Královskou oborou
Milady Horákové
Letohradská
Dobrovského
Korunovační
Sparta stadiums
LETNÁ
Former Stalin Monument
Hanavský pavilón
náb. E. Beneše
Na Zátorce
Pod kaštany
nám. Pod kaštany
Wolkerova
U Vorlíků
Slavíčkova
Krupkovo nám.
Sibiřské nám.
Pelléova
Bubenečská
Rooseveltova
Puškinovo nám.
Eliášova
Čs. armady
Hradčanská
K Brusce
Na valech
Badeniho
Bílkova vila
Chotkovy sady
Chotkova
Marianské hradby
Tychonova
Belvedér

melodramatic grotto-like memorial to the nineteenth-century Romantic poet Julius Zeyer, an elaborate monument from which life-sized characters from Zeyer's works, carved in white marble, emerge from the blackened rocks amid much drapery.

Bílkova vila

The Bílkova vila is open mid-May to mid-Oct Tues–Sun 10am–6pm; mid-Oct to mid-May Sat & Sun 10am–5pm; 80Kč.

Across the road from the park, hidden behind its overgrown garden at Mieckiewiczova 1, the **Bílkova vila** honours one of the most original of all Czech sculptors, František Bílek (1872–1941). Born in a part of South Bohemia steeped in the Hussite tradition, Bílek lived a monkish life, spending years in spiritual contemplation, reading the works of Hus and other Czech reformers. The Bílkova vila was built in 1911 to the artist's own design, intended as both a "cathedral of art" and the family home. At first sight, it appears a strangely mute red-brick building, out of keeping with the extravagant Symbolist style of Bílek's sculptures. It's meant to symbolize a cornfield, with the front porch supported by giant sheaves of corn; only the sculptural group, the fleeing Comenius and his followers, in the garden, gives a clue as to what lies within.

Inside, the brickwork gives way to bare stone walls lined with Bílek's religious sculptures, giving the impression that you've walked into a chapel rather than an artist's studio: "a workshop and temple", in Bílek's own words. In addition to his sculptural and relief work in wood and stone, often wildly expressive and spiritually tortured, there are also ceramics, graphics and a few mementoes of Bílek's life. His work is little known outside his native country, but his contemporary admirers included Franz Kafka, Julius Zeyer, and Otokar Březina, whose poems and novels provided the inspiration for much of Bílek's art. Bílek's living quarters have also been restored and opened to the public, with much of the original wooden furniture, designed and carved by Bílek himself, still in place. Check out the dressing table for his wife, shaped like some giant church lectern, and the wardrobe decorated with a border of hearts, a penis, a nose, an ear, an eye plus the sun, stars and moon.

Letná

A high plateau hovering above the city, the flat green expanse of the **Letná** plain has long been the traditional assembly point for invading and besieging armies. It was laid out as a public park in the mid-nineteenth century, but its main post-1948 function was as the site of the May Day parades. For these, thousands of citizens were dragooned into marching past the south side of the city's main football ground, the Sparta stadium, where the old Communist cronies would take the salute from a giant red podium.

On November 26, 1989, the park was the scene of a more genuine expression of popular sentiment, when over 750,000 people gathered here to join in the call for a general strike against the Communist regime. Unprecedented scenes followed in April 1990, when a million Catholics came to hear Pope John Paul II speak on his first visit to an Eastern Bloc country other than his native Poland. The present-day Communists still gather here on May 1 in rather smaller numbers.

The former Stalin monument

Letná's – indeed Prague's – most famous monument is one which no longer exists. The **Stalin monument**, the largest in the world, was once visible from almost every part of the city: a thirty-metre-high granite sculpture portraying a procession of Czechs and Russians being led to Communism by the Pied Piper figure of Stalin, but popularly dubbed *tlačenice* (the crush) because of its resemblance to a Communist-era bread queue. Designed by Jiří Štursa and Otakar Švec, it took 600 workers 500 days to erect the 14,200-tonne monster. Švec, the sculptor, committed suicide shortly before it was unveiled, as his wife had done three years previously, leaving all his money to a school for blind children, since they at least would not have to see his creation. It was eventually revealed to the cheering masses on May 1, 1955 – the first and last popular celebration to take place at the monument. Within a year, Khrushchev had denounced his predecessor and, after pressure from Moscow, the monument was blown to smithereens by a series of explosions spread over a fortnight in 1962.

All that remains above ground is the statue's vast concrete platform and steps, on the southern edge of the Letná plain, now graced with David Černý's symbolic giant red metronome (which is lit up at night); it's also a favourite spot for skateboarders and another good viewpoint, with the central stretch of the Vltava glistening in the afternoon sun. Built into the hillside below is Prague's one and only nuclear bunker, intended to preserve the Party elite, post-armageddon. For years, it was actually used to store the city's slowly rotting potato mountain; more recently it has been sporadically squatted and used as a nightclub venue.

If you're in need of some refreshment, head for the **Hanavský pavilón**, a café and restaurant (see p.228) near the metronome. Originally built for the 1891 Prague Exhibition, it looks rather like a Russian Orthodox church. It was devised by Count Hanavský as a showpiece of wrought-ironwork, in a flamboyant style which anticipated the arrival of Art Nouveau a few years later.

Národní technické muzeum

Despite its dull title, the **Národní technické muzeum** (National Technical Museum), on Kostelní, is a surprisingly interesting museum, with an interactive gallery or two, and even the odd English caption appearing here and there. Its showpiece hanger-like main hall contains an impressive gallery of motorbikes, Czech and foreign, and a wonderful collection of old planes, trains and automobiles from Czechoslovakia's industrial heyday between the wars when the country's Škoda cars and Tatra soft-top stretch limos were really something to brag about. The

The Národní technické muzeum is open Tues–Sun 9am–5pm; 40Kč.

oldest car in the collection is Laurin & Klement's 1898 *Präsident*, more of a motorized carriage than a car; the museum also boasts the oldest Bugatti in the world. Upstairs, there are interactive displays (a rarity in a Czech museum) tracing the development of early photography, and a collection of some of Kepler's and Tycho Brahe's astrological instruments. Below ground, a mock-up of a coal mine offers guided tours every other hour, at 11am, 1pm and 3pm.

Veletržní palác

The Veletržní palác is open Tues–Sun 10am–6pm, Thurs until 9pm; 120Kč.

After several decades of bureaucratic and political wrangling, the Národní galerie's vast collection of twentieth-century Czech art has finally been put on permanent display in the **Veletržní palác** (Trade Fair Palace). In addition, there's a small but judiciously chosen selection of European art from the late nineteenth and early twentieth centuries. And last but not least, there's the building itself, Prague's ultimate functionalist masterpiece, a seven-storey building constructed in 1928 by Oldřich Tyl and Josef Fuchs. The building doesn't look that great from the outside, but inside, its gleaming white vastness is suitably awesome. Even the normally hypercritical Le Corbusier, who visited the building the year it was completed, was impressed: "Seeing the Trade Fair Palace, I realised how to make large buildings, having so far built only several relatively small houses on a low budget."

Despite the fact that the Národní galerie doesn't even use the main exhibition hall, but confines itself to the north wing of the building, the museum is both big and bewildering. Special exhibitions occupy the ground, first and fourth floors; from the ground floor you can stare up at the glass-roofed atrium, a glorious space for wacky modern pieces of art, overlooked by six floors of balconies. The permanent collection occupies the second and third floors, but there is no easy way to follow it chronologically. The best approach is to take the lift to the third floor and start with the Czech art from 1900 to 1960 (as the account below does), since this was the museum's original *raison d'être*. On each floor, there's a side room, with an art studio or library, where you (and your kids, if you have any) can relax and read or draw.

Czech modern art (Ceské moderní umění) 1900–60

The collection of **Czech modern art from 1900 to 1960**, on the third floor, gives a pretty good introduction to the country's artistic peaks and troughs. To be honest, there's too much stuff here

Situated at the corner of Dukelských hrdinů and Veletržní, some distance from the nearest metro station, the Veletržní palác gets nothing like the number of visitors it should. **To get there** by public transport, catch tram #5 from náměstí Republiky, tram #12 from Malostranská metro, tram #17 from Staroměstská metro, or tram #5, #12 or #17 from Nádraží Holešovice.

– paintings, sculptures and installations – to take in at one go, and the following account aims simply to draw out the works of the most significant artists.

The collection begins with a smattering of works by two of the most successful Czech exponents of moody post-Impressionism: **Antonín Slavíček**, whose landscapes range from the Klimt-like *Birch Mood* to paintings such as *In the Rain*, which are full of foreboding; and **Antonín Hudeček**, whose canvases, such as *Moon Landscape*, are even more dream-like and ethereal.

These are followed by a whole series of works by **František Kupka**, who was Czech by birth, but lived and worked in Paris from 1896. In international terms, Kupka is by far the most important Czech painter of this century, having secured his place in the history of art by being (possibly) the first artist in the western world to exhibit abstract paintings. *Fugue in Two Colours* (*Amorpha*), one of the two abstract paintings Kupka exhibited at the Salon d'Automne in 1912, is displayed here. First, though, before you reach this seminal work are earlier, pre-abstract paintings such as *Money*, which formed part of a satirical cycle; a Munch-like portrait of a Parisian cabaret actress; and *Piano Keys – Lake*, a strange, abstracted, though by no means abstract, work from 1909. You'll come across more of Kupka's later abstract and cosmic works elsewhere in the collection.

While Kupka is thought of by many as a French artist, **Jan Preisler** couldn't be more thoroughly Czech. His mosaics and murals, which can be found on Art Nouveau buildings all over Prague, tend to be ethereal and slightly detached, whereas his oil paintings, like the cycle of *Black Lake* paintings displayed here, are more typically melancholic. Several wood sculptures by **František Bílek**, one of the country's finest sculptors, offer a taste of his anguished style, but for a more comprehensive insight into his art, you should visit the Bílkova vila (see p.164).

The Edvard Munch retrospective held in Prague in 1905 prompted the formation in 1907 of the first Czech modern art movement, Osma (The Eight), three of whose members feature in **Bohumil Kubišta**'s defiant *Triple Portrait* from the same year. Works like **Emil Filla**'s *Ace of Hearts* and *Reader of Dostoyevsky* – in which the subject appears to have fallen asleep, though, in fact, he's mind-blown – are both firmly within the Expressionist genre. However, it wasn't long before several of the Osma group were beginning to experiment with Cubism. Filla eventually adopted the style wholesale, helping found the Cubist SVU in 1911; Kubišta refused to follow suit, instead pursuing his own unique blend of Cubo-Expressionism, typified by the wonderful self-portrait, *The Smoker*. Another artist who stands apart from the crowd is **Jan Zrzavy**, who joined SVU, but during a long career pursued his own peculiarly individual style typified by paintings such as *Valley of Sorrow*, which depicts a magical, imaginary and very stylized world.

Josef Čapek, brother of the playwright, is another Czech clearly influenced by Cubism, as seen in works such as *Accordion Player*, but like Kubišta, Čapek found Filla's doctrinaire approach difficult to take, and he left SVU in 1912. Look out, too, for the sculptures of **Otto Gutfreund**, a member of SVU, whose works range from his Cubo-Expressionist *Anxiety* (1912) to the more purely Cubist *Sitting Woman* (1915). After World War I, during which he joined the Foreign Legion but was interned for three years for insubordination, Gutfreund switched to depicting everyday folk in technicolour, in a style that prefigures Socialist Realism, as in his self-portrait bust and *Business*. His life was cut short in 1927, when he drowned while swimming in the Vltava. Other sculptures worth noting are the models of **Otakar Švec**'s motorcycle and racing-car, two great three-dimensional depictions of the optimistic speed of the modern age.

Devětsil, founded in 1920 and the driving force of the Czech avant-garde between the wars, is represented here by the movement's two leading artists: **Toyen** (Marie Čermínová) and her life-long companion **Jindřich Štyrský**, whose abstract works – they dubbed them "Artificialism" – reveal the couple's interest in the French Surrealists. Predictably enough, however, there are no examples of Štyrský's pornographic photomontages, or Toyen's sexually charged drawings, which form an important part of their work. One Czech artist who had already enthusiastically embraced Surrealism was **Josef Šíma**, who settled permanently in Paris in the 1920s; several of his trademark floating torsoes and cosmic eggs can be seen here. Lastly, be sure to check out the wild kinetic-light sculpture (1936) by **Zdeněk Pešánek**, a world pioneer in the use of neon in art, who created a stir the following year at the Paris Expo with a neon fountain.

Nineteenth- and twentieth-century French art

By far the most popular section of the gallery is the **nineteenth- and twentieth-century French art section** (Francouzské umění 19. a 20. století), on the second floor, featuring anyone of note who hovered around Paris in the fifty years from 1880 onwards. There are few masterpieces here, but it's all high-quality stuff, most of it either purchased for the gallery in 1923, or bequeathed by art dealer Vincenc Kramář in 1960, and until the mid-1990s displayed in the Šternberský palác in Hradčany.

The collection kicks off with several works by **Auguste Rodin**, particularly appropriate given the ecstatic reception given to the Prague exhibition of his work in 1902. Rodin's sculptures are surrounded by works from the advance guard of Impressionism: Courbet, Delacroix, Corot and early Monet and Pissarro. Beyond, the loose brushwork, cool turquoise and emerald colours of **Auguste Renoir**'s *Lovers* are typical of the period of so-called High Impressionism. There's also a surprisingly good collection of works by **Pablo Picasso**, including several paintings and sculptures from his transitional early Cubist period (1907–08); his *Landscape with Bridge* from 1909 uses precisely the kind of prisms and geometric blocks of shading that influenced the Czech Cubist architects.

Among the other works here, there's a characteristically sunny, Provençal *Green Wheat* by **Vincent van Gogh**, a couple of paintings by Paul Cézanne and Georges Seurat, and the only known self-portrait by **Henri Rousseau**, at once both confident and comical, the artist depicting himself, palette in hand, against a boat decked with bunting and the recently erected Eiffel Tower. *Bonjour Monsieur Gauguin* is a tongue-in-cheek tribute to Courbet's painting of similar name, with Gauguin donning a suitably bohemian beret and overcoat. Another first-rate portrait is *Joaquina*, painted in 1910–11 by **Henri Matisse**, in which both Fauvist and Oriental influences are evident. There's even a painting by Le Corbusier himself, which clearly shows the influence of Fernand Léger, one of whose works hangs close by.

Twentieth-century European art

If the French art section is modest, the collection of **twentieth-century European art** (Evropské umění 20. století) is minuscule. It does, however, contain a couple of minor gems, beginning with **Gustav Klimt**'s mischievous *Virgins*, a mass of naked bodies and tangled limbs painted over in psychedelic colours, plus one of the square landscapes he used to like painting during his summer holidays in the Salzkammergut.

Although none of the artists here is Czech, many of them had close connections with Bohemia: the handful of typically vigorous landscapes by **Oskar Kokoschka** date from his brief stay here in the 1930s, when the political temperature got too hot in Vienna, while **Egon Schiele**'s mother came from Český Krumlov, the subject of a gloomy autumnal canvas, *Dead City*. The gallery also owns one of Schiele's most popular female portraits, wrongly entitled *The Artist's Wife*, an unusually graceful and gentle watercolour of a seated woman in green top and black leggings. In contrast, *Pregnant Woman and Death* is a morbidly bleak painting, in which Schiele depicts himself as both the monk of death and the life-giving mother.

Perhaps the most influential artist on show is **Edvard Munch**, whose one canvas, *Dance at the Seaside*, hardly does justice to the considerable effect he had on a generation of Czech artists after his celebrated 1905 Prague exhibition. A sculptor who clearly had an influence on Kokoschka and Schiele is the Belgian, **Georges Minne**, whose emaciated figures could happily feature on either of the Austrians' canvases. Further on, look out for Marc Chagall's *The Circus*, a typically mad work from 1927, and one of Joan Mirò's characteristically abstract Surrealist works, called simply *Composition*.

Czech art 1960–95

The collection of **Czech art from 1960 to 1995** sits rather uncomfortably on the same floor as the French and European art. Most visitors approach it the wrong way round, chronologically speaking, since the section which abuts twentieth-century European art displays Czech works from the 1980s. Still, whichever way you come at it, this is an interesting enough collection, taken at a canter.

Coming from the European art section, Ivan Kafka's *On Potent Impotence* installation should raise a smile, whereas Jiří Sozanský's photos of the destruction of the town of Most to make way for an opencast lignite mine are chilling. Surprisingly there's very little overtly political art here, with the exception of Květa Válová's *Recognition and Amazement*, featuring pairs of Big Brother eyes, and *Great Dialogue* by Karel Nepraš, in which two red figures lambast each other at close quarters with loudspeakers.

As with the 1900–60 gallery, there is a total absence of Socialist Realist works. Instead, the gallery concentrates on artists like **Mikuláš Medek**, whose surrealist and abstract works were more or less banned from public galleries throughout the Communist period. Still, you do get a chance to see a couple of pieces by **Jiří Kolář** – pronounced "collage" - who, coincidentally, specializes in collages of random words and reproductions of other people's paintings. The collection of 1990s works spills over onto the balcony, and includes an entire, hermetically sealed office, by Milan Knížák, which you can peek into.

Výstaviště

Výstaviště is open Tues–Fri 2–10pm, Sat & Sun 10am–10pm; 10Kč.

Five minutes' walk north from the Veletržní palác, up Dukelských hrdinů, takes you right to the front gates of the **Výstaviště** (Exhibition Grounds), a motley assortment of buildings, originally created for the 1891 Prague Exhibition, which have served as the city's main trade fair arena and funfair ever since. From 1948 until the late 1970s, the Communist Party held its rubber-stamp congresses in the flamboyant stained-glass and wrought-iron **Průmyslový palác** at the centre of the complex, and more recently several brand new permanent structures were built for the 1991 Prague Exhibition, including a circular theatre, **Divadlo Spirála**.

The Planetárium is open Mon–Thurs 8am–noon & 1–9pm, Sat & Sun 9.30am–noon & 1–5pm.

The grounds are at their busiest on summer weekends, when hordes of Prague families descend on the place to down hot dogs, drink beer and listen to traditional brass band music. Apart from the annual fairs and lavish special exhibitions, there are a few permanent attractions, such as the city's **Planetárium**, the **Maroldovo panorama** (Tues–Fri 1–5pm, Sat & Sun 11am–5pm), a giant diorama of the 1434 Battle of Lipany (see p.256), and the **Dětský svět** (Tues–Fri 2–5pm, Sat & Sun 11am–5pm), a run-down funfair and playground for kids. In the long summer evenings, there's also an open-air cinema (*letní kino*), and regular performances by the **Křižíkova fontána**, dancing fountains devised for the 1891 Exhibition by the Czech inventor František Křižík, which perform a music and light show to packed audiences; ask at the tourist office, or check the listings magazines, for the current schedule.

Lapidárium

Lastly, Výstaviště also contains the Národní muzeum's **Lapidárium** – immediately on the right as you enter – official depository for the city's sculptures, which are under threat either from demolition or from the weather. It's actually a much overlooked collection, ranging from the eleventh to the nineteenth centuries, arranged chronologically over the course of eight rooms.

The Lapidárium is open Tues–Fri noon–6pm, Sat & Sun 10am–6pm; 20Kč.

The first couple of rooms contain a host of salvaged medieval treasures, such as the slender columns decorated with interlacing from the Romanesque basilica that stood on the site of the city's cathedral. Some of the statues saved from the perils of Prague's polluted atmosphere like the bronze equestrian statue of **Saint George** will be familiar if you've visited Prague Castle (see p.57); others are more difficult to inspect close up in their original sites, such as the figures from the towers of the Charles Bridge; and there are even copies here, too, like the busts from the triforium of St Vitus' Cathedral.

One of the most outstanding sights is what remains of the **Krocín fountain**, in room 3, a highly ornate Renaissance work in red marble, which used to grace the Staroměstské náměstí, but failed to hold water and was eventually dismantled in 1862. The angels smiting devils, now displayed in room 5, are all that could be rescued from the **Marian Column** that used to stand on Staroměstské náměstí, after it had been attacked as a symbol of oppression by marauding Czech nationalists in 1918. Many of the original statues from **Charles Bridge** can be seen in room 6, as well as the ones that were fished out of the Vltava after the flood of 1890. The sculptural group commissioned by the Jesuits is particularly good, featuring their founder Saint Ignatius centre stage, surrounded by figures and animals representing all four known continents.

Several pompous imperial monuments that were bundled off into storage after the demise of the Habsburgs in 1918 round off the museum's collection in room 8. One of the first to be removed was the equestrian bronze statue of **Francis I**, which used to sit under the neo-Gothic baldachin that still stands on Smetanovo nábřeží. By far the most impressive, however, is the bronze statue of **Marshall Radecký**, scourge of the 1848 revolution, carried aloft on a shield by eight Habsburg soldiers, a monument which used to stand on Malostranské náměstí.

Stromovka

To the west of Výstaviště lies the *královská obora* or royal enclosure, more commonly known as **Stromovka**, originally laid out as hunting grounds for the noble occupants of the Hrad, and – again thanks to

Count Chodek – now Prague's largest and leafiest public park. If you're heading north for Troja and the city zoo (see below), a stroll through the park is by far the most pleasant approach. If you want to explore a little more of the park, head west sticking to the park's southern border and you'll come to a water tunnel, built by the surrealist court painter Giuseppe Arcimboldo as part of Rudolf II's ambitious horticultural scheme to carry water from the Vltava to the lakes he created a little to the north.

Further west still is Stromovka's main sight, the **Místodržitelský letohrádek**, one of the earliest neo-Gothic structures in the city, begun way back in 1805. Originally conceived as a royal hunting chateau, it served as the seat of the Governor of Bohemia until 1918, and now houses the Národní muzeum's periodicals collection (closed to the public). To continue on to Troja and the zoo, head north under the railway, over the canal, and on to the Císařský ostrov (Emperor's Island) – and from there to the right bank of the Vltava.

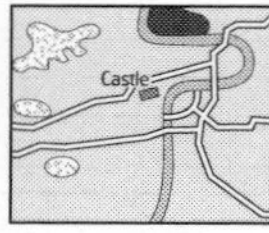

Troja

Though still well within the municipal boundaries, the suburb of **TROJA**, across the river to the north of Holešovice and Bubeneč, still has a distinctly country feel to it. Its most celebrated sight is Prague's only genuine **chateau or zámek**, perfectly situated against a hilly backdrop of vines. Troja's other attraction is the city's slightly dilapidated, but still enormously popular, **zoo**.

To get to Troja, you can either **walk** from Výstaviště (taking the route described above); catch **bus #**112, which runs hourly from metro Nádraží Holešovice; or, from April to September, you can reach Troja by boat from the boat launch between Jiráskův and Palackého most (see Nové Město map on pp.124–125).

Trojský zámek

The chateau is open April–Sept Tues–Sun 10am–6pm; Nov–March Sat & Sun 10am–5pm; 100Kč.

The **Trojský zámek** (Troja chateau) was designed by Jean-Baptiste Mathey for the powerful Šternberg family towards the end of the seventeenth century. Despite a recent renovation and rusty red repaint, its plain early Baroque facade is no match for the action-packed, blackened figures of giants and titans who battle it out on the chateau's monumental balustrades. To visit the **interior**, you'll have to join one of the guided tours. The star exhibits are the gushing frescoes depicting the victories of the Habsburg Emperor Leopold I (who reigned from 1657 to 1705) over the Turks, which cover every inch of the walls and ceilings of the grand hall; ask for the *anglický text* when you enter. You also get to wander through the chateau's pristine trend-setting French-style formal **gardens**, the first of their kind in Bohemia.

The zoo

The zoo is open daily: March & April 9am–5pm; May 9am–6pm; June–Sept 9am–7pm; Oct–Feb 9am–4pm.

On the other side of U trojského zámku, which runs along the west wall of the chateau, is the city's capacious but underfunded **zoo** (zoologická zahrada), founded in 1931 on the site of one of Troja's numerous hillside vineyards. Despite its rather weary appearance, all the usual animals are on show here, and kids, at least, have few problems enjoying themselves. Thankfully, a programme of modernization is currently under way, though some cramped cages still remain. In the summer, you can take a "ski-lift" (*lanová dráha*) from the duck pond to the top of the hill, where the prize exhibits – a rare breed of miniature horse known as Przewalski – hang out.

Dejvice, Střešovice and beyond

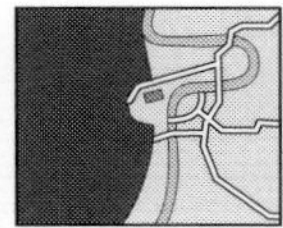

Spread across the hills to the northwest of the city centre are the leafy garden suburbs of **Dejvice** and **Střešovice**, peppered with fashionable modern villas, built between the wars for the upwardly mobile Prague bourgeoisie and commanding magnificent views across the north of the city. Both districts are short on conventional sights, but interesting to explore all the same. Some distance further west, the valley of **Šárka** is about as far as you can get from an urban environment without leaving the city. To the south of Šárka is the battlefield of **Bílá hora**, and **Hvězda**, a park containing a pretty star-shaped chateau that's well worth the effort to visit.

Dejvice

To get to the Hotel International take tram #20 or #25 from metro Dejvická.

DEJVICE was planned and built in the early 1920s for the First Republic's burgeoning community of civil servants and government and military officials. Its unappealing main square, **Vítězné náměstí** (metro Dejvická), is unavoidable if you're planning to explore any of the western suburbs, since it's a major public transport interchange. There's nothing much of note in this central part of Dejvice, though you can't help but notice the former **Hotel International** at the end of Jugoslávských partyzanů, a Stalinist skyscraper that is disturbingly similar to the universally loathed Palace of Culture in Warsaw. For followers of Socialist Realist chic, its workerist motifs merit closer inspection – somewhat incredibly, it's now part of the Holiday Inn hotel chain (see p.205).

Baba

To get to Baba, take bus #131 from metro Hradčanská.

Dejvice's most intriguing villas are located to the north in **Baba**, a model neighbourhood of 33 functionalist houses, each individually commissioned and built under the guidance of one-time Cubist and born-again functionalist, Pavel Janák. A group of leading architects affiliated to the Czech Workers' Alliance, inspired by a similar project in Stuttgart, initiated what was, at the time, a radical housing project to provide simple, single-family villas.

The idea was to use space and open-plan techniques rather than expensive materials to create a luxurious living space.

Despite the plans of the builders, the houses were mostly bought up by Prague's artistic and intellectual community. Nevertheless, they have stood the test of time better than most utopian architecture, not least because of the fantastic site – facing south and overlooking the city. Some of them remain exactly as they were when first built, others have been thoughtlessly altered, but as none of them is open to the public you'll have to be content with surreptitious peeping from the following streets: Na ostrohu, Na Babě, Nad Paťankou and Průhledová.

To reach the Müller Haus, take tram #1 or #18 from metro Hradčanská.

Střešovice is also home of the city's Transport Museum (Muzeum MHD), on Patočka, for more on which see p.246.

Střešovice

STŘEŠOVICE, southwest of Dejvice, has no central square and is dominated rather by its wealthy villa quarter, **Ořechovka,** where Havel now lives at Dělostřelecká 1. The most famous of the villas, though, is the **Müller Haus** (Loosova vila) at Nad hradním vodojemem 14, designed by the Brno-born architect, Adolf Loos. Completed in 1930 (after planning permission had been refused ten times), it was one of Loos' few commissions, a typically uncompromising white box, wiped smooth with concrete rendering. Now grey with pollution, it's nothing to look at from the outside, but then Loos believed that "a building should be dumb on the outside and reveal its wealth only on the inside". However, since you can't get inside, there's no way to appreciate the careful choice of rich materials and minimal furnishings that were Loos' hallmark. There are plans to turn the house into a museum to Loos

Šárka and Ctirad

The Šárka valley takes its name from the Amazonian **Šárka**, who, according to Czech legend, committed suicide here sometime back in the last millennium. The story begins with the death of Libuše, the founder and first ruler of Prague. The women closest to her, who had enjoyed enormous freedom and privilege in her court, refused to submit to the new patriarchy of her husband, Přemysl. Under the leadership of a woman called Vlasta, they left Vyšehrad and set up their own proto-feminist, separatist colony called Děvín, on the opposite bank of the river.

They scored numerous military victories over the men of Vyšehrad, but never managed to finish off the men's leader, a young warrior called **Ctirad**. In the end they decided to ensnare him and tied one of their own warriors naked to a tree, sure in the knowledge that Ctirad would take her to be a maiden in distress and come to her aid. Šárka offered to act as the decoy, luring Ctirad into the ambush, after which he was tortured and killed. However, in her brief meeting with Ctirad, Šárka fell madly in love with him and, overcome with grief at what she had done, threw herself off the aforementioned cliff. And just in case you thought the legend has a feminist ending, it doesn't. Roused by the cruel death of Ctirad, Přemysl and the lads had a final set-to with Vlasta and co, and butchered the lot of them.

– regarded by many as one of the founders of modern architecture – but for the moment, surrounded by hundreds of similarly boxy houses, you may well wonder what all the fuss is about.

Šárka

If you've had your fill of postcards and crowds, take tram #20 or #26 from metro Dejvice to the last stop and walk north down into the **Šárka valley**, a peaceful limestone gorge that twists eastwards back towards Dejvice. The first section (Divoká Šárka) is particularly dramatic, with grey-white crags rising up on both sides – it was here that Šárka plunged to her death (see box opposite). Gradually the valley opens up, with a grassy meadow to picnic on, and an open-air swimming pool nearby, both fairly popular with Czechs on summer weekends. There are various points further east from which you can pick up a city bus back into town, depending on how far you want to walk. The full walk to where the Šárka stream flows into the Vltava, just north of Baba, is about 6–7km all told, though none of it is particularly tough going.

The Battle of Bílá hora

The **Battle of Bílá hora** (White Mountain) may have been a skirmish of minor importance in the Thirty Years' War, but, for the Czechs, it was to have devastating consequences. The victory of the Catholic forces of Habsburg emperor Ferdinand II in 1620 set the seal on the Czech Lands for the next three hundred years. It prompted an emigration of religious and intellectual figures that relegated the country to a cultural backwater for most of modern history. The defeat also unleashed a decimation of the Bohemian and Moravian aristocracy, which meant that, unlike their immediate neighbours, the Poles and Hungarians, the Czechs had to build their nineteenth-century national revival around writers and composers, rather than counts and warriors.

The 28,000 Catholic soldiers – made up of Bavarians, Spanish, German and French troops (among them the future philosopher, René Descartes) – outnumbered the 21,000-strong Czech, Hungarian and German Protestant army, though the latter occupied the strategic chalky hill to the west of Prague. Shortly after noon on November 8 the imperial troops (under the nominal command of the Virgin Mary) began by attacking the Protestants' left flank, and, after about an hour, prompted a full-scale flight. The Protestant commander, Christian von Anhalt, went hot-foot back to the Hrad, where he met the Czech king, Frederick of Palatinate, who was late for the battle, having been delayed during lunch with the English ambassador.

Frederick, dubbed the "Winter King" for his brief reign, had once tossed silver coins to the crowd, and entertained them by swimming naked in the Vltava, while his wife, Elizabeth, daughter of James I of England, had shocked Prague society with her expensive dresses, her outlandish hairdo, and her plunging décolletage. Now, abandoned by their allies, the royal couple gathered up the crown jewels and left Prague in such a hurry they almost forgot their youngest son – later to become the dashing Prince Rupert of the English Civil War – who was playing in the nursery. The city had no choice but to surrender to the Catholics, who spent a week looting the place, before executing 27 of the rebellion's leaders on Staroměstské náměstí (see p.98).

Hvězda, Bílá hora and Břevnov

A couple of kilometres southwest of Dejvice, trams #1, #2 and #18 terminate close to the main entrance to the hunting park of **Hvězda**, one of Prague's most beautiful and peaceful parks. Wide, soft, green avenues of trees radiate from a bizarre star-shaped building (*hvězda* means "Star") that was designed by the Archduke Ferdinand of Tyrol for his wife in 1555. Recently restored, it houses a worthy but dull **museum**, devoted to the writer Alois Jirásek (1851–1930), who popularized old Czech legends during the national revival, and the artist Mikuláš Aleš (1852–1913), whose drawings were likewise inspired by Czech history. There's also a small exhibition on the Battle of Bílá hora (see box on p.175) on the top floor. It's the building itself, though – decorated with delicate stucco work and frescoes – that's the real reason for venturing inside; it makes a perfect setting for the chamber music concerts occasionally staged here.

The museum is open Tues–Sat 9am–4pm, Sun 10am–5pm; 40Kč.

A short distance southwest of Hvězda is the once entirely barren limestone summit of **Bílá hora** (White Mountain), accessible from Hvězda through one of the many holes in the park's southern perimeter wall. It was here in 1620 that the first battle of the Thirty Years' War took place, sealing the fate of the Czech nation for the following three hundred years. In little more than an hour, the Protestant forces of the "Winter King" Frederick of Palatinate were roundly beaten by the Catholic troops of the Habsburg Emperor Ferdinand. As a more or less direct consequence, the Czechs lost their aristocracy, their religion, their scholars and, most importantly, the remnants of their sovereignty. There's nothing much to see now, apart from the small monument (*mohyla*), and a pilgrims' church, just off Nad višňovkou. This was erected by the Catholics to commemorate the victory, which they ascribed to the timely intercession of the Virgin Mary – hence its name, **Panna Maria Vítězná** (St Mary the Victorious).

To get to Bílá hora, take tram #8 from metro Hradčanská or #22 from metro Malostranská to the western terminus, then walk up Nad višňovkou and across the field

If you've time to spare before heading back into town, it's only five minutes' walk east of the park, down Zeyerova alej, to the idyllic Baroque monastery of **Břevnovský klášter**. Founded as a Benedictine abbey by Saint Adalbert, tenth-century bishop of Prague, it was worked over in the eighteenth century by both Christoph and Kilian Ignaz Dientzenhofer, and bears their characteristic interconnecting ovals, inside and out. The monks have now returned, which has made it easier to gain access to the church. To get back into town, take tram #8 or #22 from just below the monastery.

There are guided tours of the monastery on Sat & Sun 10am & 2pm; at other times it's possible to peek inside through the glass doors

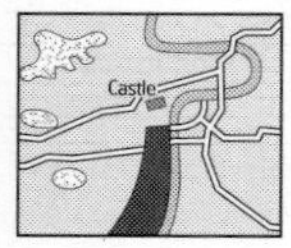

Smíchov

SMÍCHOV is for the most part a late nineteenth-century working-class suburb, home to the city's largest brewery, which produces the ubiquitous Staropramen, and a large community of Romanies, its skyline peppered with satanic chimneys dutifully belching out smoke. To the west, as the suburb gains height, the run-down tenements give way to

The Pink Tank

Smíchov's greatest claim to fame is the episode of the **pink tank**. Until 1991, Tank 23 sat proudly on its plinth in náměstí Sovětských tankistů (Soviet tank drivers' square), one of a number of obsolete tanks generously donated by the Soviets after World War II to serve as monuments to the 1945 liberation. Tank 23 was special, however, as it was supposedly the first tank to arrive to liberate Prague, on May 9, hotfoot from Berlin.

The real story of the liberation of Prague was rather different, however. When the Prague uprising began on May 5, the first offer of assistance actually came from a division of the anti-Communist Russian National Liberation Army (KONR), under the overall command of a renegade general, Andrei Vlasov. Vlasov was a high-ranking Red Army officer, who was instrumental in pushing the Germans back from the gates of Moscow, but switched sides after being captured by the Nazis in 1942. The Germans were (rightly, as it turned out) highly suspicious of the KONR, and, for the most part, the renegade Russians were kept well away from the real action. In the war's closing stages, however, the KONR switched sides once more and agreed to fight alongside the Czech resistance, making a crucial intervention against the SS troops who were poised to crush the uprising in Prague. Initially, the Czechs guaranteed Vlasov's men asylum from the advancing Soviets in return for military assistance. In reality, the Czechs were unable to honour their side of the bargain and the KONR finally withdrew from the city late on May 7 and headed west to surrender themselves to the Americans. When the Red Army finally arrived in Prague, many of Vlasov's troops were simply gunned down by the Soviets. Even those in the hands of the Americans were eventually passed over to the Russians and shared the fate of their leader Vlasov who was tried *in camera* in Moscow and hanged with piano wire on August 2, 1946.

The unsolicited reappearance of Soviet tanks on the streets of Prague in 1968 left most Czechs feeling somewhat ambivalent towards the old monument. And in the summer of 1991, situationist artist David Černý painted the tank bubble-gum pink, and placed a large phallic finger on top of it, while another mischievous Czech daubed "Vlasov" on the podium. Since the country was at the time engaged in delicate negotiations to end the Soviet military presence in Czechoslovakia, the new regime, despite its mostly dissident leanings, roundly condemned the act as unlawful. Havel, in his characteristically even-handed way, made it clear that he didn't like tanks anywhere, whether on the battlefield or as monuments.

In the end, the tank was hastily repainted khaki green and Černý was arrested under the familiar "crimes against the state" clause of the penal code, which had been used by the Communists with gay abandon on several members of the then government. In protest at the arrest of Černý, twelve members of the federal parliament turned up the following day in their overalls and, taking advantage of their legal immunity, repainted the tank pink. Finally, the government gave in, released Černý and removed the tank from public view. There's now no trace of tank, podium or plaque, and even the square has been renamed náměstí Kinských.

another of Prague's sought-after villa quarters. To the north, Smíchov borders with Malá Strana, and, officially at least, takes in a considerable part of the woods of Petřín, south of the Hladová zeď (see p.84).

Smíchov

Anděl and náměstí 14 října

There's only one important sight in Smíchov – the Bertramka (see below) – but a stroll around its busy streets is rewarding in its own way. As you leave Anděl metro station, the modern hub of Smíchov, note the Soviet-designed Socialist Realist marble **mosaic**, a relic from the days when the station was called Moskevská. Another monument to a lost era is the disused **synagogue**, adjacent to the station, up Plzeňská. Built in 1863 to serve the wealthy Jewish business folk, it was remodelled in the 1930s in functionalist style, and sports unusual crenellations on the roof – only the Hebrew inscription on the ground floor gives any indication of its former use.

If you're looking for a café to relax in, head for the Apostrof, housed in a renovated Baroque chateau by the church (see p.218).

The district's traditional heart is **náměstí 14 října**, a short walk from metro Anděl up Štefánikova. The Art Nouveau Národní dům, and the adjacent market hall (now converted into a bland supermarket), both erected around 1906, have seen better days, but the neo-Renaissance **church of sv Václav**, built in the 1880s and overlooking the square, is worth a visit. Inside, the church is a jewel box of rich Byzantine decoration, with gilded mosaics, huge Ionic pillars of red Swedish granite, a coffered ceiling and a wonderfully Turkish-looking gilded pulpit.

Bertramka (Mozart Museum)

Bertramka is open daily: April–Oct 9.30am–6pm; Nov–April 9.30am–5pm; 50Kč. For more on Mozart's links with Prague, see box on p.73.

Mozart stayed with the Dušeks at their newly acquired **Bertramka villa** on several occasions – it was here that he put the finishing touches to his *Don Giovanni* overture, the night before the premiere at the Stavovské divadlo (see p.105). It was the sort of household that would have appealed to Mozart, musical and slightly rakish: František Dušek was a well-respected pianist in his own right, while his wife, Josefa Dušková, a popular singer seventeen years younger than her husband, was one of Prague's most fashionable hostesses. As long ago as 1838, the villa was turned into a shrine to Mozart, though very little survives of the house he knew, thanks to a fire on New Year's Day, 1871 – not that this has deterred generations of Mozart lovers from flocking here. These days, what the museum lacks in memorabilia, it makes up for with its Rococo ambience, a lovely garden and regular Mozart recitals. To get to Bertramka, take the metro to Anděl, walk a couple of blocks west up Plzeňská, then left up Mozartova.

Chapter 9

Out from the city

Few capital cities can boast such extensive unspoilt tracts of woodland so near at hand as Prague. Once you leave the half-built high-rise estates of the outer suburbs behind, the traditional provincial feel of **Bohemia** (Čechy) immediately makes itself felt. Many towns and villages still huddle below the grand residences of their former lords, their street layout little changed since medieval times.

To the north, several such chateaux grace the banks of the Vltava, including the wine-producing town of **Mělník**, on the Labe (Elbe) plain. Further away, but well served by public transport, is **Terezín**, the wartime Jewish ghetto that is a living testament to the Holocaust. One of the most obvious day-trip destinations is to the east of

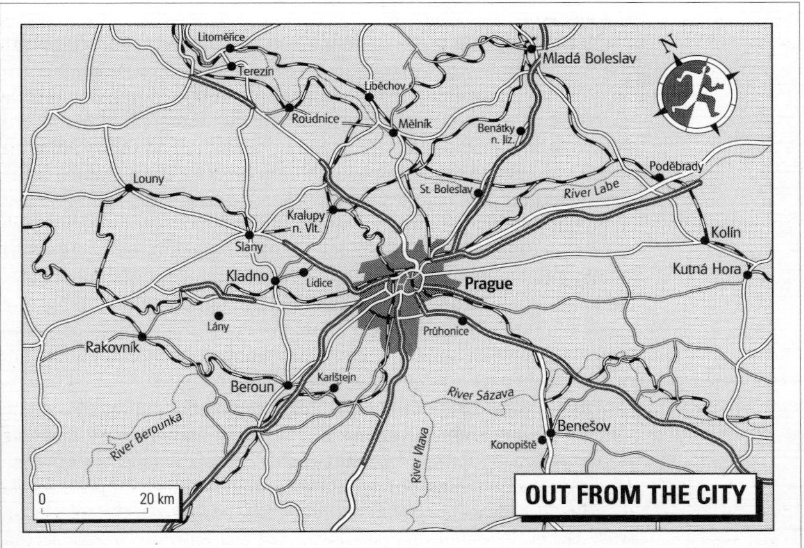

Prague: **Kutná Hora**, a medieval silver-mining town with one of the most beautiful Gothic churches in the country, and a macabre gallery of bones in the suburb of Sedlec.

Further south, the **Konopiště** chateau boasts exceptionally beautiful and expansive grounds. Southwest of Prague, a similar mix of woods and rolling hills surrounds the popular castle of **Karlštejn**, a gem of Gothic architecture, dramatically situated above the River Berounka. West of Prague, **Lidice**, razed to the ground by the SS, is another town which recalls the horror of Nazi occupation.

Getting around

For details of car rental firms, see p.43; for bike rental, see p.45.

Transport throughout Bohemia is fairly straightforward, thanks to a comprehensive network of railway lines and regional bus services, though connections can be less than smooth, and journeys slow. If you're planning to try and see more than one or two places outside Prague, or one of the more difficult destinations to reach, it might be worth considering renting a car.

By train

The most relaxing way to day-trip from Prague is by **train**; the antiquated rolling stock of Czech Railways, České dráhy (ČD), is a pleasure to travel in. However, the system, which has changed little since it was bequeathed to the country by the Habsburgs in 1918, is often a lot slower than the buses. It's also an institution that has struggled throughout the 1990s, and is in almost perpetual crisis, with a constant threat of closure hanging over much of the system.

ČD run two main **types of train**: *rychlík* (*spěšný* or Ex) trains are the faster ones which stop only at major towns, while *osobní* (or *zastavkový*) trains stop at just about every station, averaging as little as 30kph. It's also worth knowing about the existence of fast trains known as either SuperCity (SC), EuroCity (EC) or InterCity (IC), for which you need to pay a supplement. However, for the purposes of the day-trips described below, you won't need to take these fast services.

To buy a ticket, simply state your destination – if you want a return ticket (*zpáteční*), you must say so. First-class carriages (*první třída*) exist only on fast trains. There are half-price **discount fares** for children under 16, and you can take two children under 6 for free (providing they don't take up more than one seat). There are even some "crèche carriages" on the slower trains, where those with children under 10 have priority over seats.

With very few English-speakers employed on the railways, it can be difficult getting **train information**. The larger stations have a simple airport-style arrivals and departures board, which includes information on delays under the heading *zpoždění*. Many stations have poster-style displays of arrivals (*příjezd*) and departures (*odjezd*), the former on white paper, the latter on yellow, with fast trains printed in red. All but the smallest stations also have a comprehensive display of **timings and route information** on rollers. These timetables may seem daunting at first, but with a little practice they should become decipherable. First find the route you need to take on the diagrammatic map and make a note of the number printed beside it; then follow the timetable rollers through until you come to the appropriate number. The only problem now is language since everything will be written in Czech. Some of the more common notes at the side of the timetable are *jezdí jen v* (only running on), or *nejezdí v* or *nechodí v* (not running on), followed by a date or a symbol: a cross or an "N" for a Sunday, a big "S" for a Saturday, two crossed hammers for a workday, "A" for a Friday and so on. Small stations may simply have a board with a list of departures under the title *směr* (direction) followed by a town. A platform, or *nástupiště*, is usually divided into two *kolej* on either side.

By bus

Travelling by **bus** (*autobus*) tends to be quicker, and marginally cheaper, but a lot less scenic than by train. Bear in mind, though, that timetables are often designed with the working and/or school day in mind. This means that services are at their most frequent between 6am and 8am and between 4pm and 6pm during the week, with few or no services at weekends; so always check return times before you set out.

In places outside Prague, the **bus station** is often adjacent to the train station, though you may be able to pick up the bus from the centre of town, too. The bigger terminals in Prague, like Praha-Florenc, are run with train-like efficiency, though finding the right departure stand (*stání*) can be a daunting task. For most minor routes, simply buy your ticket from the driver; for popular routes, and for travel at peak times, it's best to try and book your seat in advance.

Bus **timetables** are even more difficult to figure out than train ones, as there are no maps at any of the stations. In the detailed timetables, each service is listed separately, so you may have to scour several timetables before you discover when the next bus is. A better bet is to look at the departures and arrivals board. Make sure you check on which day the service runs, since many run only on Mondays, Fridays or at the weekend (see the above section on trains for the key phrases). Minor bus stops are marked with a rusty metal sign saying *zastávka*. If you want to get off, ask *já chci vystoupit?*; "the next stop" is *příští zastávka*.

Mělník and around

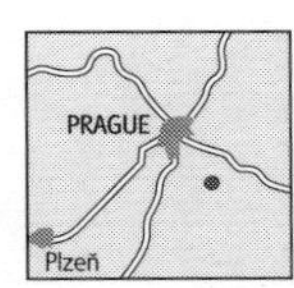

Occupying a spectacular, commanding site at the confluence of the Vltava and Labe rivers, **MĚLNÍK**, 33km north of Prague, lies at the heart of Bohemia's tiny wine-growing region. The town's history goes back to the ninth century, when it was handed over to the

Přemyslids as part of Ludmila's dowry when she married Prince Bořivoj. And it was here, too, that she introduced her heathen grandson Václav (later to become Saint Wenceslas, aka "Good King") to the joys of Christianity. Viticulture became the town's economic mainstay when the Emperor Charles IV, aching for a little of the French wine of his youth, introduced grapes from Burgundy (where he was also king).

The old town

The chateau is open daily March–Dec 10am–5pm; the museum is open April–Oct Tues–Sun 9am–5pm.

Mělník's greatest monument is its Renaissance **chateau**, perched high above the flat plains and visible for miles around. The present building, its courtyard covered in familiar sgraffito patterns, is now back in the hands of its last aristocratic owners, the Lobkowicz family, who have restored the chateau's magnificently proportioned rooms, which also provide great views out over the plain. Visits are by guided tour only, and you've a choice between exploring seven beautifully painted rooms of the castle interior, filled with artefacts and Old Masters returned to the family since 1989, or touring the wine museum in the cellars, finishing up with free samples of plonk; alternatively you can do both tours. In addition, there's a museum of prams, strollers and baby carriages, which forms part of the local **museum** on the first floor of the chateau.

Below the chateau, vines cling to the south-facing terraces, as the land plunges into the river below. From beneath the great tower of Mělník's onion-domed church of **sv Petr and Pavel**, next door to the chateau, there's an even better view of the rivers' confluence, and the subsidiary canal, once so congested with vessels that traffic lights had to be introduced to avoid accidents. The church itself contains a compellingly macabre **ossuary** or *kostnice*, filled with more than 10,000 bones of medieval plague victims, fashioned into weird and wonderful skeletal shapes by students in the early part of this century.

The ossuary is open Tues–Sun 10.30am–4pm.

The rest of the old town is pretty small, but it's pleasant enough for a casual stroll. One half of the main square, náměstí Míru, is arcaded Baroque and typical of the region, and there's an old medieval gateway nearby, the Pražská brána, which has been converted into an art gallery.

Practicalities

There's no direct train service to Mělník from Prague, but there is a regular **bus service** which leaves from metro Nádraží Holešovice and stand 18 at Florenc, and takes under an hour. On arrival at Mělník bus station, to reach the older part of town, simply head up Krombholcova in the direction of the big church tower. If your next destination is Terezín, you have the choice of either the bus or the train; the **train station** is still further from the old town, a couple of blocks northeast of the bus station, down Jiřího z Poděbrad.

As for **food and drink**, the *Zámecká restaurace* is as good (and cheap) a place as any to sample some of the local wine (and enjoy the view): the red Ludmila is the most famous of Mělník's wines, and there's even a rare Czech rosé produced by the castle vineyards, but if you prefer white, try a bottle of Tramín. Equally good views can be had from *Stará škola* restaurant, behind the church; otherwise, you could try *Na hradbách*, on náměstí Míru, which serves up big portions and local wines, not to mention Guinness and Kilkenny, in a cosy brick and wood-panelled interior.

Terezín

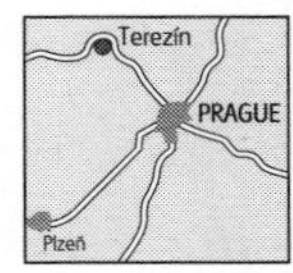

The old road from Prague to Berlin passes through the fortress town of **TEREZÍN** (Theresienstadt), just over 60km northwest of the capital. Purpose-built in the 1780s by the Habsburgs to defend the northern border against Prussia, it was capable of accommodating 14,500 soldiers and hundreds of prisoners. In 1941, the population was ejected and the whole town turned into a **Jewish ghetto**, and used as a transit camp for Jews whose final destination was Auschwitz.

A brief history of the ghetto

In October 1941, Reinhard Heydrich and the Nazi high command decided to turn the whole of Terezín into a Jewish ghetto. It was an obvious choice: fully fortified, close to the main Prague–Dresden railway line, and with an SS prison already established in the **Malá pevnost** (Small Fortress) nearby. The original inhabitants of the town – less than 3500 people – were moved out, and transports began arriving at Terezín from many parts of central Europe. Within a year, nearly 60,000 Jews were interned here in appallingly overcrowded conditions; the monthly death rate rose to 4000. In October 1942, the first transport left for Auschwitz. By the end of the war, 140,000 Jews had passed through Terezín; fewer than 17,500 remained when the ghetto was finally liberated on May 8, 1945.

One of the perverse ironies of Terezín is that it was used by the Nazis as a cover for the real purpose of the *Endlösung* or "final solution", devised at the Wannsee conference in January 1942 (at which Heydrich was present). The ghetto was made to appear self-governing, with its own council or *Freizeitgestaltung*, its own bank printing ghetto money, its own shops selling goods confiscated from the internees on arrival, and even a café on the main square. For a while, a special "Terezín family camp" was even set up in Auschwitz, to continue the deception. The deportees were kept in mixed barracks, allowed to wear civilian clothes and – the main purpose of the whole thing – send letters back to their loved ones in Terezín telling them they were OK. After six months' "quarantine", they were sent to the gas chambers.

Despite the fact that Terezín was being used by the Nazis as cynical propaganda, the ghetto population turned their unprecedented freedom to their own advantage. Since the entire population of the Protectorate

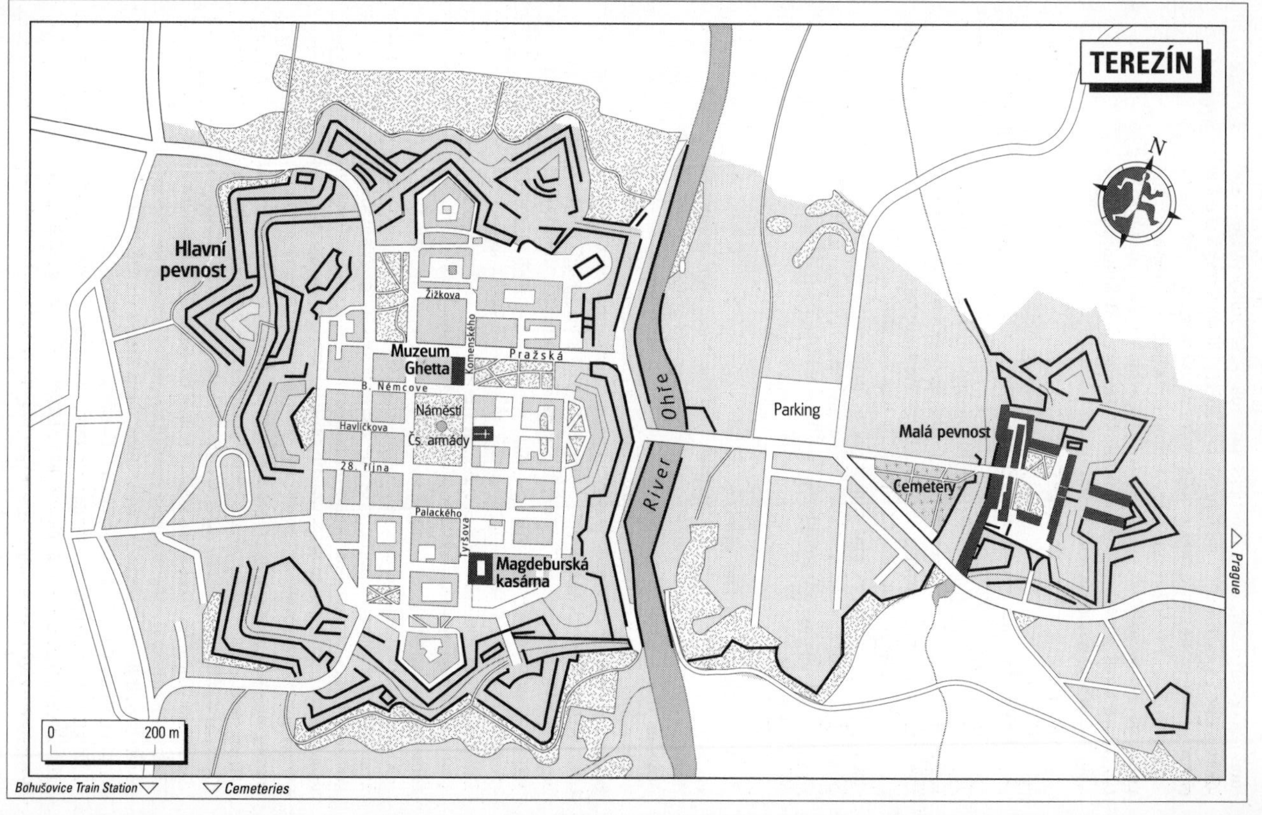
TEREZÍN
N
Hlavní pevnost
Žižkova
Komenského
Pražská
Muzeum Ghetta
B. Němcove
Náměstí Čs. armády
Havlíčkova
28. října
Palackého
Tyršova
Magdeburská kasárna
River Ohře
Parking
Malá pevnost
Cemetery
Prague
0
200 m
Bohušovice Train Station
Cemeteries

(and Jews from many other parts of Europe) passed through Terezín, the ghetto had an enormous number of outstanding Jewish artists, musicians, scholars and writers (many of whom subsequently perished in the camps). Thus, in addition to the officially sponsored activities, countless clandestine cultural events were organized in the cellars and attics of the barracks: teachers gave lessons to children, puppet theatre productions were put on, and literary evenings were held.

Towards the end of 1943, the so-called *Verschönerung* or "beautification" of the ghetto was implemented, in preparation for the arrival of the International Red Cross inspectors. Streets were given names instead of numbers, and the whole place was decked out as if it were a spa town. When the International Red Cross asked to inspect one of the Nazi camps, they were brought here and treated to a week of Jewish cultural events. A circus tent was set up in the main square; a children's pavilion erected in the park; numerous performances of Hans Krása's children's opera, *Brundibár* (Bumble Bee), staged; and a jazz band, called the Ghetto Swingers, performed in the bandstand on the main square. The Red Cross visited Terezín twice, once in June 1944, and again in April 1945; both times the delegates filed positive reports.

Hlavná pevnost (Main Fortress)

Although the **Hlavní pevnost** (Main Fortress) has never been put to the test in battle, Terezín remains intact as a garrison town. Today, it's an eerie, soulless place, built to a dour eighteenth-century grid plan, its bare streets empty apart from the residual civilian population and visitors making their way between the various museums and memorials. As you enter, the red-brick zig-zag fortifications are still an awesome sight, though the huge moat has been put to good use by local gardening enthusiasts.

Muzeum Ghetta

The museum is open daily: April–Sept 9am–6pm; Oct–March 9am–5.30pm; 100Kč; combined ticket for all sights 180Kč.

The first place to head for is the **Muzeum Ghetta** (Ghetto Museum), which was finally opened in 1991, on the fiftieth anniversary of the arrival of the first transports in Terezín. After the war, the Communists had followed the consistent Soviet line by deliberately underplaying the Jewish perspective on Terezín. Instead, the emphasis was on the Malá pevnost (see p.186), where the majority of victims were not Jewish, and on the war as an anti-fascist struggle, in which good (Communism and the Soviet Union) had triumphed over evil (Fascism and Nazi Germany). It wasn't until the Prague Spring of 1968 that the idea of a museum dedicated specifically to the history of the Jewish ghetto first emerged. In the 1970s, however, the intended building was turned into a Museum of the Ministry of the Interior instead.

Now that it's finally open, this extremely informative and well-laid-out exhibition at last attempts to do some justice to the extraordinary and tragic events which took place here between 1941 and 1945, including background displays on the measures which led inexorably to the *Endlösung*. There's also a fascinating video (with English subtitles) showing clips of the Nazi propaganda film shot in Terezín – *Hitler Gives the Jews a Town* – intercut with harrowing interviews with survivors.

Magdeburská kasárna

The exhibition is open daily: April–Sept 9am–6pm; Oct–March 9am–5.30pm.

To the south of the ghetto, the **Magdeburská kasárna** (Magdeburg Barracks), former seat of the Jewish self-governing council or *Freizeitgestaltung*, has recently been turned into a fascinating museum concentrating on the remarkable artistic life of Terezín. First off, however, there's a reconstructed women's dormitory with three-tier bunks, full of luggage and belongings, to give an idea as to the cramped living conditions endured by the ghetto inhabitants. The first exhibition room has displays on the various Jewish musicians who passed through Terezín, including Pavel Haas, a pupil of Janáček, Hans Krása, a pupil of Zemlinsky, who wrote the score for *Brundibár*, and Karel Ančerl, who survived the Holocaust to become conductor of the Czech Philharmonic. The final exhibition room concentrates on the writers who contributed to the ghetto's underground magazines. The rooms in between, however, are given over to the work of Terezín's numerous artists, many of whom were put to work by the SS, who set up a graphics department here; headed by cartoonist Bedřich Fritta, it produced visual propaganda showing how smoothly the ghetto ran. In addition, there are many clandestine works, ranging from portraits of inmates to harrowing depictions of the cramped dormitories, and the transports. These provide some of the most vivid and deeply affecting insights into the reality of ghetto life in the whole of Terezín, and it was for this "propaganda of horror" that several artists, including Fritta, were eventually deported to Auschwitz.

Malá pevnost (Small Fortress)

The Malá pevnost is open daily: April–Sept 8am–6.30pm; Oct–March 8am–4.30pm.

On the other side of the River Ohře, east down Pražská, lies the **Malá pevnost** (Small Fortress), built as a military prison in the 1780s, at the same time as the main fortress. The prison's most famous inmate was the young Bosnian Serb, Gavrilo Princip, who succeeded in assassinating Archduke Ferdinand in Sarajevo in 1914, and was interned and died here during World War I. In 1940 it was turned into an SS prison by Heydrich and, after the war, it became the official memorial and museum of Terezín. The majority of the 32,000 inmates who passed through the prison were active in the resistance (and, more often than not, Communists). Some 2500 inmates perished here, while another 8000 died subsequently in the concentration camps. The vast cemetery laid out by the entrance contains the graves of over 2300 individuals, plus numerous other corpses of unidentified victims, and is rather insensitively dominated by a large Christian cross, plus a smaller Star of David.

There are guides available (occasionally survivors of Terezín), or else you can simply use the brief guide to the prison in English, and walk around yourself. The infamous Nazi refrain *Arbeit Macht Frei* (Work Brings Freedom) is daubed across the entrance on the left, which leads to the exemplary washrooms, still as they were when built for the Red Cross tour of inspection. The rest of the camp has been left empty but intact, and graphically evokes the cramped conditions under which the prisoners were kept, half-starved and badly clothed, subject to indiscriminate cruelty and execution. The prison's main **exhibition** is housed in the SS barracks opposite the luxurious home of the camp *Kommandant* and his family. A short documentary, intelligible in any language, is regularly shown in the cinema that was set up in 1942 to entertain the SS guards.

Practicalities

Terezín is about an hour and a quarter's **bus** ride from Prague's Florenc terminal (buses leave roughly every two hours from stand 17) and therefore easy to visit on a day-trip. The nearest train station is at Bohušovice nad Ohří (slow trains from Prague's Masarykovo nádraží), 2km south of the fortress. Another alternative, albeit a more expensive one, is to sign up for one of the guided tours of Terezín that leave from Prague. The Matana travel agency, Maiselove 15, Josefov (☎232 1954; *matana@ms.anet.cz*) charges around 1000Kč for a day-trip with a guide and lunch thrown in. Foodwise, if you're on your own, you're best off either bringing a picnic or heading for *U hojtašů*, a restaurant on Komenského.

Kutná Hora

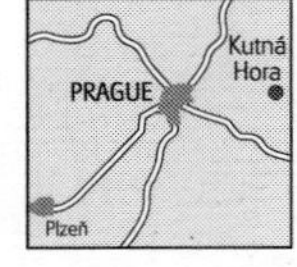

For 250 years or so, **KUTNÁ HORA** (Kuttenberg) was one of the most important towns in Bohemia, second only to Prague. At the end of the fourteenth century its population was equal to that of London, its shantytown suburbs straggled across what are now green fields, and its ambitious building projects set out to rival those of the capital itself. Today, Kutná Hora is a small provincial town with a population of just over 20,000, but the monuments dotted around it, the superb Gothic cathedral, and the remarkable monastery and ossuary in the suburb of **Sedlec**, make it one of the most enjoyable of all possible day-trips from Prague.

A brief history

Kutná Hora's road to prosperity began in the late thirteenth century with the discovery of **silver deposits** in the surrounding area. German miners were invited to settle and work the seams, and around 1300 Václav II founded the royal mint here and sent for Italian craftsmen to run it. Much of the town's wealth was used to fund the beautification of Prague, but it also allowed for the construction of one of the most magnificent churches in central Europe and a number of other prestigious Gothic monuments in Kutná Hora itself.

At the time of the Hussite Wars, the town was mostly German-speaking, and staunchly Catholic; local miners used to throw captured Hussites into the deep mine shafts and leave them to die of starvation. Word got out, and the town was besieged and eventually taken by Žižka's fanatical Táborites in 1421, only to be recaptured by Sigismund and his papal forces shortly afterwards, and again by Žižka, the following year.

While the silver stocks remained high the town was able to recover its former prosperity, but at the end of the sixteenth century the mines dried up and Kutná Hora's wealth and importance came to an abrupt end – when the Swedes marched on the town during the Thirty Years' War, they had to be bought off with beer rather than silver. The town has never fully recovered, shrivelling to less than a third of its former size, its fate emphatically sealed by a devastating fire in 1770.

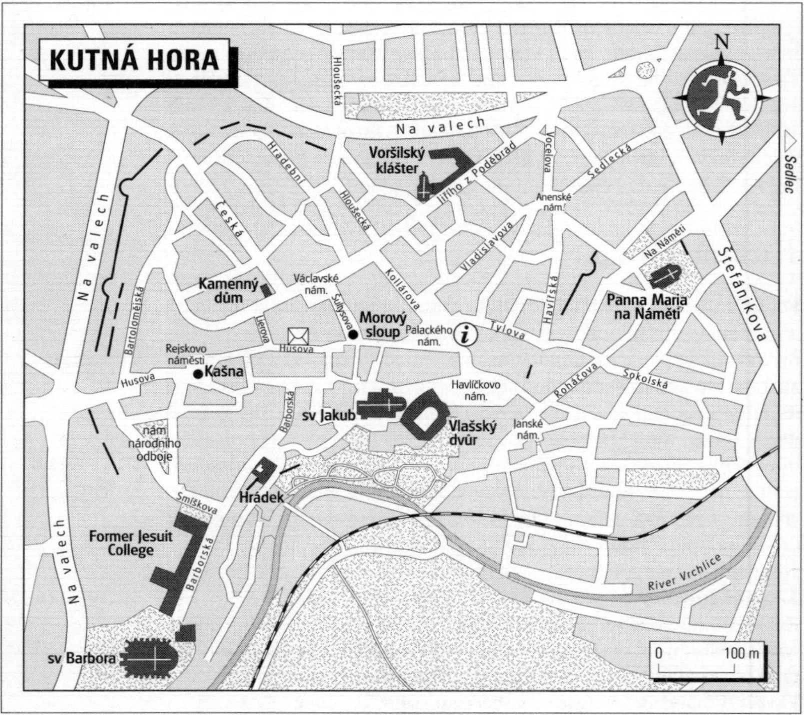

The Town

The medieval lanes and small, unassuming houses that line the town's main square, Palackého náměstí, give little idea of Kutná Hora's former glories. A narrow alleyway on the south side of the square, however, leads to leafy Havlíčkovo náměstí, on which stands the **Vlašský dvůr** (Italian Court), originally conceived as a palace by Václav II, and for three centuries the town's bottomless purse. It was here that Florentine minters produced the Prague Groschen (*pražské groše*), a silver coin widely used throughout central Europe until the nineteenth century. The building itself has been mucked about with over the years, most recently – and most brutally – by nineteenth-century restorers, who left only the chestnut trees, a fourteenth-century oriel window (capped by an unlikely looking wooden onion dome) and the statue of a miner unmolested. The original workshops of the minters have been bricked in, but the outlines of their little doors and windows are still visible in the courtyard. The short **guided tour** of the old chapel, treasury and royal palace gives you a fair idea of the building's former importance.

The Vlašský dvůr is open daily: April & Oct 10am–5pm; May–Sept 9am–6pm; Nov–April 10am–4pm; 50Kč.

Outside the court is a statue of the country's founder and first president, T. G. Masaryk, twice removed – once by the Nazis and once by the Communists – but now returned to its pride of place. Before you leave, take a quick turn in the court gardens, which climb down in steps to the River Vrchlice below. This is undoubtedly Kutná Hora's best profile, with a splendid view over to the cathedral of sv Barbora (see below).

Behind the Vlašský dvůr is **sv Jakub** (St James), the town's oldest church, begun a generation or so after the discovery of the silver deposits. Its grand scale is a clear indication of the town's quite considerable wealth by the fourteenth century, though in terms of artistry it pales in comparison with Kutná Hora's other ecclesiastical buildings. The leaning tower is a reminder of the precarious position of the town, the church's foundations being prone to subsidence from the disused mines below. If you want to see some of these, head for the **Hrádek**, an old fort which was used as a second mint and now serves as a **Mining Museum** (Muzeum a středověké důlní dílo). Here you can pick up a white coat, miner's helmet and torch, and visit some of the medieval mines that were discovered beneath the fort in the 1960s.

The museum is open Tues–Sun: April & Oct 9am–noon & 1–5pm; May–Sept 9am–noon & 1–6pm; 100Kč

Cathedral of sv Barbora

Kutná Hora's cathedral of **sv Barbora** is arguably the most beautiful church in central Europe. Not to be outdone by the great monastery at Sedlec (see p.190) or the St Vitus Cathedral in Prague, the miners of Kutná Hora began financing the construction of a great Gothic cathedral of their own, dedicated to their patron saint, Saint Barbara. The foundations were probably laid by Peter Parler in the 1380s, but work was interrupted by the Hussite wars, and the church remains unfinished, despite a flurry of building activity at the beginning of the sixteenth century by, among others, Benedikt Ried, who built the Vladislavský sál in Prague Castle.

The cathedral is open Tues–Sun: April & Oct 9–11.30am & 1–3.30pm; May–Sept 9am–5.30pm; Nov–March 9–11.30am & 2–3.30pm; 30Kč.

The approach road to the cathedral, Barborská, is lined with a parade of gesticulating Baroque saints and cherubs that rival the sculptures on the Charles Bridge; on the right-hand side is the palatial former Jesuit College. The church itself bristles with pinnacles, finials and flying buttresses which support its most striking feature, a roof of three tent-like towers, culminating in unequal needle-sharp spires. Inside, cold light streams through the plain glass windows, illuminating a playful vaulted nave whose ribs form branches and petals stamped with coats of arms belonging to Václav II and the local miners' guilds. The wide spread of the five-aisled nave is remarkably uncluttered: a Gothic pulpit – half wood, half stone – creeps tastefully up a central pillar, and black and gold Renaissance confessionals hide discreetly in the north aisle. On the south wall is the Minters' Chapel, decorated with fifteenth-century wall frescoes showing the Florentines at work, while in the ambulatory chapels some fascinating paintings – unique for their period – depict local miners at work.

The rest of the town

There are a few minor sights worth seeking out in the rest of the town. On Rejskovo náměstí, the squat, many-sided **Kašna** (fountain) by Matouš Rejsek strikes an odd pose – anything less like a fountain would be hard to imagine. At the bottom of the sloping Nultysova is a particularly fine **Morový sloup** (Plague Column), giving thanks for the end of the plague of 1713; while just around the corner, at the top of Lierova, is one of the few Gothic buildings to survive the 1770 fire, the **Kamenný dům**, built around 1480 and covered in an ornate sculptural icing. This used to contain an unexceptional local museum, which has now been moved a couple of blocks down Jiřího z Poděbrad, to Kilian Ignaz Dientzenhofer's unfinished **Voršilský klášter (Ursuline convent)**. Only three sides of the convent's ambitious pentagonal plan were completed, its neo-Baroque church added in the late nineteenth century while sv Barbora was being restored.

The museum is open April & Oct Sat & Sun 9am–4pm; May–Sept daily 9am–5pm; 30Kč.

Sedlec

Buses #1 and #4 run 3km northeast to **SEDLEC**, once a separate village but now a suburb of Kutná Hora. Adjoining Sedlec's defunct eighteenth-century Cistercian monastery (now the largest tobacco factory in Europe, owned by Phillip Morris) is the fourteenth-century church of **Panna Maria** (St Mary), imaginatively redesigned in the eighteenth century by Giovanni Santini, who specialized in melding Gothic with Baroque. Here, given a plain French Gothic church gutted during the Hussite wars, Santini set to work on the vaulting, adding his characteristic sweeping stucco rib patterns, relieved only by the occasional Baroque splash of colour above the chancel steps. For all its attractions, however, the church seems to be permanently covered in scaffolding, and closed except for the occasional service.

The church is open Tues–Sat 9am–noon & 1–5pm; 30Kč.

Cross the main road, following the signs, and you come to the monks' graveyard, where an ancient Gothic chapel leans heavily over the entrance to the macabre subterranean **kostnice** or ossuary, full to overflowing with human bones. When holy earth from Golgotha was scattered over the graveyard in the twelfth century, all of Bohemia's nobility wanted to be buried here and the bones mounted up until there were more than 40,000 complete sets. In 1870, worried about the ever-growing piles, the authorities commissioned František Rint to do something creative with them. He rose to the challenge and moulded out of bones four giant bells, one in each corner of the crypt, designed wall-to-ceiling skeletal decorations, including the Schwarzenberg coat of arms, and, as the centrepiece, put together a chandelier made out of every bone in the human body. Rint's signature (in bones) is at the bottom of the steps.

Kutná Hora

The ossuary is open daily: April & Oct 9am–5pm; May–Sept 8am–6pm; Nov–March 9am–noon & 1–4pm; 30Kč

Practicalities

The simplest way to get to Kutná Hora is to take a **bus** from outside metro Želivského (1hr 15min). Fast **trains** from Prague's Masarykovo nádraží take around an hour (there's only one in the morning); slow ones take two hours; trains from Praha hlavní nádraží involve a change at Kolín. The main **train station** (Kutná Hora hlavní nádraží) is a long way out of town, near Sedlec; bus #1 or #4 will take you into town, or there's usually a shuttle train service ready to leave for Kutná Hora město train station, near the centre of town.

The town has a highly efficient system of orientation signs, and at almost every street corner a pictorial list of the chief places of interest keeps you on the right track. Having said that, the train station signposted is not the main one. As for **eating and drinking**, *U Bakaláře*, at the junction of Husova and Nultysova, is one of the best restaurants in town, with a wide choice for vegetarians; *U Jakuba*, near the church of the same name, has an outdoor patio and a good fish menu; while *Piazza Navona*, on Palackého náměstí, is a real Italian pizzeria. There are plenty of good pubs, too, where you can get more simple fare: try *U havířů on* Šultysova (closed Mon), which offers a variety of brews including the local Dačický beer.

Konopiště

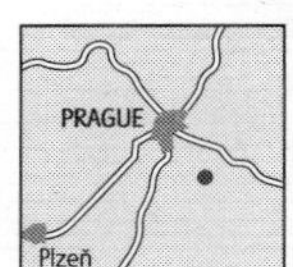

The popularity of **Konopiště**, with a quarter of a million visitors passing through its portcullis every year, is surpassed only by the likes of Karlštejn (see p.193). Of the two, Konopiště is the most interesting, though Karlštejn looks better from the outside. Coach parties from all over the world home in on this Gothic castle, which is stuffed with dead animals, weaponry and hunting trophies. Most interesting are its historical associations: King Václav IV was imprisoned for a while by

Konopiště

The chateau is open Tues–Sun: April & Oct 9am–3pm; May–Aug 9am–5pm; Sept 9am–4pm; 110Kč.

his own nobles in the castle's distinctive round tower, and the Archduke Franz Ferdinand, heir to the Habsburg throne, lived here with his wife, Sophie Chotek, until their assassination in Sarajevo in 1914. The archduke shared his generation's voracious appetite for hunting, eliminating all living creatures foolish enough to venture into the grounds. However, he surpassed all his contemporaries by recording, stuffing and displaying a significant number of the 171,537 birds and animals he shot between the years 1880 and 1906, the details of which are recorded in his *Schuss Liste* displayed inside.

There's a choice of **guided tours**. The first tour, *I okruh*, explores the period interiors, which contain some splendid Renaissance cabinets and lots of Meissen porcelain, while the *II okruh* takes you through the chapel, past the stuffed bears and deer teeth, to the assorted lethal weapons of one of the finest armouries in Europe. Both the above tours take 45 minutes, and, you'll be relieved to know, include the hunting trophies. The *III okruh* takes an hour, costs 240Kč, is restricted to just eight people per tour, and concentrates on the personal apartments of the Archduke and his wife. The couple hid themselves away in Konopiště, as they were shunned by the Habsburg court in Vienna, due to the fact that Sophie was a mere countess, and not an archduchess. Occasionally there are tours in English, French and German, too, so ask at the box office before you sign up.

The gallery of sv Jiří is open Tues–Sun: April, May, Sept & Oct 9am–1pm & 2–3pm; June–Aug 9am–1pm & 2–5pm; 20Kč.

Even if you don't fancy a guided tour, there are plenty of other things to do in Konopiště. In the main courtyard of the chateau, you can pop into the purpose-built **Střelnice** (Shooting Range), where the Archduke used to hone his skills as a marksman against moving mechanical targets, all of which have recently been lovingly restored. Tucked underneath the south terrace is the **Galerie sv Jiří**, which is stuffed to the gunnels with artefacts from paintings to statuettes and trinkets relating to Saint George, the fictional father of medieval chivalry, with whom the Archduke was obsessed. Much the best reason to come to Konopiště, though, is to explore its 555-acre **park**, which boasts several lakes, sundry statuary, an unrivalled rose garden and a deer park. There are also regular displays of falconry in the chateau's grounds (April & Oct Sat & Sun 10am, noon, 2 & 4pm; May–Sept Tues–Sun same times).

Practicalities

To get to Konopiště take a fast (50min) or slow (1hr 5min) **train** from Praha hlavní nádraží to Benešov u Prahy; the castle is a pleasant two-kilometre walk west of the railway station along the red- or yellow-marked path (buses are relatively infrequent). If the weather's fine take a picnic; otherwise, there are numerous food stalls by the main car park, and decent Czech fare in the nineteenth-century *Stará Myslivna*, on the path to the castle.

Karlštejn

PRAGUE
Křivoklát
Karlštejn
Plzeň

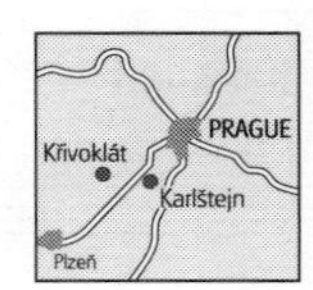

KARLŠTEJN is a small ribbon village, strung out along one of the tributaries of the Berounka – pretty, but not attractive enough to warrant a coach park the size of a football pitch. It's the **castle**, occupying a defiantly unassailable position above the village, which draws in the mass of tourists (over quarter of a million a year). Designed in the fourteenth century by Matthias of Arras for Emperor Charles IV as a giant safe-box for the imperial crown jewels and his large personal collection of precious relics, it quickly became Charles' favourite retreat from the vast city he himself had masterminded. Women were strictly forbidden to enter the castle, and the story of his third wife Anna's successful break-in (in drag) became one of the most popular Czech comedies of the nineteenth century.

The village of Karlštejn has been transformed over the last decade, with every other house offering rooms to rent or selling souvenirs.

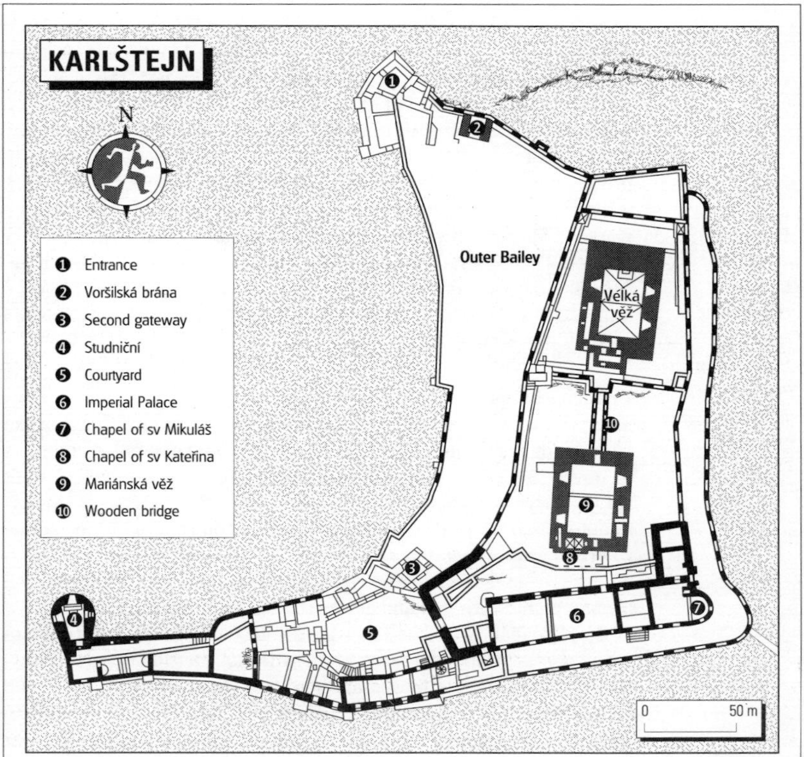
KARLŠTEJN
N
1 Entrance
2 Voršilská brána
3 Second gateway
4 Studniční
5 Courtyard
6 Imperial Palace
7 Chapel of sv Mikuláš
8 Chapel of sv Kateřina
9 Mariánská věž
10 Wooden bridge
Outer Bailey
Vélká věž
0
50 m

Most of what you see is eminently missable, with the exception of the **Muzeum Betlémů** (times as for the castle, but without a lunch break), which occupies the ground floor of a house towards the top of the village. For a modest entrance fee, you can admire an impressive array of nativity scenes dating back to the early nineteenth century. They range in size from complex mechanical set-ups to miniature affairs that can fit into small sea shells – there's even one in gingerbread.

If only the castle itself – a stunning sight from a distance – had such memorable treats in store. Sadly, centuries of neglect and generations of over-zealous restorers have taken their toll on the interior. Most of the rooms visited on the guided tour contain only the barest of furnishings, the empty spaces taken up by uninspiring displays on the history of the castle. Theoretically, the top two chambers would make the whole trip worthwhile: unfortunately, you can only look into (but not enter) the emperor's residential **Mariánská věž**. It was here that Charles shut himself off from the rest of the world, with any urgent business passed to him through a hole in the wall of the tiny ornate chapel of **sv Kateřina**.

As for the castle's finest treasure, the **Holy Rood Chapel** (*Kaple svatého kříže*), connected by a wooden bridge that leads on from here to the highest point of the castle, the **Velká věž**, this has been closed now since 1980 and it looks like it will remain so in the future as the sheer number of visitors would damage the decor irrevocably. Traditionally, only the emperor, the archbishop and the electoral princes could enter this gilded treasure house, whose six-metre-thick walls contain 2200 semiprecious stones and 128 painted panels, the work of Master Theodoric, Bohemia's greatest fourteenth-century painter. The imperial crown jewels, once secured here behind nineteen separate locks, were removed to Hungary after an abortive attack by the Hussites, while the Bohemian jewels are now stashed away in the cathedral in Prague.

A small selection of Master Theodoric's panels are exhibited in Prague's Jiřský klášter *(see p.59).*

Practicalities

Slow *osobní* or *zastavkový* **trains** leave Prague's Smíchovské nádraží for Karlštejn roughly every hour, and take about 35 minutes to cover the 28km from Prague. The village is ten minutes' walk across the river from the station, and it's a further fifteen- to twenty-minute climb up to the castle entrance. If you're looking for somewhere to grab a beer and a bite to eat, try *U Janů*, which has an outdoor terrace, or the *Koruna*, both on the main street. Alternatively, bring a picnic with you and eat by the banks of the river.

If you're feeling energetic, or have your own wheels, you could go to the popular flooded quarry, **Malá Amerika**. Getting there is tricky, however: either take the red-marked path from near the castle, and head off northwest through the woods at U dubu (you may need to ask a Czech to point you in the right direction), or head west down the track, which comes off the road between Mořina and Bubovice.

Lidice

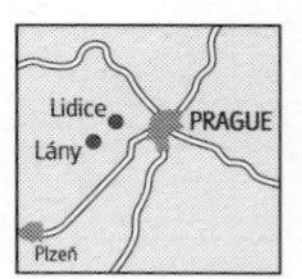

The small mining village of **LIDICE**, 18km northwest of Prague, hit world headlines on June 10, 1942, at the moment when it ceased to exist. On the flimsiest pretext, it was chosen as scapegoat for the assassination of the Nazi leader Reinhard Heydrich. All 173 men from the village were rounded up and shot by the SS, the 198 women were sent to Ravensbrück concentration camp, and the 89 children either went to the camps, or, if they were Aryan enough, were packed off to "good" German homes, while the village itself was burnt to the ground.

For a detailed account of Heydrich's assassination, see pp.144–145.

Knowing all this as you approach Lidice makes the modern village seem almost perversely unexceptional. At the end of the straight tree-lined main street, 10 Bervna 1942 (June 10, 1942), there's a dour concrete memorial with a small but horrific **museum** where you can watch a short film about Lidice, including footage shot by the SS themselves as the village was burning. The spot where the old village used to lie is just south of the memorial, now merely smooth green pasture punctuated with a few simple reminders and a new bronze memorial to the 82 local children who were gassed in the camps.

The museum is open daily: April–Oct 8am–5pm; Nov–March 8am–4pm.

After the massacre, the "Lidice shall live" campaign was launched and villages all over the world began to change their name to Lidice. The first was Stern Park Gardens, Illinois, soon followed by villages in Mexico and other Latin American countries. From Coventry to Montevideo, towns twinned themselves with Lidice, so that rather than "wiping a Czech village off the face of the earth" as Hitler had hoped, the Nazis created an international symbol of anti-fascist resistance.

There are regular buses from Florenc bus station, which pass by Lidice en route to Kladno; the journey takes 45 minutes.

7
ROW (K) SEAT 15

Part 3

Listings

Chapter 10

Accommodation

Finding a place to stay in Prague is no longer the nightmare it was back in the early 1990s when the city simply couldn't cope with the influx of new visitors. That said, the market is still top heavy with overpriced hotels and there is a chronic shortage of decent, inexpensive to middle-range hotels. Those who don't mind forgoing the pleasures of staying in a hotel, will encounter few problems getting a private room, except perhaps in July and August. All in all, though, accommodation is still likely to be by far the largest chunk of your daily expenditure, with private rooms starting at around 500Kč per person. At the extreme ends of the spectrum, you could spend as little as 200Kč per person for the cheapest youth hostel bed, or 5000Kč and upwards in the more salubrious hotels. It's worth asking about any special deals or reduced rates, though, quite honestly, unless you're in the city during a particularly slack period, demand for beds keeps prices buoyant. If you're going to Prague during high season (from Easter to September, or over the Christmas holidays), it's sensible to arrange accommodation before you arrive either directly with the hotels or through one of the specialist agencies listed on p.4 and p.12. As for camping, the main sites are a fair trek from the centre of town, and have only minimal facilities, but cheapness is their virtue: for two people and a tent pitch prices start at around 300Kč.

Accommodation agencies in Prague

AVE ☎ 24 22 35 21; *avetours@avetours.anet.cz*; daily 6am–11pm. AVE *is the largest agency in Prague, with offices at the airport and both international train stations, and is therefore an excellent last-minute fall-back.*

City of Prague Accommodation Service Haštalská 7, Staré Město; metro náměstí Republiky; ☎ 231 02 02, fax 231 66 40; daily 9am–1pm, 2–6pm. *More upmarket outfit with a good selection of centrally located private rooms.*

Pragotur Za Poříčskou bránou 7, Karlín; metro Florenc; ☎ 231 11 16; Mon–Fri 9am–6pm; Sat & Sun 8.30am–4pm. *The main office is situated just across the road from Florenc bus station, but they also operate through the various* PIS *offices. They can book anything from private rooms to hotels and hostels.*

Tom's Travel Ostrovní 7, Nové Město; metro Národní třída; ☎ 29 39 72; *toms@travel.cz*; daily 8am–8pm; June–Aug daily 8am–10pm. *Upmarket travel agency that can book you into hotels, pensions and apartments in Prague, and help with accommodation outside Prague, too.*

Accommodation

Private rooms

Renting a **private room** remains by far the most popular way to stay in Prague. Most Czechs keep their places very tidy and clean, but before agreeing to part with any money, be sure you know exactly where you're staying and check about transport to the centre – some places can be a long way out of town. Private rooms start at around 500Kč per person, and, like as not, you'll be sharing bathroom, cooking facilities, etc with your host family. This can be a great

If you're thinking of taking a private room or hotel somewhere in Prague, it's as well to know a little about the merits, or otherwise, of the various **postal districts** in the city (see map on p.36).

Prague 1
Prague 1 covers all of the old city on both sides of the river, and half of Nové Město, and consequently is the most expensive part of the capital in which to stay. Anything in this area will be within easy walking distance of the main sights, and will save you a lot of hassle, though you'll pay a higher rate for the privilege.

Prague 2
Prague 2 is another prime central area, taking in the southern half of Nové Město and western half of Vinohrady, a nineteenth-century des. res. with good metro connections.

Prague 3
The less salubrious, eastern half of Vinohrady in Prague 3 is nevertheless well served by the metro; Pižkov, on the other hand, is a crumbling, working-class district, connected to the centre only by trams.

Prague 4
Covers a wide area in the southeast of the city, stretching from half-decent, predominantly nineteenth-century suburbs such as Nusle, Podolí and Braník to the grim high-rise *panelák* buildings of Chodov and Háje. If you find yourself in either of the latter two areas, you can at least be sure of quick metro connections to the city centre.

Prague 5
Vast area in the hilly southwest of the city, with clean air and attractive family villas predominating and a metro line running through some of it. The area closest to the city, however, is Smíchov, a vibrant, polluted, working-class district, with correspondingly cheap rooms.

Prague 6
The perfect, hilly villa district to the north of the centre, a favourite with foreign embassies and their staff (not to mention Havel himself). The metro only goes as far as Dejvická, however, which means that only Dejvice and Bubeneč enjoy really fast connections with the centre.

Prague 7
The nineteenth-century suburb of Holešovice in the northeast is served by the metro and is something of a favourite ex-pat haunt. Troja, home to numerous ad hoc campsites, is almost bucolic and correspondingly difficult to get to.

Prague 8
The grid-plan streets of nineteenth-century Karlín are close to the centre and well served by the metro, which extends as far as Libeň; the rest of the area is neither aesthetically pleasing, nor easy to reach.

Prague 9
Dominated by factories, Prague 9, in the northeast of the city, is something of a last resort; however, with the extension of the metro to Černý most, it's easy enough to get into town.

Prague 10
Beware of Prague 10, which extends right into the countryside, though areas like Strašnice and Vršovice in the southeast of the city are closer to the centre of things and served, in part, by the metro.

way to meet the locals, though Czech hospitality can be somewhat overwhelming and such arrangements may not suit everyone. Most places also offer self-contained apartments, though you'll pay significantly more per person for the privilege.

The enormous supply of private accommodation in Prague means it's not really necessary to book in advance – although it can be worth doing so to save time, and for some peace of mind, especially if you're arriving in the peak season (see p.4 & p.12 for lists of travel agencies that specialize in booking accommodation in Prague). If you arrive without a room reservation, the easiest thing to do is head for one of the many **accommodation agencies** at the airport or main train stations, or, if the queues are long, one of the other agencies in town (see box on p.199). Alternatively, you're almost certain to be approached by a tout at the station, airport or sometimes outside one of the agencies. Most offers are genuine, but make sure you ask for a receipt before you pass over any money. Again, check exactly how far out of the centre you're going to be (and preferably see the room) before committing yourself.

Hotels and pensions

Pre-1989, Prague's **hotels** were much of a muchness: 1960s decor, a radio permanently tuned to the state news channel (very 1984) and sporadically hot showers. Matters have improved enormously since then, with almost all hotels now modernized to some degree, and more and more guaranteeing en-suite bathrooms, TVs and breakfast. The latter is usually included in the price of your room, and though more often than not little more than coffee and rolls, it's worth grabbing given the lack of any great alternatives out on the streets of Prague. **Pensions** are a new phenomenon and, though they tend to be smaller and less expensive, you can't guarantee it. Over all, standards still vary wildly, and don't always keep up with prices.

Since demand still exceeds supply, there's really no point in trekking around any of the hotels listed below on the off chance that they will have vacancies. Besides, Prague's cheaper hotels and pensions are scattered throughout the city, with few in the older quarters of Hradčany, Malá Strana and Staré Město. The best policy is to contact the hotel by email or phone before you leave for Prague and attempt to make a reservation that way, or use one of the agencies listed on p.199. The sub-headings used below correspond to the chapter headings in the guide. The price codes (for more on which, see box below), are followed by a grid reference to make it easy to locate the right street; the introductory notes under the sub-heading tell you which map to consult.

Hradčany

Hradčany is obviously a great area to stay in, right by the castle. The only problem is there are just two places to stay, and neither is particularly cheap. The grid references after the price codes refer to the map on pp.46–47.

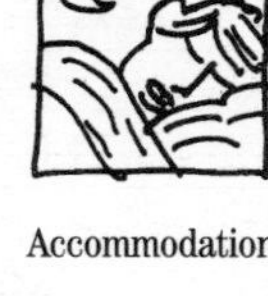

Accommodation

Accommodation prices

The accommodation lists below are divided according to area; within each section the lists are arranged alphabetically. After each entry you'll find a symbol which corresponds to one of nine price categories:

① Under 1000Kč	④ 2000–2500Kč	⑦ 3500–4000Kč
② 1000–1500Kč	⑤ 2500–3000Kč	⑧ 4000–5000Kč
③ 1500–2000Kč	⑥ 3000–3500Kč	⑨ 5000Kč and upwards

All prices are for the cheapest double room available in high season, which usually means without private bath or shower in the less expensive places. For a single room or a double in low season, expect to pay around two-thirds of the price.

Accommodation

Hotel Savoy, Keplerova 6; ☎24 30 24 30; *savoyhoprg@mbox.vol.cz*; tram #22 from metro Malostranská. Austrian-owned super-luxury hotel on the western edge of Hradčany, concealed behind a pretty Art Nouveau facade and famous for its marble bathrooms. Pretty prices too, with doubles starting at 7500Kč. ⑨. A4.

Hotel U raka, Černínská 10; ☎20 51 11 00; *uraka@login.cz*; tram #22 from metro Malostranská. The perfect hideaway, six rooms in a little half-timbered eighteenth-century cottage in Nový Svět. No children under 12 or dogs. ⑨. C1.

Malá Strana

Malá Strana is a beautiful area, and, with the exception of a few key streets, relatively traffic-free and quiet. It's also a pricey area; most places are in the higher price categories, but there are one or two bargains, for which it's worth booking ahead. The nearest **metro** station for all the places listed below is Malostranská, though some will require a further tram ride on tram #12 or #22. The grid references after the price codes refer to the map on pp.74–75.

Dům U velké boty (The Big Shoe), Vlašská 30; ☎57 31 11 07, fax 53 35 46. The sheer anonymity of this pension, in a lovely old building in the quiet backstreets, is one of its main draws. Run by a very friendly, English-speaking couple, it has a series of characterful, tastefully modernized rooms, some with en-suite, some without. Breakfast is extra, but worth it. ④. D3.

Hotel Hoffmeister, Pod Bruskou 7; ☎57 31 09 42; *hotel@hoffmeister.cz*. If you're looking for a large luxury hotel, this place, just a step away from Malostranská metro, has got to be a better bet than many of the more modern monstrosities in the outskirts. Over 6000Kč a double, not including breakfast. ⑨. J1.

Hotel pod věží, Mostecká 2; ☎53 37 10, fax 53 18 59. Even nicer than the *Hoffmeister*, this tiny luxury hotel is right by the Charles Bridge, with just twelve rooms and every possible facility you could want. ⑨. H5.

Hotel Sax, Jánský vršek 3; ☎53 84 22, fax 53 84 98. Fancy designer hotel tucked away in the backstreets off Tržiště, and a relative bargain given the location. ⑦. E3.

Hotel U krále Karla, Úvoz 4; ☎53 88 05, fax 53 88 11. Possibly the most tastefully exquisite of all the small luxury hotels in Malá Strana, with beautiful antique furnishings and stained-glass windows. ⑨. D1.

Hotel U kříže (The Cross), Újezd 20; ☎53 33 26, fax 53 34 43. No airs and graces at this modernized hotel on a busy street in the south of Malá Strana; B&B prices reduced in July and August. ⑤. E9.

Hotel U páva (The Peacock), U lužického semináře 32; ☎57 32 07 43; *hotelupava@tnet.cz*. Lovely little eight-room luxury hotel in a quiet part of Malá Strana; it's worth forking out for a room on the third floor, where you get an unrivalled view over the Vojanovy sady and up to the Hrad. ⑧. I5.

Hotel Waldstein, Valdštejnské náměstí 6; ☎53 80 08, fax 57 31 29 83. A quiet, small, secluded hotel, which retains a lovely courtyard and several original Renaissance ceilings, and is tastefully decked out. ⑧. H3.

Kampa – Stará zbrojnice, Všehrdova 16; ☎57 32 05 08, fax 57 32 02 62. Wonderful backstreet location on Kampa island, close to the Charles Bridge, but not quite as expensive (or as professional) as some of the hotels in Malá Strana. ⑥. F9.

Penzion Dientzenhofer, Nosticova 2; ☎53 16 72, fax 57 32 08 88. Birthplace of its namesake, and a very popular pension due to its price and the fact that it's one of the few reasonably priced places (anywhere in Prague) to have wheelchair access. Just seven rooms on offer. ⑤. G7.

Pension U kiliána, Všehrdova 13; ☎567 81 40, fax 73 41 10. One plain en-suite double and one triple above a snack bar down a quiet side street on Kampa. ⑤.

U tří pštrosů (The Three Ostriches),

Dražického náměstí 12; ☎24 51 07 79, fax 24 51 07 83. Exquisite Renaissance house adjacent to the Charles Bridge; the rooms have wooden floorboards and beams, and some have original ceiling frescoes and views across the river. ⑨. H5.

Staré Město

Staré Město is right in the centre of things, with lots of pubs and restaurants to choose from, all within easy walking distance. Inexpensive places to stay are few and far between, but there are a few moderately priced options – again, it's worthwhile booking ahead if possible. The grid references after the price codes refer to the map on pp.78–79.

Betlém Club, Betlémské náměstí 9; ☎24 21 68 72, fax 24 21 80 54; metro Národní třída. Small rooms, slightly tacky decor, but a perfect location and a Gothic cellar for breakfast. ⑥. D7.

Cloister Inn, Bartolomějská 9; ☎232 77 00; *cloister@cloisterinn.cz*; metro Národní třída. Pleasant, well-equipped hotel housed in a nunnery in one of the backstreets; there are cheaper rooms too, and a hostel in *Pension Unitas*, in the same building (see below). ⑥. D8.

Grand Hotel Bohemia, Kralodvorská 4; ☎24 80 41 11, fax 232 95 45; metro náměstí Republiky. Sumptuously luxurious hotel just behind the Obecní dům, with some very tasty Art Nouveau décor, and all the amenities you'd expect at 8500Kč a double. ⑨. I4.

Hotel Centrál, Rybná 8; ☎24 81 20 41, fax 232 84 04; metro náměstí Republiky. True to its name, and one of the very few reasonably priced hotels in Staré Město, partly because, despite the renovation, it's an old-style Communist hotel at heart, in terms of service and facilities. ⑥. I4.

Hotel Paříž, U Obecního domu 1; ☎24 22 21 51; *prgpariz@mbox.vol.cz*; metro náměstí Republiky. The turn-of-the-century decor here is less flamboyant than at the *Evropa*, though equally pleasing to the eye and in a lot better condition. Service, however, remains firmly stuck in the Communist past, despite the fact that doubles go for 8000Kč. ⑨. J4.

Hotel U klenotníka, Rytířská 3; ☎24 21 16 99, fax 26 17 82; metro Můstek. A former jeweller's, with ten small rooms and a slightly dubious taste in interior design. ⑦. F7.

Pension Avalon, Havelská 15; ☎26 36 43, fax 26 36 42; metro Můstek. Perfect location right over the market on Havelská, with seven small, plainly furnished but clean rooms, with or without en-suite facilities. ②. F7.

Pension U krále Jiřího, Liliová 10; ☎24 22 20 13, fax 24 22 19 83; metro Staroměstská. Eight cosy attic rooms above an "Irish" pub, hidden in the network of lanes which characterize this part of Staré Město. ⑤. D6.

Pension U medvídků (The Little Bears), Na Perštýně 7; ☎24 21 19 16, fax 24 22 09 30; metro Národní třída. Eight plainly furnished rooms (doubles and triples only) above a famous Prague pub; booking ahead essential. ③–⑥. E8.

Pension Unitas, Bartolomějská 9; ☎232 12 89; *unitas@cloisterinn.cz*; metro Národní třída. Run by the *Cloister Inn* (see above), with hostel rooms, plus bargain rooms in converted secret police prison cells (Havel stayed in P6), now owned by Franciscan nuns. No smoking and no drinking, but unbelievably cheap. ②. D8.

Penzion U zlaté studny (The Golden Well), Karlova 3; ☎ & fax 24 21 05 39; metro Staroměstská. Three apartments overlooking the tourist thoroughfare of Karlova, decked out in High Baroque style. ⑦. D6.

Nové Město

Nové Město covers a large area of the city, and some of its main thoroughfares are badly blighted by traffic. Some places listed here are literally walking distance from the old town, but in its nether regions, you'll need to hop on a tram or metro to get into the centre of town. The grid references after the price codes refer to the map on pp.124–125.

Grand Hotel Evropa, Václavské náměstí 25; ☎24 22 81 17, fax 24 22 45 44; metro Můstek/Muzeum. Without doubt, the most beautiful hotel in Prague, built

Accommodation

Price codes
① Under 1000Kč
② 1000–1500Kč
③ 1500–2000Kč
④ 2000–2500Kč
⑤ 2500–3000Kč
⑥ 3000–3500Kč
⑦ 3500–4000Kč
⑧ 4000–5000Kč
⑨ 5000Kč and upwards

Accommodation

Price codes
① Under 1000Kč
② 1000–1500Kč
③ 1500–2000Kč
④ 2000–2500Kč
⑤ 2500–3000Kč
⑥ 3000–3500Kč
⑦ 3500–4000Kč
⑧ 4000–5000Kč
⑨ 5000Kč and upwards

in the 1900s and sumptuously decorated in Art Nouveau style; the rooms are furnished in repro Louis XIV, and there are some cheaper ones without en-suite facilities. Despite its prime location and its incredible décor, this place is run like an old Communist hotel – a blast from the past in every sense. ④. G5.

Hotel Axa, Na poříčí 40; ☎24 81 25 80, fax 24 81 20 67; metro Florenc. Partially refurbished hotel with adjacent swimming pool and gym, just ten minutes' walk from náměstí Republiky – make sure you see your room before booking in, as standards in each can vary. ⑥. I2.

Hotel Hlávkova kolej, Jenštejnská 1; ☎& fax 29 00 98; metro Karlovo náměstí. Ornate late nineteenth-century hotel on the outside; former student hostel on the inside, with spartan but clean en-suite doubles. ③. C7.

Hotel Koruna, Opatovická 16; ☎24 91 51 74, fax 29 24 92; metro Národní třída. Great location in the backstreets just south of Národní, though the hotel itself is no great shakes. ⑤. D6.

Hotel 16, Kateřinská 16; ☎29 53 29, fax 29 39 56; metro Karlovo náměstí. Really friendly family-run hotel offering small en-suite rooms with TV in a quiet backstreet of southern Nové Mesto. ⑤. F8.

Hotel Legie, Sokolská 33; ☎24 92 02 54, fax 24 91 44 41; metro I. P. Pavlova. Former military R&R centre on a busy road, just one stop or a short stroll from Wenceslas Square. It looks bad from the outside, but the rooms are fine inside and are all en-suite. ④. G7.

Hotel Opera, Těšnov 13; ☎231 56 09; *htlopera@login.cz;* metro Florenc. Moderately priced nineteenth-century hotel; remarkably pleasant considering it's right by the flyover. ⑦. I1.

Hotel Palace, Panská 12; ☎24 09 31 11; *palhoprg@mbox.vol.cz;* metro Můstek. While all the other luxury hotels in Prague try their best, the *Palace*, located just off Wenceslas Square, really is the best in terms of service and facilities – but then what else would you expect at 9000Kč a double? ⑨. G4.

Hotel sv Salvator, Truhlářská 10; ☎231 22 34, fax 231 63 55; metro náměstí Republiky. Very good location, just a minute's walk from naměstí Republiky, with small but clean rooms (the cheaper ones without en-suite facilities), and a bar/breakfast/pool room. ③. H2.

Hotel Standard, Rašínovo nábřeží 38; ☎ & fax 29 87 97; metro Karlovo náměstí. An apt name for this riverside hotel; the modernized rooms are en-suite and all have TVs, but there's absolutely nothing special about them. ④. C10.

Vyšehrad and the eastern suburbs

Vinohrady is a pleasant nineteenth-century suburb, a few metro or tram stops east of Wenceslas Square, while Žižkov is a more run-down area, best-known for its riotous pubs, and large Romany population. The grid references after the price codes refer to the map on pp.150–151.

Hotel Anna, Budečská 17, Vinohrady; ☎22 51 31 11; *reception@hotelanna.cz;* metro náměstí Míru. Tastefully decorated and renovated rooms in a nice part of Vinohrady, close to Wenceslas Square. ④. E5.

Hotel Kafka, Cimburkova 24, Žižkov; ☎24 61 71 18, fax 24 22 57 69; tram #5, #9 or #26 from metro Hlavní nádraží. TVs, en-suite shower and toilet, but only sporadic hot water – still better than what the residents on the other side of the courtyard can expect. ②. G3.

Hotel Luník, Londýnská 50, Vinohrady; ☎24 25 39 74, fax 24 25 39 86; metro I. P. Pavlova. Unpretentious modernized hotel in a fairly peaceful location, just a short walk from Wenceslas Square. ④. D5.

Hotel Ostaš, Orebitská 8, Žižkov; ☎& fax 627 94 18; tram #5, #9 or #26 from metro Hlavní nádraží. Rather soulless place just off Kostnické náměstí, but offering clean, modern rooms with en-suite facilities and TVs. ③. F3.

Pension City, Belgická 10, Vinohrady; ☎691 13 34, fax 691 09 77; metro náměstí Míru. Quiet locale, cheap, clean en-suite rooms with TVs and within walking distance of Wenceslas Square. ③. D6.

Accommodation

Holešovice and the western suburbs

Holešovice is another pleasant late-nineteenth-century residential suburb, within easy walking distance of a lot of greenery, and with good metro and tram connections. Střešovice is a highly sought-after garden villa suburb, but its public transport connections aren't great. Smíchov, rather like Žižkov, has a reputation as a bit of a rough, industrial suburb, but it's well connected by metro, and, naturally enough, fairly inexpensive. The grid references after the price codes refer to the map on pp.34–35.

Gay Penzion David, Holubova 5; ☎90 01 12 93, fax 54 98 20; tram #14 from metro Anděl. Friendly gay/lesbian pension (complete with sauna) in the hills above Smíchov, with its own restaurant; advance booking essential. ④. B10.

Holiday Inn, Koulova 15, Dejvice; ☎24 39 31 11, fax 24 31 06 16; tram #20 or #25 from metro Dejvická. Prague's classic 1950s *Stalinist International Hotel*, with its dour socialist realist friezes and large helpings of marble, is now, somewhat unbelievably, a bona fide *Holiday Inn*. ⑧. B1.

Hotel Balkán, Svornosti 28, Smíchov; ☎57 32 71 80, fax 57 32 55 83; metro Anděl. One of the cheapest hotels in Prague; like Smíchov itself, it has no frills, but is clean and comfortable. ②. D9.

Hotel Coubertin, Atletická 4, Strahov; ☎33 35 31 09; bus #217, #149 or #143 to the Strahov stadión from metro Dejvická. Modern hotel attached to the south side of the Strahov stadium; only really worth it if you're coming for a sporting event. ④. B7.

Hotel Digitals, Na Petynce 106, Střešovice; ☎24 31 37 39, fax 24 31 35 83; bus #108 or #174 from metro Hradčanská. Nice en-suite rooms, located in the villa quarter fifteen to twenty minutes' walk from the Hrad. ③. A5.

Hotel Henry, U papírny 11, Holešovice; ☎& fax 80 12 57; metro Nádraží Holešovice. The purple theme is a bit worrying, but the rooms are plainly modernized, and have shower/toilet and TV; a stone's throw from Výstavištšě. ③. G1.

Hotel Julián, Elišky Peškové 11, Smíchov; ☎53 51 37, fax 54 75 25; tram #6, #9 or #12 from metro Anděl. Big hotel on the very edge of Malá Strana. Slightly dodgy decor, but all the usual facilities, and a nice lounge with a real fire. ⑤. D8.

Hotel Petr, Drtinova 17; ☎57 31 40 68, fax 57 31 00 67; tram #6, #9 or #12 from metro Anděl. Newly refurbished hotel situated at the foot of Petřín hill, close to Malá Strana. ③. C7.

Hotel Praha, Sušická 20, Dejvice; ☎24 34 11 11; *htlpraha@mbox.vol.cz*; tram #2, #20 or #26 from metro Dejvická. The old Party VIP hotel, where the likes of Ceauşescu once stayed. An appropriately grotesque 1970s concrete palace, but with wonderful views over to the Hrad. Inconveniently placed for public transport, so most guests take a taxi. ⑨. A2.

Pension Větrník, U Větrníku 40, Střešovice; ☎20 61 24 04; *milos.opatrny@telecom.cz*; tram #1 or #18 from metro Hradčanská. Six rooms in a converted eighteenth-century windmill, with a walled garden, private tennis courts and nice proprietor and dog – book early. ⑤. West of A4.

Hostels

There are a fair few **hostels** in Prague which cater for the large number of backpackers who hit the city all year round – and these are supplemented further by a whole host of more transient, high-season-only hostels. **Prices** in hostels range from 200Kč to 400Kč for a bed, usually in a dormitory. Some hostels operate **curfews** – it's worth asking before you commit yourself – and, although many rent out blankets and sheets, it's as well to bring your own sleeping bag. Note that some of the accommodation agencies in Prague also deal with hostels; see p.199 for details.

The chief Czech organization affiliated to Hostelling International is Cestovní kancelář mládeže (CKM), whose head office is at Žitná 12, Nové Město (☎24 91 57 67; metro Karlovo náměstí). They run a hostel at the same address, and can book you into the **Domov mládeže**; you can also buy HI membership from them.

Prague's university, the Karolinum, rents out over a thousand **student**

Accommodation

rooms from June to mid-September, starting at 200Kč for a bed. Go to the head booking office at Terronská 28, Dejvice (☎24 31 11 05, fax 24 31 11 07; metro Dejvická; daily 9am–7pm).

Another organization specializing in summer-only dorms is Traveller's Hostels, a chain of centrally located youth hostels which are very poular with US students. Their main booking office is round the corner at Dlouhá 33, Staré Město (☎231 13 18; *hostel@terminal.cz*), where there is a hostel (see below); dorm beds go for 350Kč and upwards per person.

Clown and Bard, Bořivojova 102, Žižkov; ☎27 24 36; tram #5, #9 or #26 from metro Hlavní nádraží. So laid-back it's horizontal, and not a place to go if you don't like hippies, but it's clean, undeniably cheap, and rents out doubles (①) as well as dorm beds for under 200Kč per person. Open all year.

Club Habitat, Na Zbořenci 10, Nové Město; ☎29 03 15, fax 29 31 01; metro Karlovo náměstí. The best of Prague's official HI hostels, located a short walk from Karlovo náměstí. Dorm beds for 350Kč per person. Open all year.

ESTEC Hostel, Vaníčkova 5, Strahov; ☎57 21 04 10; *estec@jrc.cz*; bus #217, #149 or #143 to the Strahov stadión from metro Dejvická. This is a chaotic, but cheap, hostel in the midst of student land, but only a fifteen-minute walk from Hradčany through Petřín. To find the hostel, head for block 5, opposite the east stand of the Strahov stadium. Dorms 160Kč for a bed; doubles 290Kč per person; singles 400Kč plus. Open all year.

Hotel Standart, Přístavní 2, Holešovice; ☎87 52 58, fax 80 67 52; tram #12 or #25 from metro Nádraží Holešovice. Despite the name, this is an official HI hostel. It's not conveniently located, though tram #3 will get into the centre of town quickly enough. Dorm beds (and breakfast) from around 300Kč per person (with an HI card); ask about doubles too. Open all year.

Kolej Komenského, Parléřova 6, Břevnov; ☎35 03 37, fax 35 20 10; tram #8 or #22. You can turn up on spec, but it's best to book through Universitas Tour, Opletalova 38, Nové Město (☎26 04 26, fax 24 21 22 90). Good location, just ten minutes' walk from the Hrad; dorm beds as well as doubles for around 500Kč per person. Open all year.

Libra Q, Senovážné náměstí 21; ☎24 10 55 36, fax 24 22 15 79; metro Hlavní nádraží. Friendly, centrally located, inexpensive hostel with dorm beds from 350Kč per person, and cheap doubles (①–②). Open all year.

Pension Dlouhá, Dlouhá 33, Staré Město; ☎57 21 04 10; *estec@jrc.cz*; metro Náměstí Republiky. Very centrally located hostel and booking office, so if there's not enough room here, they'll find you a bed somewhere for around 350Kč per person. Open all year.

Campsites

Prague abounds in **campsites** – there's a whole rash of them in Troja (see below) – and most are relatively easy to get to by public transport. Facilities, on the whole, are rudimentary and badly maintained, but the prices reflect this, starting at around 300Kč for a tent and two people.

Autocamp Trojská, Trojská 375, Troja; ☎& fax 854 29 45; bus #112 from metro Nádraží Holešovice. Good location in someone's large back garden, 3km north of the centre on the road to the Troja chateau. Open all year.

Kemp Džbán, Nad lávkou 5, Vokovice; ☎36 90 06, fax 36 13 65; tram #20 or #26 from metro Dejvická. Large field with tent pitches, bungalows and basic facilities, 4km west of the centre, near the Nárka valley. Open all year.

Chapter 11

Eating and drinking

The good news is that you can eat and drink very cheaply in Prague: the food is filling and the beer is divine. The bad news is that the kindest thing you can say about Czech food is that it is hearty. Forty years of culinary isolation under the Communists introduced few innovations to Czech cuisine, with its predilection for pork, gravy, dumplings and pickled cabbage. Fresh vegetables (other than potatoes) remain a rare sight on traditional Czech menus, and salads are still waiting for their day.

That said, the choice of places where you can eat has improved enormously over the last decade. You can spend a whole week eating out and never go near a dumpling, should you so wish. Czechs themselves are very keen on pizzas, and there are now some very good pizzerias in the capital – there are even some passably authentic ethnic restaurants ranging from Japanese and Lebanese to Balkan and French. In addition, there's also a whole range of new, slightly more expensive restaurants aimed at the palates (and wallets) of the passing tourist, the ex-pat community, wealthy Czechs and the diplomatic crowd.

So while it's important to sample authentic Czech food, and experience Czech eating habits, many visitors are happy to pay a bit more for food that is tastier, more imaginative, and – more often than not – not very Czech.

Where to eat

Not surprisingly, the places in the main tourist areas along Mostecká and Karlova, on either side of the Charles Bridge, and on Staroměstské náměstí and Wenceslas Square, tend to be overpriced, relying on their geographical position rather than the quality of their food, to bring in custom. Venture instead into the backstreets of Staré Město and Nové Město, or to suburbs like Vinohrady and Holešovice, just ten minutes' travel by metro from the centre, and you're likely to get much better value for money.

Czech pubs or *pivnice* are the cheapest places to eat, on the whole, though it's as well to remember that Czechs traditionally eat their main meal of the day at lunchtime, between noon and 2pm. In *pivnice*, you'll get the widest choice of dishes around this time of day, with progressively fewer available as the day goes on – kitchens in pubs can close as early as 9pm. Prices tend to climb a great deal higher in the city's restaurants, which cater for more international habits, and stay open much later in the evening.

Traditional Czech menus

Most traditional Czech menus start with **soup** (*polévka*), one of the country's culinary strong points, served mainly at lunchtimes in pubs. Some places will have a selection of starters such as *uzený jazyk* (smoked tongue) or *tresčí játra*

Eating and Drinking

(cod's liver). *Šunková rolka* is another favourite, consisting of ham topped with whipped cream and horseradish, but you're more likely to find yourself skipping the starters, which are often little more than a selection of cold meats.

Main courses tend to be divided into several separate sections. *Hotová jídla* (ready-made meals) and *jídla na objednávku* or *minutky* (meals made to order). In either case, dishes are overwhelmingly based on **meat** (*maso*), usually pork, sometimes beef. The Czechs are experts on these meats, and although the quality could often be better, the variety of sauces and preparative techniques is usually good. The difficulty lies in decoding names such as *klašterny tajemství* ("mystery of the monastery") or even a common dish like *Moravský vrabec* (literally "Moravian sparrow", but actually just roast pork).

Fish (*ryby*) is generally listed separately, or along with chicken and other fowl like duck. River trout and carp (the traditional dish at Christmas) are the cheapest and most widely available fish, and although their freshness may be questionable, they are usually served, grilled or roasted, in delicious buttery sauces or breadcrumbs.

Dumplings (*knedlíky*), though German in origin and name, are now the mainstay of Bohemian cooking. The term itself is misleading for English-speakers, since they resemble nothing like the English dumpling – more like a heavy white bread. *Houskové knedlíky* are made from flour and come in large slices (four or five to a dish), while *bramborové knedlíky* are smaller and made from potato and flour. Occasionally, you may be treated to *ovocné knedlíky* (fruit dumplings), the king of *knedlíky*. **Fresh salads** rarely rise above tomato, cucumber or cabbage (*zelí*), often swimming in a slightly sweet, watery dressing.

With the exception of *palačinky* (pancakes) filled with chocolate or fruit and cream, **desserts** (*moučníky*), where they exist at all, can be pretty unexciting. Often the ice cream and cakes on offer in restaurants aren't really up to the standards of the stuff sold on the street, so go to a café or ***cukrárna*** (confectioners) if you want a dose of sugar; for more on which see p.214.

Vegetarian eating

Czech meat consumption has dropped dramatically since 1989, but it remains one of the highest in the world. It's hardly suprisingly then that **vegetarianism** is still a minority sport. Nevertheless, you're better off in Prague than anywhere else in the country. For a start, places which cater mostly for ex-pats usually have one or two veggie options, and there are plenty of pizzerias.

Even in traditional Czech places, most menus have a section called *bezmasa* (literally "without meat") – don't take this too literally, though, for it simply means the main ingredient is not dead animal; dishes like *omeleta se šunkou* (ham omelette) regularly appear under these headings, so always check first. Emergency standbys which most Czech pubs will knock up for you without too much fuss include *knedlíky s vejci* (dumplings and egg), *omeleta s hráškem* (pea omelette), or *smažený sýr*, a slab of melted cheese (and, more often than not, ham) deep-fried in breadcrumbs. Other common deep-fried dishes include *smažené žampiony* (mushrooms) and *smažený květák* (cauliflower).

The only exclusively veggie places are *Country Life* (see p.214), *Góvinda* (see p.226), *Lotos* (see p.225), *Radost FX* (see p.227), and *U Bakaláře* (see p.214). Veggie phrases to remember are *"jsem vegeterián/vegeteriánka. Máte nejaké bezmasa?"* (I'm a vegetarian. Is there anything without meat?); for emphasis, you could add *"nejím maso nebo ryby"* (I don't eat meat or fish).

Alcohol

Alcohol consumption among Czechs has always been high, and in the decade following the events of 1968 it doubled. A whole generation found solace in drinking, mostly beer; the Czechs have been top of the world league table of beer consumption for some time now. However, it's a problem which seldom spills out onto the streets; violence in pubs is uncommon and you won't see that many drunks in public.

Czech **beer** ranks among the best in the world and the country remains the true home of most of the lager drunk around the world today. It was in the Bohemian city of Plzeň (Pilsen) that the first **bottom-fermented** beer was introduced in 1842, after complaints from the citizens about the quality of the top-fermented predecessor. The new brewing style quickly spread to Germany, and is now blamed for the bland rubbish served up in the English-speaking world as lager or Pils.

The distinctive flavour of Czech beer comes from the famous Bohemian hops, Žatec (Saaz) Red, still hand-picked and then combined with the soft local water and served with a high content of absorbed carbon dioxide – hence the thick, creamy head. Under the Communists, brewing methods in the Czech Republic remained stuck in the old ways, but the 1990s have seen many breweries opt for modernization: pasteurization, de-oxidization, rapid maturation and carbon dioxide injections – all of which mean less taste, more fizz. It's a development against which the Czech Beer Party and Britain's own Campaign for Real Ale (CAMRA) are fighting hard.

Beer (*pivo*) is served by the half-litre; if you want anything smaller, you must specifically ask for a *malé pivo* (0.3l). The average jar is medium strength, usually about 1050 specific gravity or 4.2 percent alcohol. Somewhat confusingly, the Czechs class their beers using the Balling scale, which measures the original gravity, calculated according to the amount of malt and dissolved sugar present before fermentation. The most common varieties are 10° (*desítka*), which are generally slightly weaker than 12° (*dvanáctka*). Light beer (*světlé*) is the norm, but many pubs also serve a slightly sweeter dark variety (*černé*) – or, if you prefer, you can have a mixture of the two (*řezané*).

Eating and Drinking

Czech beers

The most famous Czech beer is **Pilsner Urquell**, known to the Czechs as Plzeňský Prazdroj, the original bottom-fermented Pils from Plzeň (Pilsen), a city 80km south-west of Prague. Plzeň also boasts the **Gambrinus** brewery, whose domestic sales actually exceed those of Pilsner Urquell. The other big Bohemian brewing town is České Budějovice (Budweis), home to the country's biggest selling export beer, **Budvar**, a mildly flavoured brew for Bohemia but still leagues ahead of Budweiser, the German name for Budvar that was adopted by American brewers, Anheuser-Busch, in 1876 (and a cause of litigious grief ever since).

The biggest brewery in the country is in the Smíchov suburb of Prague where **Staropramen** (meaning "ancient spring") is produced, a typical Bohemian brew with a mild hoppy flavour. Some Staropramen is also produced at the Holešovice brewery, better known for its popular, dark **Měšťan** beer. The city's other brewery is in the southern suburb of **Braník**, a light, malty brew that was one of the first to opt for modernization. Prague also boasts several **micro-breweries** in Nové Město: the older of the two, U Fleků, which has been brewing **Flek**, a dark caramel concoction, since 1499 is now sadly a tourist trap; the beer produced at the newly established Novoměstský pivovar is vastly inferior, but the place itself is preferable, as is the nearby Pivovarský dům. It's difficult to avoid **Radegast**, a very popular drinkable brew from North Moravia, and the German-owned **Krušovice** beer, but one beer worth seeking out is the award-winning, hoppy and slightly bitter **Velkopopovický kozel**.

Eating and Drinking

Czech **wine** will never win over as many people as its beer, but since the import of French and German vines in the fourteenth century, it has produced a modest selection of medium-quality wines. The main wine region is South Moravia, though a little is produced around the Bohemian town of Mělník (see p.181). Suffice to say that most domestic wine is pretty drinkable – Frankovka is a perfectly respectable, though slightly sweet, red; Veltlínské zelené a good, dry white – and rarely much more than £1/$1.60 a bottle in shops, while the best stuff can only be had from the private wine cellars, hundreds of which still exist out in the regions. A Czech speciality to look out for is *burčák*, a very young, misty wine of varying (and often very strong) alcoholic content, which appears on the streets in the vine harvest season in September.

All the usual **spirits** are on sale and known by their generic names, with rum and vodka dominating the market. The home production of brandies is a national pastime, which results in some almost terminally strong liquors. The most renowned of the lot is **slivovice**, a plum brandy originally from the border hills between Moravia and Slovakia. You'll probably also come across *borovička*, a popular Slovak firewater, made from pine trees; *myslivec* is a rough brandy with a firm following. There's also a fair selection of intoxicating herbal concoctions: *fernet* is a dark-brown bitter drink, known as *bavorák* (Bavarian beer) when it's mixed with tonic, while *becherovka* is a supposedly healthy herbal spirit from the Bohemian spa town of Karlovy Vary, with a very unusual, almost medicinal taste.

The Czech Republic is also one of the few countries in the world where **absinthe** is still legal. The preferred poison of Parisian painters and poets in the 1920s, absinthe is a nasty green spirit made from fermented wormwood – it even gets a Biblical mention in Revelations: "and the name of the star is called Wormwood: and the third part of the waters became wormwood; and many men died of the waters, because they were made bitter". St John wasn't wrong: at 170 degrees proof, it's dangerous stuff and virtually undrinkable neat. To make it vaguely palatable, you need to set light to an absinthe-soaked spoonful of sugar, and then mix the caramalized mess with the absinthe.

There's not much to say about Czech **soft drinks**, with the exception of the high-energy drink Semtex, a can of which will amuse friends back home. Last of all, if you're looking for a decent **mineral water** (*minerální voda*), ask for the ubiquitous Mattoni, a mild and not too fizzy option.

Breakfast, snacks and fast food

Many Czechs get up so early in the morning (often around 5 or 6am) that they don't have time to start the day with anything more than a quick cup of coffee. As a result, the whole concept of **breakfast** (*snidaně*) as such is alien to the Czechs. Most hotels will serve the "continental" basics of coffee and rolls, but it's cheaper and often more enjoyable to go hunting for your own. Bear in mind, too, that if you get up much past 10am, you might as well join Prague's working population for an early lunch.

Pastries (*pečivo*) are available from Prague's bakeries (*pekářství* or *pekárna*), but rarely in bars and cafés, so you'll most likely have to eat them on the go. Traditional Czech pastry (*koláč*) is more like sweet bread, dry and fairly dense with only a little condiment to flavour it, such as almonds (*oříškový*), poppy seed jam (*mákový*), plum jam (*povidlový*) or a kind of sour-sweet curd cheese (*tvarohový*). Recently, French- and Viennese-style bakeries have started to appear in Prague, selling croissants (*loupáky*) and lighter cream cakes.

Czech **bread** (*chléb*) is some of the tastiest around when fresh. The standard loaf is *domací* or *šumava*, a dense mixture of wheat and rye, which you can buy whole, in halves (*pul*) or quarters (*čtvrtina*). *Český chléb* is a mixture of rye,

Eating and Drinking

wheat and whey, with distinctive slashes across the top; *kmínový chléb* is the same loaf packed full of caraway seeds. *Moskva* is a national favourite, despite the name – a moist, heavy, sour-dough loaf that lasts for days. Rolls come in two basic varieties: *rohlík*, a plain white finger roll, and *houska*, a rougher, tastier round bun.

Prague's stand-up **bufets** are open from as early as 6am and offer everything from light snacks to full meals. A cross between a British greasy spoon and an American diner, they're usually self-service (*samoobsluha*) and non-smoking, and occasionally have rudimentary seats. The cheapest of the tired-looking meat sausages on offer is *sekaná*, bits of old meat and bread squashed together to form a meat loaf (for connoisseurs only). *Guláš* (goulash) is popular, usually *Szegedinský* (pork with sauerkraut) but sometimes *special* (with better meat and a creamier sauce). Less substantial fare boils down to *chlebíčky* – artistically presented **open sandwiches** with combinations of gherkins, cheese, salami, ham and aspic – and mountains of mayonnaise-type **salad**, bought by weight (200 grammes is a medium-sized portion).

The ubiquitous Czech street **takeaway** is the hot dog or *párek*, a dubious-looking frankfurter (traditionally two – *párek* means a pair), dipped in mustard and served in a white roll (*v rohlíku*). A greasier option is *bramborák*, a thin potato pancake with little flecks of bacon or salami in it; *felafal* or kebabs (known as *gyros*) form another popular takeaway choice, usually with pitta bread and salad. And, of course, there are now numerous western-style fast-food joints (most notably *McDonald's*) all over Prague.

Malá Strana

Grid references after the opening times refer to the map on pp.74–75.

Bohemia Bagel, Újezd 16; tram#12 or #22 from metro Malostranská. Takeaway bagels at the side, but with a sit-down café too, where you can have an all-day breakfast or sandwiches as well as bagels. Daily 8am–midnight. E9.

Pekařství v Karmelitské, Karmelitská 20 4; tram #12 or #22 from metro Malostranská. Nice new bakery, just south of Malostranské náměstí, with a café attached where you wash down your cakes and pastries with coffee. Bakery: Mon–Fri 7am–7pm, Sun noon–6pm. Café: Mon–Fri 10am–8pm, Sat & Sun 10am–8pm. F6.

Ice cream

Whatever the season, Czechs have to have their daily fix of **ice cream** (*zmrzlina*), dispensed from window kiosks in the sides of buildings, and, more frequently now, from more substantial outlets, some with seating.

Dánská zmrzlina, Spálená 49, Nové Město; metro Národní třída. None-too-cheap option, but you're paying for the delicious cones, baked fresh on the premises. Daily 10am–8pm.

Dolce Vita, Vězenská, 15, Staré Město; metro Staroměstská. A pleasant sit-down café in the old town, which also serves excellent ice cream and cakes. Daily 8.30am–midnight.

Ovocný bar, Václavské náměstí 52, Nove Město; metro Můstek/Muzeum. Very Czech, very *Clockwork Orange* bilberry-coloured milk bar serving ice cream and huge fruit salads; located on the first floor above a grocery store on the corner of Ve Smečkách. Mon–Sat 9.30am–9.30pm, Sun noon–9pm.

Světozor, Vodičková 39, Nové Město; metro Můstek. Sit-down or takeaway, this reasonably priced *lahůdky* in the *pasáž* of the same name has over twenty varieties of ice cream, plus pastries, cakes, the lot; it's situated in the Světozor cinema passage. Mon–Sat 9am–8pm, Sun noon–8pm.

Eating and Drinking

A FOOD AND DRINK GLOSSARY

Basics

chléb	bread	*nápoje*	drinks	*sklenice*	glass
chlebíček	(open) sandwich	*nůž*	knife	*snídaně*	breakfast
		oběd	lunch	*sůl*	salt
cukr	sugar	*obloha*	garnish	*šálek*	cup
hořčice	mustard	*ocet*	vinegar	*talíř*	plate
houska	round roll	*ovoce*	fruit	*tartarská omáčka*	tartare sauce
knedlíky	dumplings	*pečivo*	pastry		
křen	horseradish	*pepř*	pepper	*večeře*	supper/ dinner
lžíce	spoon	*polévka*	soup		
maso	meat	*předkrmy*	starters	*vejce*	eggs
máslo	butter	*přílohy*	side dishes	*vidlička*	fork
med	honey	*rohlík*	finger roll	*volské oko*	fried egg
mléko	milk	*ryby*	fish	*zeleniny*	vegetables
moučník	dessert	*rýže*	rice		

Soups

boršč	beetroot soup	*kapustnica*	sauerkraut, mushroom and meat soup
bramborová	potato soup		
čočková	lentil soup		
fazolová	bean soup	*kuřecí*	thin chicken soup
hovězí vývar	beef broth	*rajská*	tomato soup
hrachová	pea soup	*zeleninová*	vegetable soup

Fish

kapr	carp	*sardinka*	sardine
losos	salmon	*štika*	pike
makrela	mackerel	*treska*	cod
platys	flounder	*zavináč*	herring/ rollmop
pstruh	trout		
rybí filé	fillet of fish		

Meat dishes

bažant	pheasant	*ledvinky*	kidneys
biftek	beef steak	*řízek*	steak
čevapčiči	spicy meat balls	*roštěná*	sirloin
dršťky	tripe	*salám*	salami
drůbež	poultry	*sekaná*	meat loaf
guláš	goulash	*skopové maso*	mutton
hovězí	beef	*slanina*	bacon
husa	goose	*svíčková*	fillet of beef
játra	liver	*šunka*	ham
jazyk	tongue	*telecí*	veal
kachna	duck	*vepřový*	pork
klobásy	sausages	*vepřové řízek*	breaded pork cutlet or schnitzel
kotleta	cutlet		
kuře	chicken	*zajíc*	hare
kýta	leg	*žebírko*	ribs

Eating and Drinking

Vegetables

brambory	potatoes	*hranolky*	chips, French fries	*lilek*	aubergine
brokolice	broccoli			*okurka*	cucumber
celer	celery	*hrášek*	peas	*pórek*	leek
cibule	onion	*karot*	carrot	*rajče*	tomato
česnek	garlic	*květák*	cauliflower	*ředkev*	radish
chřest	asparagus	*kyselá okurka*	pickled gherkin	*řepná bulva*	beetroot
čočka	lentils			*špenát*	spinach
fazole	beans	*kyselé zelí*	sauerkraut	*zelí*	cabbage
houby	mushrooms	*lečo*	ratatouille	*žampiony*	mushrooms

Fruit, cheese and nuts

banán	banana	*oříšky*	peanuts
borůvky	blueberries	*ostružiny*	blackberries
broskev	peach	*oštěpek*	heavily smoked, curd cheese
brusinky	cranberries		
bryndza	goat's cheese in brine	*parenica*	rolled strips of lightly smoked, curd cheese
citrón	lemon		
grejp	grapefruit	*pivní sýr*	cheese flavoured with beer
hermelín	Czech brie		
hrozny	grapes	*pomeranč*	orange
hruška	pear	*rozinky*	raisins
jablko	apple	*švestky*	plums
jahody	strawberries	*třešně*	cherries
kompot	stewed fruit	*tvaroh*	fresh curd cheese
maliny	raspberries	*urda*	soft, fresh, whey cheese
mandle	almonds		
meruňka	apricot	*uzený sýr*	smoked cheese
niva	semi-soft, crumbly, blue cheese	*vlašské ořechy*	walnuts

Common terms

čerstvý	fresh	*s.m. (s máslem)*	with butter
domácí	home-made	*sladký*	sweet
dušený	stew/casserole	*slaný*	salted
grilovaný	roast on the spit	*smažený*	fried in breadcrumbs
kyselý	sour	*studený*	cold
na kmíně	with caraway seeds	*syrový*	raw
na roštu	grilled	*sýrový*	cheesey
na zdraví	cheers!	*teplý*	hot
nadívaný	stuffed	*uzený*	smoked
nakládaný	pickled	*vařený*	boiled
(za)pečený	baked/roast	*znojmský*	with gherkins
plněný	stuffed		

Drinks

čaj	tea	*mléko*	milk	*svařené víno*	mulled wine
destiláty	spirits	*pivo*	beer		
káva	coffee	*presso*	espresso	*tonic*	tonic
koňak	brandy	*s ledem*	with ice	*vinný střik*	white wine with soda
láhev	bottle	*soda*	soda		
minerální (voda)	mineral (water)	*suché víno*	dry wine	*víno*	wine
		šumivý	fizzy		

Eating and Drinking

Staré Město

Grid references after the opening times refer to the map on pp.78–79.

Country Life, Melantrichova 15; metro Můstek. Health food shop up front, and large sit-down self-service buffet, serving veggie slop and salads in the courtyard behind. Mon–Fri 9am–9.30pm, Sun 11am–9.30pm. F6.

Dům lahůdek, Malé náměstí; metro Staroměstská. Prague's largest and best delicatessen on several levels, with great picnic fodder plus traditional *chlebičky*, salads, coffee and cakes. Mon–Sat 9.30am–7pm, Sun noon–7pm. E5.

Safir, Havelská 12; metro Můstek. Inexpensive centrally located Middle Eastern kebab and *felafal* outlet. Mon–Sat 10am–8pm. F7.

U Bakaláře, Celetná 13; metro Staroměstská/náměstí Republiky. Very central, cheap self-service veggie hole-filler, serving typical Czech fry-up food to hungry tourists. Mon–Fri 9am–9pm, Sat & Sun 10am–9pm. H5.

Nové Město

Grid references after the opening times refer to the map on pp.124–125.

Adonis, Jungmannova 21; metro Národní třída. Cheap Middle Eastern fare – stuffed vine leaves, *felafal, taboule* and a salad bar – sit-in or takeaway, a stone's throw from Wenceslas Square and Národní třída. Daily 11am–7pm. E5.

Le Gourmand, Václavské náměstí 18; metro Můstek. Neither French nor gourmet, but a large, cheap, convenient self-service salad bar with a few standard hot Czech dishes on offer, too. Daily 8am–2am. F5.

Poříčská pekárna, Na poříčí 30; metro náměstí Republiky. Viennese-style bakery selling coffee and pastries, with a few stand-up tables for munching in the warmth. Mon–Fri 7am–7pm, Sat until 1pm. I2.

U české koruny, Vodičkova 30; metro Národní třída. Classic Czech stand-up *bufet*, inside the arcade at no. 30, with a sit-down restaurant section tacked on. Mon–Fri 10am–10pm, Sat & Sun 11am–8pm. F5.

U rozvařilů, Na poříčí 26; metro náměstí Republiky/Florenc. New old-style *bufet* where everything is under 50kč, you perch at zinc-top tables and the beer flows freely. Mon–Fri 7.30am–7.30pm, Sat 7.30am–7pm, Sun 10am–5pm. I2.

Cafés

Prague can no longer boast a café society to rival that of Vienna or Paris, as it could at the beginning of this century and between the wars, as only a handful of classic haunts survive. Nevertheless, many Praguers still spend a large part of the day smoking and drinking in the cafés, and in the summer, the tables spill out onto the streets and squares. The cafés listed below are a mixed bunch. The majority serve just coffee and cakes, and more often than not, alcohol; others also serve up cheap and filling (though by no means gourmet) meals.

Like the Austrians who once ruled over them, the Czechs have a grotesquely sweet tooth, and the coffee-and-cake hit is part of the daily ritual. The more traditional cafés offer a wide range of **cakes**: *dort*, like the German *Torte*, consist of a series of custard cream, chocolate and sponge layers, while *řez* are lighter, square cakes, usually containing a bit of fruit. A *věneček*, filled with "cream", is the nearest you'll get to an éclair; a *větrník* is simply a larger version with a bit of fresh cream added. One speciality to look out for is *rakvička*, which literally means "little coffin", an extended piece of sugar with cream, moulded vaguely into the shape of a coffin.

Coffee is drunk black and is usually available in espresso (*presso*) form: small, black and strong, though by no means as diminutive as in Italy. The original Czech coffee, called somewhat hopefully *turecká* (Turkish) – it's really just hot water poured over coffee grains – is fast becoming obsolete, in Prague at least. Downmarket *bufet*s sell *ledová káva*, a weak, cold black coffee, while at the other end of the scale *Viděňská káva* (Viennese coffee) is a favourite with the older generation, served with a dollop of whipped cream. Another

Eating and Drinking

Prague's tea-houses

According to local legend, the Russian anarchist Mikhail Bakunin entered a Prague café in 1848 and ordered tea. When the owner said that he'd never heard of the drink, Bakunin marched into the kitchen and made the city's first cup of tea. Eighty years later, there were an estimated 150 **tea-houses** or *čajovny* in Prague, but the culture died out under the Communists. Today's tea-houses are a 1990s' phenomenon, though they have their historical roots in the First Republic. Partly a reaction to the smoke-filled, alcohol-driven atmosphere of the ubiquitous Czech pub, and partly a reaction against the multinational, fast-food culture that has recently arrived in Prague, tea-houses are non-smoking, slightly hippified places to enjoy a quiet cuppa and chill out. The tea-drinking is taken very seriously, and several of the places listed below stock a staggering array of leaves.

Dobrá čajovna, Boršov 2, Staré Město; metro Staroměstská. Probably the most successful of all the tea-houses at re-creating a distinctively mellow, rarefied atmosphere, with hookah smoking permitted. An astonishing variety of teas (and a few Middle Eastern snacks) are served by young male proto-Buddhist waiters who slip by silently in their sandals. This place is very difficult to find (it's off Karoliny Světlé) and the door is frequently locked, so you'll need to ring the bell to find out if there's any space available (or if they like the look of you). Daily 8am–noon & 4–10pm.

Dobrá čajovna, Václavské náměstí 14, Nové Město; metro Můstek/Muzeum. The pioneering tea-house with a slightly less rarefied but equally relaxing ambience. It's set back from the square, has world music wafting through it, floor seating and a vast range of teas. Mon–Sat 10am–9pm, Sun 3–9pm.

Malý Buddha, Úvoz 44, Malá Strana; tram #12 or #22 from metro Malostranská. Typical Prague tea-house décor, with a Buddhist altar in one corner. A very useful haven just down from the Hrad. Tues–Sun 11am–10pm.

Růžová čajovna, Růžová 8, Nové Město; metro Můstek/Muzeum. The "pink tea-house" is a lighter, more modern version that caters for a less hippified clientele, and doesn't play exclusively non-western music. Daily 11am–9pm.

U zeleného čaje, Nerudova 19, Malá Strana; tram #12 or #22 from metro Malostranská. The "green tea" is a great little stop-off for a pot of tea or a veggie snack en route to or from the Hrad; the only problem is getting a place at one of the four tables. Daily 11am–9.30pm.

U zlatého kohouta, Michalská 3, Staré Město; metro Můstek. Hidden away in a courtyard off Michalská, this is another secretive, relaxing *čajovna* worth knowing about, located in the heart of Staré Mesto. Mon–Fri 10am–9.30pm, Sat & Sun 2–9.30pm.

rather rich option is a mix with advocaat, *Alžírská káva*. **Tea** is drunk weak and without milk, although you'll usually be given a glass of boiling water and a tea bag so you can do your own thing – if you want milk, say *"s mlékem"*.

Malá Strana

Grid references after the opening times refer to the map on pp.74–75. The nearest **metro** for all the following places is Malostranská.

Baraka, Míšenská 2. A smoky little art gallery/café conveniently hidden away beside the Charles Bridge. Daily 11am–midnight. H5.

Chiméra, Lázeňská 6. Coffee, toast and cigarettes are the defining features of this pleasant art gallery/café, which has a few comfy armchairs to crash out in. Daily 11am–11pm. G5.

Malostranská kavárna, Malostranské náměstí 28. A time-honoured café founded in 1874 in a late eighteenth-century

Eating and Drinking

palace, recently refurbished yet despite its prime position still a very pleasant place inside. Daily 9am–11pm. G4.

St Nicholas Café, Tržiště 10. Cellar café/bar that pulls in wealthy, posey, beautiful Czechs and the diplomatic crowd in some numbers. Mon–Fri noon–1am, Sat & Sun 4pm–1am. F4.

Savoy, Vítězná 5. Renovated nineteenth-century café with high, gilded ceiling, but rather unfortunate modern fittings and little atmosphere. Daily 9am–midnight. F10.

U zavěšenýho kafe, Radnické schody 7. A "hanging coffee" is one that has been paid for by the haves for the have-nots who drop in. That apart, this place is a pleasant smoky cross-over café/pub, serving cheap Měšťan beer and traditional Czech food in a handy spot on the steps down from the Hrad. Daily 11am–midnight. D1.

Staré Město

Grid references after the opening times refer to the map on pp.78–79.

Barock, Pařížská 24; metro Staroměstská. Deeply fashionable, candle-lit and popular French-style café in russet with framed photos of supermodels on the walls. The breakfasts and the Thai, Japanese and Chinese food are all good, but pricey. Mon–Fri 8.30am–1am, Sat & Sun 10am–2am. E3.

Blatouch, Vězeňská 7; metro Staroměstská. Smoky, literary café, frequented mostly by Czech students. Olives, jazz, dubious snacks and alcoholic/non-alcoholic cocktails available. Mon–Fri 11am–midnight, Sat 2pm–1am, Sun 2pm–midnight. F3.

Café Érra, Konviktská 11; metro Národní třída. Golden-brown designer café in the backstreets off Betlémské náměstí that's popular with Prague's young, arty, professional mobile-phone users. Tasty salads and snacks on offer too. Mon–Fri 10am–midnight, Sat & Sun 11am–midnight. C8.

Café Milena, Staroměstské náměstí 22; metro Staroměstská. A stab at a 1920s-style café, situated opposite the astronomical clock, named after Kafka's famous and talented lover, Milena Jesenská (see p.142), and by far the nicest café in this part of the old town. Daily 10am–9pm. F5.

Chez Marcel, Haštalská 12; metro náměstí Republiky. Effortlessly chic French café. A good place to grab a coffee, a *tarte tatin*, read a French mag or eat some moderately priced bistro-style food. Mon–Fri 8am–1am, Sat & Sun 9am–1am. I2.

Gulu Gulu, Betlémské náměstí 8; metro Národní třída. Centrally located popular café/pub with bare floorboards, Míró-style murals, newspapers and friendly bar staff. Radegast beer on offer. Daily 10am–midnight. D7.

Hogo Fogo, Salvátorská 4; metro Staroměstská. Monochrome café tucked into the backstreets off Pařížská serving cheap, filling student-style pasta and meat dishes – very popular with young Czechs. Mon–Thurs & Sun noon–midnight, Fri & Sat noon–2am. F4.

Konírna, Anenská 11; metro Staroměstská. Very popular vaulted stable building, with cheap drinks and a salad bar. Mon–Fri noon–midnight, Sat & Sun 6pm–midnight. C6.

O' Ché's, Liliová 14; metro Staroměstská. Prague's premier Irish-run Cuban-themed café/bar. Daily 10am–1am. D7.

Paříž, U obecního domu 1; metro náměstí Republiky. The prices are sky-high for Prague, and the service can be surly, but there's a certain rather formal elegance about this hotel's Art Nouveau *kavárna*. Daily 8am–1am. J4.

Reno, UPM, 17 listopadu; metro Staroměstská. Great place to relax after taking in the treasures of the Applied Art Museum (see p.122). Mon–Fri 10am–6pm, Sat & Sun 11am–6pm. C3.

Rudolfinum, Alšovo nábřeží 12; metro Staroměstská. Gloriously grand nineteenth-century café on the first floor of the old parliament building (see p.1222) – you don't have to go to the exhibition to go to the café. Tues–Sun 10am–6pm. C3.

Internet cafés

You can now get on-line at numerous cafés in Prague, including unlikely places such as the Obecní dům (see below), and several tea-houses. The two cafés listed below are the pick of the bunch, however.

Pl@neta, Vinohradská 102, Vinohrady; metro Jiřího z Poděbrad. A business-like place that's not somewhere to linger, but the English-speaking staff will help you pick up and write email happily enough. Daily 8am–10pm.

Terminal Bar, Soukenická 6, Nové Město; metro Náměstí Republiky. Definitely the number one choice in terms of atmosphere, this is a funky, loud bar, with a groovy chill-out basement littered with kitsch sofas and weird lighting. English-speakers can help with any technical problems. Daily 10am–2am.

Eating and Drinking

Nové Město

Grid references after the opening times refer to the map on pp.124–125.

Archa, Na poříčí 26; metro náměstí Republiky/Florenc. Designer café belonging to the avant-garde venue of the same name, with big fishbowl windows for street-watching. Mon–Fri 9am–10.30pm, Sat 10am–8pm, Sun 1–10pm. I2.

Káva Káva Káva, Národní 37; metro Národní třída. You're guaranteed good coffee in this pleasant little café in the Platýz pasáž between Národní and Uhelný trh. Daily 7am–8pm. E5.

Louvre, Národní 20; metro Národní třída. High ceiling, mirrors, daily papers, lots of cakes, a billiard hall and window seats overlooking Národní make this a popular re-fuelling spot for tourists and shoppers alike. Daily 8am–11pm. E5.

Grand Hotel Evropa, Václavské náměstí 25; metro Můstek/Muzeum. To truly appreciate the sumptuous Art Nouveau decor, you'll have to forsake the terrace and step inside – still worth it even if the coffee and staff are below par, and they slap a surcharge on for the music. Daily 10am–midnight. G5.

Institut Français, Štěpánská 35; metro Muzeum. Housed in the French cultural centre – great coffee and superb French pastries, plus of course the chance to pose with a French newspaper, make this one of Prague's best cafés. Mon–Fri 9am–6pm. F6.

Le Patio, Národní 22, metro Národní třída. Strange mixture of high ceilings and bare-brick vaults plus a clutter of *objets d'art* help to create a slightly kooky but sophisticated atmosphere that goes down well with the local shoppers. Mon–Sat 8am–11pm, Sun 10am–11pm. D5.

Marathon, Černá 9; metro Národní třída. Self-styled, smoky "library café" in the university's 1920s-style religious faculty, hidden in the backstreets, south of Národní. Mon–Fri 10am–10pm. D6.

Obecní dům, náměstí Republiky; metro náměstí Republiky. The *kavárna*, with its famous fountain, is in the more restrained south hall of this huge Art Nouveau complex, and has recently been glitteringly restored – an absolute aesthetic treat. Daily 7.30am–11pm. G3.

Paris-Praha, Jindřišská 7; metro Můstek. Small café serving good French coffee, adjacent to the Communist-era French delicatessen of the same name. Mon–Fri 10.30am–7.30pm. G4.

Praha-Roma, V jámě 5; metro Muzeum. Small *pasticceria* with dubious pink 1920s-style decor, serving authentic Italian pastries, coffee and ice cream. Daily 9am–11pm. F6.

Slavia, Národní 1; metro Národní třída. An enduring and endearing Prague institution (see p.136) that still pulls in a mixed crowd from shoppers and tourists to older folk and the pre-and post-theatre mob. Mon–Fri 8am–midnight, Sat & Sun 9am–midnight. C5.

Eating and Drinking

U sv Vojtěcha, Vojtěšská 14; metro Karlovo náměstí. Lively coffee place not far from the Národní divadlo and Pofín, with big windows that open out on to the street in summer. Mon–Fri 8am–10pm, Sat & Sun 10am–10pm. C6.

Velryba (The Whale), Opatovická 24; metro Národní třída. One of the most determinedly cool cafés in Prague, not intended as an ex-pat joint (and not keen to entice tourists), serving cheap, post-revolutionary Czech food (several veggie options) and a stunning range of malt whiskies. Daily 11am–2am. D6.

Vyšehrad and the eastern suburbs

Grid references after the opening times refer to the map on pp.150–151.

G plus G, Čerchovská 4, Vinohrady; metro Jiří z Poděbrad. Czech literary café housed in an arty bookshop, off Polská, with a busy programme of readings, discussions and folk/jazz/blues concerts. Mon–Fri 10am–10pm. F5.

Medúza, Belgická 17, Vinohrady; metro náměstí Míru. Trendy young crowd hang-out in this deliberately faded, inexpensive café, which serves breakfast all day and gets packed out most evenings. Mon–Fri 11am–1am, Sat & Sun noon–1am. D5.

U knihomola (The Bookworm), Mánesova 79, Vinohrady; metro Jiřího z Poděbrad. Basement café in one of Prague's main ex-pat bookstores, with foreign papers to browse and art exhibitions to admire. Mon–Thurs 10am–11pm, Fri & Sat 10am–midnight, Sun 11am–8pm. F5.

Holešovice and the western suburbs

Grid references after the opening times refer to the map on pp.34–35.

Café Apostrof, Matoušova, Smíchov. Smart café in a pristinely renovated Dientzenhofer palace on náměstí 28 října, with lots of violins and art on the walls. A positive oasis in Smíchov. Daily 11am–11pm. D8.

The Globe, Janovského 14, Holešovice; metro Vltavská. This laid-back café – like the adjoining English-language bookstore of the same name – is one big ex-pat hang-out, but enjoyable nevertheless. Daily 10am–midnight. G2.

Pubs and bars

Traditional Czech *pivnice* are smoky, male-dominated places, where 99 percent of the customers are drinking copious quantities of Czech beer by the half-litre – but they're a dying breed. Pubs with a more youthful clientele, and ex-pat bars, tend to be a bit more mixed, but if you're not interested in drinking (and preferably smoking), you're going to have a hard time having a good time in many of them. Still, as with British pubs, whatever their faults, they remain deeply embedded in the local culture, and to sample that, you'll need to sample the amber nectar. Food is almost always of the traditional Czech variety (for more on Czech cuisine, see p.207) – cheap and filling, but ultimately it could shorten your life by a couple of years.

Hradčany

Grid references after the opening times refer to the map on pp.46–47.

U černého vola (The Black Ox), Loretánské náměstí 1; tram #22 from metro Malostranská. Great traditional Prague pub doing a brisk business providing the popular light beer Velkopopovický kozel in huge quantities to thirsty local workers, plus a few basic pub snacks. Daily 10am–10pm. C4.

Malá Strana

Grid references after the opening times refer to the map on pp.74–75. The nearest metro is Malostranská, followed either by a short walk or a stop or two on tram #12 or #22.

Baráčnická rychta, Na tržiště 22 (down a narrow passageway leading south off Nerudova). A real survivor – a small backstreet *pivnice* squeezed in between the embassies, with a cheap and filling menu. Daily 11am–11pm. E3.

Jo's Bar, Malostranské náměstí 7. A narrow bar in Malá Strana that is the archetypal

Czech etiquette

It's common practice in Prague to share a table with other eaters or drinkers; *je tu volno*? (Is this seat free?) is the standard question. Waiter service is the norm even in pubs, where if you sit tight a beer should come your way. From this point on your beer should hopefully be replenished by a waiter as soon as you near the bottom of your glass. Note that pouring beer from one glass into an another is a social no-no. You may have to ask for the menu (*jídelní lístek*) in pubs – and some cafés – to indicate that you wish to eat. When food arrives for your neighbours, it's common practice to wish them *bon appetit* (*dobrou chuť*). When you want to leave, simply say *zaplatím, prosím* (literally "I'll pay, please"), and your tab will be totted up. A modest form of **tipping** exists in all establishments, generally done by rounding up the bill to the nearest few crowns, though beware that the waiters haven't already done this for you. On leaving, bid your neighbours farewell (*na shledanou*).

Eating and Drinking

ex-pat/backpacker hang-out. Tex-Mex food served all day, bottled beer only and a heaving crowd guaranteed most evenings. Daily 11am–2am. F4.

Na Kampě, Na Kampě 15. Round the corner from the formal restaurant of the same name is this friendly (and even child-friendly) *pivnice* offering tasty pub snacks; you can sit outside or wander down to the riverside with your Pilsner Urquell. Daily noon–midnight. H7.

Scarlett O'Hara's, Mostecká 21. One of Prague's many Irish-theme pubs, better than the *James Joyce*, but not as cosy as *Molly Malone's*. One of the better places to watch sports on TV. Daily noon–2am. G5.

U bílé kuželky (The White Bowling Pin), Míšeňská 12. Not a bad pub considering its touristy location right by the Charles Bridge. Reasonably priced Pilsner Urquell and Czech pub food. Daily noon–10pm. H5.

U černého orla (The Black Eagle), Újezd 33. Popular student pub with cheap food and Staropramen 10° beer, across the bridge from the Národní divadlo. Mon–Fri 10am–10pm, Sat & Sun 11am–10pm. E9.

U hrocha (The Hippo), Thunovská 10. A genuine Czech pub in the heart of Malá Strana – difficult to believe but true. Cheap grub and beer. Daily noon–11pm. G3.

U kocoura (The Cat), Nerudova 2. One of the few surviving pubs on Nerudova, owned by the Beer Party, but, for the most part, abandoned by its old clientele. Some of the best Budvar in town, plus the obvious Czech stomach-fillers. Daily 11.30am–midnight. G3.

U malého Glena, Karmelitská 23. Smart-looking pub/jazz bar that attracts a fair mixture of Czechs and ex-pats thanks to its better-than-average food and live music in the basement. Daily 10am–2am. F5.

Staré Město

Grid references after the opening times refer to the map on pp.78–79.

Banana Café, Štupartská 9; metro náměstí Republiky. Strange kitsch disco bar above *La Provence* restaurant deep in the heart of ex-pat territory. It has table-top dancers (of both sexes) and gets absolutely packed out with Czech thirtysomethings in suits. Worth experiencing once (perhaps). Daily 8pm–1am. H4.

Chapeau Rouge, Malá Štupartská; metro náměstí Republiky. Loud, posey, boozer with wooden floorboards and red hat on door in the heart of the so-called French Quarter or "Bermuda Triangle", absolutely packed out with non-Czechs. Daily 4pm–4am. H4.

Divadlo na zabradlí, Anenské náměstí 5. Lovely pale pea-green wood fittings to this theatre bar that attracts an intellectual crowd. Braník on tap and lots of spirits to choose from. Mon–Fri 10am–1am, Sat & Sun 3pm–1am. B7.

James Joyce, Liliová 10; metro Staroměstská. A soulless and expensive re-creation of an Irish pub, with prices

Eating and Drinking

that only foreign businessmen think are reasonable – go to *U krále Jiřího* or *Molly Malone's* instead (see below). Daily 11am–1am. D7.

Konvikt, Bartolomějská 11; metro Národní třída. New, but very normal smoky Czech pub serving Pilsner and Czech food. Mon–Fri 9am–11pm, Sat & Sun 11am–11pm. D8.

Kozička, Kozí 4; metro Staroměstská. Designer bare-brick cellar bar with cheap Czech food, tucked away just a short walk from Staroměstské náměstí. Daily noon–4am. G3.

Marquis de Sade, Templová 8; metro náměstí Republiky. Great space: huge high ceiling, big comfy sofas, and a mostly ex-pat crowd. Crap beer and limited snacks, but a good place to start the evening, before the live band kicks in, or end it, after they've packed up. Daily 11am–2am. I4.

Molly Malone's, U Obecního dvora 4; metro Staroměstská. Best of Prague's Irish pubs with real Irish staff (who speak very little Czech), an open fire and draught Kilkenny and Guinness (neither of them very cheap), and decent Irish-themed food. Mon–Thurs & Sun noon–12.45am, Fri & Sat noon–1.45am. G2.

Na Ovocném trhu, Ovocný trh 17; metro náměstí Republiky. New pub behind the Stavovské divadlo – perfect for a pre-theatre bite and a jar of Velkopopovický kozel. Mon–Sat 10am–10pm, Sun 11am–10pm. H5.

Radegast, Templová 2; metro náměstí Republiky. Typically smoky boozy pub divided into booths, serving its namesake plus decent Czech food. Attracts Czechs and ex-pats. Daily 11am–midnight. I4.

U krále Jiřího (The King George), Liliová 10; metro Staroměstská. Forget the more visible *James Joyce* (see p.219), and head down the steps to this nice Czech pub serving Gambrinus beer instead. Mon–Fri 11am–midnight, Sat & Sun noon–midnight. D7.

U medvídků (The Little Bears), Na Perštýně 7; metro Národní třída. A Prague institution going back to the thirteenth century and still much as it ever was (make sure you turn right when you enter, and avoid the new bar to the left). The Budvar comes thick and fast, and the food is absolutely standard. Mon–Sat 11am–11pm, Sun 11am–10pm. E8.

U milosrdných, Kozí 21; metro Staroměstská. Refurbished pub far enough away from the tourist crowds, serving typical Czech food and Plzeň beers. Daily 10am–10pm. G2.

U pivrnce, Maiselova 3; metro Staroměstská. No-frills basic Czech food and Radegast beer, which is something of a boon in the heart of Josefov; shame about the unfunny cartoons on the walls. Daily 11am–11.30pm. E4.

U radnice, U radnice 2; metro Staroměstská. Incredibly, given the location, this is an alright Czech pub, serving the three most famous Czech beers and typical Czech pub food at reasonable prices. Daily 11am–10.30pm. E5.

U železného dveře (The Iron Doors), Michalská 19; metro Staroměstská. Funky cellar bar sprayed with gold, offering a good selection of cocktails, and popular with the TEFL crowd. Daily 8pm–4am. F6.

U zlatého tygra (The Golden Tiger), Husova 17; metro Staroměstská. Small *pivnice* with nearly every seat taken by regulars. Once frequented by Prague's literary in-crowd – the late writer and bohemian, Bohumil Hrabal, was a semi-permanent resident. Daily 3–11pm. D6.

V Blatnici, Michalská 6; metro Můstek. Popular basement *vinárna* bang in the old town, serving Moravian wines and cheap Czech food. Daily 3pm–midnight. F6.

Nové Město

Grid references after the opening times refer to the map on pp.124–125.

Billiard Club, Trojická 10, Nove Město; tram #3, #7, #7 or #17 from Karlovo náměstí. Theatre converted into a pool and billiard hall with cheap beer and long hours. Daily 1pm–4am.

Branický sklípek, Vodičkova 26; metro Můstek. One of the few places in the

Eating and Drinking

centre where you can down Prague's Braník beers. Mon–Fri 9am–11pm, Sat & Sun 11am–11pm. F5.

Jáma (The Hollow), V jámě 7; metro Můstek/Muzeum. Loud ex-pat pub with lots of cocktails and a range of passable attempts at Tex-Mex dishes. Daily 11am–1am. F6.

John Bull, Senovážná 8; metro náměstí Republiky. A real imitation British pub, serving indifferent John Bull ale and cheap Czech food; popular with the local bank clerks. Mon–Fri 8am–10pm, Sat 11am–2am, Sun 11am–midnight. G3.

Novoměstský pivovar, Vodičkova 20; metro Národní třída. New micro-brewery, which serves its own misty home brew, plus Czech food, in a series of bright, sprawling modern beer halls. Mon–Sat 11.30am–11.30pm, Sun noon–10pm. E6.

Pivovarksý dům, corner of Lipová/Ďečná; metro Karlovo náměstí. Busy micro-brewery dominated by its big shiny copper vats, serving light, mixed and dark unfiltered beer (plus banana, coffee and wheat varieties), and all the standard Czech pub dishes (including *pivný sýr*). Daily 11am–11.30pm. F7.

U bubeníčků, Myslíkova 8; metro Karlovo náměstí. Good, unpretentious place to down a few halves of Gambrinus and eat some simple Czech cuisine after visiting the Mánes gallery. Daily 11am–11pm. C6.

U Fílů, Klimentská 2; metro náměstí Republiky. New, cheap Czech place on the edge of Revoluční that calls itself a café-bar, but is really just a normal pub. Serves Krušovice beer and basic Czech food. Mon–Sat 9am–10pm. G1.

U Fleků, Křemencova 11; metro Karlovo náměstí. Famous medieval *pivnice* where the unique dark 13° beer, Flek, has been exclusively brewed and consumed since 1499. Seats over 500 German tourists at a go, serves short measures (0.4l) for high prices, slaps an extra charge on for the music and still you have to queue. This is a tourist trap and the only reason to visit is to sample the beer, which you're best off doing during the day. Daily 9am–11pm. D6.

U havrana (The Crow), Hálkova 8; metro I. P. Pavlova. Surprisingly unseedy, normal pub serving food and Měšťan and Kozel beer throughout the night. Mon–Fri 24hr, Sat & Sun 6pm–6am. G7.

U kotvy (The Anchor), Spalená 11; metro Národní třída. All-night spot that's perfect for a last beer before you attempt to work out how to catch a night tram home. Daily 24 hours. D5.

U Pinkasů, Jungmannovo náměstí 15; metro Můstek. Famed as the first *pivnice* in Prague to serve Pilsner Urquell (which it still does). It still manages to keep its Czech regulars, but seems pretty hostile to everyone else. Mon–Fri 8am–11pm, Sat 10am–11pm, Sun 11am–9pm. F4.

U pravdu (The Truth), Žitná 15; metro Karlovo náměstí/Muzeum. Cheap Czech food and Staropramen at this local boozer, which has a separate restaurant section and a garden out back. Mon–Fri 10am–11pm, Sat & Sun 11am–11pm. F7.

U staré pošty, Opletalova 19; metro Muzeum/Hlavní nádraží. Czech pub serving Staropramen and typical Czech grub, conveniently located near the main station, and popular with local Czech workers. Mon–Fri 9am–11pm, Sat & Sun 11am–10pm. H5.

U zpěváčků (The Choir Boy), Na struze 7; metro Národní třída. Loud and smoky workers/musicians' pub just around the corner from the Národní divadlo, with an ironic line in Marxist-Leninist tracts, and the local Staropramen on tap. Mon–Thurs 10am–2am, Fri 10am–3am, Sat 11am–3am & Sun 11am–2am. C6.

Zlatá Hvězda (Golden Star), Ve Smečkách 12; metro Muzeum. The main reason to hit this big, loud pub is to watch the match you want on the numerous satellite TV screens. Mon–Wed 11am–midnight, Thurs 11am–1am, Fri 11am–2.30am, Sat noon–1am, Sun noon–midnight. G6.

Vyšehrad and the eastern suburbs

Grid references after the opening times refer to the map on pp.150–151.

Eating and Drinking

Akropolis, Kubelíkova 27, Žižkov; metro Jiřího z Poděbrad. Funkily decked out and very popular smoke-filled pub that plays half-decent music and serves cheap Czech food and Kozel beer; also puts on lots of live gigs. Mon–Fri 10am–1am, Sat & Sun 4pm–1am. F4.

Hostinec pod Vyšehradem, Vratislavova 4, Vyšehrad; tram #3, #7 or #17 from metro Karlovo náměstí. Neo-Gothic on the outside but perfectly normal inside, serving cheap mugs of Gambrinus. Daily 11am–11pm. A6.

Na zvonařce (The Bell), Šafaříkova, Vinohrady; tram #6 or #11 from metro I. P. Pavlova. Cheap Czech cuisine, Pilsner Urquell, Radegast, billiards, occasional dancing, and great views from the terrace over the Nuselské schody and Botič valley. Daily 10am–11pm. D6.

U Bergnerů, Slezská 134, Žižkov; metro Flora. For beer connoisseurs: one of the few pubs serving the slightly bitter, unfiltered beer from the recently resurrected brewery in Kacov; good, simple Czech food available, too. Daily 11am–midnight. H6.

U Bulinů, Budečská 2, Vinohrady; metro náměstí Míru. Fine Czech pub with equally good pub food on offer, situated on the corner of Francouzská. Daily 10am–10pm. E5.

U koleje (The College), Slavíkova 24, Vinohrady; metro Jiřího z Poděbrad. Thriving local: cigarette smoke, Kozel beer, meat and dumplings all guaranteed. Mon–Fri 11am–10pm. F5.

U růžového sadu (The Rose Garden), Mánesova 89, Vinohrady; metro Jiřího z Poděbrad. Imaginatively decorated for a Czech pub, with old shop signs and the like, and perfectly situated if you're visiting the Plečnik Church or the Bookworm bookstore; Gambrinus and dark Purkmistr beer on tap. Daily 11am–10pm. F5.

U vystřelenýho oka (The Shot-Out Eye), U božích bojovníků, Žižkov; metro Florenc. Big, loud, smoky, heavy-drinking pub just south of Žižkov Hill, off Husitská, with (unusually) good music playing and lashings of Radegast beer, plus absinthe chasers. Daily 3.30pm–1am. G3.

U zlaté kotvy, Vratislavova 19, Vyšehrad; tram #3, #7 or #17 from metro Karlovo náměstí. New pub with dubious colour scheme, but excellent, cheap Gambrinus, Pilsner and Punkmistr dark beer. Daily 11am–midnight. A6.

Holešovice and the western suburbs

Grid references after the opening times refer to the map on pp.34–35.

Na slamníku (The Straw Bed), Schwaigrova 7, Bubeneč; bus #131 from metro Hradčanská. The perfect place to end up after a stroll in Stromovka: a *pivnice* serving good Czech grub and Krušovice beer. Daily 4pm–midnight. D2.

Na staré kovárně v Braníku (The Old Blacksmith's in Braník), Kamenická 17, Holešovice; tram #26 from metro náměstí Republiky. Nicely refurbished pub that's popular with the locals and a

Czech menus

In pubs and inexpensive restaurants, the **menu** (*jídelní lístek*), which should be displayed outside, is often in Czech only and deciphering it without a grounding in the language can be quite a feat. Just bear in mind that the general rule is for the right-hand column to list the prices, while the far left column often gives you the estimated weight of every dish in grammes; if what you get weighs more or less, the price alters accordingly.

The menu is usually divided into various sections beginning with *předkrmy* (starters) or *polévky* (soups), followed by the main courses: *jídla na objednávku* (food to order), *hotová jídla* (ready-made food), *drůbez a ryby* (fowl and fish) and, if you're lucky, *bezmasa* (vegetarian dishes). Side dishes are listed under *přílohy*; puddings, where available, are listed under the heading *moučníky*.

crowd of young Czechs. Small menu of meaty daily dishes, Radegast beer and good music. Mon–Sat 11.30am–1am, Sun 11.30am–11.30pm. F3.

Nad královskou oborou (The Royal Game Preserve), Nad královskou oborou 31, Bubeneč; bus #1255 from the northern end of Revoluční. Another place to head for after a stroll in Stromovka; good Czech food, Purkmistr dark and Gambrinus light beers on tap, the world's cheapest pint of Guinness, plus live bands (Fri & Sat). Daily noon–11pm.

U buldoka (The Bulldog), Preslova 1, Smíchov; metro Anděl. A half-decent Smíchov pub is hard to find, so here's one, serving Gambrinus. Mon–Fri 11am–midnight, Sat & Sun noon–midnight. D8.

U váhy (The Weight), Nádražní 88, Smíchov; metro Anděl. Right by the Staropramen brewery and therefore the unofficial brewery tap; it also does food. Mon–Fri 10am–10pm, Sat & Sun 11am–10pm. D8.

Ullman, Kostelní, Holešovice; ☎37 16 78; tram #1 from metro Vltavská. Convenient Letná pub in the Letenský zámeček, opposite the Národní technické muzeum, serving typical slightly upgraded Czech food, including some veggie options, with Velkopopovický kozel on draught. Daily 11am–11pm. F3.

Restaurants

Prague's **restaurant** scene has greatly improved in the last few years in terms of both choice and quality. The influx of tourists has, of course, pushed the prices out of the reach of many Czechs, who tend more than ever to stick to pubs when eating out. However, even in the city's top restaurants, you can't guarantee faultless food and service, so keep an open mind. Service is gradually becoming more sophisticated, though surly staff are still no rarity, nor are unscrupulous waiters who exercise dubious arithmetics when totting up the bill. Beware of extras in the pricier restaurants, where you will be charged for everything you touch, including the almonds you thought were courtesy of the house.

Hradčany

The grid references after the opening times refer to the map on pp.46–47; the nearest **metro** for the places listed below is Malostranská, after which you can either walk up to the castle area or catch tram #22.

INEXPENSIVE

Saté, Pohořelec 3. One of the few places you can fill your belly for very little in the vicinity of the Hrad. Simple veggie and non-veggie noodle dishes prepared, all with a vaguely Indonesian bent. Daily 11am–10pm. C4.

U Lorety, Loretánské náměstí 8. Familiar Czech menu, bang next door to the Loreto chapel, and facing the monster Černínský palác – a great place to eat outside in summer. Daily 11am–11pm. C4.

Eating and Drinking

For a glossary of Czech terms for food and drink, see pp.212–213.

The restaurant listings are divided into geographical areas that correspond to the chapters, and into price categories, too – inexpensive, moderate and expensive. As a rough guide, you'll be able to get a soup, main course and pudding with a couple of beers thrown in for:

Inexpensive under 250Kč a head
Moderate 250–500Kč a head
Expensive 500Kč and upwards

While 500kč for a meal is hardly extravagant compared to meal prices in the EU or US, it's still pricey for most Czechs. Note that at restaurants where we have included phone numbers, it is advisable to book beforehand.

Eating and Drinking

MODERATE

U Fevce Matouše (The Cobbler), Loretánské náměstí 4; ☎20 51 45 36. The cobbler's been made redundant and the prices have quadrupled, but this is still the best steak house in Prague. Daily noon–4pm & 6–11pm. C4.

EXPENSIVE

U zlaté hrušky (The Golden Pear), Nový Svět 3; ☎20 51 53 56. Romantic, exclusive, intimate, the setting is perfect, the menu is imaginative, and the bill (after careful massaging by the management) will probably exceed 1000Kč a head. Daily 11.30am–3pm & 6.30pm–midnight. C2.

Malá Strana

The grid references after the opening times refer to the map on pp.74–75. The nearest **metro** for all the places listed below is Malostranská, followed by a tram ride on tram #12 or #22 or a short walk.

INEXPENSIVE

Bar Bar, Všehrdova 17. Arty crêperie with big cheap salads, savoury and sweet crêpes and Jamaican *palačinky* on offer. Mon–Fri 11am–11pm, Sat & Sun noon–11pm. F8.

MODERATE

Avalon, Malostranské náměstí 12. American-style brasserie upstairs from *Circle Line* (see below), offering a California-inspired menu with everything from burgers to fresh salads, but particularly strong on shellfish and the finned variety; tables outside in the summer. Daily 11am–1am. F4.

Bazaar, Nerudova 40. Big labyrinthine candle-lit complex on several levels, with bare brick vaults and an al fresco rooftop section. The Med food usually hits the spot. Daily noon–11pm. E2.

Faros, Šporkova 5; ☎53 34 82. Cosy little Greek restaurant in the backstreets of Malá Strana that makes a nice change from other Prague restaurants and is fairly veggie-friendly. Daily noon–11pm. D2.

Palffy palác, Valdštejnská 14. Grand candle-lit room on the first floor of the conservatoire, with okay food (stick to the salads and desserts) and a wonderful outdoor terrace from which to survey the red rooftops of Malá Strana. Daily 11am–midnight. H2.

U Maltézských rytířů, Prokopská 10; ☎53 63 57. One of the best Gothic cellars in Prague to sample faultless local cuisine (particularly game) and excellent apple strudel. Daily 11am–11pm. G5.

U Mecenáše, Malostranské náměstí 10; ☎53 38 81. Vaulted Gothic *vinárna* where Václav IV used to drink (a lot) and which now pulls in hungry tourists. The menu features the usual Czech favourites, all well prepared. Mon–Fri 5–11.30pm, Sat & Sun 1pm–11.30pm. G4.

U modré kachničky (The Blue Duckling), Nebovidská 6; ☎57 32 03 08. Cosy little restaurant, decorated with murals and antiques, and offering a mouth-watering selection of dishes, including many Czech favourites, given the gourmet treatment. Daily noon–4pm & 6.30–11.30pm. F7.

U patrona, Dražického náměstí 4. An excellent restaurant very close to the Charles Bridge, offering beautifully prepared local dishes. Daily 11.30am–2.30pm & 5.30–11.30pm. H5.

EXPENSIVE

Circle Line, Malostranské náměstí 12; ☎57 53 00 23. The fresh seafood and sumptuous salads are the main draw, though the meat and veggie courses are equally good. Approaching 1000Kč a head and situated below the less expensive *Avalon* (see above). Mon–Sat 6–11pm. F4.

David, Tržiště 21; ☎53 93 25. Very formal, small, family-run restaurant which specializes in doing Bohemian cuisine full justice for around 1000Kč a head. Daily 11.30am–11pm. F4.

Kampa Park, Na Kampě 8b; ☎53 48 00. Pink house exquisitely located right by the Vltava on Kampa Island with a superb international menu and tables outside in summer. Daily noon–midnight. H6.

Nebozízek (Little Auger), Petřínské sady 411; ☎53 79 05. Situated at the halfway stop on the funicular up Petřín. The view is superb, and the traditional Czech menu heavy with game dishes. Daily 11am–11pm. C7.

U malířů (The Artist's), Maltézské náměstí 11; ☎57 32 03 17. Prague's most expensive French restaurant is a converted sixteenth-century house that used to belong to an artist called Jiří Šic (pronounced "Shits"). The food *can* be delicious, but your bill will head towards 1500Kč a head regardless. Daily 7–10pm. G6.

Staré Město and Josefov

The grid references after the opening times refer to the map on pp.78–79.

INEXPENSIVE

Klub architektů, Betlémské náměstí 5a; metro Národní třída. Sweaty Gothic cellar by the side of the Betlémská kaple, packed full of smart and sophisticated locals enjoying the excellent choice of cheap veggie food and meat dishes; some tables outside in the summer. Daily 11.30am–midnight. D7.

Lotos, Platnéřská 13; metro Staroměstská. The decor's an odd mixture of tie-dye and ultra-tidy sterility, and the food's bizarre too, including banana ragout. Some veggie wholefood versions of Czech cuisine too, though – this is your chance to have a meat-free pork and dumplings. No smoking but there is alcohol. Daily 11am–10pm. C5.

Maestro, Křižovnická 10; metro Staroměstská. Very good pizza place close to the metro (and to Charles Bridge); the chicken dishes are also worth sampling, as are the profiteroles. Daily 11am–11pm. C4.

Modrá zahrada (Blue Garden), Pařížská 14; metro Staroměstská. Given its location, right by the Jewish sights, this is a surprisingly pleasant, stylish and inexpensive pizzeria (the entrance is on Niroká) serving big portions washed down with Radegast or wine. You have to ask specifically for mozzarella, otherwise you'll get Czech Edam. Daily 11am–midnight. E3.

Pizzeria Rugantino, Dušní 4; metro Staroměstská. This pizzeria, just off Dlouhá, is the genuine article: an oak-fired oven, gargantuan thin bases, nineteen toppings to choose from, and Bernard on tap. Mon–Sat 11am–11pm, Sun 6–11pm. F3.

MODERATE

Le Saint-Jacques, Jakubská 4; metro náměstí Republiky. Excellent French brasserie cuisine on offer here in the heart of the so-called "French quarter". Daily noon–3pm & 6pm–midnight. I4.

Massada, Michalská 16; metro Můstek. Smart kosher restaurant, offering some unusual dishes such as *latkes*, aubergines and fruit dumplings, though I'm not sure what the Talmud says about microwaves. Flesh-based dishes upstairs; dairy and veggie dishes downstairs. Daily except Fri & Sat 8am–midnight. F6.

Red, Hot & Blues, Jakubská 12; metro náměstí Republiky. Laid-back joint deep in the heart of ex-pat territory serving chilli-hot Tex-Mex – *burritos, étouffées* and Creole food – to the sound of jazz and blues. Daily 9am–11pm. I4.

U supa (The Vulture), Celetná 22; metro náměstí Republiky. Lively fourteenth-century pub-style restaurant serving typical Czech food and Braník beer, either inside or on the cobbles of its cool, vaulted courtyard. Daily 11.30am–10.30pm. H5.

EXPENSIVE

Bellevue, Smetanovo nábřeží 18; ☎24 22 76 14; metro Národní třída. The view of Charles Bridge and the Hrad is outstanding and they serve imaginative Czech-centred cuisine – hardly surprising then that it's around 1000Kč a head and you need to book ahead to eat here. Mon–Sat noon–3pm & 7–11.30pm, Sun 11am–3.30pm & 5.30–11pm. B9.

Le Café Colonial, Široká 6; metro Staroměstská. Situated right opposite the Klausová synagoga, this café/restaurant

Eating and Drinking

is a classy place. The colonial theme isn't overplayed, though the menu has a touch of Chinese and Indian. Mon–Sat 7.30am–1am, Sun 8.30am–5pm. D4.

Metamorphosis, Týn/Ungelt; ☎24 82 70 58; metro Staroměstská/náměstí Republiky. Ground-floor café serving pasta, desserts and drinks, plus an atmospheric Gothic cellar restaurant specializing in Mediterranean dishes and live jazz. The best of the swish new outfits that inhabit the restored courtyard hidden behind the Týn church. Daily 9am–1am. H4.

Praha Tamura, Havelská 6; ☎24 23 20 56; metro Můstek. Authentic Japanese sashimi and sushi at authentic Japanese prices (around 750Kč a head); there's a street-level buffet that costs a lot less. Daily 11am–midnight. F7.

Reykjavik, Karlova 20; ☎24 22 92 51; metro Staroměstská. Its prime tourist location and pleasant décor and service make this Icelandic-owned restaurant a very popular place. The best feature is the wonderful variety of fresh fish, flown in from you know where. Daily 11am–midnight. D6.

V zátiší (Still-Life), Liliová 1; ☎24 22 89 77; metro Národní třída. Exquisitely prepared international cuisine with fresh vegetables, fresh pasta, and regular non-meat dishes, all served in *nouvelle cuisine*-sized portions by professional waiters. Daily noon–3pm & 5.30–11pm. D7.

Nové Město

The grid references after the opening times refer to the map on pp.124–125.

INEXPENSIVE

Góvinda, Soukenická 27; metro náměstí Republiky. Hare Krishna (*Haré Kršna* in Czech) restaurant serving organic Indian veggie slop for knock-down prices. Mon–Sat 11am–5pm. H1.

Pizzeria Coloseum, Vodičkova 32; metro Můstek. Basement pizzeria in the passage beside *Kentucky Fried Chicken*, dishing up big pizzas and pasta dishes, washed down with Krušovice beer and Moravian wine – good for a pre-cinema filler. Daily noon–11.30pm. F5.

Pizzeria Kmotra (Godmother), V jirchářích 12; ☎24 91 58 09; metro Národní třída. This sweaty basement pizza place is one of Prague's most popular, and justifiably so – if possible book a table in advance. Daily 11am–1am. D6.

Pizzeria Mamma Mia, Na poříčí 13; metro náměstí Republiky. The main feature here is the restaurant's very own in-house tree. Otherwise it's easier to get a seat than at *Kmotra* and not quite so stiflingly hot. Daily 11am–11pm. H2.

Taverna, Revoluční 16; metro náměstí Republiky. Cheap Greek place in a pretty central location, a stone's throw from the Roxy. Daily 11am–midnight. G2.

MODERATE

Bella Napoli, V jámě 8; metro Národní třída. One of Prague's better Italian restaurants, situated above a tacky disco, offering pasta and pizza dishes, plus a great antipasti buffet. Mon–Sat 11.30am–11.30pm, Sun 6–11.30pm. F6.

Cerberus, Soukenická 19; ☎231 09 85; metro náměstí Republiky. Cosy, pristine little joint serving up Czech favourites, including plenty of imaginative pork dishes. Daily 11.30am–4pm & 5–11.30pm. G2.

Cicala, Žitná 43; metro I. P. Pavlova. Very good little Italian basement restaurant that does a good range of pasta and pizza, has an appetizing antipasti selection, and specializes (mid-week) in fresh seafood. Mon–Sat 11.30am–10.30pm. G7.

Sergej, Zlatnická 11; metro náměstí Republiky. Good range of Russian, Georgian and Ukrainian dishes, from kebabs to borsch, all washed down with Czech beer. Daily 11am–1am. H2.

U Čížků, Karlovo náměstí 34; ☎29 88 91; metro Karlovo náměstí. Cosy restaurant on the east side of the square, dishing up seriously large meaty helpings of beef, pork, goose, duck and anything else that moves, washed down with Plzeň beers. Daily noon–3.30pm & 5–11pm. E7.

EXPENSIVE

Casablanca, Na příkopě 10; ☎24 21 05 19; metro Můstek. The full Moroccan monty, both in terms of décor, belly dancing and food (at around 750Kč a head). Daily 6–10pm. F4.

Fakhreldine, Klimentská 48; ☎232 79 70; metro Florenc. Lebanese restaurant that charges a high price for its authentic Middle Eastern cuisine, in which the starters outnumber the main courses. Daily noon–midnight. I1.

Francouzská restaurace, **Obecní dům**, náměstí Republiky; metro náměstí Republiky. The Art Nouveau decor in this cavernous hall is absolutely stunning; the setting is formal and therefore puts a lot of tourists off, though the food's actually not that expensive. Daily noon–3pm & 6–11pm. G3.

La Perle de Prague, Rašínovo nábřeží 80; ☎21 98 41 60; metro Karlovo náměstí. Very formal French restaurant with plenty of pretensions, situated on the top floor of the notorious Tančící dům (see p.146) – well over 1500Kč a head. Mon–Sat noon–4pm & 7pm–midnight. C7.

Le Bistrot de Marlène, Plavecká 4; ☎29 10 77; metro Karlovo náměstí. Very good rustic French cuisine in a pleasant little restaurant with excellent service, in the backstreets near Vyšehrad. Daily noon–3pm & 7–11.30pm. C10.

Ostroff, Střelecký ostrov; tram #6, #9 or #22. Top-notch Italian restaurant in a great location on one of the islands in the Vltava (over 1000Kč a head); this place also has a great riverside bar that stays open until 3am. Daily noon–2pm & 7pm–midnight. A5.

Vyšehrad and the eastern suburbs

The grid references after the opening times refer to the map on pp.150–151.

INEXPENSIVE

Myslivna (The Hunting Lodge), Jagellonská 21, Žižkov; ☎627 02 09; metro Flora. One of Prague's best game restaurants, serving up excellent venison and quail. Daily 11.30am–3.30pm & 6–11pm. G5.

Na rybárně, Gorazdova 17; metro Karlovo náměstí. Dependable Czech fish restaurant near the river, that's cosy, unpretentious and, depending on the fish you choose, pretty cheap. Mon–Sat noon–midnight, Sun 5pm–midnight. C7.

U pastýřky (The Shepherdess), Bělehradská 15, Vinohrady; tram #6 or #11. Unashamedly themed Slovak restaurant, with grilled meats, folk music and outdoor seating. Daily 6pm–1am. D5.

MODERATE

Dolly Bell, Neklanova 20, Vyšehrad; ☎29 88 15; tram #3, #7, #17, #18 or #24 from metro Karlovo náměstí. Yugoslav restaurant, named after a film (it sounds more promising in Serbo-Croat), which serves up excellent Balkan grub, and features upside-down tables stuck to the ceiling. Daily 2–11pm.

Il Ritrovo, Lublaňská 11, Vinohrady; tram #6 from metro I. P. Pavlova. Excellent Italian-run outfit with a wide range of pasta dishes and good salads, a great antipasti bar in the centre of the restaurant and delicious *tiramisu* for dessert. Mon–Sat noon–3pm & 6pm–midnight. C6.

Kongzi, Seifertova 18, Žižkov; tram #5, #9 or #26 from metro Hlavní nádraží. Very reasonable Chinese restaurant in deepest Pižkov. Daily 11am–3pm & 6–11pm.

Radost FX Café, Bělehradská 120, Vinohrady; metro I. P. Pavlova. Without doubt the best choice of vegetarian dishes in town (okay, so there's not much competition), that draws in a large ex-pat posse, particularly for the Sunday brunch. Daily 11.30am–4am. D6.

Shalimar, Balbínova 10, Vinohrady; metro Muzeum. Prague's best-value curry restaurant, situated behind the Národní muzeum, serving the real thing: poppadums, bhajees, samosas and an excellent chicken kerahi. Mon–Thurs & Sun 5pm–midnight, Fri & Sat noon–midnight. D4.

Eating and Drinking

Holešovice and the western suburbs

The grid references after the opening times refer to the map on pp.34–35.

INEXPENSIVE

La Crêperie, Janovského 4, Holešovice; tram #5, #12 or #17. Stylish French-run crêperie serving sweet and savoury pancakes, French liqueurs and even the rare Nová Paka beer. Mon–Sat noon–11pm. G3.

U Matouše, Preslova 17, Smíchov; metro Anděl. Unpretentious restaurant serving good Czech cuisine with a few surprises aside from the staples: *smažený Olomoucský sýr*, a pungent deep-fried cheese and *špekové knedlíky*, bacon and onion dumplings, to name but two. Daily 11am–11pm. D8.

MODERATE

Thajský restaurant, V Holešovičkách 22a, Troja; bus #102, #156 or #175 from metro Nádraží Holešovice. A bit of a trek, unless you're camping at Troja, but inexpensive authentic Thai food is the reward. Mon–Sat 11am–3pm & 6–10.30pm.

U cedru (The Cedar), Na hutích 13, Dejvice; metro Dejvická. Much better value and even more delicious than the *Fakhreldine* in town is this reasonable Lebanese joint in the suburbs. Daily 11am–11pm. C3.

EXPENSIVE

Hanavský pavilón, Letenské sady 173, Letná; ☎32 57 92; tram #18 or #22 from metro Malostranská. Highly ornate Art Nouveau pleasure pavilion high above the Vltava, with stunning views and a bill that is unlikely to be less than 1000Kč per person. Daily 11.30am–3.30pm & 6pm–1am. D4.

Chapter 12

Clubs and live venues

The great thing about going out for the night in Prague is that the beer flows cheaply, entry to most late-night places is pretty negligible, and there are one or two venues open until 5 or 6am. That said, Prague has nothing like the number of **clubs** you'd expect from a European capital. The dance craze has a small but dedicated following, and there are a few good one-off raves over the summer (a case of scouring the fly posters around), but pure dance clubs are the exception. The continuing survival of timeless tacky discos around Wenceslas Square is remarkable; less so, the more recent arrival of a bevy of thriving strip clubs.

Many nightclubs double as live music venues, with lots of world music bands finding their way to Prague in recent years, along with Czech bands that span the entire range of musical tastes from (mostly white) reggae to thrash. To find out the latest on the city's up-and-coming events, check the listings sections in *Prague Post*, the bilingual bi-weekly free listings handout *Do města/Downtown*, or the Czech listings monthly *Přehled*, and, once again, keep your eyes peeled for flyers and posters. To buy tickets in advance, try one of the agencies like Ticketpro, which has branches all over the city, with its main branch at Salvátorská 10, Staré Město (☎24 81 40 20; Mon–Fri 8am–6pm).

Rock, Pop, Dance & World Music

Major western **bands** are beginning to include Prague in their European tours and, to be sure of a full house, many offer tickets at a fraction of their price in the West. There are gigs by Czech bands almost every night in the city's clubs and discos – a selection of the better ones is listed below. Be warned that many clubs in Prague appear to be under constant threat of closure, so always check in the local listings before setting out.

Larger live venues

Výstaviště, U Výstaviště, Holešovice; tram #5, #12 or #17; ☎20 10 311 11. The 1891 Exhibition Hall at Výstaviště is an atmospheric aircraft hangar of a place to watch a band.

Palác kultury, 5 května 65, Nusle; metro Vyšehrad; ☎61 17 22 63. The 1970s concrete centre for the old Communist Party congresses, situated near Vyšehrad.

Strahov Stadion, Vaníčkova, Břevnov; bus #176 from metro Karlovo náměstí; ☎53 99 51. Europe's largest stadium, which can hold 200,000 spectators.

Smaller live venues and club

Akropolis, Kubelíkova 27, Žižkov; tram #5, #9 or #26. Decent live venue space adjacent to the café/bar of the same name in Pižkov, that attracts some very good bands – everything from world

Clubs and live venues

music to avant-garde Czech stuff – and a discerning, mostly Czech crowd. *Doors open 7pm.*

Fromin, Václavské náměstí 21, Nové Město; metro Můstek. If you're going to hit one of the discos on Wenceslas Square, this is the one to go for, as it has all the usual ingredients, plus stunning views over the rooftops of the square. *Daily 9pm–3am.*

Jo's Garáž, Malostranské náměstí 7; tram #12 or #22 from metro Malostranská. Loud, sweaty and packed backpacker and ex-pat free disco in the cellar next door to *Jo's Bar. Daily 9pm–late.*

La Habana, Míšenská 12, Malá Strana; tram #12 or #22 from metro Malostranská. Cellar salsa disco below a small bar in the backstreets of Malá Strana. *Daily 5pm–5am.*

Lucerna music bar, Vodičkova 36, Nové Město; metro Můstek. Without doubt the best gig venue in Prague, a gilded turn-of-the-century hall with balcony, situated underneath the Lucerna *pasáž. Gigs start at 9pm.*

Mánes, Masarykovo nábřeží, Nové Město; metro Karlovo náměstí. Riverside disco, often with a Latin influence, above the functionalist art gallery of the same name. *Fri & Sat only.*

Radost FX, Bělehradská 120, Vinohrady; metro I. P. Pavlova. Still by far the slickest (and longest-running) dance club in Prague, attracting a mix of clubbers and despots; good veggie café upstairs (see p.227). *Daily 10pm–5am.*

Rock Café, Národní 22, Nové Město; metro Národní třída. The *Rock Café* has had its day. It made its name in the early 1990s, but is now considered passé. Still, its frequent "revival" bands continue to pull in plenty of tourists and out-of-town Czechs, and it shows rockumentaries all afternoon in the bar. *Daily 4pm–3am.*

Roxy, Dlouhá 33, Staré Město; metro náměstí Republiky. The *Roxy* is a great little venue: a rambling old theatre with an interesting programme of events from arty films and exhibitions to live acts and dance nights. *Tues–Sun 8pm–late.*

Újezd, Újezd 18, Malá Strana; tram #12 or #22 from metro Malostranská. Like *Rock Café*, this place has a long pedigree, but unlike Rock Café it still hosts real low-tech Czech bands – the only problem is they're usually grim. *Daily 7pm–3am.*

Jazz

Prague has a surprisingly long indigenous tradition, and is home to a handful of good jazz clubs. With little money to attract acts from abroad, the artists are almost exclusively Czech and tend to do the entire round of venues each month. The one exception to all this is the annual **international jazz festival** in October, which attracts at least one big name; previous greats have included Wynton Marsalis, B. B. King and Jan Garbarek. More often than not, it's a good idea to book a table at the jazz clubs listed below – this is particularly true of *AghaRTA* and *Reduta.*

AghaRTA Jazz Centrum, Krakovská 5, Nové Město; metro Muzeum; ☎ 24 21 29 14. Probably the best jazz club in Prague, with a good mix of Czechs and foreigners and a consistently good programme of gigs; situated in a side street off the top end of Wenceslas Square. *Daily 7pm–1am.*

Malostranská beseda, Malostranské náměstí 21, Malá Strana; tram #12 or #22 from metro Malostranská; ☎ 53 90 24. Ramshackle, inexpensive venue that attracts lots of Czechs, despite its location. The programme is by no means exclusively jazz. *Daily until 1am; gigs start at 8pm.*

Metropolitan Jazz Club, Jungmannova 14, Nové Město; metro Můstek; ☎ 24 21 60 25. Small jazz restaurant that tends to stick to a traditional menu, on stage and in the kitchen. Daily until 1am; gigs start at 9pm.

Reduta, Národní 20, Nové Město; metro Národní třída; ☎ 24 91 22 46. Prague's best-known jazz club – Bill Clinton played his sax here in front of Havel. *Live jazz daily from 9pm.*

U malého Glena, Karmelitská 23, Malá Strana; tram #12 or #22 from metro Malostranská. Tiny downstairs stage worth checking out for its eclectic mix of bluegrass, acid jazz, be-bop and blues. Sunday jam sessions start at 6pm; all other gigs begin at 9pm. *Daily 10am–2am.*

U staré paní, Michalská 9, Staré Město; metro Můstek; ☎26 49 20. Decent jazz restaurant that really gets going when the live music kicks in from 9pm onwards. *Daily 7pm–4am.*

Železná, Železná 16, Staré Město; metro Můstek; ☎24 21 25 41. Inexpensive, centrally located cellar venue that puts on a regular live programme of mostly trad jazz bands. *Daily from 5pm.*

Clubs and live venues

Gay and Lesbian Nightlife

Prague Post does the occasional update on **gay and lesbian nightlife** in Prague, otherwise you'll need to get hold of the monthly gay magazine *SOHO Revue*, which has an English summary; *Amigo*, another bi-monthly listings mag; or the lesbian monthly, *ProFem*. You'll also find useful flyers at the places listed below (for more on gay life, see p.248).

"A" Klub, Milíčova 32, Žižkov; tram #5, #9 or #26. The city's premier lesbian bar with women-only Friday nights. It's small but stylish and definitely worth checking out. *Mon–Sat 6pm–6am, Sun 3pm–midnight.*

Babylona, Martinská 6, Staré Město; metro Národní třída. Prague's most centrally located gay sauna, with steam baths, pools and massage on offer. *Daily 2pm–2am.*

Connections, Husitská 7, Žižkov; metro Florenc. Mixed gay/lesbian disco with a sauna and popular, occasional drag nights. *Daily 9pm–4am.*

Drake's, Petřínská 5, Smíchov; tram #6, #9 or #12 from metro Anděl. Expensive, almost exclusively male hangout, which bills itself as a "really big cruise facility"; twenty private video booths are the biggest draw. *Open 24 hours a day.*

L Club, Lublaňská 48, Vinohrady; metro I. P. Pavlova. Mixed lesbian/gay crowd at this restaurant, which turns into a cruisy disco after 10pm. *Daily 8pm–4am.*

Meďúza, Belgick 17, Vinohrady; metro náměstí Míru. Laid-back café run by women for women; the best gynocentric spot in Prague. *Mon–Fri 11am–1am, Sat & Sun noon–1am.*

Stella, Lužická 10, Vinohrady; metro náměstí Míru. Currently one of the most popular mixed gay/lesbian hot spots in the capital. *Daily 8pm–5am.*

Tom's Bar, Pernerova 4, Karlín; metro Florenc. Small but popular restaurant and downstairs disco frequented almost exclusively by Czech gay men. *Tues–Thurs 9pm–2am, Fri & Sat 9pm–4am.*

U dubu, Záhřebská 14, Vinohrady; metro náměstí Míru. Typical, cheap Czech pub with a predominantly gay male clientele. *Daily 10am–3pm & 6pm–midnight.*

U kapra, Žatecká 7, Staré Město; metro Staroměstská. Perfectly normal, very central Czech restaurant that attracts a small, loyal coterie of gay men. *Daily 11am–1am.*

U Petra Voka, Na bělidle 40, Smíchov; metro Anděl. Pre-1989 mixed gay/lesbian nightspot that features a disco and drag nights. *Daily 8pm–late.*

U střelce, Karoliny Světlé 12, Staré Město; ☎24 23 82 78; metro Národní třída. Sweaty cellar club whose drag shows pull in a mixed straight/gay crowd. *Wed–Sat 9.30pm–late.*

Chapter 13

The arts

Alongside the city's numerous cafés, pubs and clubs, there's a rich **cultural life** in Prague. Music is everywhere in the city: especially in the summer, when the streets, churches, palaces, opera houses, concert halls and even the gardens are filled with the strains of classical music. True, there are too many Mozart concerts pandering to the tourist trade, but equally there are some very high-quality chamber concerts.

Czech theatre and film have recovered significantly since the early 1990s, when subsidies and censorship both disappeared more or less overnight. Even if you don't understand Czech, there are theatre performances worth catching – Prague has a strong tradition of mime, "black theatre" and puppetry, and many cinemas show films in their original language. Rock, pop and jazz gigs are covered in the previous chapter.

Tickets

You can obtain **tickets** from the box office (*pokladna*) of the venue concerned, but you might find it easier to go to one of the city's numerous **ticket agencies** – it will cost you more, but might save you a lot of hassle. Ticketpro has branches all over the city, with its main branch at Salvátorská 10, Staré Město (☎24 81 40 20; Mon–Fri 8am–6pm). Another option is Bohemia Ticket International, which has several offices, including one at Na příkopě 16, Nové Město (☎24 21 50 31; Mon–Fri 9am–6pm, Sat 9am–4pm, Sun 10am–3pm). Ticket **prices**, with a few notable exceptions, are still extremely cheap, ranging from 250–500Kč. Lastly, don't despair if everything is officially sold out (*vyprodáno*), as stand-by tickets are often available at the venue's box office on the night.

Listings and information

The English-language **listings** in *Prague Post* are selective, but they do at least pick out the events which may be of particular interest to the non-Czech speaker, and list all the major venues and their addresses. Also in English is the monthly handout, *Culture In Prague*, also available in Czech as *Kultura v Praze*, which, along with the bilingual fortnightly listings fold-out *Do města/Downtown* and the Czech monthly listings booklet *Přehled*, are available from any PIS office. Any additional **information** you might need can usually be obtained from one of the PIS offices around town: at Na příkopě 20, or in the Staroměstská radnice.

Classical Music, Opera and Ballet

Folk songs lie at the heart of Czech music and have found their way into much of the country's **classical music**, of which the Czechs are justifiably proud, having produced four composers of international stature – Dvořák, Janáček, Smetana and Martinů – and a fifth, Mahler, who, though German-speaking,

The arts

was born in Bohemia. If the music of Mozart appears rather too often in the city's monthly concert programme, it's partly because the tourists love him, but also because of his special relationship with Prague (for more on which see p.73).

The city boasts three large-scale theatres where opera is regularly staged, and has several resident orchestras, the most illustrious of which are the Czech Philharmonic (*Česká filharmonie*), which is based at the Rudolfinum and is currently under the baton of Vladimir Ashkenazy, and the Prague Symphony Orchestra (*Symfonický orchestr hl. m. Prahy*), whose home is the Smetanova síň in the Obecní dům. The country continues to produce top-class conductors, a host of singers, and virtuoso violinists.

By far the biggest annual event is the *Pražské jaro* (Prague Spring), the country's most prestigious **international music festival**. It traditionally begins on May 12, the anniversary of Smetana's death, with a performance of *Má vlast*, and finishes on June 2 with a rendition of Beethoven's *Ninth Symphony*. Tickets for the festival sell out fast – try your luck by writing, a month before the festival begins, to the Prague Spring Festival box office at Hellichova 18, Malá Strana; *festival@login.cz*. The main venues are listed below, but keep an eye out for concerts in the city's churches and palaces, gardens and courtyards (the main ones are listed separately below); note that evening performances tend to start fairly early, either at 5 or 7pm.

The major venues

Národní divadlo (National Theatre), Národní 2, Nové Město; ☎24 91 34 37; metro Národní třída. Prague's grandest nineteenth-century theatre is the living embodiment of the Czech national revival movement, and continues to put on a wide variety of mostly, though by no means exclusively, Czech plays, opera and ballet. Worth visiting for the decor alone. *Box office Mon–Fri 10am–6pm, Sat & Sun 10am–12.30pm & 3–6pm.*

Obecní dům – Smetanova síň, náměstí Republiky 5, Nové Město; metro náměstí Republiky. Fantastically ornate and recently renovated Art Nouveau concert hall which usually kicks off the Prague Spring festival, and is home to the excellent Prague Symphony Orchestra. *Box office Mon–Fri 10am–12.30pm & 1.30–6pm.*

Rudolfinum, Alšovo nábřeží 12, Staré Město; ☎24 89 33 52; metro Staroměstská. A truly stunning Neo-Renaissance concert hall from the late nineteenth century, and home base for the Czech Philharmonic. The Dvořákova síň is the large hall; the Sukova síň is the chamber concert hall. *Box office Mon–Fri 10am–12.30pm & 1.30–6pm, plus an hour before the performance.*

Státní opera (State Opera), Wilsonova 4, Nové Město; ☎24 22 76 93; metro Muzeum. A sumptuous nineteenth-century opera house, built by the city's German community, which once attracted star conductors such as Mahler and Zemlinsky. Now it's the number two venue for opera, with a repertoire that tends to focus on Italian pieces. *Box office Mon–Fri 10am–5.30pm, Sat & Sun 10am–noon & 1–5.30pm.*

Stavovské divadlo (Estates Theatre), Ovocný trh 1, Staré Město; ☎24 21 50 01; metro Můstek. Prague's oldest opera house, which witnessed the première of Mozart's *Don Giovanni*, puts on a mixture of opera, ballet and straight theatre (with simultaneous headphone translation available). *Box office Mon–Fri 10am–6pm, Sat & Sun 10am–12.30pm & 3–6pm.*

Concert venues

Anežký klášter (Convent of sv Anežka), U milosrdných 17, Staré Město; ☎24 81 08 35; metro náměstí Republiky. Regular Czech chamber concerts, often of the big four Czech composers, are given in the convent's atmospheric Gothic chapel (see p.104).

Bazilika sv Jakuba (St James), Malá Štupartská, Staré Město; metro náměstí Republiky. Choral church music, sung mass and Prague's finest organ used for regular recitals (see p.104).

The arts

Bertramka, Mozartova 169, Smíchov; ☎54 38 93; metro Anděl. Occasional concerts given at the Mozart Museum (see p.178), mostly though not entirely of the composer's own music.

Chrám sv Mikuláše (St Nicholas), Malostranské náměstí, Mala Strána; metro Malostranská. Prague's most sumptuous Baroque church is the perfect setting for choral concerts and organ recitals (see p.76).

Dûm U kamenného zvonu (House at the Stone Bell), Staroměstské náměstí 13, Staré Město; ☎24 81 00 36; metro Staroměstská. An adventurous programme of modern and classical concerts is staged at this contemporary art gallery, housed in an old building on Old Town Square (see p.101).

Kostel sv Martina ve zdi, Martinská, Staré Město; metro Národní třída. Daily chamber music concerts mostly, though not exclusively, of eighteenth-century composers, held in a bare medieval church.

Lichtenštejnský palác (Liechtenstein Palace), Malostranské náměstí 13, Malá Strana; metro Malostranská. The Czech Academy of Music lives here and puts on mostly Baroque music by chamber orchestras and string quartets.

Lobkovický palác (Lobkovic Palace), Jiřská 3, Hradčany; ☎53 73 06; metro Malostranská. Concerts held in the palace's main be-frescoed hall at the eastern edge of Prague Castle (see p.62).

Míčovna, U prašného mostu, Hradčany; tram #22 from metro Malostranská. Renaissance ball game court in the Královská zahrada of Prague Castle (see p.63).

Nostický palác (Nostitz Palace), Maltézské náměstí 1, Malá Strana; metro Malostranská. Chamber concerts here start at the civilized hour of 8pm, and include a glass of wine as part of the ticket price.

Pražský Hlahol, Masarykovo nábřeží 16, Nové Město; ☎29 34 30; Karlovo náměstí. Home to the Hlahol Choir, the hall holds occasional concerts on Wednesday evenings and is decorated by, among others, the Art Nouveau artist Alfons Mucha.

Valdštejnská zahrada (Valdštejn Gardens), Letenská, Malá Strana; metro Malostranská. Probably the finest of the summer-only outdoor venues (see p.78).

Zrcadlová kaple, Klementinum, Mariánské náměstí, Staré Město; metro Staroměstská. Regular chamber and organ concerts held in the ornate pink Baroque Mirrored Chapel (see p.96).

Theatre

Theatre has always had a special place in Czech culture, one which the events of 1989 only strengthened. Not only did the country end up with a playwright as president, but it was the capital's theatres that served as information centres during those first few crucial weeks. After the revolution, however, the whole theatre scene, for so long heavily subsidized – and censored – by the authorities, went through a difficult patch. More recently, audiences figures have picked up considerably; tourists are also a lucrative source of income and there are several English-language theatre companies now based in Prague. Ticket prices have risen dramatically, though you can still get into most theatres for less than 250kč; tickets are available from the venues themselves, or for considerably more from the ticket agencies listed on p.232.

Prague also has a strong tradition of **mime** and **"černé divaldo"** or "black light theatre" (visual trickery created by "invisible" actors dressed all in black) ranging from the classical style of the late Ladislav Fialka and his troupe to the more experimental work of Boris Polívka. However, along with Prague's long-running multimedia company, Laterna magika, many of these shows are deliberately geared towards tourists, and can make for disappointing viewing.

Puppet theatre (*loutkové divadlo*) also has a long indigenous tradition, as an art form for both adults and children, and is currently enjoying something of a renaissance, thanks to its accessibility to non-Czech audiences. Unfortunately, this has meant never-ending performances of Mozart's *Don Giovanni* in period costume specifically aimed at passing tourists. At the other end of the spectrum, few companies now maintain the traditional puppets-only set-up, instead featuring live actors in their productions, many of which can be very wordy, making the shows less accessible if you don't speak the language.

Selected theatres: dance, experimental, fringe, mime and musicals

The Stavovské divadlo and the Národní divadlo both put on plays as well as opera and ballet, and are listed on p.233. Below is a selection of Prague's other main theatres; the phone numbers given are for box offices.

Divadlo Alfred ve dvoře, Fr. Křížka 36, Holešovice; ☎20 57 15 84; metro Vltavská. Experimental theatre run by mime theatre guru, Ctibor Turba, and an occasional student drama venue. *Box office opens from 5pm on the day of performance.*

Divadlo Archa, Na poříčí 26, Nové Město; ☎232 88 00; metro Florenc. By far the most innovative venue in Prague, with two very versatile spaces, an art gallery and a café. The programming includes music, dance and theatre with an emphasis on the avant-garde. *Box office Mon–Fri 10am–6pm.*

Divadlo na Klárově, nábřeží Edvarda Beneša 3, Malá Strana; ☎53 98 37; metro Malostranská. This is a good place to catch traditional Czech folk songs and dancing. Shows begin at 7.30pm.

Divadlo na zábradlí, Anenské náměstí 5, Staré Město; ☎24 22 19 33; metro Staroměstská. Havel's old haunt and a centre of absurdist theatre back in the 1960s, it's still a provocative rep theatre, with a wide variety of shows (in Czech) and a lively bar. *Box office Mon–Fri 2–7pm, Sat & Sun two hours before performance.*

Divadlo Spirála, Výstaviště, Holešovice; ☎10 67; tram #5, #12 or #17 from nádraží Holešovice. Spectacular 360-degree theatre that puts on suitably stagey shows (mostly musicals). *Box office Mon–Fri 8am–8pm, Sat noon–8pm, Sun noon–4pm.*

Divadlo v Celetné, Celetná 17, Nové Město; ☎232 68 43; metro náměstí Republiky. Home of several fringe companies (including an English-language one), and a student drama venue, which puts on tourist-friendly productions (occasionally puppetry and *černé divadlo*). *Box office daily 9am–midnight.*

Duncan Centre, Branická 41, Braník; ☎44 46 18 10; tram#3, #16, #17 or #21, stop Přístaviště. Interesting dance pieces by resident and visiting artists at this theatre based in a school for contemporary dance in the southern suburb of Braník. *Tickets from Ticketpro.*

Laterna magika (Magic Lantern), Nová scéna, Národní 4, Nové Město; ☎24 91 41 29; metro Národní třída. The National Theatre's *Nová scéna*, one of Prague's most modern and versatile stages, is now the main base for Laterna magika, founders of multimedia theatre way back in 1958, now content just to pull in crowds of tourists. *Box office Mon–Fri 10am–8pm, Sat & Sun 3–8pm.*

Ta Fantastika, Karlova 8, Staré Město; ☎24 22 90 78; metro Staroměstská. Probably the best of the "black theatre" venues, albeit strategically located close to the Charles Bridge, offering dialogue-free shows specifically aimed at tourists. *Box office daily 11am–9pm.*

Puppet theatre

Divadlo minor, Senovážné náměstí 28, Nové Město; ☎24 22 96 75; metro náměstí Republiky. The former state puppet theatre puts on children's puppet shows most days, plus adult shows on occasional evenings – sometimes with English subtitles. *Box office Mon–Fri 2–5pm and one hour before performance.*

The arts

Divadlo na královské cestě, Karlova 12, Staré Město; ☎26 93 83; metro Staroměstská. Prague is the international headquarters of UNIMA, the international marionette organization, so the productions staged at their centrally located theatre should, by rights, be brilliant – sadly, that's seldom the case. *Box office daily noon–7pm.*

Divadlo Spejbla a Hurvínka, Dejvická 38, Dejvice; ☎31 21 24 13; metro Dejvická/Hradčanská. Features the indomitable puppet duo, Spejbl and Hurvínek, created by Josef Skupa earlier this century and still going strong at one of the few puppets-only theatres in the country. *Box office Tues, Thurs & Fri 10am–2pm & 3–6pm, Wed 10am–2pm & 3–7pm, Sat & Sun 1–5pm.*

Umělecká scéna říše loutek, Žatecká 1, Staré Město; ☎232 45 65; metro Staroměstská. This company's rather dull marionette version of Mozart's *Don Giovanni* has proved extremely popular and has been running without a break for several years now, but they also put on regular kids' shows at the weekends. *Box office Wed 3.30–7pm, Sat & Sun 1–5pm.*

Film

As with the theatre, **cinema** (*kino*) attendances have been steadily decreasing over the last decade. The advent of video machines, more TV stations and steadily rising ticket prices are to blame for the most part. Nevertheless, the cinema remains a relatively cheap (around 100Kč a ticket) and popular form of entertainment, and although Hollywood blockbusters form a large part of the weekly fare, the Czech film industry continues to chug along, bolstered by the odd success story, such as Jan Svěrák's Oscar-winning *Kolja*. For more on Czech film, see p.271.

Hollywood films do tend to be shown dubbed (*český dabing*), but there's usually at least one cinema where films are shown in their original language with subtitles (*titulky*). And thanks to Prague's large ex-pat community, some Czech films are occasionally shown with English subtitles – these are all listed in *Prague Post*, but for a comprehensive rundown of the week's films, check out the bilingual *Do města/Downtown*. Film titles are nearly always translated into Czech, so you'll need to have your wits about you to identify films such as *Královna Alžběta* as *Elizabeth*.

The city's main **cinemas** are concentrated around Wenceslas Square, while the list below is confined to the best screens, plus Prague's art-house film clubs, where you may need to buy a membership card (*legitimace*) in order to purchase tickets. Keep a look out, too, for films shown at the various foreign cultural institutions around town (see p.247 for addresses), and for the summer-only open-air *letní kina* which is held on the Střelecký ostrov and in Výstaviště. The city's short-lived international film festival failed to dislodge Karlovy Vary's annual bash as the country's leading film festival. More interesting is the newly established annual **Days of European Film**, which takes place over ten days at the end of April.

Aero, Biskupcova 31, Zižkov; ☎89 36 01; tram #1, #9 or #16. Crumbling art-house cinema that shows rolling mini-festivals, interspersed by more popular movies.

Cinema Broadway, Na příkopě 31, Nové Město; ☎21 61 32 78; metro náměstí Republiky. The second largest screen in the city, and the best sound system, Broadway is the most central of Prague's newly refurbished cinemas and shows mainstream films.

Dlabačov, Bělohorská 24, Břevnov; ☎33 35 90 58; tram #22 from metro Malostranská. Excellent film club (membership 20Kč) on the ground floor of the ugly *Hotel Pyramid*, showing a discerning selection of new releases and plenty of art-house classics.

Illusion, Vinohradská 48, Vinohrady; ☎25 02 60; metro náměstí Míru. A regular programme of old and new Czech movies, though sadly without English subtitles.

Jalta, Václavské náměstí 43, Nové Město; ☎24 22 88 14; metro Museum. Two screens here, including the only *kinokavárna* left in Prague, where you can have a drink and smoke while watching the film.

Lucerna, Vodičkova 36, Nové Město; ☎24 21 69 72; metro Můstek. Without doubt the most ornate film theatre in Prague, decked out in Moorish style by Havel's grandfather.

MAT, Karlovo náměstí 19, Nové Město; ☎24 91 57 65; metro Karlovo náměstí. Café and cinema popular with the film crowd, with an eclectic programme of shorts, documentaries and Czech films with English subtitles.

Ponrepo – Bio Konvikt, Bartolomějská 11, Staré Město; metro Národní třída. Really old classics from the black-and-white era, dug out from the National Film Archives. Membership cards (150Kč) can only be bought Mon–Fri 2–5pm.

The Visual Arts

The Národní galerie (National Gallery) or NG runs the city's main **permanent art collections**, in the Anežský klášter, Jiřský klášter, Šternberský palác and Veletržní palác, each of which is described in detail in the guide section. Most of these galleries also give over space for **temporary exhibitions**, and there are several which only ever stage special exhibitions. *Prague Post* has selective listings, and there's a list of foreign cultural institutes, which also put on regular exhibitions, on p.247, but as ever you'll find the fullest listings in the Czech monthly listings magazine *Přehled*. After years of fairly dull state-approved art, there have been some illuminating and challenging exhibitions in recent years. Dozens of **commercial galleries** have also sprung up, only a handful of which can be relied on regularly to show interesting stuff; below is a selection of the best (the "galerie a výstavy" section of *Přehled* will have a full rundown).

Exhibitions spaces

Belvedér, Mariánské hradby 1, Hradčany; tram #22 from metro Malostranská. One of the most beautiful Renaissance buildings in Prague (see p.63), which usually shows works by contemporary artists. *Tues–Sun 10am–6pm.*

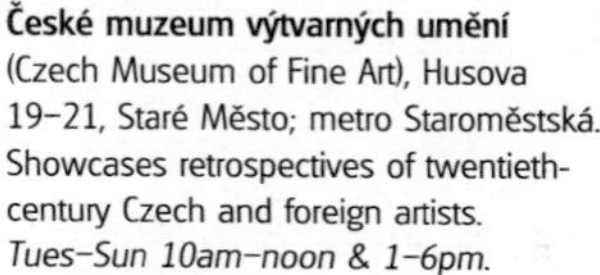

České muzeum výtvarných umění (Czech Museum of Fine Art), Husova 19–21, Staré Město; metro Staroměstská. Showcases retrospectives of twentieth-century Czech and foreign artists. *Tues–Sun 10am–noon & 1–6pm.*

Císařská konírna (Imperial Stables), druhé nádvoří, Hradčany; tram #22 from Malostranská. Temporary exhibition space in Rudolf II's stables, situated in the second courtyard of Prague Castle. *Tues–Sun 10am–6pm.*

Dům U černé Matky boží, Celetná 34, Staré Město; metro náměstí Republiky. The first two floors of this Cubist museum are given over to exhibitions of twentieth-century Czech artists; the top floor has a permanent exhibition on Czech Cubism (see p.103). *Tues–Sun 10am–6pm.*

Dům U kamenného zvonu, Staroměstské náměstí 13, Staré Město; metro Staroměstská. A real range from Baroque to avant-garde sees the light of day in the small Gothic rooms and courtyard of this ancient building (see p.101). *Tues–Sun 10am–6pm.*

Galerie Hollar, Smetanovo nábřeží 6, Nové Město; metro Národní třída. The main exhibition space for Czech graphic artists is situated on the noisy river embankment, but there are plenty of old prints for sale. *Tues–Sun 10am–1pm & 2–6pm.*

Galerie Jaroslav Fragnera, Betlémské náměstí 5a, Staré Město; metro Národní třída. Gallery space next door to the Betlémská kaple used for free architectural exhibitions. *Tues–Sun 10am–6pm.*

Galerie Václava Špály, Národní 30; metro Národní třída. Large exhibition space which hosts exhibitions of Czech modern and contemporary artists' works. *Tues–Sun 10am–1pm & 2–6pm.*

The arts

Jízdárna pražkého hradu (Prague Castle Riding School), U prašného mostu, Hradčany; tram #22 from Malostranská. One of the Národní galerie's main temporary exhibition spaces, often used to display twentieth-century Czech art. *Tues–Sun 10am–6pm.*

Karolinum, Ovocný trh 3, Staré Město; metro Můstek. Gothic vaulted room in Prague's Charles University, which puts on shows by Czech and foreign artists. *Tues–Sun 10am–5pm.*

Mánes, Masarykovo nábřeží 250, Nové Město; metro Karlovo náměstí. White functionalist building spanning a channel in the Vltava, with an open-plan gallery and a tradition of excellent exhibitions. *Tues–Sun 10am–6pm.*

Městská knihovna, Mariánské náměstí 1, Staré Město; metro Staroměstská. Slightly off the Staré Město beaten track, exhibitions at the Municipal Library's gallery space are usually devoted to Czech artists and are well worth checking out. *Tues–Sun 10am–6pm.*

Obecní dům, náměstí Republiky 5, Nové Město; metro Náměstí Republiky. Exhibitions on a turn-of-the-century theme in the luscious surroundings of the Art Nouveau Obecní dům (see p.137). *Daily 10am–6pm.*

Palác Goltz-Kinských (Goltz-Kinsky Palace), Staroměstské náměstí 12, Staré Město; metro Staroměstská. Prints and drawings from the Národní galerie's collection. *Tues–Sun 10am–6pm.*

Rudolfinum, Alšovo nábřeží 12, Staré Město; metro Staroměstská. One of the few galleries in Prague which can take large-scale international exhibitions. *Tues–Sun 10am–6pm.*

UPM, 17 listopadu 2, Staré Město; metro Staroměstská. The UPM, the city's museum of applied art (see p.122), owns some of the finest Czech art in the world, much of which is hidden away in the vaults due to lack of space – be sure to catch their generally excellent temporary exhibitions. *Tues–Sun 10am–6pm.*

Valdštejnská jízdárna, Valdštejnská 3, Malá Strana; metro Malostranská. The Národní galerie's most provocative exhibitions tend to be housed here. *Tues–Sun 10am–6pm.*

Veletržní palác, Dukelských hrdinů 47, Holešovice; tram #5, #12 or #17. Prague's vast new modern art museum puts on excellent temporary exhibitions and retrospectives in its first-floor galleries (see p.166). *Tues–Sun 10am–6pm, Thurs until 9pm.*

Commercial galleries

Galerie Behémot, Elišky Krásnohorské 6, Josefov; metro Staroměstská. Avant-garde installations by up-and-coming Czech and Slovak contemporary artists. *Tues–Sun 1–7pm.*

Galerie jednorožec s harfou, Průchodní 4, Staré Město; metro Národní třída. The "Unicorn with a Harp" gallery is located in an alleyway off Konviktská, and showcases works in a variety of media by contemporary disabled artists. *Mon–Fri 11am–11pm, Sat & Sun 1–10pm.*

Galerie MXM, Nosticova 6, Malá Strana; metro Malostranská. Prague's pioneering and highly influential private gallery puts on consistently good shows by contemporary Czech artists in its one, small vaulted room. *Tues–Sun noon–6pm.*

Galerie na Jánském Vršku, Jánský vršek 15; metro Malostranská. Art gallery, situated just off Nerudova, devoted to glassmaking, for which the Czechs have an enviable reputation. *Tues–Sun 10.30am–5.30pm.*

Galerie Peithner-Lichtenfels, Michalská 12, Staré Město; metro Můstek. Tiny gallery which regularly shows works by leading Czech and Central European artists of the twentieth century. *Daily 10am–7pm.*

Gambra-surrealisticka galerie, Černínská 5, Hradčany; tram #22 from metro Malostranská. The gallery of Prague's small, but persistent surrealist movement, past and present, hidden in the enchanted backstreets of Hradčany, also provides a window for the works of animator extraordinaire, Jan Švankmajer, and his wife, the artist Eva Švankmajerová. *Wed–Sun noon–6pm.*

Photographic galleries

Galerie Josefa Sudka, Úvoz 24, Malá Strana; metro Malostranská. Confusingly there are now two photography galleries named after the father of the modern Czech art form – this one's the only photo space on the left bank. *Tues–Sun 10am–noon & 1–6pm.*

Komorní galerie domu fotografie Josefa Sudka, Maiselova 2 & U Radnice 5, Staré Město; metro Staroměstská. There are two bits to this gallery: the exhibition space is on Maiselova 2, while the commercial section, where you can buy stuff, is at U Radnice 5. *Tues–Sun 10am–7pm.*

Pražský dům fotografie, U Řečických, Vodičkova 10, Nové Město; metro Můstek/Museum. Puts on consistently good exhibitions drawn from the group's extensive collections, plus visiting photographic shows. *Daily 11am–6pm.*

Chapter 14

Sports

The Czech Republic is equally famous for its world-class tennis players, its national football squad and its ice hockey players; however, the sport which pulls the biggest crowds, by far, is soccer. Getting tickets to watch a particular sport is easy (and cheap) enough on the day – even big matches rarely sell out. If you want to check forthcoming sports events, read the sports pages in *Prague Post*, or ask at a PIS office. Participating in sports activities is also becoming much easier, though the Czechs are only very slowly getting into the health kick.

Soccer

The Czech national team have enjoyed mixed fortunes since splitting from the Slovaks in 1993. After losing the Euro 96 final in extra time, they failed even to qualify for the 1998 World Cup. On the domestic front, however, things have been much worse. As with most former Eastern Bloc countries, the best home-grown players have, almost without exception, chosen to seek fame and fortune abroad. As a result, domestic teams have underperformed in all European competitions, and four-figure crowds remain the norm.

Big money was pumped into certain clubs by local entrepreneurs, but a combination of mismanagement and corruption has spelled disaster for several of the big clubs. Despite a decade of turmoil, however, the most consistent teams in the *Českomoravského liga* are still arch rivals Sparta Praha and Slavia Praha. The season runs from August to late November and late February to early June, and matches are usually held on Sundays. And the best thing, of course, is that, somewhat unbelievably, you can still drink inexpensive and delicious beer on the terraces.

The most successful club in the country is **Sparta Praha**, who won eight league titles in the 1990s, and look set to maintain their hold over Czech football for some time to come. That said, in 1996, they had to endure the embarrassment of being saved from bankruptcy by the Slovak steelworks VSŽ Košice, and are currently owned by a German publishing group. They play at the country's finest, and newly renovated, Sparta stadium, by the Letná plain (five minutes' walk from metro Hradčanská); international matches are also regularly played there.

Sparta's closest rivals, **Slavia Praha**, majority-owned by a British investment firm, won the league title in 1996 for the first time in nearly fifty years. It has not, however, heralded a new dawn for Slavia, who remain second best to Sparta. Their ground, optimistically called Eden, is on Vladivostocká in Vršovice, just off U Slavie (tram #4 or #22 from metro náměstí Míru). **Viktoria Žižkov**, based in the traditionally working-class district of Prague 3, enjoyed a brief period of glory when they won the Czech cup in 1994. Sadly, the man who helped get them there, Vratislav Čekan, was forced to pull out in 1996 after a financial scandal. Viktoria's ground is on

Seifertova (tram #5, #9 or #26 from metro Hlavní nádraží). Prague's least successful professional side, **Bohemians**, were relegated to the second division in 1997; they play at a ground just south of Vršovické náměstí (tram #4 or #22 from metro náměstí Míru).

The old army team, **Dukla Praha** – immortalized in the pop song *All I Want for Christmas is a Dukla Prague Away-Kit* by British band Half Man Half Biscuit – were forced to leave the capital in 1997, and merge with the local team at Příbram, 60km southwest of Prague. Dukla have since bounced back into the first division, but continue to play rent-free in the town of Příbram.

Ice hockey

Ice hockey runs soccer a close second as the nation's most popular sport. It's not unusual to see kids playing their own form of the game in the street, rather than kicking a football around. As with soccer, the fall of Communism prompted an exodus by the country's best players who left to seek fame and fortune in North America's National Hockey League (NHL). In fact, Jaromír Jágr, by far the most famous Czech player, is one of the NHL's top scorers, and currently plays for the Pittsburgh Penguins. In 1998, the Czech national team surprised everyone by taking the gold medal in the Winter Olympics.

Games take place on Saturdays and can take anything up to three hours; they are fast and physical and make for cold but compelling viewing. The season starts at the end of September and culminates in the annual World Championships the following summer, when the fortunes of the national side are subject to close scrutiny, especially if pitched against the old enemy Russia, not to mention their former bed-mate and new rival, Slovakia. A double victory against the Soviets in 1969 precipitated riots in towns across the country, culminating in the torching of the Soviet airline Aeroflot's offices in Prague.

Unlike in football, **Sparta Praha** are only one of a number of successful teams, and the *Extraliga* is usually hotly contested. Sparta's *zimní stadión* (winter stadium) is next door to the Výstaviště exhibition grounds in Holešovice (metro nádraží Holešovice). Prague's only other first division team are **Slavia Praha**, who play at the *zimní stadión* to the south of the Havlíčkovy sady in Vršovice (tram #4 or #22 from metro náměstí Míru).

Ice skating

Given the nation's penchant for ice hockey, it's not surprising that **ice skating** (*bruslení*) is Prague's most popular winter activity. There's no shortage of rinks (*zimní stadión*) in the city, although public opening hours are limited, and of course there are the city's two reservoirs, Hostivář and Nárka, which regularly freeze over in winter. Most rinks don't rent out skates, and those that do have only a limited selection, so your best bet is to buy a pair downtown; men's skates tend to be for ice hockey, women's for figure skating, and either will set you back around £25/$40.

Štvanice, Štvanice ostrov, Holešovice; five-minute walk on to the island from metro Florenc. Skate rental is available, but the rink is only open to the public for a very limited period. Fri 7.30–10pm, Sat 1–3.30pm, Sun 7.30–10pm.

Tennis

Tennis has been one of the country's most successful exports, with the likes of Martina Navrátilová and Ivan Lendl among the game's all-time greats. The glory days of Czech tennis may well be over, though the country still provides a smattering of world-class players each year. Contrary to what you might read in the western press, however, the Swiss player and top seed Martina Hingis is of Slovak, not Czech, descent. Any home-grown talent there is will be on domestic display only in the Škoda Czech Open, the country's only ATP event, held every August on Prague's Štvanice ostrov, the island on the Hlávkův most (metro Florenc).

Sports

Sports

If you fancy a quick game yourself, you'll have to bring your own racket and balls with you, or buy them downtown. The most central tennis courts are listed below.

Slavia Praha, Letenské sady, Holešovice; ☎33 37 40 33; tram #1, #18 or #25 from metro Hradčanská. Indoor and outdoor floodlit clay courts situated opposite the Národní technické muzeum. Daily 7am–8pm.

Střelecky ostrov, Nové Město; ☎224 92 01 36; tram #6, #9 or #22. Outdoor courts on one of the islands in the Vltava, situated opposite the National Theatre. Daily 9am–dusk.

Horse racing

Prague's main racecourse is at **Velká Chuchle**, 5km or so south of the city centre; bus #129, #172, #241, #244, or *osobní* train from metro Smíchovské nádraží. Steeplechases and hurdles take place on Tuesday and Sunday afternoons from May to October. There are also less frequent races at a smaller trot course on **Císařský ostrov** (May–Oct only); walk through the Stromovka park and across the river to the island from metro Nádraží Holešovice.

Swimming

The waters of the Vltava, Beroun and Labe are all pretty polluted – the Sázava is marginally better – so for a clean swim it's best to head for one of the city's swimming pools (*koupaliště*), though these, too, can be of varying water quality.

Hotel Axa, Na poříčí 40, Nové Město; metro Florenc. Has a 25-metre indoor pool, the oldest and largest of the hotel pools in Prague. Mon–Fri 7am–10pm, Sat & Sun 9am–9pm.

Divoká Nárka, Divoká Nárka, Vokovice; tram #20 or #26 from metro Dejvická. Idyllically located in a craggy valley to the northwest of Prague, with two small oudoor pools filled with cold but fresh and clean water – great for a full, hot day out. Food and drink and plenty of shade available, too. May–Oct daily 9am–7pm.

Podolí, Podolská, Podolí; tram #3, #17 or #21 from metro Karlovo náměstí, stop Kublov. Well-heated fifty-metre indoor pool, plus two smaller outdoor ones and a children's wading pool and water slide. Mon–Fri 6am–9.45pm, Sat & Sun 8am–7.45pm.

Slavia, Vladivostocká 2, Vršovice; tram #7 from metro Strašnická. Clean, indoor pool in winter, and a very popular summer-only outdoor pool. Mon–Fri 10am–10pm, Sat & Sun 10am–6pm.

Strahov, Vaníčkova, Břevnov; bus#176 from metro Karlovo náměstí, or walk from the top of the Petřín funicular. Big indoor training pool for Olympic hopefuls in the big Strahov complex. Mon–Fri 6am–8pm, Sat 8am–2pm.

Gyms and saunas

There's no shortage of fitness centres and hotels in Prague with good gyms, saunas and masseurs. Rates are generally very low compared to the West, but hours are erratic so check before you go.

Erpet Golf Centrum, Strakonická 510, Smíchov; ☎54 80 86; metro Smíchovské nádraží. Non-members can only come for a squash, solarium and massage, while members can use the whirlpool, sauna, weights and eighteen-hole golf course. Daily 8am–11pm.

Hotel Intercontinental Fitness, náměstí Curieových, Staré Město; ☎24 88 15 25; metro Staroměstská. Well-equipped gym and friendly staff in this very central posh hotel. Mon–Fri 6am–11pm, Sat & Sun 9am–10pm.

Hotel Forum Fitness, Kongresová 4, Nusle; ☎61 19 13 26; metro Vyšehrad. Pool, sauna, weights, solarium and massage – pricey, but luxurious, with an amazing view over Prague. Mon–Fri 7am–10pm, Sat & Sun 9am–9pm.

Chapter 15

Shopping

Despite enormous improvements over the past few years, service in Prague's shops is still surly, and the variety and quality of a lot of the goods suspect. The few bargains that still exist are in goods like glass, ceramics, wooden toys, cutlery, CDs, cassettes, LPs and books and, of course, smoked meats, salamis and alcohol, all of which the Czechs continue to produce at a fraction of western prices. If it's multinational goods you want, then you should encounter few problems, all the big players from Body Shop to DKNY have branches here in Prague, charging prices that are roughly the same as in the EU.

Department stores

For most basic goods, you're best off heading for a department store (*obchodní dům*), which will stock most things – including toiletries, stationery and usually an extensive food and drink selection. The prices are low, but so, often, is the quality.

Bílá labuť, Na poříčí 23, Nové Město; metro Florenc. Built in the 1930s, when its functionalist design turned more than a few heads, but nowadays in need of serious renovation. Mon–Fri 8am–7pm, Sat 8am–6pm.

Kotva, náměstí Republiky 8, Nové Město; metro náměstí Republiky. Ugly, Swedish-built store, spread over five floors, with a food section in the basement. Mon–Fri 9am–8pm, Sat 9am–6pm, Sun 10am–6pm.

Tesco, Národní 26, Nové Město; metro Národní třída. Neo-functionalist store on four floors, selling a good mix of Czech and imported goods, though it bears absolutely no resemblance to its British supermarket namesake, beyond its neon sign. Mon–Fri 8am–8pm, Sat 9am–6pm, Sun 10am–6pm.

Markets and food stores

Prague is chronically short of good **markets** of all types, despite the introduction of free enterprise. For bread, butter, cheese, wine and beer, you should simply go to the nearest *potraviny* or supermarket. These have changed enormously since 1989 in terms of what they stock, but are still a long way from the superstores of the western world. Again, low prices are the main draw. For health-food-starved visitors, a few outlets now stock some basic items, as listed below.

Markets

Havelská, Staré Město; metro Můstek. Food, flowers and wooden toys are sold in the only open-air fruit and veg market in central Prague. Mon–Fri 8am–6pm, Sat & Sun 9am–6pm.

Pražská tržnice, Bubenské nábřeží, Holešovice; metro Vltavská. Prague's largest market, a sprawling mass of cheap stalls housed in a disused abattoir. Mon–Fri 8am–6pm, Sat 8am–2pm.

Specialist food stores

Country Life, Melantrichova 15, Staré

Shopping

Město; metro Můstek. All the health food staples, from dried bananas to seaweed, plus freshly baked wholemeal bread. Mon–Thurs 8am–7pm, Fri 8.30am–3pm, Sun 11am–6pm.

Dům lahůdek, Malé náměstí 3, Staré Město; metro Staroměstská. Prague's number one deli is spread over several floors; the smoked fish and caviar section is particularly good. Mon–Sat 9.30am–7pm, Sun noon–7pm.

Fruits de France, Jindřišská 9, Nové Město; metro Můstek. Unusually good selection of fruit and vegetables, plus various other longer-lasting delights flown in fresh from France. Mon–Wed & Fri 9.30am–6.30pm, Thurs 11.30am–6.30pm, Sat 9.30am–1pm.

Ocean, Zborovská 49, Smíchov; tram #6, #9 or #22. Fresh fish and seafood arrives from Belgium on Wednesdays at this fishmonger's. Mon–Sat 10am–8pm.

Books, maps and graphics

Prague is now home to numerous English-language bookstores (*knihkupectví*), which thrive on the large ex-pat community. The city is also replete with second-hand bookstores (*antikvariát*), though these are often pricey antiquarian-type places rather than cheap, rambling stores; however, many also stock a good selection of old prints and posters.

Academia, Václavské náměstí 34, Nové Město; metro Muzeum/Můstek. One of the best bookstores in town for Czech books, with a good selection of English-language books, too. Mon–Fri 9am–8pm, Sat & Sun 10am–8pm.

Anagram, Týn 4, Nové Město; metro náměstí Republiky. Well-stocked, central English-language bookstore near Staroměstské náměstí, which also boasts a small second-hand section. Mon–Sat 10am–8pm, Sun 10am–6pm.

Big Ben Book Shop, Malá Štupartská 5, Staré Město; metro náměstí Republiky. Bookstore that specializes in TEFL material, but also stocks cheap paperbacks. Mon–Fri 9am–7pm, Sat & Sun 10am–6pm.

The Globe, Janovského 14, Holešovice; tram #5 or #26 from metro náměstí Republiky. *The* ex-pat bookstore *par excellence*: both a social centre and superbly well-stocked ramshackle store, with an adjacent café and friendly staff. Daily 10am–midnight.

Judaica, Široká 7, Staré Město; metro Staroměstská. Probably the best-stocked of all the places flogging Jewish books to passing tourists, with books and prints, second-hand and new. Mon–Fri 10am–6pm, Sun 10am–4pm.

Karel Křenek, Celetná 31, Staré Město; metro náměstí Republiky. High-quality second-hand and antiquarian dealer, with a handful of English books, and lots of old maps, graphics and art books. Mon–Fri 10am–noon & 2–6pm, Sat 10am–2pm.

U knihomola (The Bookworm), Mánesova 79, Vinohrady; metro Jiřího z Poděbrad. Much larger selection of art and coffee-table books and a classier range all round, than its rival, The Globe. The café in the basement is quiet and relaxed. Mon–Thurs 10am–11pm, Fri & Sat 10am–midnight, Sun 11am–8pm.

Music

Czech CDs are no longer the bargain they once were, though they are still priced a tad lower than in the West; cassettes and LPs are significantly cheaper. Classical buffs will fare best of all, not just with the Czech composers, but with cheap copies of Mozart, Vivaldi and other favourites on sale at just about every street corner.

Bontonland Megastore, palác Koruna, Václavské náměstí 1; metro Můstek. Prague's biggest record store in the newly renovated *pasáž* at the bottom of Wenceslas Square, with rock, folk, jazz and classical, and headphones for previews to boot. Mon–Sat 9am–8pm, Sun 10am–7pm.

Maximum Underground, Jilská 22, Staré Město; metro Staroměstská. The best indie record shop in town, very strong on dance music, and also reggae, ragga, punk and world music. Mon–Sat 10am–7pm, Sun 2–7pm.

Music antikvariát, Národní 25, Nové Město; metro Národní třída. The best second-hand record store in Prague, particularly good for jazz and folk, but also rock/pop – not much in the way of classical. Mon–Sat 10.30am–7pm.

Popron, Jungmannova 30, Nové Město; metro Můstek. Calls itself a "megastore", though it's nowhere near as big as Bonton's store – strongest on pop and rock CDs, though it does stock jazz and classical (not to mention video games). Mon–Sat 9am–7pm, Sun 10am–6pm.

Supraphon, Jungmannova 20, Nové Město; metro Můstek. Former state record company with a pretty good selection of classical CDs, cassettes and even LPs. Mon–Fri 9am–7pm, Sat 9am–noon.

Souvenirs, toys, camera equipment and antiques

Tacky tourist gifts – Kafka T-shirts, Mucha merchandise and matrioshka dolls – are mostly sold from market stalls set up along the main tourist thoroughfares. For better quality goods and more specialist gifts, try some of the shops listed below.

Antique, Pohořelec 7, Hradčany; tram #22 from metro Malostranská. Great little shop filled with glassware, malachite objets and icons – one of several in this area. Daily 9am–8pm.

Art Deco, Michalská 21, Staré Město; metro Můstek. Clothes, shoes, coffee sets, lamps and accessories, all dating from the turn of the century or between the wars (at a price). Mon–Fri 2–7pm.

Česká lidová řemesla, Jilská 22, Karlova 12 & 26 (plus many more), Staré Město; metro Staroměstská. It's impossible to miss this chain of shops as they've got a branch on just about every main tourist thoroughfare in Prague. Each one stocks wooden toys and Czech folk art from painted eggshells and linen to straw and corn dolls. Daily 10am–6pm.

Fototechnika a video, Vodičkova 36, Nové Město; metro Můstek. New gear, plus an excellent selection of second-hand East German and Soviet equipment. Mon–Fri 9am–7pm, Sat 9am–2pm.

Granát, Dlouhá 30, Staré Město; metro Muzeum. Czech garnets are among the best in the world, and this shop has some interesting pendants and brooches. Mon–Fri 10am–5pm, Sat 10am–1pm.

Keramika, Václavské náměstí 60, Nové Město; metro Muzeum. All kinds of glazed pottery cups, mugs and bowls at reasonable prices. Mon–Fri 10am–7pm, Sat 10am–4pm.

Manhartský dům, Celetná 12, Staré Město; metro náměstí Republiky. Performance-quality marionettes at high prices. Mon–Sat 10am–6pm.

Moser, Na příkopě 12, Nové Město; metro Můstek. The most famous glass and crystal manufacturers in the country – however, you won't find many bargains here (or anywhere else in Prague). Mon–Fri 9am–7pm, Sat 9am–4pm.

Sparta Praha, Betlémské náměstí 7, Staré Město; metro Národní třída. Everything from a Sparta Praha shirt to an ashtray, and even some Slavia souvenirs, too. Mon–Thurs 10am–5pm, Fri 10am–4pm.

Zerba, Vodičkova 37, Nové Město; metro Můstek. Come here for your Czech trams, trains and wind-up metal toys. Mon–Fri 10am–6pm, Sat 9am–noon.

Chapter 16

Directory

AIRLINES Austrian Airlines, Revoluční 15, Nové Město; ☎231 18 72. British Airways, Ovocný trh 8, Staré Město; ☎22 11 44 44; metro Můstek. British Midland, Washingtonova 17, Nové Město; ☎24 23 92 80; metro Muzeum. Czech Airlines (ČSA), V celnici 5, Nové Město; ☎20 10 43 10; metro náměstí Republiky. Delta, Národní 32, Nové Město; ☎24 23 22 58; metro Národní třída. KLM, Na příkopě 13 37, Nové Město; ☎24 21 69 50; metro Můstek. Lufthansa, Pařížská 28, Staré Město; ☎24 81 10 07; metro Staroměstská.

AMERICAN EXPRESS Amex, Václavské náměstí 56, Nové Město; ☎24 22 98 83; metro Muzeum. May–Sept Mon–Fri 9am–6pm, Sat 9am–2pm; Oct–April Mon–Fri 9am–5pm, Sat 9am–noon; exchange office daily 9am–7pm.

BOTTLES The Czech Republic has yet to become a fully paid-up member of the throwaway culture and many drinks still come in glass bottles with a deposit on them. For non-deposit bottles, or if you simply can't be bothered to retrieve the deposit, there are now numerous bottle banks scattered around Prague.

CHILDREN The Czech attitude to kids is generally very positive. That said, you'll see few Czech babies out in the open, unless snuggled up in their giant old-fashioned perambulators, and almost no children in pubs, cafés or even most restaurants. Czechs generally expect children to be unreasonably well-behaved and respectful to their elders, and many of the older generation may frown at over-boisterous behaviour. Nevertheless, most kids will enjoy Prague, with its hilly cobbled streets and trams, especially in the summer, when the place is positively alive with buskers and street performers. The obvious attractions for children are the Petřín hill, with its funicular and mirror maze (see p.84); the Zoo (see p.173); the Národní technické muzeum (see p.165); and the MHD Muzeum, a short walk west of Hradčany at Patočkova 4 (April–Oct Sat & Sun 9am–5pm), which houses a collection of historic trams and trolleybuses; take tram #1 or #8 from metro Hradčanská. Another year-round option is to hop aboard the regular tram #22, as it goes round some great hairpins, across the river and past a fair few city landmarks. In the summer a historic tram (#91) also criss-crosses the city; tickets are slightly more expensive than normal, and it runs less frequently.

CIGARETTES Loosely packed and lethal, the only virtue of Czech cigarettes is their cheapness. Top of the domestic range is **Sparta**, named after the country's leading soccer team. The workers smoke Mars or Start, while the rest smoke Petra. Havel switched from the latter to Marlboro once he became president and has since given up.

Duma rolling tobacco is widely available; domestic brands and their cigarette papers are worth avoiding. Matches are *zápalky*.

CONTRACEPTIVES Condoms (*kondom* or *prezervativ*) are available in metro stations in the centre of Prague from machines marked *Men's Shop, Easy Shop* or some such euphemism. They're also on sale from pharmacies.

CULTURAL INSTITUTES

Austrian Cultural Institute (Rakouský kulturní institut), Jungmannovo náměstí 18, Nové Město; ☎24 23 48 75; metro Můstek. Very good exhibitions of Austrian art, plus the odd concert, film and talk. Gallery Mon–Fri 8am–4.30pm; library Mon–Fri 10am–1pm & 2–4pm.

British Council (Britská rada), Národní 10, Nové Město; ☎24 91 21 79; metro Národní třída. A window gallery for temporary exhibitions; newspapers and magazines in the foyer and the top-floor reading room; Sky TV in the auditorium and various films, concerts and events during the year. There's an English-language teaching library and resource centre in the basement (Mon–Thurs 10am–1pm & 3–8pm, Fri 10am–1pm). Mon–Thurs 9am–7pm, Fri 9am–4pm.

Goethe Institut, Masarykovo nábřeží 32, Nové Město; ☎21 96 21 11; metro Národní třída. Weekly film showings and more frequent lectures; small exhibition space and café. Mon–Fri 9am–7pm; library Mon–Thurs 2–6pm.

Hungarian Cultural Centre (Maďarské kulturní středisko), Rytířská 25–27, Staré Město; ☎24 22 24 24; metro Můstek. Weekly film showings and regular exhibitions and concerts. Mon–Thurs 10am–6pm.

Institut Français (Francouzský institut), Štěpánská 35, Nové Město; ☎22 23 05 78; metro Muzeum. Great exhibitions and a great café, with croissants and *journaux*; also puts on more or less daily screenings of classic French films, plus lectures and even the odd concert. Café: Mon noon–6pm, Tues–Sun 9am–6pm. Library: Tues–Fri 10am–6pm, Sat 10am–1pm.

Polish Institute (Polský institut), Václavské náměstí 51, Nové Město; ☎24 21 47 08; metro Muzeum. Weekly film showings, occasional concerts and lectures. Mon–Fri 9am–5pm, Sat 9am–noon.

ELECTRICITY This is the standard continental 220 volts AC. Most European appliances should work as long as you have an adaptor for European-style two-pin round plugs. North Americans will need this plus a transformer.

EMBASSIES/CONSULATES

Australia, Na Ořechovce 38, Střešovice; ☎24 31 07 43; tram #1, #8 or #18 from metro Hradčanská.

Belgium, Valdštejnská 6, Malá Strana; ☎57 32 03 89; metro Malostranská.

Britain, Thunovská 14, Malá Strana; ☎57 32 03 55; metro Malostranská.

Canada, Mickiewiczova 6, Hradčany; ☎24 31 11 08; metro Hradčanská.

Denmark, Maltézské náměstí, Malá Strana; ☎57 31 66 30; metro Malostranská.

Finland, Hellichova 1, Malá Strana; ☎57 00 71 30; tram #12 or #22 from metro Malostranská.

France, Velkopřevorské náměstí 2, Malá Strana; ☎57 32 03 52; metro Malostranská.

Germany, Vlašská 19, Malá Strana; ☎57 32 01 90; metro Malostranská.

Ireland, Tržiště 13, Malá Strana; ☎53 09 11; metro Malostranská.

Norway, Na Ořechovce 69, Střešovice; ☎311 13 94; tram #1, #8 or #18 from metro Hradčanská.

Poland, Valdštejnská 8, Malá Strana; ☎57 32 06 78; metro Malostranská.

Slovakia, Pod hradbami 1, Dejvice; ☎32 05 21; metro Dejvická.

Sweden, Úvoz 13, Malá Strana; ☎20 31 32 00; metro Malostranská.

USA, Tržiště 15, Malá Strana; ☎57 32 06 63; metro Malostranská.

Directory

EXCHANGE 24-hour service at 28 října 13, Nové Město, metro Můstek.

GAY/LESBIAN There is no great "scene" in Prague as such, but there are a few bars and clubs that have become an established part of Prague nightlife (see p.231) and even a gay-friendly hotel (see p.205). A good source of information is the *SOHO revue*, a monthly Czech gay magazine, with a brief section in English and some useful listings. Lambda, the first organization for Czech gays and lesbians which started up in 1989, is based at Krakovská 2, Nové Město; ☎73 92 76; metro Muzeum. The age of consent in the Czech Republic is 15, whatever your sexual orientation.

LANGUAGE SCHOOLS Angličtina expres, ýáhřebská 32, Vinohrady (☎24 25 14 82); Státní jazyková škola, Školská 15, Nové Město (☎22 23 22 38).

LAUNDRIES Most Czechs still wash their clothes by hand or leave them at a *čistírna*, where they are washed, dried, ironed and neatly folded. If time isn't a problem, try Čistírna oděvů, Opletalova 16, Nové Město; metro Muzeum/Hlavní nádraží; Mon–Fri 8am–6pm. Ex-pats tend to head for self-service launderettes: Laundry Kings, Dejvická 16 (☎312 37 43; metro Hradčanská; daily 8am–10pm), is very much part of the ex-pat scene. Other American-style launderettes include Laundryland, Londýnská 71, Vinohrady (☎25 11 24; metro I. P. Pavlova; daily 8am–10pm) and Prague Laundromat, Korunní 14, Vinohrady (☎25 55 41; metro náměstí Míru; daily 8am–8pm).

LEFT LUGGAGE Most bus and train stations have lockers and/or a 24-hour left-luggage office, which officially only take bags under 15kg. If your bag is very heavy, say *promiňte, je těžký* and offer to carry it to the locker yourself – *já to vezmu*. The modern lockers have instructions in English. To work the old-fashioned lockers, put the money in the slot on the inside of the door and set the code (choose a number you can easily remember and make a note of it), then shut the door. To re-open it, set the code on the outside and wait a few seconds before trying the door. The lockers are usually checked every night, and the contents of any still occupied are taken to the 24-hour left-luggage office. If you forget your number, you'll have to go through a lengthy bureaucratic procedure, involving the police, in order to retrieve your luggage.

LOST PROPERTY The main train stations have lost property offices (*ztráty a nálezy*).

RELIGIOUS SERVICES Anglican, Sun 11am, sv Kliment, Klimentská 18, Nové Město; metro náměstí Republiky. Baptist, Sun 11am, Vinohradská 68, Vinohrady; metro Jiřího z Poděbrad. Greek/Russian Orthodox, Sun 9.30am, sv Cyril & Metoděj, Resslova 9, Nové Město. Interdenominational, Sun 10.30am, Peroutkova 57; bus #137 from metro Anděl. Jewish Orthodox, Mon–Thurs & Sun 8am, Fri dusk, Sat 9am, Staronová synagóga, Maiselova, Josefov; metro Staroměstská. Jewish Reform, Fri dusk, Sat 8.45am; Jubilejní synagóga, Jeruzalemská 7, Nové Město; metro Hlavní nádraží. Lutheran, Sun 11am, sv Michal, V jirchářích 4, Nové Město; metro Národní třída. Roman Catholic (in English), Sun 11am, sv Tomáš, Josefská 8, Malá Strana; metro Malostranská.

TAMPONS Tampons (*tampóny*) and sanitary towels (*dámské vložky*) are cheap and easy to get hold of in major department stores (see p.243).

THOMAS COOK Staroměstské náměstí 5, Staré Město; ☎24 81 71 73; metro Staroměstská; Mon–Fri 9am–9pm, Sat 9am–4pm, Sun 10am–2pm.

TIME The Czech Republic is generally one hour ahead of Britain and six hours ahead of EST, with the clocks going forward as late as May and back again some time in September – the exact date changes from year to year. Generally speaking, Czechs use the 24-hour clock.

TOILETS Apart from the automatic ones in central Prague, toilets (*záchody, toalety* or *WC*) are few and far between. In some, you still have to buy toilet paper (by the sheet) from the attendant, whom you will also have to pay as you enter. Standards of hygiene can be low. Gentlemen should head for *muži* or *páni*; ladies should head for *ženy* or *dámy*.

WOMEN The Czech Republic remains a deeply conservative and patriarchal society, despite the upheaval of 1989. The atmosphere in Prague is slightly more liberated than in the rest of the country, however, and street-level sexual harasssment rarely approaches levels experienced in some western countries. Pubs are about the only places where men always predominate; the usual common-sense precautions apply here and elsewhere. Feminism and women's issues keep a very low profile in the Czech Republic. The city's main feminist organizations are to be found at the Ženské centrum, Národní dům, náměstí 14 října 16, Smíchov; metro Anděl.

Metric Weights and Measures

1 ounce = 28.3 grammes (g)
1 inch = 2.54 centimetres (cm)
1 pound = 454g
1 foot = 0.3 metres (m)
2.2 pounds = 1 kilogramme (kg)
1 yard = 0.91m
1 pint = 0.47 litres (l)
1.09 yards = 1m
1 quart = 0.94l
1 mile = 1.61 kilometres (km)
1 gallon = 3.78l
0.62 miles = 1km

Directory

Part 4

The Contexts

A History of Prague

The pronouncement (attributed to Bismarck) that "he who holds Bohemia holds mid-Europe" gives a clear indication of the pivotal role the region has played in European history. As the capital of Bohemia, Prague has been fought over and occupied by German, Austrian, French and even Swedish armies. Consequently, it is virtually impossible to write a historical account of the city without frequent reference to the wider events of European history. One of the constant themes that runs throughout Prague's history, however, are the conflicts between the city's religious factions, and, much later, between the German-speaking community and the Czech nationalists. The history of Prague as the capital of, first Czechoslovakia, and now the Czech Republic, is, in fact, less than a hundred years old, beginning only with the foundation of the country in 1918. Since then, the country's numerous tragedies, mostly focused on Prague, have been exposed to the world at regular intervals – 1938, 1948, 1968 and, most recently (and most happily), 1989.

Legends

The Czechs have a **legend** for every occasion, and the founding of Bohemia and Prague is no exception. The mythical mound of Říp, the most prominent of the pimply hills in the Labe (Elbe) plain, north of Prague, is where **Čech**, the leader of a band of wandering Slavs, is alleged to have founded his new kingdom, Čechy (Bohemia). His brother Lech, meanwhile, headed further north to found Poland. Some time in the seventh or eighth century AD, **Krok** (aka Pace), a descendant of **Čech**, moved his people south from the plains to the rocky knoll that is now Vyšehrad (literally "High Castle").

Krok was succeeded by his youngest daughter, **Libuše**, the country's first and last female ruler, who, handily enough, was endowed with the gift of prophecy. Falling into a trance one day, she pronounced that the tribe should build a city "whose glory will touch the stars", at the point in the forest where they found an old man constructing the threshold of his house. He was duly discovered on the Hradčany hill, overlooking the Vltava, and the city was named *Praha,* meaning threshold. However, it wasn't long before Libuše's subjects began to demand that she take a husband. As Cosmas, the twelfth-century chronicler put it, "resting on her elbow like one who is giving birth, she lay there on a high pile of soft and embroidered pillows, as is the lasciviously wanton habit of women when they do not have a man at home whom they fear". Again she fell into a trance, this time pronouncing that they should follow her horse to a ploughman, with two oxen, whose descendants (the ploughman's, that is) would rule over them. Sure enough, a man called **Přemysl** (which means ploughman) was discovered, and became the mythical founder of the Přemyslid dynasty which ruled Bohemia until the fourteenth century.

Early history

So much for the legend. According to Roman records, the area now covered by Bohemia was inhabited as early as 500 BC by a Celtic tribe, the **Boii**, who gave their name to the region. Very little is known about the Boii except that around 100 BC they were driven from their territory by a Germanic tribe, the **Marcomanni**, who occupied Bohemia. The Marcomanni were a semi-nomadic people and later proved awkward opponents for the Roman Empire, which wisely chose to use the River Danube as its natural eastern border, thus leaving Bohemia outside the empire.

The disintegration of the Roman Empire in the fifth century AD corresponded with a series of raids into central Europe by eastern tribes: first the **Huns** and later the **Avars**, around the sixth century, settling a vast area including the Hungarian plains and parts of what is now Slovakia. Around the same time, the Marcomanni disappear from the picture to be replaced by **Slav tribes** who entered Europe from somewhere east of the Carpathian mountains. To begin with, at least, they appear to have been subjugated by the Avars. The first successful Slav rebellion against the Avars seems to have taken place in the seventh century, under the Frankish leadership of **Samo**, though the kingdom he created, which was centred on Bohemia, died with him around 658 AD.

The Great Moravian Empire

The next written record of the Slavs in the region isn't until the eighth century, when East Frankish (Germanic) chroniclers report a people known as the **Moravians** as having established themselves around the River Morava, a tributary of the Danube. It was an alliance of Moravians and Franks (under Charlemagne) which finally expelled the Avars from central Europe in 796 AD. This cleared the way for the establishment of the **Great Moravian Empire**, which at its peak included Slovakia, Bohemia and parts of Hungary and Poland. Its significance in political terms is that it was the first and last time (until the establishment of Czechoslovakia, for which it served as a useful precedent) that the Czechs and Slovaks were united under one ruler.

The first attested ruler of the empire, **Mojmír**, found himself at the political and religious crossroads of Europe under pressure from two sides: from the west, where the Franks and Bavarians (both Germanic tribes) were jostling for position with the papacy; and from the east, where the Patriarch of Byzantium was keen to extend his influence across eastern Europe. Mojmír's successor, **Rastislav** (850–870), plumped for Byzantium, and invited the missionaries Cyril and Methodius to introduce Christianity, using the Slav liturgy and Eastern rites. Rastislav, however, was ousted by his nephew, **Svätopluk** (871–894), who captured and blinded his uncle, allying himself with the Germans instead. With the death of Methodius in 885, the Great Moravian Empire fell decisively under the influence of the Roman Catholic Church.

Svätopluk died shortly before the **Magyar invasion** of 896, an event which heralded the end of the Great Moravian Empire and a significant break in Czecho-Slovak history. The Slavs to the west of the River Morava (the Czechs) swore allegiance to the Frankish Emperor, Arnulf, while those to the east (the Slovaks) found themselves under the yoke of the Magyars. This separation, which continued for the next millennium, is one of the major factors behind the redundant social, cultural and political differences between Czechs and Slovaks, which culminated in the separation of the two nations in 1993.

The Přemyslid Dynasty

There is evidence that Bohemian dukes were forced in 806 to pay a yearly tribute of 500 pieces of silver and 120 oxen to the Carolingian empire (a precedent the Nazis were keen to exploit as proof of German hegemony over Bohemia). These early Bohemian dukes "lived like animals, brutal and without knowledge", according to one chronicler. All that was to change when the earliest recorded Přemyslid duke **Bořivoj** (852/53–888/89), appeared on the scene. The first Christian ruler of Prague, Bořivoj was baptized, along with his wife Ludmila, in the ninth century by the Byzantine missionaries Cyril and Methodius (see above). Other than being the first to build a castle on Hradčany, nothing very certain is known about Bořivoj, nor about any of the other early Přemyslid rulers, although there are numerous legends, most famously that of **Prince Václav** (Saint Wenceslas), who was martyred by his pagan brother Boleslav the Cruel in 929 (see p.55).

Cut off from Byzantium by the Hungarian kingdom, Bohemia lived under the shadow of the **Holy Roman Empire** from the start. In 950, Emperor Otto I led an expedition against Bohemia, making the kingdom officially subject to the empire and its king one of the seven electors of the emperor. In 973, under Boleslav the Pious (967–999), a bishopric was founded in Prague, subordinate to the archbishopric of Mainz. Thus, by the end of the first millennium, German influence was already beginning to make itself felt in Bohemian history.

The **thirteenth century** was the high point of Přemyslid rule over Bohemia. With Emperor Frederick II preoccupied with Mediterranean affairs and dynastic problems, and the

Hungarians and Poles busy trying to repulse the Mongol invasions from 1220 onwards, the Přemyslids were able to assert their independence. In 1212, Otakar I (1198–1230) managed to extract a **"Golden Bull"** (formal edict) from the emperor, securing the royal title for himself and his descendants (who thereafter became kings of Bohemia). Prague prospered too, benefiting from its position on the central European trade routes. Czechs, Germans, Jews and merchants from all over Europe settled there, and in 1234 the first of Prague's historic five towns, **Staré Město**, was founded to accommodate them.

As a rule, the Přemyslids welcomed **German colonization**, none more so than King Otakar II (1253–78), the most distinguished of the Přemyslid kings, who systematically encouraged German craftsmen to settle in the kingdom. At the same time, the gradual switch to a monetary economy and the discovery of copper and silver deposits heralded a big shift in population from the countryside to the towns. German immigrants founded whole towns in the interior of the country, where German civic rights were guaranteed them, for example Kutná Hora, Mělník and, in 1257, **Malá Strana** in Prague. Through battles, marriage and diplomacy, Otakar managed to expand his territories so that they stretched (almost) from the Baltic to the Adriatic. In 1278, however, Otakar met his end on the battlefield of Marchfeld, defeated by Rudolf of Habsburg.

The beginning of the fourteenth century saw a series of dynastic disputes – messy even by medieval standards – beginning with the death of Václav II from consumption and excess in 1305. The following year, the murder of his son, the heirless, teenage Václav III, marked the **end of the Přemyslid dynasty** (he had four sisters, but female succession was not recognized in Bohemia). The nobles' first choice of successor, the Habsburg Albert I, was murdered by his own nephew, and when Albert's son, Rudolf I, died of dysentery not long afterwards, Bohemia was once more left without any heirs.

Carolinian Prague

The crisis was finally solved when the Czech nobles offered the throne to **John of Luxembourg** (1310–46), who was married to Václav III's youngest sister. German by birth, but educated in France, King John spent most of his reign participating in foreign wars, with Bohemia footing the bill, and John himself paying for it first with his sight, and finally with his life, on the field at Crécy in 1346.

His son, **Charles IV** (1346–78), was wounded in the same battle, but thankfully for the Czechs lived to tell the tale. It was Charles who ushered in Prague's **golden age** (see p.93). Although born and bred in France, Charles was a Bohemian at heart (his mother was Czech and his real name was Václav). In 1344, he had wrangled an archbishopric for Prague, independent of Mainz, and two years later he became not only king of Bohemia, but also, by election, Holy Roman Emperor. In the thirty years of his reign, Charles transformed Prague into the new capital of the empire. He established institutions and buildings that still survive today and founded an entire new town, **Nové Město**, to accommodate the influx of students and clergy. He promoted Czech as the official language alongside Latin and German and, perhaps most importantly of all, presided over a period of peace in central Europe while western Europe was tearing itself apart in the Hundred Years' War.

Sadly, Charles' son, **Václav IV** (1378–1419), was no match for such an inheritance. Stories that he roasted an incompetent cook alive on his own spit, shot a monk whilst hunting, and tried his own hand at lopping off people's heads with an axe, are almost certainly myths. Nevertheless, he was a legendary drinker, prone to violent outbursts, and so unpopular with the powers that be that he was imprisoned twice – once by his own nobles, and once by his brother, Sigismund. His reign was also characterized by religious divisions within the Czech Lands and in Europe as a whole, beginning with the **Great Schism** (1378–1417), when rival popes held court in Rome and Avignon. This was a severe blow to Rome's centralizing power, which might otherwise have successfully combated the assault on the Church that was already under way in the Czech Lands towards the end of the fourteenth century.

The Bohemian Reformation

Right from the start, Prague was at the centre of the Bohemian reform movement. The increased influence of the Church, and its independence from Mainz established under Charles, led to a sharp increase in debauchery, petty theft and alcoholism among the clergy – a fertile climate for militant reformers like Jan Milič of Kroměříž, whose fiery sermons drew crowds of people to hear him at Prague's Týn church. In Václav's reign, the attack was led by the peasant-born preacher **Jan Hus**, who gave sermons at Prague's Betlémská kaple (see p.109).

Hus's main inspiration was the English reformist theologian John Wycliffe, whose heretical works found their way to Bohemia via Václav's sister, Anne, who married King Richard II. Worse still, as far as Church traditionalists were concerned, Hus began to preach in the language of the masses (ie Czech) against the wealth, corruption and hierarchical tendencies within the Church at the time. A devout, mild-mannered man himself, he became embroiled in a dispute between the conservative clergy led by Archbishop Zbyněk and backed by the pope, and the Wycliffian Czechs at the university. When Archbishop Zbyněk gave the order to burn the books of Wycliffe, Václav backed Hus and his followers, for political and personal reasons (Hus was, among other things, the confessor to his wife, Queen Sophie).

There can be little doubt that King Václav used Hus and the Wycliffites to further his own political cause. He had been deposed as Holy Roman Emperor in 1400, and, as a result, bore a grudge against the current emperor, Ruprecht of the Palatinate, and his chief backer, Pope Gregory XII in Rome. His chosen battleground was Prague's university, which was divided into four "nations" with equal voting rights: the Saxons, Poles and Bavarians, who supported Václav's enemies, and the Bohemians, who were mostly Wycliffites. In 1409 Václav issued the **Kutná Hora Decree**, which rigged the voting within the university giving the Bohemian "nation" three votes, and the rest a total of one. The other "nations", who made up the majority of the students and teachers, left Prague in protest.

Three years later the alliance between the King and the Wycliffites broke down. Widening his attacks on the Church, Hus began to preach against the sale of religious indulgences to fund the inter-papal wars, thus incurring the enmity of Václav, who received a percentage of the sales. In 1412 Hus and his followers were expelled from the university, excommunicated and banished from Prague, and spent the next two years as itinerant preachers spreading their reformist gospel throughout Bohemia. In 1414 Hus was summoned to the **Council of Constance** to answer charges of heresy. Despite a guarantee of safe conduct from Emperor Sigismund, Hus was condemned to death and, having refused to renounce his beliefs, was burned at the stake on July 6, 1415.

Hus's martyrdom sparked off **widespread riots** in Prague, initially uniting virtually all Bohemians – clergy and laity, peasant and noble (including many of Hus's former opponents) – against the decision of the council, and, by inference, against the established Church and its conservative clergy. The Hussites immediately set about reforming church practices, most famously by administering communion *sub utraque specie* ("in both kinds", ie bread and wine) to the laity, as opposed to the established practice of reserving the wine for the clergy.

The Hussite Wars: 1419–34

In 1419, Václav inadvertently provoked further large-scale rioting by endorsing the readmission of anti-Hussite priests to their parishes. In the ensuing violence, several councillors (including the mayor) were thrown to their death from the windows of Prague's Novoměstská radnice, in Prague's **first defenestration** (see p.143). Václav himself was so enraged (not to say terrified) by the mob that he suffered a stroke and died, "roaring like a lion", according to a contemporary chronicler. The pope, meanwhile, declared an international crusade against the Czech heretics, under the leadership of Emperor Sigismund, Václav's brother and, since Václav had failed to produce an heir, chief claimant to the Bohemian throne.

Already, though, cracks were appearing in the Hussite camp. The more radical reformers, who became known as the **Táborites** after their south Bohemian base, Tábor, broadened their attacks on the Church hierarchy to include all figures of authority and privilege. Their message found a ready audience among the oppressed classes in Prague and the Bohemian countryside, who went around eagerly destroying church property and massacring Catholics. Such actions were deeply disturbing to the Czech nobility and their supporters who backed the more moderate Hussites – known as the **Utraquists** (from the Latin *sub utraque specie*) – who confined their criticisms to religious matters.

For the moment, however, the common Catholic enemy prevented a serious split developing amongst the Hussites, and under the inspirational military leadership of the Táborite **Jan Pižka**, the Hussites' (mostly peasant) army enjoyed some miraculous early victories over the numerically superior "crusaders", most notably at the Battle of Vítkov in Prague in 1420. The Bohemian Diet quickly drew up the **Four Articles of Prague**, a compromise between the two Hussite camps, outlining the basic tenets about which all Hussites could agree, including communion "in both kinds". The Táborites, meanwhile, continued to burn, loot and pillage ecclesiastical institutions from Prague to the far reaches of the kingdom.

At the **Council of Basel** in 1433, Rome reached a compromise with the Utraquists over the Four Articles, in return for ceasing hostilities. The peasant-based Táborites rightly saw the deal as a victory for the Bohemian nobility and the status quo, and vowed to continue the fight. However, the Utraquists, now in cahoots with the Catholic forces, easily defeated the remaining Táborites at the **Battle of Lipany**, outside Kolín, in 1434. The Táborites were forced to withdraw to the fortress town of Tábor. Poor old Sigismund, who had spent the best part of his life fighting the Hussites, died only three years later.

Compromise

Despite the agreement of the Council of Basel, the pope refused to acknowledge the Utraquist church in Bohemia. The Utraquists nevertheless consolidated their position, electing the gifted **George of Poděbrady** first as Regent and then King of Bohemia (1458–71). The first and last Hussite king, George (Jiří to the Czechs) is remembered primarily for his commitment to promoting religious tolerance and for his far-sighted, but ultimately futile, attempts to establish some sort of "Peace Confederation" in Europe.

On George's death, the Bohemian Estates handed the crown over to the **Polish Jagiellonian dynasty**, who ruled *in absentia*, effectively relinquishing the reins of power to the Czech nobility. In 1526, the last of the Jagiellonians, King Louis, was decisively defeated by the Turks at the Battle of Mohács, and died fleeing the battlefield, leaving no heir to the throne. The Roman Catholic Habsburg, Ferdinand I (1526–64), was elected king of Bohemia – and what was left of Hungary – in order to fill the power vacuum, marking the **beginning of Habsburg rule** over what is now the Czech Republic. Ferdinand adroitly secured automatic hereditary succession over the Bohemian throne for his dynasty, in return for which he accepted the agreement laid down at the Council of Basel back in 1433. With the Turks at the gates of Vienna, he had little choice but to compromise at this stage, but in 1545, the international situation eased somewhat with the establishment of an armistice with the Turks.

The following year, the Utraquist Bohemian nobility provocatively joined the powerful Protestant Schmalkaldic League in their (ultimately successful) war against the Holy Roman Emperor, Charles V. After a brief armed skirmish in Prague, however, victory fell to Ferdinand, who took the opportunity to extend the influence of Catholicism in the Czech Lands, executing several leading Protestant nobles, persecuting the reformist Unity of Czech Brethren, who had figured prominently in the rebellion, and inviting Jesuit missionaries to establish churches and seminaries in the Czech Lands.

Like Václav IV, **Emperor Rudolf II** (1576–1611), Ferdinand's eventual successor, was moody and wayward, and by the end of his reign Bohemia was once more rushing headlong into a major international confrontation. But Rudolf also shared characteristics with Václav's father, Charles, in his genuine love of the arts, and in his passion for Prague, which he re-established as the royal seat of power, in preference to Vienna, which was once more under threat from the Turks. He endowed Prague's galleries with the best Mannerist art in Europe, and, most famously, invited the respected astrologists Tycho Brahe and Johannes Kepler, and the infamous English alchemists John Dee and Edward Kelley, to Prague (see p.61).

Czechs tend to regard Rudolfine Prague as a second golden age, but as far as the Catholic Church was concerned, Rudolf's religious tolerance and indecision were a disaster. In the early 1600s, Rudolf's melancholy began to veer dangerously close to insanity, a condition he had inherited from his Spanish grandmother, Joanna the Mad. And in 1611, the heirless Rudolf was forced to abdicate by his brother **Matthias**, to save the Habsburg house from ruin. Ardently Catholic, but equally heirless, Matthias proposed his cousin **Ferdinand II** as his successor in 1617. This was the last straw for Bohemia's mostly Protestant nobility, and the following year conflict erupted again.

The Thirty Years' War: 1618–48

On May 23, 1618, two Catholic governors appointed by Ferdinand were thrown out of the windows of Prague Castle (along with their secretary) – the country's **second defenestration** (see p.58) – an event that's now taken as the official beginning of the complex religious and dynastic conflicts collectively known as the **Thirty Years' War**. Following the defenestration, the Bohemian Diet expelled the Jesuits and elected the youthful Protestant "Winter King", Frederick of the Palatinate, to the throne. In the first decisive set-to of the war, on November 8, 1620, the Czech Protestants were utterly defeated at the **Battle of Bílá hora** or Battle of the White Mountain (see p.175) by the imperial Catholic forces under Count Tilly. In the aftermath, 27 Protestant nobles were executed on Prague's Staroměstské náměstí, and the heads of ten of them displayed on the Charles Bridge.

It wasn't until the Protestant Saxons occupied Prague in 1632 that the heads were finally taken down and given a proper burial. The Catholics eventually drove the Saxons out, but for the last ten years of the war, Bohemia became the main battleground between the new champions of the Protestant cause – the Swedes – and the imperial Catholic forces. In 1648, the final battle of the war was fought in Prague, when the Swedes seized Malá Strana, but failed to take Staré Město, thanks to the stubborn resistance of Prague's Jewish, and newly Catholicized student populations on the Charles Bridge.

The Counter-Reformation and the Dark Ages

The Thirty Years' War ended with the **Peace of Westphalia**, which, for the Czechs, was as disastrous as the war itself. An estimated five-sixths of the Bohemian nobility went into exile, their properties handed over to loyal Catholic families from Austria, Spain, France and Italy. Bohemia had been devastated, with towns and cities laid waste, and the total population reduced by almost two-thirds; Prague's population halved. On top of all that, Bohemia was now decisively within the Catholic sphere of influence, and the full force of the **Counter-Reformation** was brought to bear on its people. All forms of Protestantism were outlawed, the education system was handed over to the Jesuits and, in 1651 alone, more than two hundred "witches" were burned at the stake in Bohemia.

The next two centuries of Habsburg rule are known to the Czechs as the **Dark Ages**. The focus of the empire shifted back to Vienna, the Habsburgs' absolutist grip over the Czech Lands catapulted the remaining nobility into intensive Germanization, while fresh waves of German immigrants reduced Czech to a despised dialect spoken only by peasants, artisans and servants. The situation was so bad that Prague and most other urban centres became practically German-speaking cities. By the end of the eighteenth century, the Czech language was on the verge of dying out, with government, scholarship and literature carried out exclusively in German. For the newly ensconced Germanized aristocracy, and for the Catholic Church, of course, the good times rolled and Prague was endowed with numerous Baroque palaces, churches, monasteries and monuments, many of which still grace the city today.

The Enlightenment

After a century of iron-fisted Habsburg rule, dispute arose over the accession of Charles VI's daughter, **Maria Theresa** (1740–80), to the Habsburg throne, and Prague, as usual, found itself at the centre of the battlefield. In November 1741, Prague was easily taken by Bavarian, French and Saxon troops, but the French occupation force quickly found itself besieged in turn by a Habsburg army, and in January 1743 was forced to abandon the city. By November 1744, Prague found itself once more besieged, this time by the Prussian army, who bombed the city into submission in a fortnight. After a month of looting, they left the city to escape the advancing Habsburg army. During the Seven Years' War, in 1757, Prague was once more besieged and bombarded by the Prussian army, though this time the city held out, and following their defeat at the Battle of Kolín, the Prussians withdrew.

Maria Theresa's reign also marked the beginning of the **Enlightenment** in the Habsburg Empire. Despite her own personal attachment to the Jesuits, the empress acknowledged the need for reform, and followed the lead of Spain, Portugal and France in expelling the order from the empire in 1773. But it was her son, **Joseph II** (1780–90), who, in the ten short years of his reign, brought about the most radical changes to the social structure of the Habsburg lands. His 1781 Edict of Tolerance allowed a large degree of freedom of worship for the first time in over 150 years, and went a long way towards lifting the restrictions on Jews within the empire. The following year, he ordered the dissolution of the monasteries, and embarked upon the abolition of serfdom. Despite all his reforms, Joseph was not universally popular. Catholics – some ninety percent of the Bohemian population – viewed him with disdain, and even forced him to back down when he decreed that Protestants, Jews, unbaptized children and suicide victims should be buried in consecrated Catholic cemeteries. His centralization and bureaucratization of the empire placed power in the hands of the Austrian civil service, and thus helped entrench the **Germanization** of Bohemia. He also offended the Czechs by breaking with tradition and not bothering to hold an official coronation ceremony in Prague.

The Czech national revival

The Habsburgs' enlightened rule inadvertently provided the basis for the economic prosperity and social changes of the **Industrial Revolution**, which in turn fuelled the Czech national revival of the nineteenth century. The textile, glass, coal and iron industries began to grow, drawing ever more Czechs from the countryside and swamping the hitherto mostly German-speaking towns and cities, including Prague. A Czech working class, and even an embryonic Czech bourgeoisie emerged, and, thanks to Maria Theresa's reforms, new educational and economic opportunities were given to the Czech lower classes.

For the first half of the century, the Czech **national revival** or *národní obrození* was confined to the new Czech intelligentsia, led by philologists like Josef Dobrovský and Josef Jungmann at the Charles University or *Karolinum* in Prague. Language disputes (in schools, universities and public offices) remained at the forefront of Czech nationalism throughout the nineteenth century, only later developing into demands for political autonomy from Vienna. The leading figure of the time was the historian **František Palacký**, a Moravian Protestant who wrote the first history of the Czech nation, rehabilitating Hus and the Czech reformists in the process. He was in many ways typical of the early Czech nationalists – pan-Slavist, virulently anti-German, but not yet entirely anti-Habsburg.

1848 and all that

The fall of the French monarchy in February 1848 prompted a crisis in the German states and in the Habsburg Empire. The new Bohemian bourgeoisie, both Czech and German, began to make political demands: freedom of the press, of assembly, of religious creeds. In March, when news of the revolutionary outbreak in Vienna reached Prague, the city's Czechs and Germans began organizing a joint national guard, while the students formed an Academic Legion, in imitation of the Viennese. Eventually, a National Committee of Czechs and Germans was formed, and Prague itself got its own elected mayor.

However, it wasn't long before cracks began to appear in the Czech-German alliance. Palacký and his followers were against the dissolution of the empire and argued instead for a kind of multinational federation. Since the empire contained a majority of non-Germans, Prague's own Germans were utterly opposed to Palacký's scheme, campaigning for unification with Germany to secure their interests. On April 11, Palacký refused an invitation to attend the Pan-German National Assembly in Frankfurt. The Germans immediately withdrew from the National Committee, and Prague's other revolutionary institutions began to divide along linguistic lines. On June 2, Palacký convened a **Pan-Slav Congress** the following month, which met on Prague's Slovanský ostrov, an island in the Vltava. Czechs and Slovaks made up the majority of the delegates, but there were also Poles, Croats, Slovenes and Serbs in attendance.

On June 12, the congress had to adjourn, as fighting had broken out on the streets the previous day between the troops of the local Habsburg commander, Alfred Prince Windischgrätz, and Czech protesters. The radicals and students took to the streets of Prague, barricades went up overnight, and martial law was declared. During the night of June 14, Windischgrätz withdrew his troops to the left bank and proceeded to bombard the right bank into submission. On the morning of June 17 the city capitulated – the counter-revolution in Bohemia had begun. The upheavals of 1848 left the absolutist Habsburg Empire shaken but fundamentally unchanged and served to highlight the sharp differences between German and Czech aspirations in Bohemia.

Dualism

The Habsburg recovery was, however, short-lived. In 1859, and again in 1866, the new emperor, Franz-Joseph II, suffered humiliating defeats at the hands of the Italians and Prussians respectively, the latter getting their hands on Prague yet again. In order to buy some more time, the compromise or *Ausgleich* of 1867 was drawn up, establishing the so-called **Dual Monarchy** of Austria-Hungary – two independent states united by one ruler.

For the Czechs, the *Ausgleich* came as a bitter disappointment. While the Magyars became the Austrians' equals, the Czechs remained second-class citizens. The Czechs' failure in bending the emperor's ear was no doubt partly due to the absence of a Czech aristocracy that could bring its social weight to bear at the Viennese court. Nevertheless, the *Ausgleich* did mark an end to the absolutism of the immediate post-1848 period, and, compared to the Hungarians, the Austrians were positively enlightened in the wide range of civil liberties they granted, culminating in universal male suffrage in 1907.

The industrial revolution continued apace in Bohemia, bringing an ever-increasing number of Czechs into the newly founded suburbs of Prague, such as Smíchov and Pižkov. Thanks to the unfair voting system, however, the German-speaking minority managed to hold onto power in the Prague city council until the 1880s. By the turn of the century, German-speakers made up just five percent of the city's population – fewer than the Czechs in Vienna – and of those more than half were Jewish. Nevertheless, German influence in the city remained considerable, far greater than their numbers alone warranted; this was due in part to economic means, and in part to overall rule from Vienna.

Under Dualism, the Czech *národní obrození* flourished. Towards the end of the century, Prague was endowed with a number of symbolically significant Czech monuments, like the Národní divaldo (National Theatre), the Národní muzeum (National Museum) and the Rudolfinum. Inevitably, the movement also began to splinter, with the liberals and conservatives, known as the **Old Czechs**, advocating working within the existing legislature to achieve their aims, and the more radical **Young Czechs** favouring a policy of non-cooperation. The most famous political figure to emerge from the ranks of the Young Czechs was the Prague university professor **Tomáš Garrigue Masaryk**, who founded his own Realist Party in 1900 and began to put forward the (then rather quirky) concept of closer cooperation between the Czechs and Slovaks.

The Old Czechs, backed by the new Czech industrialists, achieved a number of minor legislative successes, but by the 1890s, the Young Czechs had gained the upper hand and conflict between the Czech and German communities became a daily ritual in the boulevards of the capital – a favourite spot for confrontations being the promenade of Na příkopě. Language was also a volatile issue, often fought out on the shop and street signs of Prague. In 1897 the **Badeni Decrees**, which put Czech on an equal footing with German in all dealings with the state, drove the country to the point of civil war, before being withdrawn by the cautious Austrians.

World War I

At the outbreak of **World War I**, the Czechs and Slovaks showed little enthusiasm for fighting alongside their old enemies, the Austrians and Hungarians, against their Slav brothers, the Russians and Serbs. As the war progressed, large numbers defected to form the **Czechoslovak Legion**, which fought on the Eastern Front against the Austrians. Masaryk travelled to the USA to curry favour for a new Czechoslovak state, while his two deputies, the Czech Edvard Beneš and the Slovak Milan Štefánik, did the same in Britain and France.

Meanwhile, the Legion, which by now numbered some 100,000 men, became embroiled in the Russian revolutions of 1917, and, when the Bolsheviks made peace with Germany, found itself cut off from the homeland. The uneasy cooperation between the Reds and the Legion broke down when Trotsky demanded that they hand over their weapons before heading off on their legendary **anabasis**, or march back home, via Vladivostok. The soldiers refused and became further involved in the Civil War, for a while controlling large parts of Siberia and, most importantly, the Trans-Siberian Railway, before arriving back to a tumultuous reception in the new republic.

Meanwhile, during the course of the summer of 1918, the Slovaks finally threw in their lot with the Czechs, and the Allies recognized Masaryk's provisional Czechoslovak government. On October 28, 1918, as the Habsburg Empire began to collapse, the first **Czechoslovak Republic** was declared in Prague. In response, the German-speaking border regions (later to become known as the Sudetenland) declared themselves autonomous provinces of the new republic of *Deutsch-Österreich* (German-Austria), which, it was hoped, would eventually unite with Germany itself. The new Czechoslovak government was having none of it, but it took the intervention of Czechoslovak troops before control of the border regions was rested from the secessionists.

Last to opt in favour of the new republic was **Ruthenia** (officially known as Sub-Carpatho Ruthenia), a rural backwater of the old Hungarian Kingdom which became officially part of Czechoslovakia by the Treaty of St Germain in September 1919. Its incorporation was largely due to the campaigning efforts of Ruthenian emigrés in the USA. For the new republic the province was a strategic bonus, but otherwise a huge drain on resources.

The First Republic

The new nation of Czechoslovakia began postwar life in an enviable economic position – **tenth in the world industrial league table** – having inherited seventy to eighty percent of Austria-Hungary's industry intact. Prague regained its position at the centre of the country's political and cultural life, and in the interwar period was embellished with a rich mantle of Bauhaus-style buildings. Less enviable was the diverse make-up of the country's population – a melange of minorities which would in the end prove its downfall. Along with the six million Czechs and two million Slovaks who initially backed the republic, there were more than three million Germans and 600,000 Hungarians, not to mention sundry other Ruthenians (Rusyns), Jews and Poles.

That Czechoslovakia's democracy survived as long as it did is down to the powerful political presence and skill of **Masaryk**, the country's president from 1918 to 1935, who shared executive power with the cabinet. It was his vision of social democracy that was stamped on the nation's new constitution, one of the most liberal of the time (if a little bureaucratic and centralized), aimed at ameliorating any ethnic and class tensions within the republic by means of universal suffrage, land reform and, more specifically, the Language Law, which ensured bilinguality to any area where the minority exceeded twenty percent.

The elections of 1920 reflected the mood of the time, ushering in the left-liberal alliance of the **Pětka** (The Five), a coalition of five parties led by the Agrarian, Antonín Švehla, whose slogan, "we have agreed that we will agree", became the keystone of the republic's consensus politics between the wars. Gradually all the other parties (except the Fascists and the Communists) – including even Andrej Hlinka's Slovak People's Party and most of the Sudeten German parties – began to participate in (or at least not disrupt) parliamentary proceedings. On the eve of the Wall Street Crash, the republic was enjoying an economic boom, a cultural renaissance and a temporary *modus vivendi* among its minorities.

The Thirties

The 1929 Wall Street Crash plunged the whole country into crisis. Economic hardship was quickly followed by **political instability**. In Slovakia, Hlinka's People's Party fed off the anti-Czech resentment that was fuelled by Prague's manic centralization, consistently polling around thirty percent, with an increasingly nationalist/separatist message. In Ruthenia, the elections of 1935 gave only 37 percent of the vote to parties supporting the republic, the rest going to the Communists, pro-Magyars and other autonomist groups.

But without doubt the most intractable of the minority problems was that of the Sudeten Germans, who occupied the heavily industrialized border regions of Bohemia and Moravia. Nationalist sentiment had always run high in the Sudetenland, whose German-speakers resented having been included in the new republic, but it was only after the Crash that the extremist parties began to make significant electoral gains. Encouraged by the rise of Nazism in Germany, and aided by rocketing Sudeten German unemployment, the proto-Nazi **Sudeten German Party** (SdP), led by a gym teacher called Konrad Henlein, was able to win over sixty percent of the German-speaking vote in the 1935 elections.

Although constantly denying any wish to secede from the republic, the activities of Henlein and the SdP were increasingly funded and directed from Nazi Germany. To make matters worse, the Czechs suffered a severe blow to their morale with the death of Masaryk late in 1937, leaving the country in the less capable hands of his Socialist deputy, Edvard Beneš. With the Nazi annexation of Austria (the *Anschluss*) on March

11, 1938, Hitler was free to focus his attention on the Sudetenland, calling Henlein to Berlin on March 28 and instructing him to call for outright autonomy.

The Munich crisis

On April 24, 1938, the SdP launched its final propaganda offensive in the **Karlsbad Decrees**, demanding (without defining) "complete autonomy". As this would clearly have meant surrendering the entire Czechoslovak border defences, not to mention causing economic havoc, Beneš refused to bow to the SdP's demands. Armed conflict was only narrowly avoided and, by the beginning of September, Beneš was forced to acquiesce to some sort of autonomy. On Hitler's orders, Henlein refused Beneš's offer and called openly for the secession of the Sudetenland to the German Reich.

On September 15, as Henlein fled to Germany, the British prime minister, Neville Chamberlain, flew to Berchtesgaden on his own ill-conceived initiative to "appease" the Führer. A week later, Chamberlain flew again to Germany, this time to Bad Godesburg, vowing to the British public that the country would not go to war (in his famous words) "because of a quarrel in a far-away country between people of whom we know nothing". Nevertheless, the French issued draft papers, the British Navy was mobilized, and the whole of Europe fully expected war. Then, in the early hours of September 30, in one of the most treacherous and self-interested acts of modern European diplomacy, prime ministers Chamberlain (for Britain) and Daladier (for France) signed the **Munich Diktat** with Mussolini and Hitler, agreeing – without consulting the Czechoslovak government – to all of Hitler's demands. The British and French public were genuinely relieved, and Chamberlain flew back to cheering home crowds, waving his famous piece of paper that guaranteed "peace in our time".

The Second Republic

Betrayed by his only Western allies and fearing bloodshed, Beneš capitulated, against the wishes of most Czechs. Had Beneš not given in, however, it's doubtful anything would have come of Czech armed resistance, surrounded as they were by vastly superior hostile powers. Beneš resigned on October 5 and left the country. On October 15, **German troops occupied Sudetenland**, to the dismay of the forty percent of Sudeten Germans who hadn't voted for Henlein (not to mention the half a million Czechs and Jews who lived there). The Poles took the opportunity to seize a sizeable chunk of North Moravia, while in the short-lived "rump" **Second Republic** (officially known as Czecho-Slovakia), the one-eyed war veteran Jan Sýrový became prime minister and Emil Hácha became president, Slovakia and Ruthenia electing their own autonomous governments.

The Second Republic was not long in existence before it too collapsed. On March 15, 1939, Hitler informed Hácha of the imminent Nazi occupation of what was left of the Czech Lands, and persuaded him to demobilize the army, again against the wishes of many Czechs. The Germans encountered no resistance (nor any response from the Second Republic's supposed guarantors, Britain and France) and swiftly set up the Nazi **Protectorate of Bohemia and Moravia**. The Hungarians effortlessly crushed Ruthenia's brief independence, while the Slovak People's Party, backed by the Nazis, declared **Slovak independence**, under the leadership of the clerical fascist Jozef Tiso.

World War II

In the first few months of the occupation, left-wing activists were arrested, and Jews were placed under the infamous Nuremberg Laws, but Nazi rule in the Protectorate was not as harsh as it would later become – the economy even enjoyed something of a mini-boom. In late October and November 1939, Czech students in Prague began a series of demonstrations against the Nazis, who responded by closing down all institutions of higher education. In 1941 a leading SS officer, **Reinhard Heydrich**, was put in charge of the Protectorate. Arrests and deportations followed, reaching fever pitch after Heydrich himself was assassinated by the Czech resistance in June 1942 (see p.144). The "final solution" was meted out on the country's remaining Jews, who were transported first to the ghetto in Terezín (see p.183), and then on to the extermination camps. The rest of the population were frightened into submission – very few acts of active resistance being undertaken in the Czech Lands until the Prague Uprising of May 1945 (see below).

By the end of 1944, Czechoslovak and Russian troops had begun to liberate the country, starting with Ruthenia, which Stalin decided to take as war booty despite having guaranteed to maintain Czechoslovakia's pre-Munich borders. On April 4, 1945, under Beneš's leadership, the provisional National Front or **Národní fronta** government – a coalition of Social Democrats, Socialists and Communists – was set up in Košice. On April 18, the US Third Army, under General Patton, crossed the border in the west, meeting very little German resistance. The people of Prague finally rose up against the Nazis on May 5, many hoping to prompt an American offensive from Plzeň, which the Third Army were on the point of taking. In the end, the Americans made the politically disastrous (but militarily wise) decision not to cross the demarcation line that had been agreed between the Allies at Yalta. Two crack German armoured divisions, not to mention some extremely fanatical SS troops, remained in position near the capital. Some 1600 barricades were erected, and around 30,000 Praguers held out against the numerically superior German troops, backed up by tanks and artillery, until they finally capitulated on May 8. The Russians entered the city the following day.

The Third Republic

Violent reprisals against suspected collaborators and the German-speaking population in general began as soon as the country was liberated. All Germans were immediately given the same food rations as the Jews had been given during the war. Starvation, summary executions and worse resulted in the deaths of countless thousands of ethnic Germans. With considerable popular backing and the tacit approval of the Red Army, Beneš began to organize the forced **expulsion of the German-speaking population**, referred to euphemistically by the Czechs as the *odsun* (transfer). Only those Germans who could prove their anti-fascist credentials were permitted to stay – the Czech community was not called on to prove the same – and by the summer of 1947, nearly 2.5 million Germans had been expelled or had fled in fear. On this occasion, Sudeten German objections were brushed aside by the Allies, who had given Beneš the go-ahead for the *odsun* at the postwar Potsdam Conference. Attempts by Beneš to expel the Hungarian-speaking minority from Slovakia in similar fashion, however, proved unsuccessful.

On October 28, 1945, in accordance with the leftist programme thrashed out at Košice, sixty percent of the country's industry was nationalized. Confiscated Sudeten German property was handed out by the largely Communist-controlled police force, and in a spirit of optimism and/or opportunism, people began to join the Communist Party (KSČ) in droves; membership more than doubled in less than a year. In the **May 1946 elections**, the Party reaped the rewards of their enthusiastic support for the *odsun*, of Stalin's vocal opposition to Munich, and of the recent Soviet liberation, emerging as the strongest single party in the Czech Lands with up to forty percent of the vote (the largest ever for a European Communist Party in a multi-party election). In Slovakia, however, they achieved just thirty percent, thus failing to push the Democrats into second place. President Beneš appointed the KSČ leader, **Klement Gottwald**, prime minister of another *Národní fronta* coalition, with several strategically important cabinet portfolios going to Party members, including the ministries of the Interior, Finance, Labour and Social Affairs, Agriculture and Information.

Gottwald assured everyone of the KSČ's commitment to parliamentary democracy, and initially at least even agreed to participate in the Americans' Marshall Plan (the only Eastern Bloc country to do so). Stalin immediately summoned Gottwald to Moscow, and on his return the KSČ denounced the Plan. By the end of 1947, the Communists were beginning to lose support, as the harvest failed, the economy faltered and malpractices within the Communist-controlled Ministry of the Interior were uncovered. In response, the KSČ began to up the ante, constantly warning the nation of imminent "counter-revolutionary plots", and arguing for greater nationalization and land reform as a safeguard.

Then in February 1948 – officially known as **"Victorious February"** – the latest in a series of scandals hit the Ministry of the Interior, prompting the twelve non-Communist cabinet ministers to resign en masse in the hope of forcing a physically weak President Beneš to dismiss Gottwald. No attempt was made, however, to rally popular support against the Communists. Beneš received more than 5000 resolutions supporting the Communists and just 150 opposing them. Stalin sent word to Gottwald to take advantage of the crisis and ask for military assistance – Soviet troops began massing on the Hungarian border. It was the one time in his life when Gottwald disobeyed Stalin; instead, by exploiting the divisions within the Social Democrats he was able to maintain his majority in parliament. The KSČ took to the streets (and the airwaves), arming "workers' militia" units to defend the country against counter-revolution, calling a general strike and finally, on February 25, organizing the country's biggest ever demonstration in Prague. The same day Gottwald went to an indecisive (and increasingly ill) Beneš with his new cabinet, all Party members or "fellow travellers". Beneš accepted Gottwald's nominees and the most popular Communist coup in Eastern Europe was complete, without bloodshed and without the direct intervention of the Soviets. In the aftermath of the coup, thousands of Czechs and Slovaks fled abroad.

The People's Republic

Following Victorious February, the Party began to consolidate its position, a relatively easy task given its immense popular support and control of the army, police force, workers' militia and trade unions. A **new constitution** confirming the "leading role" of the Communist Party and the "dictatorship of the proletariat" was passed by parliament on May 9, 1948. President Beneš refused to sign it, resigned in favour of Gottwald, and died (of natural causes) shortly afterwards. Those political parties that were not banned or forcibly merged with the KSČ were prescribed fixed-percentage representation within the so-called "multi-party" *Národní fronta*.

With the Cold War in full swing, the **Stalinization** of Czechoslovak society was quick to follow. In the Party's first Five Year Plan, ninety percent of industry was nationalized, heavy industry (and in particular the country's defence industry) was given a massive boost and compulsory collectivization forced through. Party membership reached an all-time high of 2.5 million, and "class-conscious" Party cadres were given positions of power, while "class enemies" (and their children) were discriminated against. It wasn't long, too, before the Czechoslovak mining "gulags" began to fill up with the regime's political opponents – "kulaks", priests and "bourgeois oppositionists" – numbering more than 100,000 at their peak.

Having incarcerated most of its non-Party opponents, the KSČ, with a little prompting from Stalin, embarked upon a ruthless period of internal blood-letting. As the economy nose-dived, calls for intensified "class struggle", rumours of impending "counter-revolution" and reports of economic sabotage by fifth columnists filled the press. An atmosphere of fear and confusion was created to justify **large-scale arrests of Party members** with an "international" background: those with a wartime connection with the West, Spanish Civil War veterans, Jews and Slovak nationalists.

In the early 1950s, the Party organized a series of Stalinist **show trials** in Prague, the most spectacular of which was the trial of Rudolf Slánský, who had been second only to Gottwald in the KSČ before his arrest. He and thirteen other leading Party members (eleven of them Jewish, including Slánský) were sentenced to death as "Trotskyist-Titoist-Zionists". Soon afterwards, Vladimír Clementis, the former KSČ foreign minister, was executed along with other leading Slovak comrades (Gustáv Husák, the post-1968 president, was given life imprisonment).

After Stalin

Gottwald died in mysterious circumstances in March 1953, nine days after attending Stalin's funeral in Moscow (some say he drank himself to death). The whole nation heaved a sigh of relief, but the regime seemed as unrepentant as ever. The arrests and show trials continued. Then, on May 30, the new Communist leadership announced a drastic currency devaluation, effectively reducing wages by ten percent, while raising prices. The result was a wave of isolated **workers' demonstrations** and rioting in Plzeň and Prague. Czechoslovak army units called in to suppress the demonstrations proved unreliable, and it was left to the heavily armed workers' militia and police to disperse the crowds and make the predictable arrests and summary executions.

So complete were the Party purges of the early 1950s, so sycophantic (and scared) was the surviving leadership, that Khrushchev's 1956 thaw was virtually ignored by the KSČ. An attempted rebellion in the Writers' Union Congress was rebuffed and an enquiry into the show trials made several minor security officials scapegoats for the "malpractices". The genuine mass base of the KSČ remained blindly loyal to the Party for the most part; Prague basked under the largest statue of Stalin in the world; and in 1957, the dull, unreconstructed neo-Stalinist **Antonín Novotný** – recently alleged to have been a spy for the Gestapo during the war – became First Secretary and President.

Reformism and invasion

The first rumblings of protest against Czechoslovakia's hardline leadership appeared in the official press in 1963. At first, the criticisms were confined to the country's worsening economic stagnation, but soon developed into more generalized protests against the KSČ leadership. Novotný responded by ordering the belated release and rehabilitation of victims of the 1950s purges, permitting a slight cultural thaw and easing travel restrictions to the West. In effect, he was simply buying time. The half-hearted economic reforms announced in the 1965 **New Economic Model** failed to halt the recession, and the minor political reforms instigated by the KSČ only increased the pressure for greater changes within the Party.

In 1967, Novotný attempted a pre-emptive strike against his opponents. Several leading writers were imprisoned, Slovak Party leaders were branded as "bourgeois nationalists" and the economists were called on to produce results or else forego their reform programme. Instead of eliminating the opposition, though, Novotný unwittingly united them. Despite Novotný's plea to the Soviets, Brezhnev refused to back a leader whom he saw as "Khrushchev's man in Prague", and on January 5, 1968, the young Slovak leader **Alexander Dubček** replaced Novotný as First Secretary. On March 22, the war hero Ludvík Svoboda dislodged Novotný from the presidency.

1968: The Prague Spring

By inclination, Dubček was a moderate, cautious reformer – the perfect compromise candidate – but he was continually swept along by the sheer force of the reform movement. The virtual **abolition of censorship** was probably the single most significant step Dubček took. It transformed what had been until then an internal Party debate into a popular mass movement. Civil society, for years muffled by the paranoia and strictures of Stalinism, suddenly sprang into life in the dynamic optimism of the first few months of 1968, the so-called **"Prague Spring"**. In April, the KSČ published their Action Programme, proposing what became popularly known as "socialism with a human face" – federalization, freedom of assembly and expression, and democratization of parliament.

Throughout the spring and summer, the reform movement gathered momentum. The Social Democrat Party (forcibly merged with the KSČ after 1948) re-formed, anti-Soviet polemics appeared in the press and, most famously of all, the writer and lifelong Party member Ludvík Vaculík published his personal manifesto entitled **"Two Thousand Words"**, calling for radical de-Stalinization within the Party. Dubček and the moderates denounced the manifesto and reaffirmed the country's support for the Warsaw Pact military alliance. Meanwhile, the Soviets and their hardline allies – Gomulka in Poland and Ulbricht in the GDR – viewed the Czechoslovak developments on their doorstep very gravely, and began to call for the suppression of "counter-revolutionary elements" and the reimposition of censorship.

As the summer wore on, it became clear that the Soviets were planning military intervention. Warsaw Pact manoeuvres were held in Czechoslovakia in late June, a Warsaw Pact conference (without Czechoslovak participation) was convened in mid-July and, at the beginning of August, the Soviets and the KSČ leadership met for **emergency bilateral talks** at Čierná nad Tisou on the Czechoslovak–Soviet border. Brezhnev's hardline deputy, Alexei Kosygin, made his less than subtle threat that "your border is our border", but did agree to withdraw Soviet troops (stationed in the country since the June manoeuvres) and gave the go-ahead to the KSČ's special Party Congress scheduled for September 9.

In the early hours of August 21, fearing a defeat for the hardliners at the forthcoming KSČ Congress, and claiming to have been invited to provide "fraternal assistance", the Soviets gave the order for the **invasion of Czechoslovakia** to be carried out by all the Warsaw Pact forces (only Romania refused to take part). Dubček and the KSČ reformists immediately condemned the invasion before being arrested and flown to Moscow for "negotiations". President Svoboda refused to condone the formation of a new government under the hardliner Alois Indra, and the people took to the streets in protest, employing every form of non-violent resistance in the book. Individual acts of martyrdom, like the self-immolation of **Jan Palach** on Prague's Wenceslas Square, hit the headlines, but casualties were light compared to the Hungarian uprising of 1956 – the cost in terms of the following twenty years was much greater.

Normalization

In April 1969, there were anti-Soviet riots during the celebrations of the country's double ice hockey victory over the Soviets. On this pretext, another Slovak, **Gustáv Husák**, replaced the broken Dubček as First Secretary, and instigated his infamous policy of **"normalization"**. More than 150,000 fled the country before the borders closed, around 500,000 were expelled from the Party, and an estimated one million people lost their jobs or were demoted. Inexorably, the KSČ reasserted its absolute control over the state and society. The only part of the reform package to survive the invasion was **federalization**, which gave the Slovaks greater freedom from Prague (on paper at least), though even this was severely watered down in 1971. Dubček, like countless others, was forced to give up his job, working for the next twenty years as a minor official in the Slovak forestry commission.

An unwritten social contract was struck between rulers and ruled during the 1970s, whereby the country was guaranteed a tolerable standard of living (second only to that of the GDR in Eastern Europe) in return for its passive collaboration. Husák's security apparatus quashed all forms of dissent during the early 1970s, and it wasn't until the middle of the decade that an organized opposition was strong enough to show its face. In 1976, the punk rock band *The Plastic People of the Universe* was arrested and charged with the familiar "crimes against the state" clause of the penal code. The dissidents who rallied to their defence – a motley assortment of people ranging from former KSČ members to right-wing intellectuals – agreed to form **Charter 77** (*Charta 77* in Czech), with the purpose of monitoring human rights abuses in the country. One of the organization's prime movers and initial spokespeople was the absurdist Czech playwright **Václav Havel**. Havel, along with many others, endured relentless persecution (including long prison sentences) over the next decade in pursuit of Charter 77's ideals. The initial gathering of 243 signatories had increased to more than 1000 by 1980, and caused panic in the moral vacuum of the Party apparatus, but consistently failed to stir a fearful and cynical populace into action.

The Eighties

In the late 1970s and early 1980s, the inefficiencies of the economy prevented the government from fulfilling its side of the social contract, as living standards began to fall. Cynicism, alcoholism, absenteeism and outright dissent became widespread, especially among the younger (post-1968) generation. The **Jazz Section** of the Musicians' Union, who disseminated "subversive" western pop music (like pirate copies of "Live Aid"), highlighted the ludicrously harsh nature of the regime when they were arrested and imprisoned in the mid-1980s. Pop concerts, religious pilgrimages and, of course, the anniversary of the Soviet invasion all caused regular confrontations between the security forces and certain sections of the population. Yet still a mass movement like Poland's Solidarity failed to emerge.

With the advent of **Mikhail Gorbachev**, the KSČ was put in an extremely awkward position, as it tried desperately to separate *perestroika* from comparisons with the reforms of the Prague Spring. Husák and his cronies had prided themselves on being second only to Honecker's GDR as the most stable and orthodox of the Soviet satellites – now the font of orthodoxy, the Soviet Union, was turning against them. In 1987, **Miloš Jakeš**, the hardliner who oversaw Husák's normalization purges, took over from Husák as General (First) Secretary and introduced *přestavba* (restructuring), Czechoslovakia's lukewarm version of *perestroika*.

The Velvet Revolution

Everything appeared to be going swimmingly for the KSČ as it entered 1989. Under the surface, however, things were becoming more and more strained. As the country's economic performance worsened, divisions were developing within the KSČ leadership. The protest movement was gathering momentum: even the Catholic Church had begun to voice dissatisfaction, compiling a staggering 500,000 signatures calling for greater freedom of worship. But the twenty-first anniversary of the Soviet invasion produced a demonstration of only 10,000, which was swiftly and violently dispersed by the regime.

During the summer, however, more serious cracks began to appear in Czechoslovakia's staunch hardline ally, the GDR. The trickle of East Germans fleeing to the West turned into a mass exodus, with thousands besieging the West German embassy in Prague. Honecker, the East German leader, was forced to resign and, by the end of October, nightly mass demonstrations were taking place on the streets of Leipzig and Dresden. The opening of the Berlin Wall on November 9 left Czechoslovakia, Romania and Albania alone on the Eastern European stage still clinging to the old truths.

All eyes were now turned upon Czechoslovakia. Reformists within the KSČ began plotting an internal coup to overthrow Jakeš, in anticipation of a Soviet denunciation of the 1968 invasion. In the end, events overtook whatever plans they may have had. On Friday, **November 17**, a 50,000-strong peaceful demonstration organized by the official Communist youth organization was viciously attacked by the riot police. More than 100 arrests, 500 injuries and one death were reported (the fatality was later retracted) in what became popularly known as the *masakr* (massacre). Prague's students immediately began an occupation strike, joined soon after by the city's actors, who together called for an end to the Communist Party's "leading role" and a general strike to be held for two hours on November 27.

Civic Forum and the VPN

On Sunday, November 19, on Václav Havel's initiative, the established opposition groups, like Charter 77, met and agreed to form *Občanské fórum* or **Civic Forum**. Their demands were simple: the resignation of the present hardline leadership, including Husák and Jakeš; an enquiry into the police actions of November 17; an amnesty for all political prisoners; and support for the general strike. In Bratislava, a parallel organization, *Veřejnosť proti nasiliu* or **People Against Violence** (VPN), was set up to coordinate protest in Slovakia.

On the Monday evening, the first of the really big **nationwide demonstrations** took place – the biggest since the 1968 invasion – with more than 200,000 people pouring into Prague's Wenceslas Square. This time the police held back and rumours of troop deployments proved false. Every night for a week people poured into the main squares in towns and cities across the country, repeating the calls for democracy, freedom and an end to the Party's monopoly of power. As the week dragged on, the Communist media tentatively began to report events, and the KSČ leadership started to splinter under the strain, with the prime minister, **Ladislav Adamec**, alone in sticking his neck out and holding talks with the opposition.

The end of one-party rule

On Friday evening, Dubček, the ousted 1968 leader, appeared alongside Havel, before a crowd of 300,000 in Wenceslas Square, and in a matter of hours the entire Jakeš leadership had resigned. The weekend brought the largest demonstrations the country had ever seen – more than 750,000 people in Prague alone. At the invitation of Civic Forum, Adamec addressed the crowd, only to be booed off the platform. On Monday, November 27, eighty percent of the country's workforce joined the two-hour **general strike**, including many of the Party's previously stalwart allies, such as the miners and engineers. The following day, the Party agreed to an end to one-party rule and the formation of a new "coalition government".

A temporary halt to the nightly demonstrations was called and the country waited expectantly for the "broad coalition" cabinet promised by Prime Minister Adamec. On December 3, another Communist-dominated line-up was announced by the Party and immediately denounced by Civic Forum and the VPN, who called for a fresh wave of demonstrations and another general strike for December 11. Adamec promptly resigned and was replaced by the Slovak Marián Čalfa. On December 10, one day before the second threatened general strike, Čalfa announced his provisional **"Government of National Understanding"**, with Communists in the minority for the first time since 1948 and multi-party elections planned for June 1990. Having sworn in the new government, President Husák, architect of the post-1968 "normalization", finally threw in the towel.

By the time the new Čalfa government was announced, the students and actors had been on strike continuously for over three weeks. The pace of change surprised everyone involved, but there was still one outstanding issue: the election of a new president. Posters shot up all round the capital urging **"HAVEL NA HRAD"** (Havel to the Castle – the seat of the presidency). The students were determined to see his election through, continuing their occupation strike until Havel was officially elected president by a unanimous vote of the Federal Assembly, and sworn in at the Hrad on December 29.

The 1990 elections

Czechoslovakia started the new decade full of optimism for what the future would bring. On the surface, the country had a lot more going for it

Princes, kings, emperors and presidents

The Přemyslid dynasty

Princes

Bořivoj I d. 895
Spytihněv I 895–905
Vratislav I 905–921
Václav I 921–929
Boleslav I 929–972
Boleslav II 972–999
Boleslav III 999–1002
Vladivoj 1002–1003
Jaromir 1003–1012
Ulrich 1012–1034
Břetislav I 1034–1055
Spytihněv II 1055–1061
Vratislav II (king from 1086) 1061–1092
Břetislav II 1092–1110
Bořivoj II 1110–1120
Vladislav I 1120–1125
Soběslav I 1125–1140
Vladislav II (as king, I) 1140–1173
Soběslav II 1173–1189
Otho 1189–1191
Václav II 1191–1192
Otakar I (king from 1212) 1192–1230

Kings

Václav I 1230–1253
Otakar II 1253–1278
Václav II 1278–1305
Václav III 1305–1306

Habsburgs

Rudolf I 1306–1307
Henry of Carinthia 1307–1310

The Luxembourg dynasty

John 1310–1346
Charles I (as emperor, IV) 1346–1378
Václav IV 1378–1419
Sigismund 1436–1437

Habsburgs

Albert 1437–1439
Ladislav the Posthumous 1439–1457

Czech Hussite

George of Poděbrady 1458–1471

The Jagiellonian dynasty

Vladislav II 1471–1516
Louis I 1516–1526

The Habsburg dynasty

Ferdinand I 1526–1564
Maximilian 1564–1576
Rudolf II 1576–1612
Matthias 1612–1619
Ferdinand II 1619–1637
Ferdinand III 1637–1657
Leopold I 1657–1705
Joseph I 1705–1711
Charles II (as emperor, VI) 1711–1740
Maria Theresa 1740–1780
Joseph II 1780–1790
Leopold II 1790–1792
Franz 1792–1835
Ferdinand IV (I) 1835–1848
Franz Joseph 1848–1916
Charles III 1916–1918

Presidents

Tomáš Garrigue Masaryk 1918–1935
Edvard Beneš 1935–1938 & 1945–1948
Klement Gottwald 1948–1953
Antonín Zápatocký 1953–1957
Antonín Novotný 1957–1968
Ludvík Svoboda 1968–1975
Gustáv Husák 1975–1989
Václav Havel 1989–1992 & 1993–

than its immediate neighbours (with the possible exception of the GDR). The Communist Party had been swept from power without bloodshed, and, unlike the rest of Eastern Europe, Czechoslovakia had a strong interwar democratic tradition with which to identify – Masaryk's First Republic. Despite Communist economic mismanagement, the country still had a relatively high standard of living, a skilled workforce and a manageable foreign debt.

In reality, however, the situation was somewhat different. Not only was the country economically in a worse state than most people had imagined, it was also environmentally devastated, and its people were suffering from what Havel described as "post-prison psychosis" – an inability to think or act for themselves. The country had to go through the painful transition "from being a big fish in a small pond to being a sickly adolescent trout in a hatchery". As a result, it came increasingly to rely on its new-found saviour, the humble playwright-president, Václav Havel.

In most people's eyes, "Saint Václav" could do no wrong, though he himself was not out to woo his electorate. His call for the rapid withdrawal of Soviet troops was popular enough, but his apology for the postwar expulsion of Sudeten Germans was deeply resented, as was his generous amnesty which eased the country's overcrowded prisons. The amnesty was blamed by many for the huge **rise in crime** in 1990. Every vice in the book – from racism to homicide – raised its ugly head in the first year of freedom.

In addition, there was still a lot of talk about the possibility of "counter-revolution", given the thousands of unemployed StČ (secret police) at large. Inevitably, accusations of previous StČ involvement rocked each political party in turn in the run-up to the first elections. The controversial ***lustrace*** (literally "lustration" or cleansing) law, which barred all those on StČ files from public office for the following five years, ended the career of many public figures, often on the basis of highly unreliable StČ reports.

Despite all the inevitable hiccups and the increasingly vocal Slovak nationalists, Civic Forum/VPN remained high in the opinion polls. The **June 1990 elections** produced a record-breaking 99 percent turnout. With around sixty percent of the vote, Civic Forum/VPN were clear victors (the Communists got just 13 percent) and Havel immediately set about forming a broad "Coalition of National Sacrifice", including everyone from Christian Democrats to former Communists.

The main concern of the new government was how to transform an outdated command-system economy into a **market economy**. The argument over the speed and model of economic reform eventually caused Civic Forum to split into two main camps: the centre-left *Občánské hnutí* or Civic Movement (OH), led by the foreign minister and former dissident Jiří Dienstbier, who favoured a more gradualist approach; and *Občánská democratická strana*, the right-wing **Civic Democratic Party** (ODS), headed by the finance minister **Václav Klaus**, whose pronouncement that the country should "walk the tightrope to Thatcherism" sent shivers up the spines of those familiar with the UK in the 1980s.

One of the first acts of the new government was to pass a **restitution law**, handing back small businesses and property to those from whom it had been expropriated after the 1948 Communist coup. This proved to be a controversial issue, since it excluded Jewish families driven out in 1938 by the Nazis, and, of course, the millions of Sudeten Germans who were forced to flee the country after the war. A law was later passed to cover the Jewish expropriations, but the Sudeten German issue remains a tricky one, despite the subsequent conclusion of an agreement over the issue.

The Slovak crisis

One of the most intractable issues facing post-Communist Czechoslovakia turned out to be the **Slovak problem**. Having been the victim of Prague-inspired centralization from Masaryk to Gottwald, the Slovaks were in no mood to suffer second-class citizenship any longer. In the aftermath of 1989, feelings were running high in Slovakia, and more than once the spectre of a "Slovak UDI" was threatened by Slovak politicians, who hoped to boost their popularity by appealing to voters' nationalism. Despite the tireless campaigning and negotiating by both sides, a compromise failed to emerge.

The **June 1992 elections** soon became an unofficial referendum on the future of the federation. Events moved rapidly towards the break-up of the republic after the resounding victory of the Movement for a Democratic Slovakia (HZDS), under the wily, populist politician Vladimir Mečiar, who, in retrospect, was quite clearly seeking Slovak independence, though he never explicitly said so during the campaign. In the Czech Lands, the right-wing ODS emerged as the largest single party, under Václav Klaus, who – ever the economist – was clearly not going to shed tears over losing the economically backward Slovak half of the country.

Talks between the two sides got nowhere, despite the fact of opinion polls in both countries consistently showing majority support for the federation. The HZDS then blocked the re-election of Havel, who had committed himself entirely to the pro-federation cause. Havel promptly resigned, leaving the country president-less and Klaus and Mečiar to talk over the terms of the divorce. On January 1, 1993, after 74 years of troubled existence, Czechoslovakia was officially divided into two new countries: the Czech Republic and Slovakia.

Czech politics since 1993

Generally speaking, life was much kinder to the Czechs than the Slovaks in the immediate period following the break-up of Czechoslovakia. While the Slovaks had the misfortune of being led by the increasingly wayward and isolated Mečiar, the Czechs enjoyed a long period of political stability under Klaus. Under his guidance, the country jumped to the front of the queue for the EU, joined NATO, and was held up as a shining example to all other former Eastern Bloc countries. Prague attracted more foreign investment than anywhere else in the country – plus thousands of American ex-pats into the bargain – and was transformed beyond all recognition, its main thoroughfares lined with brand new hotels, shops and restaurants.

Klaus and his party, the ODS, certainly proved themselves the most durable of all the new political forces to emerge in the former Eastern Bloc. Nevertheless, in the **1996 parliamentary elections**, although the ODS again emerged as the largest single party, they failed to gain an outright majority. They repeated the failure again in November 1996 during the elections for the Czech Senate, the upper house of the Czech parliament. The electorate was distinctly unenthusiastic about the whole idea of another chamber full of overpaid politicians, and a derisory thirty percent turned out to vote in the second round. In the end, however, it was – predictably enough – a series of allegations of corruption over the country's privatization that eventually prompted **Klaus's resignation** as prime minister in November 1997.

The **1998 elections** proved that the Czechs had grown sick and tired of Klaus's dry, rather arrogant, style of leadership. However, what really did for Klaus was that for the first time since he took power, the economy had ground to a halt. The Social Democrats (ČSSD), under Miloš Zeman, emerged as the largest single party, promising to pay more attention to social issues, though their record so far is less than impressive.

Havel, Czech President since 1993, secured another five-year term in 1998, though his health remains dodgy. Havel still commands considerable moral authority in politics, though he is by no means as popular at home as he is abroad. His marriage to the actress Dagmar Veškrnová, seventeen years his junior, in January 1997, less than a year after his first wife, Olga, died of cancer, was frowned upon by many. And his very public fall-out with his sister-in-law, Olga Havlová, over the family inheritance of the multi-million crown Lucerna complex in Prague, didn't do his reputation any favours either.

The Czech Romanies

Nevertheless, the Czechs look like they are going to need Havel's moral guidance more than ever, if they are to have any hope of tackling the biggest problem to emerge in the late 1990s. The present crisis began in late 1997, when a misleading documentary broadcast on Czech TV showed life for the handful of Czech Romanies who had emigrated to Canada as a proverbial bed of roses. At last, the documentary seemed to be suggesting, they had found a life free from the racism and unemployment that is the reality for most of the Czech Republic's estimated quarter of a million gypsies. The programme prompted a minor exodus of up to one thousand Czech Romanies to Canada. Another Nova documentary, this time extolling life for Czech Romanies in Britain, had a similar effect, with several hundred Czech and Slovak Romanies seeking political asylum on arrival at Dover.

Needless to say, in both cases, the Czech Romanies were given a very cold reception. Fascists in both countries demonstrated to have the Czechs repatriated immediately, while the Canadians reimposed visa restrictions on all Czechs, and British Foreign Office officials appeared on Czech and Slovak TV to try and dissuade any further applicants. While racists back in the Czech Republic gleefully plastered up "Gypsies to Canada" graffiti, the positive side effect of all this media attention has been to force Czechs to focus on the institutionalized racism of their society and the casual racism that is acceptable in almost every walk of life.

Further controversy broke out in 1999 over the planned building of a wall to separate Romanies and non-Romanies in the north Bohemian city of Ústí nad Labem. While the central government, under pressure from the EU, condemned the construction of the wall, the local council have so far proved determined to press on. All this merely highlights the continued need for a concerted campaign of anti-racism in order to try and counter the prevalent prejudices of the vast majority of Czechs. In addition, a great deal more grass roots social work needs to be done within Romany communities, and equal opportunities policies put in place, if Czech Romanies are to be persuaded that staying in the country is a viable option.

Czech cinema

A new "New Wave"?

Whenever a couple of Czech films attract critical attention there is a temptation to declare the return of the New Wave, the extraordinary collection of Czech and Slovak films that emerged in the mid- and late 1960s.

In 1996 Jan Svěrak won international acclaim with *Kolja*, a sentimental tale of a worldly cellist (played by his script-writer father Zdeněk), tamed by a charming Russian boy. It was the first Czech film to win an Oscar since Jiří Menzl's delightful wartime tale of incompetent authorities and young men losing their virginity, *Closely Observed Trains*, in 1968, at the height of the New Wave. Critics and audiences hoped that this was just the beginning of a similar outpouring of world-class Czech cinema. In 1997 Petr Zelenka's black comedy about forgiveness, *Knoflíkáři* (*Buttoners*), picked up a clutch of trophies at international film festivals and soon every Czech premiere was being greeted with announcements of the new New Wave. However, it is probably premature to make such claims. For a start, the sheer range of talent in the 1960s is hard to match.

The Czech New Wave

Almost everybody in Czech cinema seems to have been at FAMU, the Prague film academy, at the same time during the 1960s. There was **Miloš Forman**, who made witty comedies like *Loves of a Blonde* (1965) and *The Fireman's Ball* (1967) before emigrating in the 1970s and going on to direct *Amadeus*, *One Flew Over the Cuckoo's Nest* and, most recently, *The People v Larry Flint* (all of which take on a different meaning when viewed as the work of a refugee from Communist censorship). In the same graduation class was **Věra Chýtilová**, whose outrageous *Daisies* (1966), where two young women take on the political and sexual restrictions in a Dadaist orgy of destruction, still has the power to shock. **Jan Němec** made the chilling *Party and the Guests* (1966) about an impromptu birthday party from which you are not allowed to leave.

And of course, the New Wave was not just made up of film directors. They were supported by world-class film technicians such as editor Miloš Hájek, art director Ester Krumbahová, and most crucially cameramen like **Miroslav Ondříček** and **Jan Kučera**. They brought a daring new look to cinema, full of lyrical images, but bold in use of stylized colour or hand-held camera.

Animation

Animation has always been a genre where the Czechs have excelled, partly thanks to having a nightly spot for children reserved on television to this day. **Jiří Trnka** had established the ground rules of 3-D animation using native puppet skills with *A Czech Year* back in 1947. His teaching had inspired **Karel Zeman** to combine puppets, animation and live action in *Journey into Prehistory* (1954). In the depths of normalization, animation was sometimes the only Czech cinema seen abroad. In the early 1980s, **Jiří Bárta** collected a string of awards for the endearing *The Extinct World of Gloves* (1982). Although he was not at FAMU, **Jan Švankmajer** emerged at the same time as the other directors of the New Wave with early shorts like *The Apartment* (1967) and *The Garden* (1968). He moved briefly to Bratislava to evade official restrictions, but survived the Soviet occupation chiefly by adapting himself as a surrealist to whatever medium was available, turning to pottery, painting or poetry when he could not make films. He acquired a world-wide following with his full-length masterpiece *Alice* (1987), and greeted the Velvet Revolution of 1989 with a slogan draped on his house calling for "More imagination, please".

However, what characterized the films of the New Wave more than anything was their irreverent humour, poignant satire and warm, wry human observation. Often they focused on the difficulty for young people to integrate into an alien or hostile world, like Němec's visceral *Diamonds of the Night* (1964). Frequently they created absurd allegories of life under Communism as in the openly Kafkaesque *Joseph Kilián* (1964) about the increasing frustrations of a man vainly trying to find the shop from where he had borrowed a cat.

Some of the big names from the 1960s are still active today. **Vojtěch Jásny** has returned from American exile to make a sequel to his devastatingly beautiful *All My Good Countrymen* (1969). It was one of the first films to be banned "forever" by the authorities for depicting, with the force of a biblical parable, the disastrous consequences of the Communist takeover in a small Moravian village. **Jaromír Jireš**, the director of *The Joke* in 1969 (based on Milan Kundera's bleak tale of the lack of humour in Communist officialdom), another of the most controversial films of the Prague Spring, has also resumed his career. And Menzl, Chýtilová and Němec are all still making Czech films.

Sadly, the new work from the greats of the New Wave has largely been embarrassingly bad, ignored by domestic audiences and patronized by foreign critics. One possible exception is **Dragomír Výhanová**, who made a documentary about young men loathing compulsory military service just before the Soviet invasion. Not only was the film banned, but she was prevented from pursuing her promising career as a director. For twenty years, the nearest she could get to it was inspiring and challenging students as an editing tutor at FAMU. When her feature film debut *Fortress* (1996) finally emerged, it was very much in New Wave tradition. While commercial audiences no longer flock to political parables, her poignant tale of an individual's attempt to preserve his identity – and his cat – in the face of arbitrary attacks by authorities, has much more contemporary relevance than its ravishing black and white photography would suggest.

Interwar cinema: avant-garde to erotica

The New Wave did not spring out of nowhere. Czech cinema was already thriving before the war. Films ranged from the expressionist classic *The Golem* (1920) by Paul Wagner, to **Gustáv Machatý's** notorious *Extase* (1933), famous less for its use of graphic motifs and expressive montages than its briefly naked appearance of the young Slovak actress who was to achieve worldwide fame as **Hedy Lamarr**.

There were also the comedies of Jiří Voskovec and **Jan Werich**, whose films like *Your Money or Your Life* (1932) and *The World is Ours* (1937) brought their blend of politics and farce from the Liberated Theatre (now ABC Theatre) off Wenceslas Square to the screen. Their domestic popularity was enormous, comparable to Chaplin in the West. Werich in particular remained a powerful figure in Czech cinema long after the war. He played most of the key roles in **Martin Frič**'s two-part intellectual comedy about the limits of absolute power, based on the golem myth, *in The Emperor's Baker* and *The Baker's Emperor* (1951). Werich later featured as the genial narrator in *Cassandra Cat* (1963), telling an unforgettable fable about a cat that could see people in their true colours. The authorities only stopped him making records, performances and films in the 1970s by threatening to prevent him receiving vital throat surgery.

Film under the Nazis and Communists

World War II did not end Czech film production. The largest film studios in Europe had been built at **Barrandov** by Václav Havel's architect grandfather in the 1920s, and the Nazis decided to use them to make domestic propaganda films, perhaps to enable Göbbels to maintain a relationship with the Czech actress, Lara Baarova. Many Czech film makers took their talents into exile, such as Jiří Weiss, who joined the British Crown Film Unit, but others continued to work during the Nazi occupation, notably the director **E.F. Burian**, who was famous for riding up to the studios through wartime Prague in his own carriage.

After the war, President Beneš declared, "If there is anything ripe for nationalization in our country, it is film!" The **Prague Film Academy (FAMU)** was founded in 1945 and Czech film students started to gather at the *Café Slavia*. Initially Communist governments were wary of anything that strayed from the official policy of social realism, laid down by the Russian Minister of Culture, Zhadnov, in 1946. Czech cinema produced an unappetizing diet of girls in love with tractors, imperialist saboteurs foiled by worthy shop stewards and wartime epics. Some unusual gems emerged however, long before the New Wave of the mid-1960s. **Zdeněk Brnych** made a case for "dirty realism" that was not necessarily uplifting in *Local Romance* (1957), and **František Vlačil** bewildered the censors by producing a masterly historical epic, *Markéta Lazarska* (1960), in Old Slavonic. Recently restored and reissued, it remains one of the supreme achievements of Czech cinema.

Czech films of the late 1990s

Younger Czech film makers who started producing films after the fall of Communism are uneasy about being saddled with the mantle of their forebears. They are more aware than foreign critics of how different the film-making environment is now. In the 1960s, Czech audiences were hungry for films that evaded official censorship and appealed to their specific circumstances. They knew who *The Uninvited Guest* (1969) was supposed to be, in the marvellous short with Pavel Landovsky as the mysterious visitor who arrives one night and then refuses to leave; they recognized the world of *The Ear* (1970) by Jan Kadar, which depicted an entire society under surveillance. By contrast, contemporary Czech audiences are just as enthusiastic and willing consumers of heavily promoted American cinema as their Western counterparts.

Few of the new Czech films so far are likely to make an international impact beyond film festivals and esoteric art houses. Some of the directors, however, are definitely talents to watch. **Saša Gedeon**, for example, with *Indian Summer* (1995) and *Return of the Idiot* (1999), has demonstrated his ability to develop mature performances that turn small stories into powerful films. **David Ondříček** (son of the cameraman) captured the confused world of young people in *Whispers* (1998) and promises to acquire a cult following with *Loners* (2000) in collaboration with Petr Zelenka. Meanwhile, their classmate at FAMU **Jan Hřebek** has concentrated on stories with specifically Czech themes, like *Big Beat* (1993), a musical about the arrival of rock and roll in Dejvice, or *Cosy Dens* (1999), yet another reminiscence about life on the eve of the Soviet invasion.

Foreign audiences are likely to encounter the enduring strengths of Czech cinema without necessarily being aware of them. Many **international advertisements** are now made in Prague, sometimes with Czech directors like Ivan Zachariáš or Tomáš Mašin, usually drawn by untapped locations and cheap facilities. These have also attracted scores of **foreign feature films** and TV movies from *Mission Impossible* to *Les Misérables*. They have exploited a range of film-making talent across diverse professions. Czech pyrotechnic experts and make-up artists are now flown in to work around the world, even on productions that have no Czech connection.

The Czech cinema industry has also trained some of the region's finest film makers. **Emir Kusturica** is the best known of dozens of Yugoslav directors who trained in Prague, returning there in 1995 to shoot most of *Underground*. Slovaks, Germans, Poles and even Britons like **Lindsey Anderson** have picked up their film-making craft at the studios on Klímenská and lecture rooms on Smetanovo nábreli.

Documentary-making has tended to be overshadowed by drama and animation in Czech cinema. It proved very vulnerable to political censors demanding morale-boosting tales of Socialist Czechoslovakia. Nevertheless, Miloš Forman managed to produce a hilarious portrait of the otherwise tragic Munich Olympics in *Decathalon* (1972), and Jan Sparta produced a range of moving documentary portraits working as both cameraman and director. Recent work like *The Unseen* (1997) by Miroslav Janek about the world of blind children, and Mira Erdevički's intimate portrait of the Romany singer Věra Bílá, *Black and White in Colour* (1999), suggest that the quality Czech documentary has far from vanished.

The Czechs take their cinema seriously and show more signs of maintaining their cinematic traditions than most of their European neighbours. Czech film actors who are unknown or barely known in the west are hugely popular back home. Also, every cinema ticket sold includes a levy to the state fund for the support of Czech cinematography. Czech television recognized that it was often cheaper to support local production rather than import films, and almost all new Czech cinema has significant television funding. Like ice hockey, beer and dumplings, cinema is recognized as a significant way of promoting the country. Unlike in the 1960s, however, new Czech films have to compete at the box office with the strenuous marketing campaigns from Hollywood blockbusters, while the domestic market is too small to make Czech films a viable proposition unless they are heavily subsidized. These commercial pressures both on productions and on individual film makers themselves combine to make a New Wave unlikely.

David Charap

Books

The upsurge of interest in all things eastern European in the 1990s has had a number of positive repercussions in the publishing world. There's certainly a much wider choice of Czech fiction than ever before, and art and architecture don't lag too far behind. There's now a whole load of books published only in Prague, which cater for the city's large English-speaking ex-pat community, and which are well-nigh impossible to obtain anywhere else (a list of English-language bookstores in Prague can be found on p.244). Where two publishers are given in the selection below, the first is the UK publisher, the second the US; o/p means the publication is out of print.

History, politics and society

Peter Demetz *Prague in Black and Gold; Scenes from the Life of a European City* (Penguin/Hill & Wang). Demetz certainly knows his subject, both academically and at first hand, having been brought up here before World War II (where his account ends). His style can be a little dry, but he is determinedly un-partisan, and refreshingly anti-nationalist in his reading of history.

R. J. W. Evans *Rudolf II and his World* (Thames & Hudson, UK). First published in 1973, and still the best account there is of the alchemy-mad emperor, but not as salacious as one might hope.

Jan Kaplan and Krystyna Nosarzewska *Prague: The Turbulent Century* (Könemann, Prague). This is the first real attempt to cover the twentieth-century history of Prague with all its warts. The text isn't as good as it should be, but the book is worth it just for the incredible range of photographs and images from the century.

Karel Kaplan *The Short March: The Communist Takeover in Czechoslovakia, 1945–48* (C. Hurst Co, UK); *Report on the Murder of the General Secretary* (I. B. Tauris/Ohio State University Press, o/p). *The Short March* is an excellent account of the electoral rise and rise of the Communists in Czechoslovakia after the war, which culminated in the bloodless coup of February 1948. *Report on the Murder of the General Secretary* is a detailed study of the most famous of the anti-Semitic Stalinist show trials, that of Rudolf Slánský, number two in the Party until his arrest.

Callum MacDonald *The Killing of SS Obergruppenführer Reinhard Heydrich* (Macmillan/Da Capo). Gripping account of the build-up to the most successful and controversial act of wartime resistance, which took place in May 1942, and prompted horrific reprisals by the Nazis on the Czechs.

Callum MacDonald and Jan Kaplan *Prague in the Shadow of the Swastika* (Quartet, UK). Excellent account of the city under Nazi occupation, with an incisive, readable text illustrated by copious black-and-white photos.

Jan Musil (ed) *The End of Czechoslovakia* (Central European University Press). Academics from both the Czech and Slovak Republics attempt to explain why Czechoslovakia split into two countries just at the point when it seemed so successful.

Derek Sayer *The Coasts of Bohemia* (Princeton). A very readable cultural history, concentrating on Bohemia and Prague, which aims to dispel the ignorance shown by the Shakespearean quote of the title, and particularly illuminating on the subject of twentieth-century artists.

R. W. Seton-Watson *The History of the Czechs and Slovaks* (Shoe String Press US, o/p). Seton-Watson's informed and balanced account, written during World War II, is hard to beat. The Seton-Watsons were lifelong Slavophiles but maintained a scholarly distance in their writing, rare amongst émigré historians.

Kieran Williams *The Prague Spring and its Aftermath: Czechoslovak Politics, 1968-70* (CUP). Drawing on declassified archives, this book analyzes the attempted reforms under Dubček and takes a new look at the Prague Spring.

Elizabeth Wiskemann *Czechs and Germans* (Macmillan, o/p/AMS Press, o/p). Researched and written in the build-up towards Munich, this is the most fascinating and fair treatment of the Sudeten problem. Meticulous in her detail, vast in her scope, Wiskemann manages to suffuse the weighty text with enough anecdotes to keep you gripped. Unique.

Essays, memoirs and biographies

Margarete Buber-Neumann *Milena* (Schocken/Arcade). A moving biography of Milena Jesenská, one of interwar Prague's most beguiling characters, who befriended the author while they were both interned in Ravensbrück concentration camp.

Karel Čapek *Talks with T. G. Masaryk* (Catbird Press). Čapek was a personal (and political) friend of Masaryk, and his diaries, journals, reminiscences and letters give great insights into the man who personified the First Republic.

Jana Cerná *Kafka's Milena* (Souvenir Press/Northwestern University Press). Another biography of Milena Jesenská, this time written by her daughter, a surrealist poet, whose own works were banned under the Communists.

Timothy Garton Ash *We The People: The Revolutions of 89* (Penguin/Vintage). A personal, anecdotal, eye-witness account of the Velvet Revolution (and the events in Poland, Berlin and Budapest). By far the most compelling of all the post-1989 books. Published as *The Magic Lantern* in the US.

Patrick Leigh Fermor *A Time of Gifts* (Penguin). The first volume of Leigh Fermor's trilogy based on his epic walk along the Rhine and Danube rivers in 1933–34. In the last quarter of the book he reaches Czechoslovakia, indulging in a quick jaunt to Prague before crossing the border into Hungary. Written forty years later in dense, luscious and highly crafted prose, it's an evocative and poignant insight into the culture of *Mitteleuropa* between the wars.

Václav Havel *Living in Truth* (Faber); *Letters to Olga* (Faber/Holt); *Open Letters: Selected Prose; Disturbing the Peace; Summer Meditations* (all Faber/Vintage); *The Art of the Impossible* (Fromm, US). The first essay in *Living in Truth* is "Power of the Powerless", Havel's lucid, damning indictment of the inactivity of the Czechoslovak masses in the face of "normalization". *Letters to Olga* is a collection of Havel's letters written under great duress (and heavy censorship) from prison in the early 1980s to his wife, Olga – by turns philosophizing, nagging, effusing, whingeing. *Disturbing the Peace* is probably Havel's most accessible work yet: a series of autobiographical questions and answers in which he talks interestingly about his childhood, the events of 1968 when he was in Liberec, and the path to Charter 77 and beyond (though not including his reactions to being thrust into the role of president). *Summer Meditations* are post-1989 essays by the playwright-president, while *The Art of the Impossible: Politics as Morality in Practice*, is a collection of speeches given since he became the country's president in 1990.

Václav Havel et al *Power of the Powerless* (M. E. Sharpe, US). A collection of essays by leading Chartists, kicking off with Havel's seminal title-piece. Other contributors range from the dissident Marxist Petr Uhl to devout Catholics like Václav Benda.

Miroslav Holub *The Dimension of the Present Moment* (Faber & Faber, UK); *Shedding Life: Disease, Politics and Other Human Conditions* (Milkweed, US). Two books of short philosophical musings/essays on life and the universe by this unusual and clever scientist-poet.

John Keane *Vaclav Havel: A Political Tragedy in Six Acts* (Bloomsbury, UK). The first book to tell both sides of the Havel story: Havel the dissident playwright and civil rights activist who played a key role in the 1989 Velvet Revolution, and Havel the ageing and increasingly ill president, who has, in many people's opinion, simply stayed on the stage too long.

Antonín Klimek and Zbyněk Zeman *The Life of Edvard Bene Beneš: Czechoslovakia in Peace & War* (Clarendon Press). Beneš is a fascinating figure in Czech history, revered as number two to Masaryk while the latter was alive, only to find himself held responsible firstly for the Munich debacle, and secondly for allowing the Communists into power in 1948.

Heda Margolius Kovaly *Prague Farewell* (Orion/Holmes & Meier). An autobiography that starts in the concentration camps of World War II, ending with the author's flight from Czechoslovakia in 1968. Married to one of the Party officials executed in the 1952 Slánský trial, she tells her story simply and without bitterness. The best account there is on the fear and paranoia whipped up during the Stalinist terror. Published as *Under a Cruel Star* in the US.

Angelo Maria Ripellino *Magic Prague* (Picador/University of California Press). A wide-ranging look at the bizarre array of historical and literary characters who have lived in Prague, from the mad antics of the court of Rudolf II to the escapades of Jaroslav Hašek. Scholarly, rambling, richly and densely written – unique and recommended.

William Shawcross *Remember Dubček: Dubček and Czechoslovakia 1918–1990* (Hogarth Press, o/p/Simon & Schuster, o/p). Biography of the most famous figure of the 1968 Prague Spring, updated to include Dubček's role in the 1989 Velvet Revolution.

Josef Škvorecký *Talkin' Moscow Blues* (Faber/Ecco Press). Without doubt the most user-friendly of Škvorecký's works, containing a collection of essays on his wartime childhood, Czech jazz, literature and contemporary politics, all told in his inimitable, irreverent and infuriating way. Published as *Head for the Blues* in the US.

Ludvík Vaculík *A Cup of Coffee with My Interrogator* (Readers International). A Party member until 1968, and signatory of Charter 77, Vaculík revived the *feuilleton* – a short political critique once much loved in central Europe. This collection dates from 1968 onwards.

Zbyněk Zeman *The Masaryks – The Making of Czechoslovakia* (I. B. Tauris, UK). Written in the 1970s while Zeman was in exile, this is a very readable, none-too-sentimental biography of the country's founder Tomáš Garrigue Masaryk, and his son Jan Masaryk, the postwar Foreign Minister who died in mysterious circumstances shortly after the 1948 Communist coup.

Czech fiction

Josef Čapek *Stories about Doggie and Cat* (Albatros, Prague). Josef Čapek (Karel's older brother) was a Cubist artist of some renown, and also a children's writer. These simple stories about a dog and a cat are wonderfully illustrated, and seriously postmodern.

Karel Čapek *Towards a Radical Centre* (Catbird Press); *The War with the Newts* (Penguin/Catbird Press); *Nine Fairy Tales* (Catbird Press). Karel Čapek was the literary and journalistic spokesperson for Masaryk's First Republic, but he's better known in the West for his plays, some of which feature in the anthology, *Towards a Radical Centre*.

Ladislav Fuks *The Cremator* (Marion Boyars); *Mr Theodore Mundstock* (Four Walls Eight Windows, US). Two readable novels – the first about a man who works in a crematorium in occupied Prague, and is about to throw in his lot with the Nazis when he discovers that his wife is half-Jewish. The second is set in 1942 Prague, as the city's Jews wait to be transported to Terezín.

Jaroslav Hašek *The Good Soldier Švejk* (Penguin/Viking). The former, by Bohemia's most bohemian writer, is a rambling, picaresque tale of Czechoslovakia's famous fictional fifth columnist, *Švejk*, who wreaks havoc in the Austro-Hungarian army during World War I.

Václav Havel *The Memorandum* (Eyre-Methuen, o/p/Grove-Atlantic, o/p); *Three Vaněk Plays* (Faber, o/p); *Selected Plays 1984–87* (Faber, UK). Havel's plays are not renowned for being easy to read (or watch). *The Memorandum* is one of his earliest works, a classic absurdist drama that, in many ways, sets the tone for much of his later work, of which the *Three Vaněk Plays*, featuring Ferdinand Vaněk, Havel's alter ego, are perhaps the most successful. The 1980s collection includes *Largo Desolato*, *Temptation* and *Redevelopment*; freedom of thought, Faustian opportunism and town planning as metaphors of life under the Communists.

Bohumil Hrabal *Closely Observed Trains/Closely Watched Trains* (Abacus/Northwestern University Press); *I Served the King of England* (Picador/Vintage); *Too Loud a Solitude* (Deutsch/Harcourt Brace); *The Little Town Where Time Stood Still* (Abacus/Pantheon, o/p); *Dancing Lessons* (Harvill/Harcourt Brace). A thoroughly mischievous writer, Hrabal's slim but superb *Closely Observed Trains* is a postwar classic, set in the last days of the war and relentlessly unheroic; it was made into an equally brilliant film by Jiří Menzl. *I Served the King of England* follows the antihero Dítě, who works at the *Hotel Paříž*, through the decade after 1938. *Too Loud a Solitude*, about a waste-paper disposer under the Communists, has also been made into a film, again by Menzl. *The Little Town Where Time Stood Still* was the last work Hrabal completed before his death in 1997. *Dancing Lessons* is a short tale from 1964, composed of a single sentence, a rambling monologue by a 70-year-old shoemaker to six sunbathing women.

Alois Jirásek *Old Czech Legends* (Forest Books/Dufour). A major figure in the nineteenth-century Czech *národní obrození*, Jirásek popularized Bohemia's legendary past. This collection includes all the classic texts, as well as the story of the founding of the city by the prophetess Libuše.

Franz Kafka *The Collected Novels of Franz Kafka*; *The Complete Short Stories*; *Letters to Felice*; *Diaries* (all Penguin/Vintage). A German-Jewish

Praguer, Kafka has drawn the darker side of central Europe – its claustrophobia, paranoia and unfathomable bureaucracy – better than anyone else, both in a rural setting, as in *The Castle*, and in an urban one, in one of the great novels of the twentieth century, *The Trial*.

Ivan Klíma *A Summer Affair* (Penguin, UK); *My Merry Mornings: Stories from Prague* (Readers International); *My First Loves* (Penguin/Norton); *Love and Garbage* (Penguin/Vintage); *Judge on Trial* (Vintage); *My Golden Trades* (Penguin/Macmillan); *Waiting for the Dark, Waiting for the Light* (Penguin/Picador); *The Spirit of Prague* (Granta); *Ultimate Intimacy* (Granta/Grove-Atlantic). A survivor of Terezín, Klíma is another writer in the Kundera mould as far as sexual politics goes, but his stories are a lot lighter. *Judge on Trial*, written in the 1970s, is one of his best, concerning the moral dilemmas of a Communist judge. *Waiting for the Dark, Waiting for the Light* is a pessimistic novel set before, during and after the Velvet Revolution of 1989. *The Spirit of Prague* is a very readable collection of biographical and more general articles and essays on subjects ranging from Klíma's childhood experiences in Terezín to the current situation in Prague. *Ultimate Intimacy* is his latest novel, set in the cynical post-revolutionary Czech Republic.

Milan Kundera *Laughable Loves; The Farewell Party; The Joke; The Book of Laughter and Forgetting; The Unbearable Lightness of Being; The Art of the Novel; Immortality; Slowness; Identity; Testaments Betrayed* (all Faber/HarperCollins); *Life is Elsewhere* (Faber/Penguin). Milan Kundera is the country's most popular writer – at least with non-Czechs. His books are very obviously "political", particularly *The Book of Laughter* and *Forgetting*, which led the Communists to revoke Kundera's citizenship. *The Joke*, written while he was still living in Czechoslovakia and in many ways his best work, is set in the very unfunny era of the Stalinist purges. Its clear, humorous style is far removed from the carefully poised posturing of his most famous work, *The Unbearable Lightness of Being*, set in and after 1968, and successfully turned into a film some twenty years later. *Slowness* is a slim volume set in France, and his first work written in French; *Identity* is his latest novel, a series of slightly detached musings on the human condition that is typical of his later works. *Testaments Betrayed*, on the other hand, is a fascinating series of essays about a range of subjects from the formation of historical reputation to the problems of translations.

Arnošt Lustig *Diamonds of the Night; Night and Hope* (both Quartet/Northwestern University Press); *Darkness Casts No Shadow* (Quartet/Avon, o/p); *A Prayer for Kateřina Horovitová* (Overlook Press in US); *Indecent Dreams* (Northwestern University Press in US). A Prague Jew exiled since 1968, Lustig spent World War II in Terezín, Buchenwald and Auschwitz, and his novels and short stories are consistently set in the Terezín camp.

Gustav Meyrink *The Golem* (Dedalus/Ariadne); *The Angel of the West Window* (Dedalus/Ariadne). Meyrink was another of Prague's weird and wonderful characters who started out as a bank manager, but soon became involved in cabalism, alchemy and drug experimentation. His *Golem*, based on Rabbi Löw's monster, is one of the classic versions of the tale, set in the Jewish quarter. *The Angel at the West Window* is a historical novel about John Dee, an English alchemist invited to Prague in the late sixteenth century by Rudolf II.

Jan Neruda *Prague Tales* (Central European University Press). Not to be confused with the Chilean Pablo Neruda (who took his name from the Czech writer), these are short, bittersweet snapshots of life in Malá Strana at the close of the last century.

Karel Poláček *What Ownership's All About* (Catbird Press/Independent Publishers Group). A darkly comic novel set in a Prague tenement block, dealing with the issue of fascism and appeasement, by a Jewish-Czech Praguer who died in the camps in 1944.

Rainer Maria Rilke *Two Stories of Prague* (University Press of New England, US). Both tales deal with the artificiality of Prague's now defunct German community, whose claustrophobic parochialism drove the author into self-imposed exile in 1899 (for more on Rilke see *Poetry*, p.278).

Peter Sís *The Three Golden Keys* (Pavilion/Doubleday). Short, hauntingly illustrated children's book set in Prague, by Czech-born American Sís.

Josef Škvorecký *The Cowards; The Miracle Game* (both Faber/Norton); *The Swell Season; The Bass Saxophone* (both Vintage/Ecco Press); *Miss Silver's Past; Dvořák in Love* (both Vintage/Norton); *The Engineer of Human Souls*

(Vintage/Dalkey Archive); *The Republic of Whores* (Faber/Ecco Press). A relentless anti-Communist, Škvorecký is typically Bohemian in his bawdy sense of humour and irreverence for all high moralizing. *The Cowards* (which briefly saw the light of day in 1958) is the tale of a group of irresponsible young men in the last days of the war, an antidote to the lofty prose from official authors at the time, but hampered by its dated Americanized translation.

Josef Škvorecký *The Mournful Demeanor of Lieutenant Boruvka; Sins for Father Knox; The Return of Lieutenant Boruvka; The End of Lieutenant Boruvka* (all Faber & Faber/Norton). Less well-known (and understandably so) are Škvorecký's detective stories featuring a podgy, depressive Czech cop, which he wrote in the 1960s at a time when his more serious work was banned. The later book, *The Return of Lieutenant Boruvka,* is set in Škvorecký's new home, Canada.

Zdena Tomin *Stalin's Shoe; The Coast of Bohemia* (both Dent, UK, o/p). Although Czech-born, Tomin writes in English (the language of her exile since 1980); she has a style and fluency all her own. *Stalin's Shoe* is the compelling and complex story of a girl coming to terms with her Stalinist childhood, while *The Coast of Bohemia* is based on Tomin's experiences of the late 1970s dissident movement, when she was an active member of Charter 77.

Ludvík Vaculík *The Guinea Pigs* (Northwestern University Press, US). Vaculík was expelled from the Party in the midst of the 1968 Prague Spring; this novel, set in Prague, catalogues the slow dehumanization of Czech society in the aftermath of the Soviet invasion.

Jiří Weil *Life With a Star* (Northwestern University Press); *Mendelssohn is on the Roof* (Collins, o/p/Farra, Straus & Giroux). Two novels written just after the war and based on Weil's experiences as a Czech Jew in hiding under Nazi-occupied Prague.

Poetry

Jaroslav Čejka, Michal Černík and Karel Sys *The New Czech Poetry* (Bloodaxe/Dufour). Slim, but interesting volume by three Czech poets; all in their late forties, all very different. Čejka is of the Holub school, and comes across simply and strongly; Černík is similarly direct; Sýs the least convincing.

Sylva Fischerová *The Tremor of Racehorses: Selected Poems* (Bloodaxe/Dufour). Poet and novelist, Fischerová is one of the new generation of Czech writers, though in many ways she is continuing in the Holub tradition. Her poems are by turns powerful, obtuse and personal, as was necessary to escape censorship during the late 1980s.

Josef Hanzlík *Selected Poems* (Bloodaxe/Dufour). Refreshingly accessible collection of poems written over the last 35 years by a poet of Havel's generation.

Miroslav Holub *Supposed to Fly; The Jingle Bell Principle; Poems Before and After* (all Bloodaxe/Dufour); *Vanishing Lung Syndrome* (Faber/Oberlin College Press). Holub is a scientist and scholar, and his poetry reflects this unique fusion of master poet and chief immunologist. Regularly banned in his own country, he is the Czech poet *par excellence* – classically trained, erudite, liberal and westward-leaning. *Vanishing Lung Syndrome* is his latest volume; the other two are collections.

Rainer Maria Rilke *Selected Poetry* (Picador/Vintage). Rilke's upbringing was unexceptional, except that his mother brought him up as a girl until the age of six. In his adult life, he became one of Prague's leading authors of the interwar period and probably the best-known poet outside Czechoslovakia.

Jaroslav Seifert *The Poetry of Jaroslav Seifert* (Catbird Press, US). Czechoslovakia's only author to win the Nobel prize for literature, Seifert was a founder-member of the Communist Party and the avant-garde arts movement *Devětsil*, later falling from grace and signing the Charter in his old age. His longevity means that his work covers some of the most turbulent times in Czechoslovak history, but his irrepressible lasciviousness has been known to irritate.

Literature by foreign writers

David Brierley *On Leaving a Prague Window* (Warner UK). A very readable thriller set in post-Communist Prague, which shows that past connection with dissidents can still lead to violence.

Bruce Chatwin *Utz* (Penguin). Chatwin is from the "exotic" school of travel writers, hence this slim, intriguing and mostly true-to-life account of an avid crockery collector from Prague's Jewish quarter.

Lionel Davidson *The Night of Wenceslas* (Reed Consumer Books/St Martin's Press). A Cold War thriller set in pre-1968 Czechoslovakia that launched Davidson's career as a spy-writer.

Sue Gee *Letters from Prague* (Arrow, UK). The central character in this book falls in love with a Czech student in England in 1968, but returns home when the Russians invade. Twenty years later, together with her ten-year-old daughter, she goes in search of him.

Martha Gellhorn *A Stricken Field* (Virago, o/p /Penguin, o/p). The story of an American journalist who arrives in Prague just as the Nazis march into Sudetenland. Based on the author's own experiences, this is a fascinating, if sentimental, insight into the panic and confusion in "rump" Czecho-Slovakia after the Munich Diktat. First published in 1940.

Philip Roth *Prague Orgy* (Vintage). A novella about a world-famous Jewish novelist (ie Roth) who goes to Communist Prague to recover some unpublished Jewish stories. Prague "is the city I imagined the Jews would buy when they had accumulated enough money for a homeland", according to Roth. A coda to Roth's Zuckerman trilogy.

Art, photography and film

The Castle of Prague and its Treasures (Flint River Press o/p/Vedome o/p). Heavy, coffee-table book with excellent colour photos of all the main sights, plus exclusive coverage of the castle interiors – many by Plečnik – which remain closed to the public.

Czech Modernism 1900–1945 (Little Brown o/p/Museum of Fine Arts, Houston). Wide-ranging and superbly illustrated, this American publication records the journey of the Czech modern movement through Cubism and Surrealism to Modernism and the avant-garde. The accompanying essays by leading art and film critics cover fine art, architecture, film, photography and theatre.

Devětsil – Czech Avant-Garde Art, Architecture and Design of the 1920s and 30s (Museum of Modern Art, Oxford, UK). Published to accompany the 1990 Devětsil exhibition at Oxford, this is the definitive account of interwar Czechoslovakia's most famous left-wing art movement, which attracted artists from every discipline.

Disorientations – Eastern Europe in Transition (Thames & Hudson, UK). A self-explanatory book of photos accompanied by Pavel Kohout's text.

Ivan Margolius *Prague – A guide to Twentieth-century Architecture* (Ellipsis London/Knickerbocker). Dinky little pocket guide to all the major modern landmarks of Prague (including a black-and-white photo of each building), from the Art Nouveau Obecní dům, through functionalism and Cubism, to the Fred & Ginger building, currently in construction.

Language

The official language of the Czech Republic is Czech (český), a highly complex western Slav tongue. Any attempt to speak Czech will be heartily appreciated, though don't be discouraged if people seem not to understand, as most will be unaccustomed to hearing foreigners stumble through their language. If you don't know any Czech, brush up on your German, since, among the older generation at least, this is still the most widely spoken second language. Russian, once the compulsory second language, has been practically wiped off the school curriculum, and the number of English-speakers has been steadily increasing, especially among the younger generation.

Pronunciation

English-speakers often find Czech impossibly difficult to pronounce. In fact, it's not half as daunting as it might first appear from the "traffic jams of consonants", as Patrick Leigh-Fermor put it, which crop up on the page. An illustration of this is the Czech tongue-twister, *strč prst skrz krk* (stick your finger down your neck). Apart from a few special letters, each letter and syllable is pronounced as

BASIC WORDS AND PHRASES

Yes	*ano*	Yesterday	*včera*
No	*ne*	Tomorrow	*zítra*
Excuse me/don't mention it	*prosím/není zač*	The day after tomorrow	*pozítří*
Sorry	*pardon*	Now	*hnet*
Thank you	*děkuju*	Later	*později*
Bon appétit	*dobrou chuť*	Leave me alone	*dej mi pokoj*
Bon voyage	*šťastnou cestu*	Go away	*jdi pryč*
Hello/goodbye (informal)	*ahoj*	Help!	*pomoc!*
Goodbye (formal)	*na shledanou*	This one	*tento*
Good day	*dobrý den*	A little	*trochu*
Good morning	*dobré ráno*	Large/small	*velký/malý*
Good evening	*dobrý večer*	More/less	*více/méně*
Good night (when leaving)	*dobrou noc*	Good/bad	*dobrý/špatný*
How are you?	*jak se máte?*	Hot/cold	*horký/studený*
Today	*dnes*	With/without	*s/bez*

GETTING AROUND

Over here	*tady*	By taxi	*taxíkem*
Over there	*tam*	Ticket	*jízdenka/lístek*
Left	*nalevo*	Return ticket	*zpateční*
Right	*napravo*	Railway station	*nádraží*
Straight on	*rovně*	Bus station	*autobusové nádraží*
Where is . . .?	*kde je . . .?*	Bus stop	*autobusová zastávka*
How do I get to Prague?	*jak se dostanu do Prahy ?*	When's the next train to Prague?	*kdy jede další vlak do Prahy?*
How do I get to the university?	*jak se dostanu k univerzitě?*	Is it going to Prague?	*jede to do Prahy?*
By bus	*autobusem*	Do I have to change?	*musím přestupovat?*
By train	*vlakem*	Do I need a reservation?	*musím mit místenku?*
By car	*autem*		
On foot	*pěšky*		

QUESTIONS AND ANSWERS

Do you speak English?	*mluvíte anglicky?*
I don't speak German	*nemluvím německy*
I don't understand	*nerozumím*
I understand	*rozumím*
Speak slowly	*mluvíte pomalu*
How do you say that in Czech?	*jak se tohle řekne česky?*
Could you write it down for me?	*mužete mí to napsat?*
What	*co*
Where	*kde*
When	*kdy*
Why	*proč*
How much is it?	*kolík to stojí?*
Are there any rooms available?	*máte volné pokoje?*
I would like a double room	*chtěl bych dvou lůžkovy pokoj*
For one night	*na jednu noc*
With shower	*se sprchou*
Is this seat free?	*je tu volna?*
May we (sit down)?	*můžeme (se sednout)?*
The bill please	*zaplatím prosím*
Do you have . . .?	*máte . . .?*
We don't have	*nemáme*
We do have	*máme*

SOME SIGNS

Entrance	*vchod*
Exit	*východ*
Toilets	*záchody/toalety*
Men	*muži*
Women	*ženy*
Ladies	*dámy*
Gentlemen	*pánové*
Open	*otevřeno*
Closed	*zavřeno*
Danger!	*pozor!*
Hospital	*nemocnice*
No smoking	*kouření zakázáno*
No bathing	*koupání zakázáno*
No entry	*vstup zakázán*
Arrival	*příjezd*
Departure	*odjezd*
Police	*policie*

DAYS OF THE WEEK

Monday	*pondělí*
Tuesday	*uterý*
Wednesday	*středa*
Thursday	*čtvrtek*
Friday	*pátek*
Saturday	*sobota*
Sunday	*neděle*
Year	*rok*
Week	*týden*
Month	*měsíc*
Day	*den*

MONTHS OF THE YEAR

Many Slav languages have their own highly individual systems in which the words for the names of the months are descriptive nouns – sometimes beautifully apt for the month in question.

January	*leden* – ice
February	*únor* – hibernation
March	*březen* – birch
April	*duben* – oak
May	*květen* – blossom
June	*červen* – red
July	*červenec* – redder
August	*srpen* – sickle
September	*září* – blazing
October	*říjen* – rutting
November	*listopad* – leaves falling
December	*prosinec* – slaughter of pigs

NUMBERS

1	*jeden*
2	*dva*
3	*tří*
4	*čtyři*
5	*pět*
6	*šest*
7	*sedm*
8	*osm*
9	*devět*
10	*deset*
11	*jedenáct*
12	*dvanáct*
13	*třináct*
14	*čtrnáct*
15	*patnáct*
16	*šestnáct*
17	*sedmnáct*
18	*osmnáct*
19	*devatenáct*
20	*dvacet*
21	*dvacetjedna*
30	*třicet*
40	*čtyřicet*
50	*padesát*
60	*šedesát*
70	*sedmdesát*
80	*osmdesát*
90	*devadesát*
100	*sto*
101	*sto jedna*
155	*sto padesát pět*
200	*dvě stě*
300	*tři sta*
400	*čtyři sta*
500	*pět set*
600	*šest set*
700	*sedm set*
800	*osm set*
900	*devět set*
1000	*tisíc*

it's written – the trick is always to **stress the first syllable** of a word, no matter what its length; otherwise you'll render it unintelligible.

The Alphabet

In the Czech alphabet, letters which feature a **háček** (as in the *č* of the word itself) are considered separate letters and appear in Czech indexes immediately after their more familiar cousins. More confusingly, the consonant combination *ch* is also considered as a separate letter and appears in Czech indexes after the letter *h*. In the index in this book, we use the English system, so words beginning with *c*, *č* and *ch* all appear under *c*.

Short and long vowels

Czech has both short and long vowels (the latter being denoted by a variety of accents). The trick here is to lengthen the vowel without affecting the principal stress of the word, which is invariably on the first syllable.

a like the u in c**u**p
á as in f**a**ther
e as in p**e**t
é as in f**ai**r
ě like the ye in **ye**s
i or y as in p**i**t
í or ý as in s**ea**t
o as in n**o**t
ó as in d**oo**r
u like the oo in b**oo**k
U or ú like the oo in f**oo**l

Vowel combinations and diphthongs

There are very few diphthongs in Czech, so any combinations of vowels other than those below should be pronounced as two separate syllables.

au like the ou in f**ou**l
ou like the oe in f**oe**

A Czech language guide

There are very few **teach-yourself Czech** courses available and each has drawbacks. *Colloquial Czech* by James Naughton is good, but a bit fast and furious for most people; *Teach Yourself Czech* is a bit dry for some. The best portable **dictionary for Czech** is the *kapesní slovník*, most easily purchased in Prague. The *Rough Guides* also produces a useful Czech phrasebook.

Consonants and accents

There are no silent consonants, but it's worth remembering that *r* and *l* can form a syllable if standing between two other consonants or at the end of a word, as in Brno (Br–no) or Vltava (Vl–ta–va). The consonants listed below are those which differ substantially from the English. Accents look daunting – particularly the háček, which appears above *c, d, l, n, r, s, t* and *z* – but the only one which causes a lot of problems is ř, probably the most difficult letter to say in the entire language – even Czech toddlers have to be taught how to say it.

c like the **ts** in boats
č like the **ch** in chicken
ch like the **ch** in the Scottish loch
ď like the **d** in duped
g always as in goat, never as in general
h always as in have, but more energetic
j like the **y** in yoke
kd pronounced as **gd**
ľ like the **lli** in colliery
mě pronounced as mnye
ň like the **n** in nuance
p softer than the English **p**
r as in rip, but often rolled
ř like the sound of **r** and **ž** combined
š like the **sh** in shop
ť like the **t** in tutor
ž like the **s** in pleasure; at the end of a word like the **sh** in shop

Prague's leading personalities – past and present

Beneš, Edvard (1884–1948). Hero to some, traitor to others, Beneš was president from 1935 until 1938 – when he resigned, having refused to lead the country into bloodshed over the Munich Crisis – and again from 1945 until 1948, when he aquiesced to the Communist coup.

Čapek Josef (1887–1945). Cubist artist and writer and illustrator of children's books, Josef was older brother to the more famous Karel (see below); he died in Belsen concentration camp.

Čapek, Karel (1890–1938). Czech writer, journalist and unofficial spokesperson for the First Republic. His most famous works are *The Insect Play* and *R.U.R.*, which introduced the word *robot* into the English language.

Dobrovský, Josef (1753–1829). Jesuit-taught pioneer in Czech philology. Wrote the seminal text *The History of Czech Language and Literature*.

Dubček, Alexander (1921–92). Slovak Communist who became First Secretary in January 1968, at the beginning of the Prague Spring. Expelled from the Party in 1969, but returned to become speaker in the federal parliament after 1989, before being killed in a car crash in 1992.

Dvořák, Antonín (1841–1904). Perhaps the most famous of all Czech composers. His best-known work is the *New World Symphony*, inspired by an extensive sojourn in the USA.

Fučík, Julius (1903–43). Communist journalist murdered by the Nazis, whose prison writings, *Notes from the Gallows*, were obligatory reading in the 1950s. Hundreds of streets were named after him, but doubts about the authenticity of the work, and general hostility towards the man, have made him *persona non grata*.

Gottwald, Klement (1896–1953). One of the founders of the KSČ, General Secretary from 1927, Prime Minister from 1946 to 1948, and President from 1948 to 1953, Gottwald is universally abhorred for his role in the show trials of the 1950s.

Hašek, Jaroslav (1883–1923). Anarchist, dog-breeder, lab assistant, bigamist, cabaret artist and People's Commissar in the Red Army, Hašek was one of prewar Prague's most colourful characters, who wrote the famous *Good Soldier Nvejk* and died from alcohol abuse in 1923.

Havel, Václav (1936–). Absurdist playwright of the 1960s, who became a leading spokesperson of Charter 77 and, following the Velvet Revolution, the country's first post-Communist president.

Havlíček-Borovský, Karel (1821–56). Satirical poet, journalist and nationalist, exiled to the Tyrol by the Austrian authorities after 1848.

Hrabal, Bohumil (1936–97). Writer and bohemian, whose novels were banned under the Communists, but revered worldwide.

Hus, Jan (1370–1415). Rector of Prague University and reformist preacher who was burnt at the stake as a heretic by the Council of Constance.

Husák, Gustáv (died 1991). Slovak Communist who was sentenced to life imprisonment in the show trials of the 1950s, released in 1960, and eventually became General Secretary and President following the Soviet invasion. Resigned in favour of Havel in December 1989.

Jirásek, Alois (1851–1930). Writer who popularized Czech legends for both children and adults and became a key figure in the Czech national revival.

Jungmann, Josef (1773–1847). Prolific Czech translator and author of the seminal *History of Czech Literature* and the first Czech dictionary.

Kafka, Franz (1883–1924). German-Jewish Praguer who worked as an insurance clerk in Prague for most of his life, and also wrote some of the most influential novels of the twentieth century, most notably *The Trial*.

Kelley, Edward. English occultist who was summoned to Prague by Rudolf II, but eventually incurred the wrath of the emperor and was imprisoned in Kokořín castle.

Kepler, Johannes (1571–1630). German Protestant forced to leave Linz for Denmark because of the Counter-Reformation. Succeeded Tycho de Brahe as Rudolf II's chief astronomer. His observations of the planets became the basis of the laws of planetary motion.

Kisch, Egon Erwin (1885–1948). German-Jewish Praguer who became one of the city's most famous investigative journalists.

Klaus, Václav. Known somewhat bitterly as "Santa Klaus". Prime Minister from 1992 to 97, confirmed Thatcherite, and driving force behind the country's present economic reforms.

Komenský, Jan Amos (1592–1670). Leader of the Protestant Czech Brethren. Forced to flee the country and settle in England during the Counter-Reformation. Better known to English-speakers as Comenius.

Mácha, Karel Hynek (1810–36). Romantic nationalist poet, great admirer of Byron and Keats and, like them, died young. His most famous poem is *Maj*, published just months before his death.

Masaryk, Jan Garrigue (1886–1958). Son of the founder of the republic (see below), Foreign Minister in the postwar government and the only non-Communist in Gottwald's cabinet when the Communists took over in February 1948. Died ten days after the coup in suspicious circumstances.

Masaryk, Tomáš Garrigue (1850–1937). Professor of Philosophy at Prague University, President of the Republic from 1918 to 1935. His name is synonymous with the First Republic and was removed from all street signs after the 1948 coup. Now back with a vengeance.

Mucha, Alfons (1860–1939). Moravian graphic artist and designer whose Art Nouveau posters and artwork for Sarah Bernhardt brought him international fame. After the founding of Czechoslovakia, he returned to the country to design stamps, bank notes, and complete a cycle of giant canvases on Czech nationalist themes.

Němcová, Božena (1820–62). Highly popular writer who became involved with the nationalist movement and shocked many with her unorthodox behaviour. Her most famous book is *Grandmother*.

Neruda, Jan (1834–91). Poet and journalist for the *Národní listy*. Wrote some famous short stories describing Prague's Malá Strana.

Palacký, František (1798–1876). Nationalist historian, Czech MP in Vienna and leading figure in the events of 1848.

Purkyně, Jan Evangelista (1787–1869). Czech doctor, natural scientist and pioneer in experimental physiology who became professor of physiology at Prague and then at Wrocław University.

Rieger, Ladislav (1818–1903). Nineteenth-century Czech politician and one of the leading figures in the events of 1848 and the aftermath.

Rilke, Rainer Maria (1876–1926). Despite having been brought up as a girl for the first six years of his life, Rilke ended up as an officer in the Austrian army, and wrote some of the city's finest German *fin-de-siècle* poetry.

Smetana, Bedřich (1824–84). Popular Czech composer and fervent nationalist whose *Má vlast* (My Homeland) traditionally opens the Prague Spring Music Festival.

Svoboda, Ludvík (1895–1979). Victorious Czech General from World War II, who acquiesced to the 1948 Communist coup and was Communist President from 1968 to 1975.

Tycho Brahe (1546–1601). Ground-breaking Danish astronomer, who was summoned to Prague by Rudolf II in 1597, only to die from overdrinking in 1601.

Tyl, Josef Kajetán (1808–56). Czech playwright and composer of the Czech half of the national anthem, *Where is my Home?*

Werfel, Franz (1890–1945). One of the German-Jewish literary circle, which included Kafka, Kisch and Brod.

Pižka, Jan (died 1424). Brilliant, blind military leader of the Táborites, the radical faction of the Hussites.

A glossary of Czech words and terms

brána gate.
český Bohemian.
chata chalet-type bungalow, country cottage or mountain hut.
chrám large church.
divadlo theatre.
dóm cathedral.
dům house.
dům kultury generic term for local arts and social centre; literally "House of Culture".
hora mountain.
hospoda pub.
hostinec pub.
hrad castle.
hřbitov cemetery.
kaple chapel.
katedrála cathedral.
kavárna coffee house.
klášter monastery/convent.
kostel church.
koupaliště swimming pool.
Labe River Elbe.
lanovka funicular or cable car.
les forest.
město town.
most bridge.
muzeum museum.
nábřeží embankment.
nádraží train station.
náměstí square.
ostrov island.
palác palace.
památník memorial or monument.
pasáž indoor shopping mall.
pivnice pub.
radnice town hall.
restaurace restaurant.
sad park.
sál room or hall (in a chateau or castle).
schody steps.
svatý saint; often abbreviated to sv.
třída avenue.
ulice street.
věž tower.
vinárna wine bar or cellar.
Vltava River Moldau.
vrchy hills.
výstava exhibition.
zahrada garden.
zámek chateau.

An Architectural Glossary

Ambulatory Passage round the back of the altar, in continuation of the aisles.

Art Nouveau French term for the sinuous and stylized form of architecture dating from 1900 to 1910; known as the Secession in the Czech Republic and as *Jugendstil* in Germany.

Baroque Expansive, exuberant architectural style of the seventeenth and mid-eighteenth centuries, characterized by ornate decoration, complex spatial arrangement and grand vistas.

Chancel The part of the church where the altar is placed, usually at the east end.

Empire Highly decorative Neoclassical style of architecture and decorative arts, practised in the early 1800s.

Fresco Mural painting applied to wet plaster, so that the colours immediately soak into the wall.

Functionalism Plain, boxy, modernist architectural style, prevalent in the late 1920s and 1930s in Czechoslovakia, often using plate-glass curtain walls and open-plan interiors.

Gothic Architectural style prevalent from the fourteenth to the sixteenth century, characterized by pointed arches and ribbed vaulting.

Loggia Covered area on the side of a building, often arcaded.

Nave Main body of a church, usually the western end.

Neoclassical Late eighteenth- and early-nineteenth-century style of architecture and design returning to classical Greek and Roman models as a reaction against Baroque and Rococo excesses.

Oriel A bay window, usually projecting from an upper floor.

Rococo Highly florid, fiddly, though (occasionally) graceful, style of architecture and interior design, forming the last phase of Baroque.

Romanesque Solid architectural style of the late tenth to thirteenth century, characterized by round-headed arches and geometrical precision.

Secession Linear and stylized form of architecture and decorative arts imported from Vienna as a reaction against the academic establishment.

Sgraffito Monochrome plaster decoration effected by means of scraping back the first white layer to reveal the black underneath.

Stucco Plaster used for decorative effects.

Trompe l'oeil Painting designed to fool the onlooker into believing that it is actually three-dimensional.

INDEX

D

E

F

G

P

R

S

T

U

V

W

ROUGH NEWS
THE ROUGH GUIDES
TRAVEL NOTES p.2
SOUTHWEST USA p.3
READERS' LETTERS p.4
NEPAL p.5
MUSIC & WEB REVIEWS p.6
RESEARCHING KINGSTON p.7
The view from Johannesburg
ARE WE IN AFRICA YET?
ROUGHNEWS • Winter 1997
SUBSCRIBE TO ROUGHNEWS NOW. See back page for details
The Final Countdown: The Last Days of
COLONIAL HONG KONG
RAINFOREST TOURISM

ROUGH GUIDES: Reference and Music CDs

REFERENCE

Classical Music
Classical:
100 Essential CDs
Drum'n'bass
House Music
Jazz
Music USA

Opera
Opera:
100 Essential CDs
Reggae
Reggae:
100 Essential CDs
Rock
Rock:
100 Essential CDs
Techno
World Music
World Music:
100 Essential CDs
English Football
European Football
Internet
Millennium

ROUGH GUIDE MUSIC CDs

Music of the Andes
Australian Aboriginal
Brazilian Music
Cajun & Zydeco

Classic Jazz
Music of Colombia
Cuban Music
Eastern Europe
Music of Egypt
English Roots Music
Flamenco
India & Pakistan
Irish Music
Music of Japan
Kenya & Tanzania
Native American
North African
Music of Portugal

Reggae
Salsa
Scottish Music
South African Music
Music of Spain
Tango
Tex-Mex
West African Music
World Music
World Music Vol 2
Music of Zimbabwe

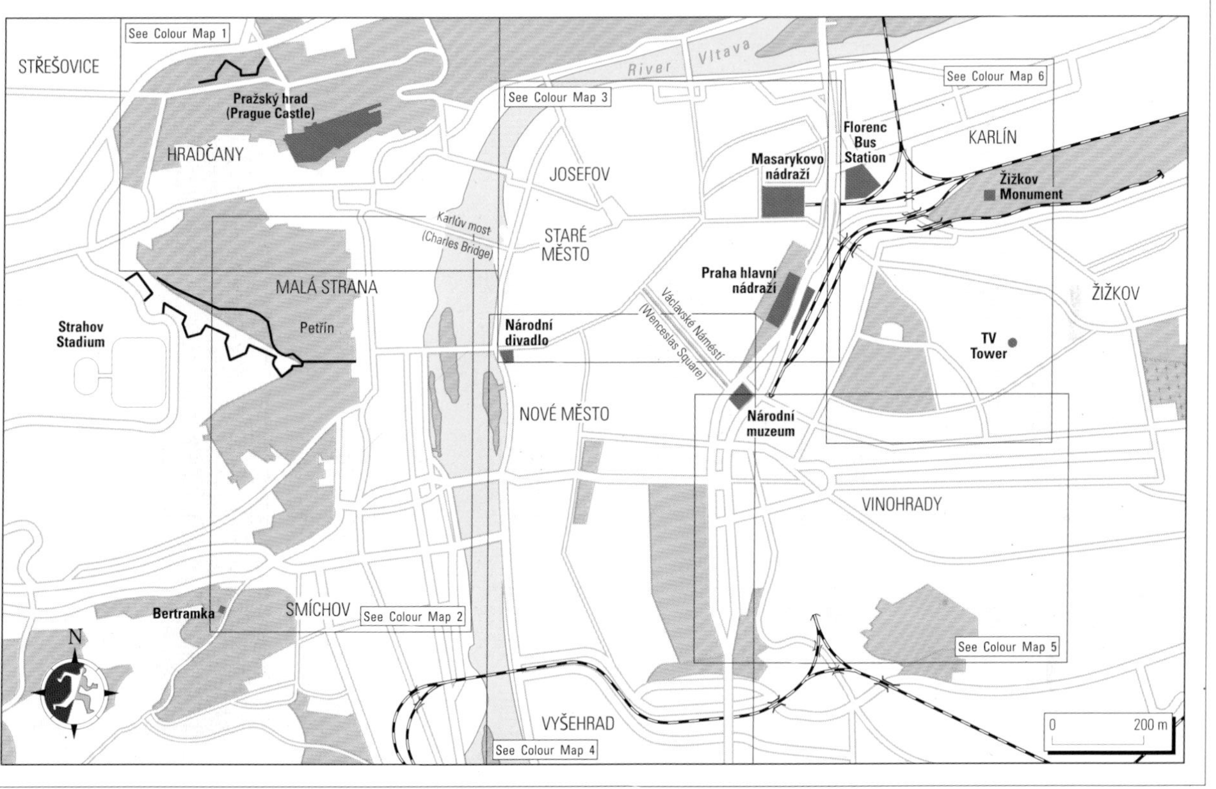

See Colour Map 1
STŘEŠOVICE
Pražský hrad
(Prague Castle)
HRADČANY
River Vltava
See Colour Map 3
See Colour Map 6
Florenc
Bus
Station
KARLÍN
Masarykovo
nádraží
Žižkov
Monument
JOSEFOV
Karlův most
(Charles Bridge)
STARÉ
MĚSTO
MALÁ STRANA
Praha hlavní
nádraží
ŽIŽKOV
Strahov
Stadium
Petřín
Národní
divadlo
Václavské Náměstí
(Wenceslas Square)
TV
Tower
NOVÉ MĚSTO
Národní
muzeum
VINOHRADY
Bertramka
SMÍCHOV
See Colour Map 2
See Colour Map 5
N
VYŠEHRAD
0
200 m
See Colour Map 4

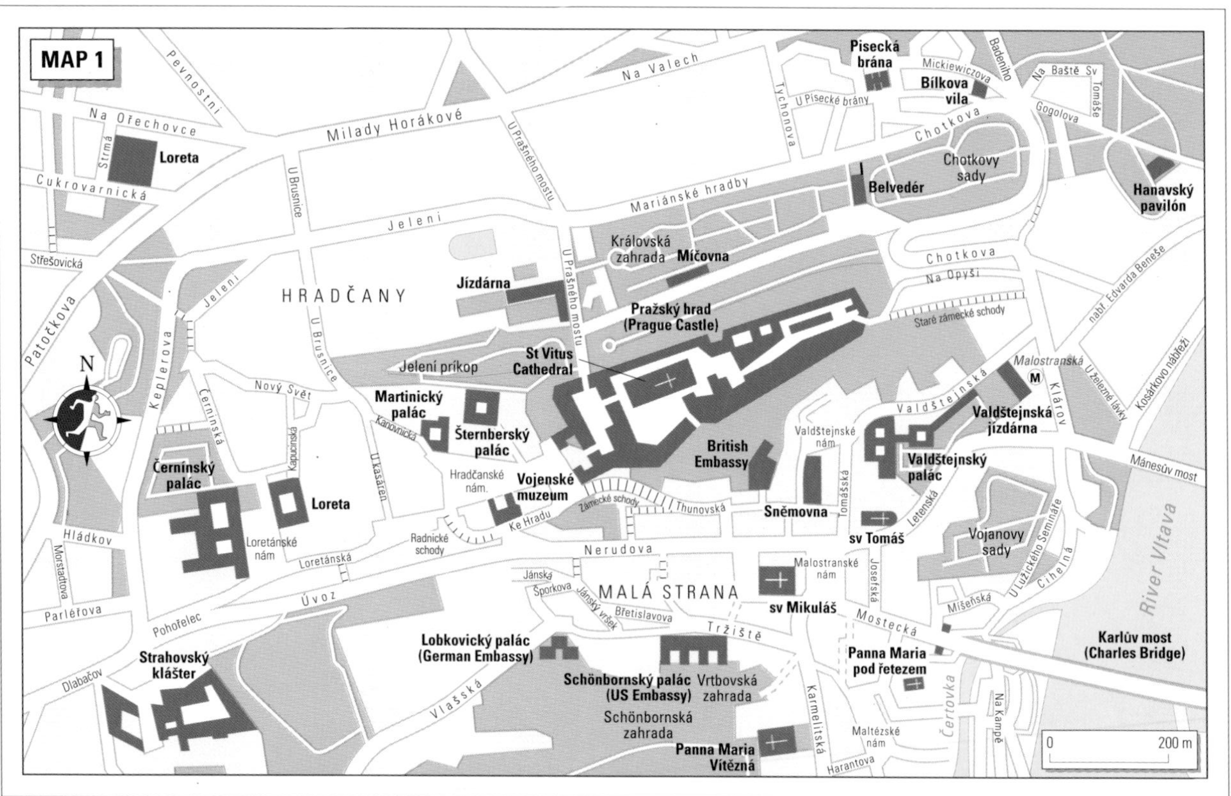
MAP 1
N
0
200 m
HRADČANY
MALÁ STRANA
River Vltava
Loreta
Pisecká brána
Bílkova vila
Belvedér
Chotkovy sady
Hanavský pavilón
Královská zahrada
Míčovna
Jízdárna
Pražský hrad (Prague Castle)
St Vitus Cathedral
Jelení příkop
Martinický palác
Šternberský palác
Černínský palác
Loreta
Vojenské muzeum
British Embassy
Sněmovna
sv Tomáš
Valdštejnský palác
Valdštejnská jízdárna
Vojanovy sady
sv Mikuláš
Lobkovický palác (German Embassy)
Schönbornský palác (US Embassy)
Vrtbovská zahrada
Schönbornská zahrada
Panna Maria Vítězná
Panna Maria pod řetezem
Karlův most (Charles Bridge)
Strahovský klášter
Na Ořechovce
Pevnostní
Strmá
Cukrovarnická
Střešovická
Patočkova
Keplerova
Milady Horákové
U Brusnice
Jelení
Na Valech
U Prašného mostu
Mariánské hradby
Tychonova
U Písecké brány
Mickiewiczova
Badeniho
Na Baště Sv Tomáše
Gogolova
Chotkova
Na Opyši
Staré zámecké schody
nábř. Edvarda Beneše
Kosárkovo nábřeží
U železné lávky
Malostranská
Klárov
Valdštejnská
Mánesův most
Černínská
Nový Svět
Kapucínská
Kanovnická
U kasáren
Hradčanské nám.
Ke Hradu
Zámecké schody
Thunovská
Valdštejnské nám
Tomášská
Letenská
U Lužického Semináře
Cihelná
Hládkov
Morstadtova
Parléřova
Pohořelec
Loretánské nám
Loretánská
Radnické schody
Nerudova
Úvoz
Jánská
Šporkova
Jánský vršek
Břetislavova
Tržiště
Malostranské nám
Josefská
Mišeňská
Mostecká
Dlabačov
Vlašská
Karmelitská
Čertovka
Na Kampě
Maltézské nám
Harantova

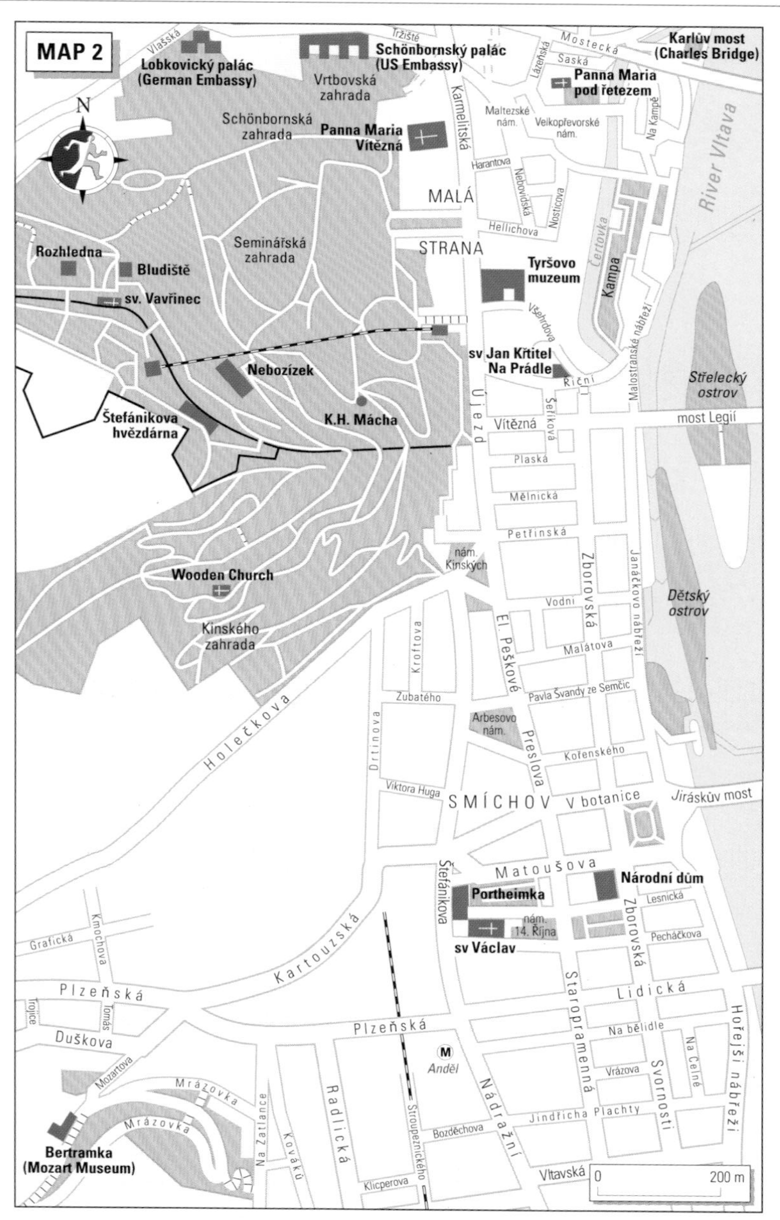

MAP 2
Lobkovický palác (German Embassy)
Schönbornský palác (US Embassy)
Karlův most (Charles Bridge)
Vrtbovská zahrada
Schönbornská zahrada
Panna Maria Vítězná
Panna Maria pod řetezem
MALÁ STRANA
River Vltava
Seminářská zahrada
Rozhledna
Bludiště
sv. Vavřinec
Tyršovo muzeum
Kampa
Nebozízek
sv Jan Křtitel Na Prádle
Střelecký ostrov
Štefánikova hvězdárna
K.H. Mácha
most Legií
Wooden Church
Kinského zahrada
Dětský ostrov
Arbesovo nám.
SMÍCHOV
Jiráskův most
Národní dům
Portheimka
nám. 14. Října
sv Václav
Anděl
Bertramka (Mozart Museum)
0 200 m

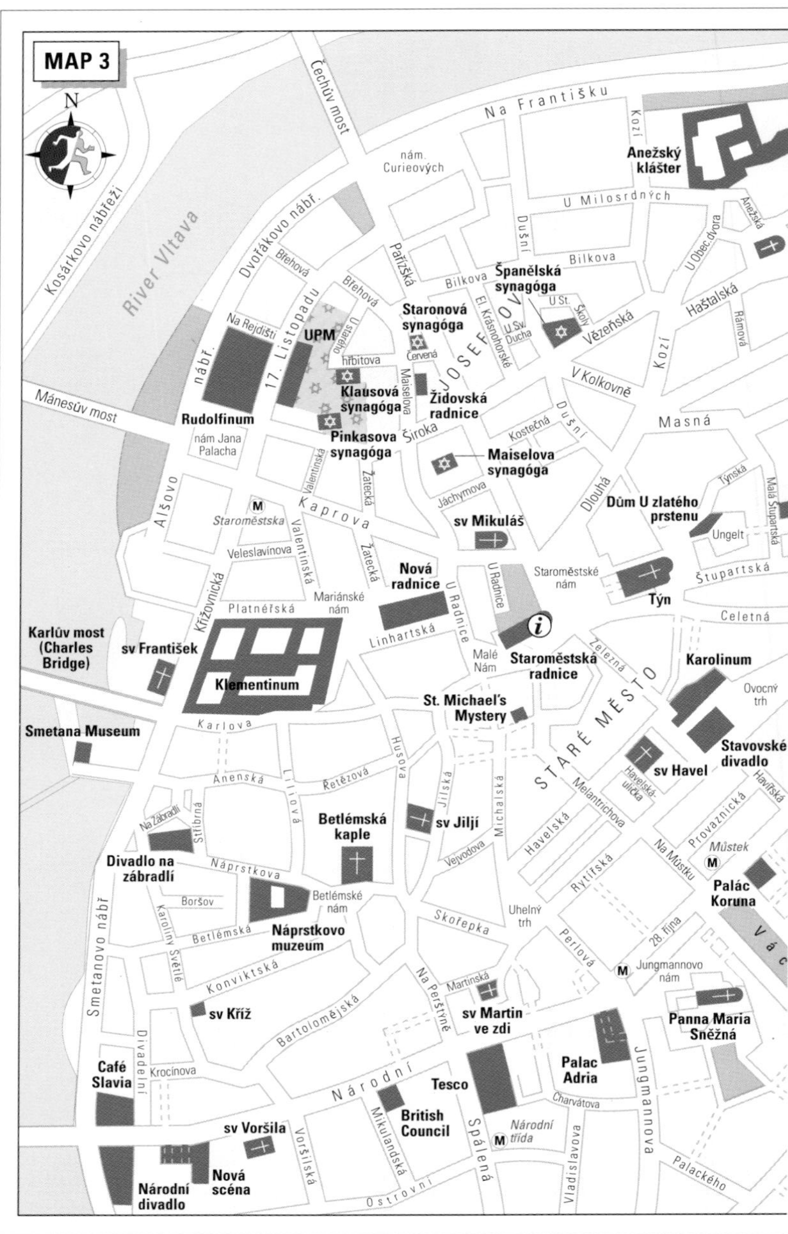
MAP 3
N
River Vltava
Kosárkovo nábřeží
Čechův most
Mánesův most
Karlův most (Charles Bridge)
Na Františku
nám. Curieových
Anežský klášter
Dvořákovo nábř.
Břehová
Pařížská
Bilkova
Španělská synagóga
Staronová synagóga
UPM
17. Listopadu
Na Rejdišti
Rudolfinum
Klausová synagóga
Židovská radnice
Pinkasova synagóga
Maiselova synagóga
nám Jana Palacha
JOSEFOV
Široká
Kaprova
Staroměstska
sv Mikuláš
Dům U zlatého prstenu
Nová radnice
Staroměstské nám
Týn
Mariánské nám
Platnéřská
Linhartská
sv František
Klementinum
Staroměstská radnice
Karolinum
St. Michael's Mystery
STARÉ MĚSTO
Smetana Museum
Karlova
Celetná
Ovocný trh
Stavovské divadlo
sv Havel
Betlémská kaple
sv Jiljí
Divadlo na zábradlí
Náprstkovo muzeum
Betlémské nám
Můstek
Palác Koruna
Uhelný trh
Jungmannovo nám
Panna Maria Sněžná
sv Kříž
sv Martin ve zdi
Café Slavia
Tesco
Palac Adria
British Council
Národní třída
Národní
sv Voršila
Nová scéna
Národní divadlo
Smetanovo nábř
Jungmannova
Spálená
Vladislavova
Palackého
Ostrovní
Mikulandská
Voršilská
Bartolomějská
Konviktská
Skořepka
Perlová
28. října
Na Můstku
Rytířská
Havelská
Melantrichova
Michalská
Husova
Jilská
Liliová
Anenská
Řetězová
Náprstkova
Křižovnická
Alšovo
Valentinská
Žatecká
Veleslavínova
U Radnice
Malé Nám
Železná
Masná
Dlouhá
Dušní
Kozí
Haštalská
Vězeňská
V Kolkovně
U Milosrdných
Štupartská
Ungelt
Týnská
Provaznická
Havířská
Charvátova
Krocínova
Divadelní
Boršov
Karoliny Světlé
Betlémská
Na Perštýně
Martinská

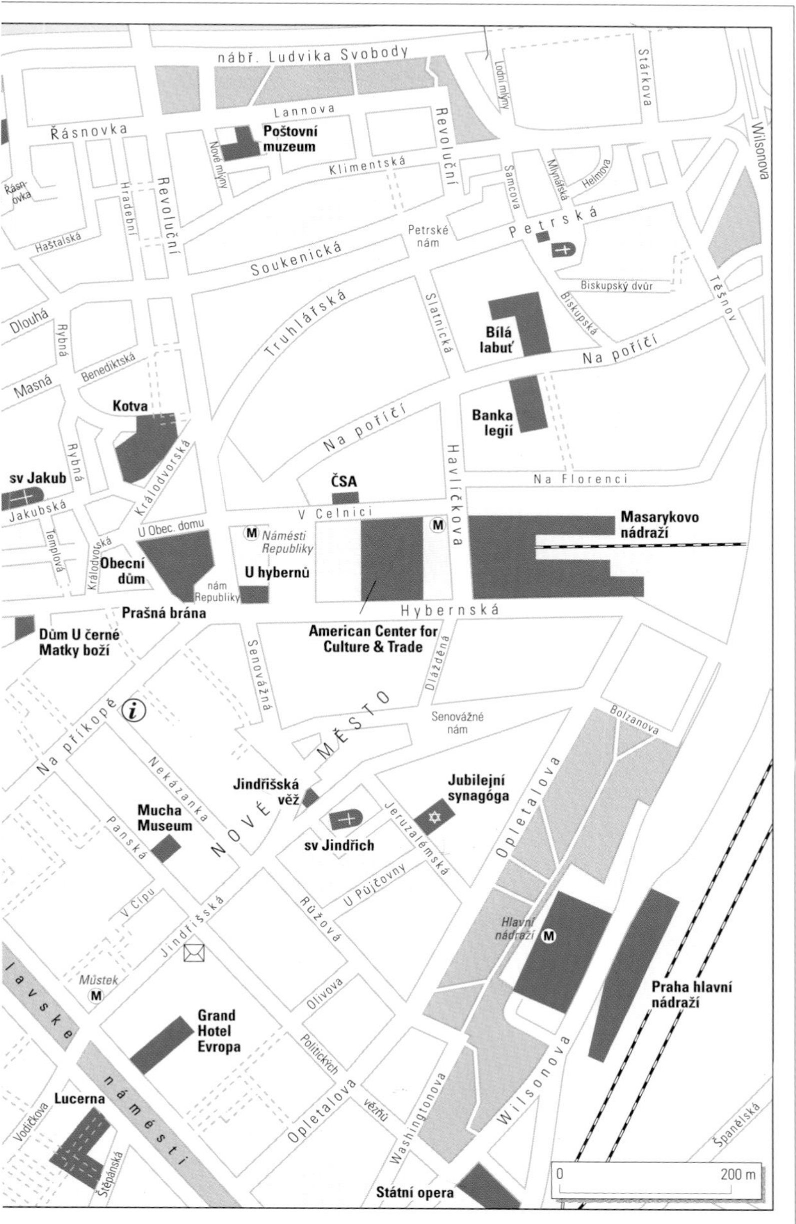
nábř. Ludvika Svobody
Lannova
Řásnovka
Poštovní muzeum
Nové mlýny
Revoluční
Klimentská
Lodní mlýny
Stárkova
Wilsonova
Řásnovka
Hradební
Revoluční
Samcova
Mlynářská
Helmova
Haštalská
Petrská nám
Petrská
Soukenická
Biskupský dvůr
Těšnov
Dlouhá
Truhlářská
Slatnická
Biskupská
Bílá labuť
Rybná
Benediktská
Na poříčí
Masná
Kotva
Na poříčí
Banka legií
Rybná
Královdvorská
Havlíčkova
sv Jakub
ČSA
Na Florenci
Jakubská
V Celnici
U Obec. domu
Náměstí Republiky
Masarykovo nádraží
Templová
Králodvorská
Obecní dům
U hybernů
nám Republiky
Prašná brána
Hybernská
Dům U černé Matky boží
American Center for Culture & Trade
Senovážná
Dlážděná
Na příkopě
NOVÉ MĚSTO
Senovážné nám
Bolzanova
Nekázanka
Jindřišská věž
Jubilejní synagóga
Opletalova
Mucha Museum
Panská
sv Jindřich
Jeruzalémská
U Půjčovny
V Cípu
Jindřišská
Růžova
Hlavní nádraží
Jindřišská
Můstek
Olivova
Praha hlavní nádraží
Grand Hotel Evropa
Václavské náměstí
Politických vězňů
Wilsonova
Opletalova
Washingtonova
Lucerna
Vodičkova
Štěpánská
Španělská
Státní opera
0
200 m

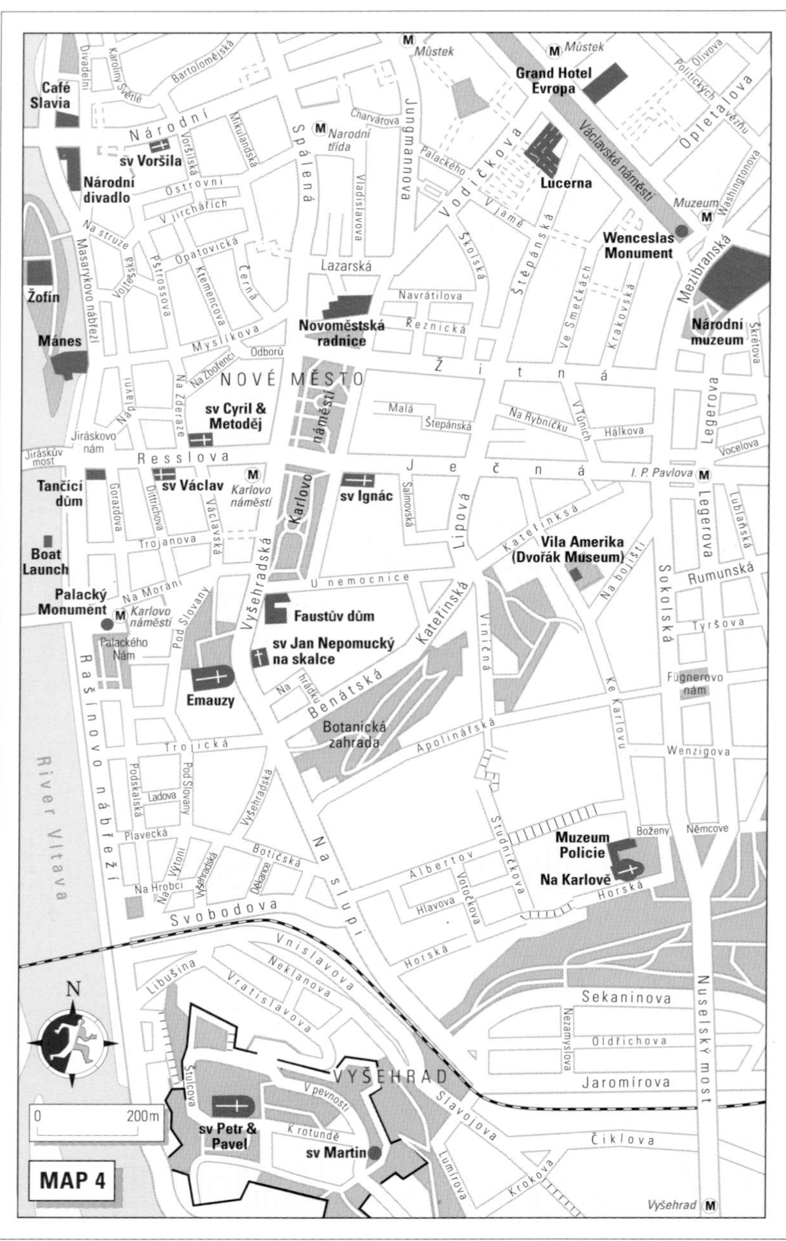

MAP 4
Café Slavia
Národní divadlo
sv Voršila
Žofín
Mánes
Jiráskovo nám
Jiráskův most
Tančící dům
Boat Launch
Palacký Monument
Palackého Nám
NOVÉ MĚSTO
Novoměstská radnice
sv Cyril & Metoděj
sv Václav
sv Ignác
Karlovo náměstí
Faustův dům
sv Jan Nepomucký na skalce
Emauzy
Botanická zahrada
Grand Hotel Evropa
Lucerna
Wenceslas Monument
Národní muzeum
Vila Amerika (Dvořák Museum)
Muzeum Policie
Na Karlově
VYŠEHRAD
sv Petr & Pavel
sv Martin
River Vltava
Můstek
Národní třída
Muzeum
I. P. Pavlova
Vyšehrad
Národní
Ostrovní
V jirchářích
Opatovická
Myslíkova
Resslova
Trojanova
Na Moráni
Rašínovo nábřeží
Masarykovo nábřeží
Václavské náměstí
Vodičkova
Jungmannova
Spálená
Žitná
Ječná
Lipová
Kateřinská
Benátská
Apolinářská
Na slupi
Vyšehradská
Svobodova
Vnislavova
Neklanova
Vratislavova
Libušina
Slavojova
Sekaninova
Oldřichova
Jaromírova
Čiklova
Krokova
Nuselský most
Sokolská
Legerova
Mezibranská
Opletalova
Washingtonova
Štěpánská
Ve Smečkách
Krakovská
Navrátilova
Řeznická
Lazarská
Na Rybníčku
Hálkova
Vocelova
Rumunská
Tyršova
Fügnerovo nám
Wenzigova
Ke Karlovu
Albertov
Horská
Studničkova
Viničná
Na bojišti
U nemocnice
Trojická
Plavecká
Botičská
Dittrichova
Gorazdova
Václavská
Na Zderaze
Vojtěšská
Pštrossova
Křemencova
Černá
Mikulandská
Vladislavova
Charvátova
Palackého
Školská
V jámě
Bartolomějská
Karoliny Světlé
Divadelní
Na struze
Odborů
Na Zbořenci
Na Poříčním
Malá Štěpánská
V Tůních
Salmovská
Lublaňská
Škrétova
Pod Slovany
Podskalská
Ladova
Na Výtoni
Na Hrobci
Děkanská
Hlavova
Votočkova
Boženy Němcove
Nezamyslova
Lumírova
Štulcova
V pevnosti
K rotundě
Politických vězňů
Olivova
0 200m
N

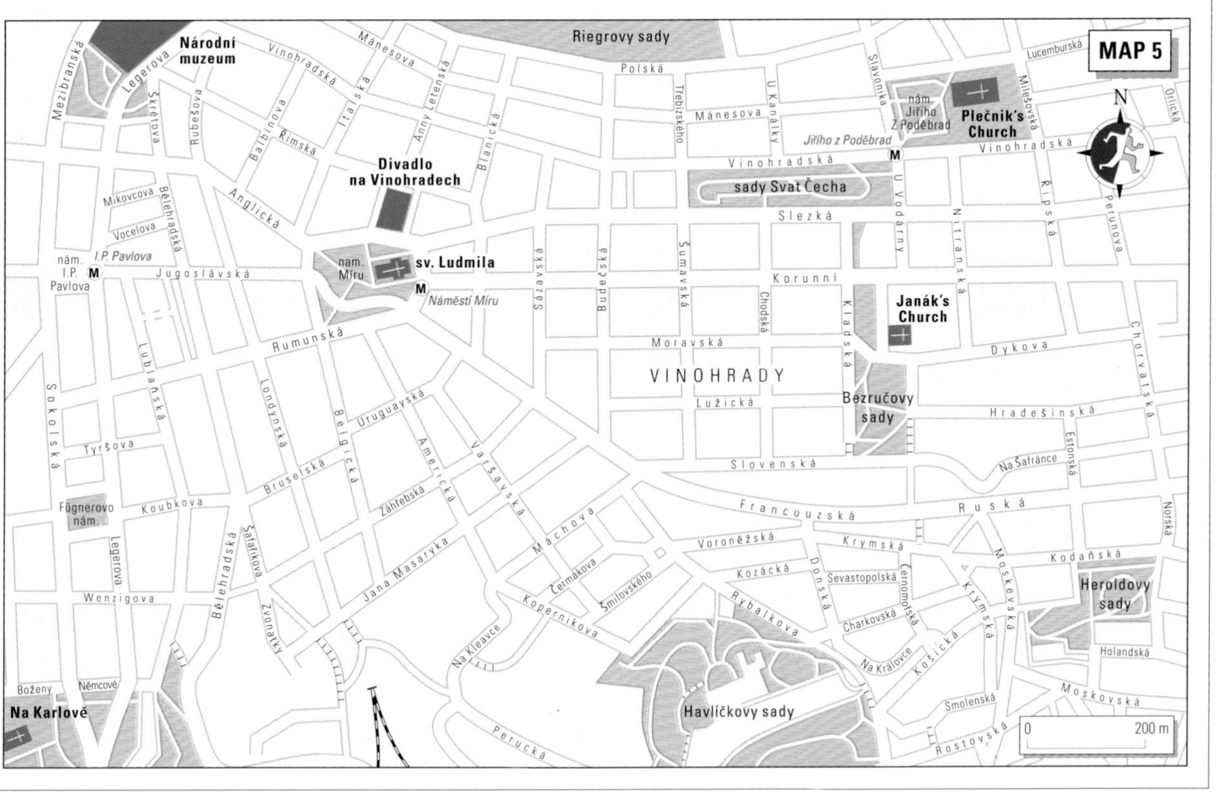
MAP 5
N
0
200 m
Národní muzeum
Divadlo na Vinohradech
sv. Ludmila
nam. Míru
Náměstí Míru
nám. I.P. Pavlova
I.P. Pavlova
Plečnik's Church
nám. Jiřího z Poděbrad
Jiřího z Poděbrad
Janák's Church
Riegrovy sady
sady Svat Čecha
Bezručovy sady
Heroldovy sady
Havlíčkovy sady
Fügnerovo nám.
Na Karlově
VINOHRADY
Mezibranská
Legerova
Škrétova
Rubešova
Vinohradská
Mánesova
Balbínova
Římská
Italská
Anny Letenská
Blanická
Polská
Třebízského
U Kanálky
Slavonika
Lucemburská
Milešovská
Orlická
Perunova
Řipská
Anglická
Mikovcova
Vocelova
Bělehradská
Jugoslávská
Slezká
U Vodárny
Nitranská
Sázavská
Budečská
Šumavská
Chodská
Korunní
Kladská
Dykova
Chorvatská
Rumunská
Moravská
Lužická
Hradešinská
Estonská
Na Šafránce
Slovenská
Lublaňská
Londynská
Uruguayská
Belgická
Sokolská
Tyršova
Bruselská
Americká
Varšavská
Francouzská
Ruská
Norská
Koubkova
Záhřebská
Machova
Voroněžská
Krymská
Moskevská
Kodaňská
Šafaříkova
Jana Masaryka
Čermákova
Kozácká
Donská
Sevastopolská
Černomořská
Wenzigova
Zvonařky
Kopernikova
Šmilovského
Rybalkova
Charkovská
Holandská
Na Kleavce
Na Královce
Košická
Moskovská
Boženy Němcové
Smolenská
Perucká
Rostovská

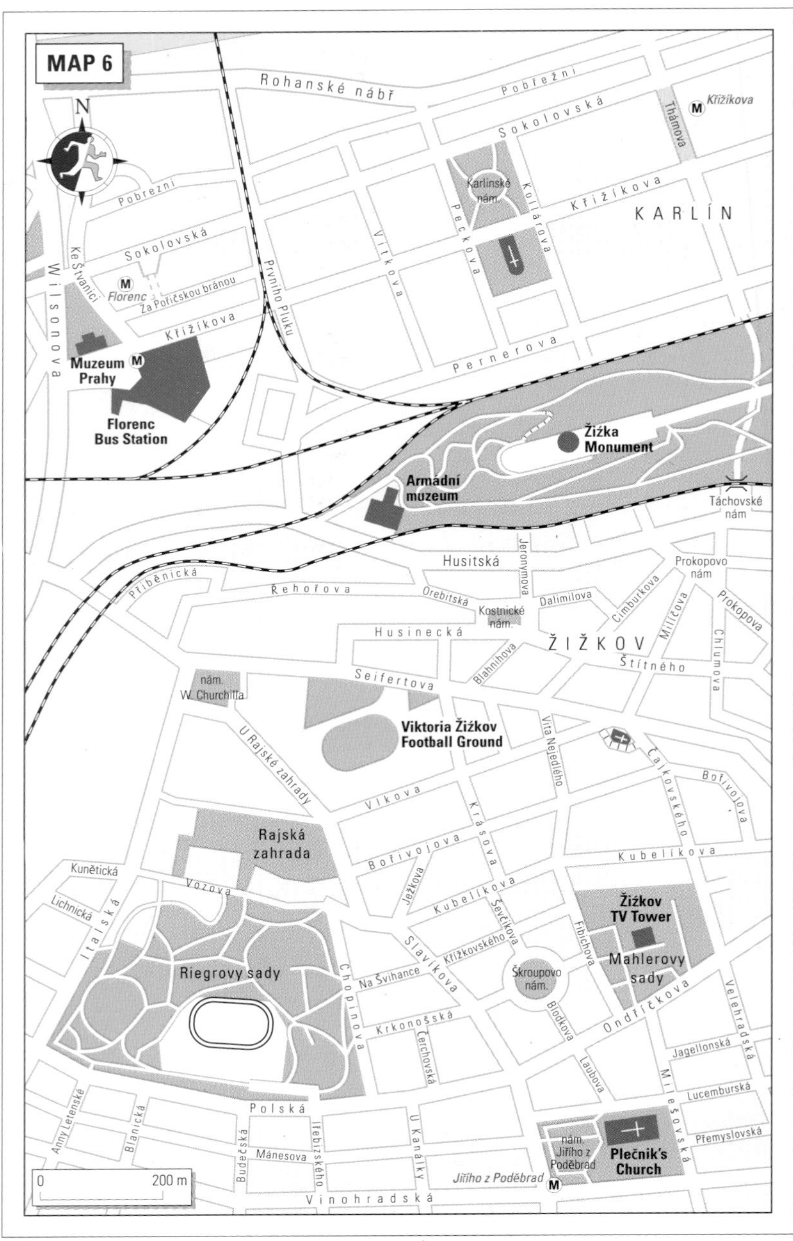
MAP 6
N
Rohanské nábř
Pobřežní
Sokolovská
Thámova
Křižíkova
Karlínské nám.
Kollárova
Křižíkova
KARLÍN
Pecková
Vítkova
Prvního Pluku
Pobrezni
Sokolovská
Ke Štvanici
Wilsonova
Florenc
Za Poříčskou bránou
Křižíkova
Pernerova
Muzeum Prahy
Florenc Bus Station
Žižka Monument
Armádní muzeum
Táchovské nám
Husitská
Jeronymova
Prokopovo nám
Přiběnická
Řehořova
Orebitská
Dalimilova
Cimburkova
Prokopova
Kostnické nám.
Husinecká
Miličova
Chlumova
ŽIŽKOV
Blahníkova
Štítného
Seifertova
nám. W. Churchilla
Viktoria Žižkov Football Ground
Víta Nejedlého
U Rajské zahrady
Čajkovského
Bořivojova
Vlkova
Krásova
Rajská zahrada
Bořivojova
Kubelíkova
Kunětická
Vozová
Ježkova
Kubelíkova
Lichnická
Italská
Ševčíkova
Žižkov TV Tower
Slavíkova
Křížkovského
Fibichova
Mahlerovy sady
Riegrovy sady
Chopinova
Na Švihance
Škroupovo nám.
Ondříčkova
Velehradská
Blodkova
Krkonošská
Čerchovská
Jagellonská
Laubova
Lucemburská
Anny Letenské
Polská
Miešovská
Blanická
U Kanálky
Budečská
Mánesova
Ilrebízského
nám. Jiřího z Poděbrad
Plečnik's Church
Přemyslovská
Jiřího z Poděbrad
0
200 m
Vinohradská